STUDIES IN EVANGELICAL HISTORY AND THOUGHT

Revival, Renewal,

and the Holy Spirit

STUDIES IN EVANGELICAL HISTORY AND THOUGHT

Revival, Renewal, and the Holy Spirit

Edited by
Dyfed Wyn Roberts

WIPF & STOCK · Eugene, Oregon

Wipf and Stock Publishers
199 W 8th Ave, Suite 3
Eugene, OR 97401

Revival, Renewal, and the Holy Spirit
By Roberts, Dyfed Wyn
Copyright©2009 Paternoster
ISBN 13: 978-1-60899-168-6
Publication date 10/9/2009
Previously published by Paternoster, 2009

This Edition published by Wipf and Stock Publishers by arrangement with Paternoster

Series Preface

The Evangelical movement has been marked by its union of four emphases: on the Bible, on the cross of Christ, on conversion as the entry to the Christian life and on the responsibility of the believer to be active. The present series is designed to publish scholarly studies of any aspect of this movement in Britain or overseas. Its volumes include social analysis as well as exploration of Evangelical ideas. The books in the series consider aspects of the movement shaped by the Evangelical Revival of the eighteenth century, when the impetus to mission began to turn the popular Protestantism of the British Isles and North America into a global phenomenon. The series aims to reap some of the rich harvest of academic research about those who, over the centuries, have believed that they had a gospel to tell to the nations.

STUDIES IN EVANGELICAL HISTORY AND THOUGHT

Series Editors

David Bebbington, Professor of History, University of Stirling, Stirling, Scotland, UK

John H.Y. Briggs, Senior Research Fellow in Ecclesiastical History and Director of the Centre for Baptist History and Heritage, Regent's Park College, Oxford, UK

Timothy Larsen, Professor of Theology, Wheaton College, Illinois, USA

Mark A. Noll, McAnaney Professor of History, University of Notre Dame, Notre Dame, Indiana, USA

Ian M. Randall, Senior Research Fellow, International Baptist Theological Seminary, Prague, Czech Republic

For Helen and new beginnings

Contents

Contributors	xv
Preface	xvii
Acknowledgements	xix

Chapter 1
Revival and Renewal Amongst the Eighteenth-Century Welsh Methodists
Eryn White — 1

Chapter 2
John Lewis and the Promotion of the International Evangelical Revival, 1735–56
David Ceri Jones — 13

Chapter 3
'Tinkers and other vermin': Methodists and the Established Church in Wales, 1735–1800
John Morgan Guy — 27

Chapter 4
The Effect of Charles Finney's Revivalism on the 1858-60 Awakening in Wales
Dyfed Wyn Roberts — 36

Chapter 5
The Significance of Hymnody in the First Evangelical Revivals, 1730–1760
Mark A. Noll — 45

The Prominence of Singing in the Early Revivals	47
The Innovative Character of the New Evangelical Hymns	56
Hymns as Agents of Egalitarianism	62
The Heightened Meaning of Song in Early Evangelical Movements	63

Chapter 6
Revival and the Clash of Cultures:
Ferryden, Forfarshire, in 1859
D. W. Bebbington — 65

Chapter 7
'Preserved from Erroneous Views?': The Contribution of Francis Johnston as a Baptist Voice in the Scottish Evangelical Debate, in the Mid-Nineteenth Century, on the Work of the Holy Spirit
Brian Talbot — 95

Chapter 8
Evan Roberts: Blessings and Burnout
Gaius Davies — 107

Some Burning Questions	108
'A Personal Statement'	109
Evan Roberts before the Revival	109
Two Contemporary Accounts	111
Unanswered Questions	113
The Breakdown: Mrs Penn-Lewis and the Long Silence	114
Forgive Our Foolish Ways	115

Chapter 9
Jessie Penn-Lewis
Peter Prosser — **116**

Introduction	116
Who was Jessie Penn-Lewis?	116
Her Self-Commissioning	117
Her Experience of Being 'In the Spirit'	118
In Russia, 1898	119
Jessie Penn-Lewis and the Tripartite Nature of Human-Kind	120
War on the Saints	120

Roberts's Breakdowns	123
Last Services, 1905 and Enter Penn-Lewis	125
Conclusion	127

Chapter 10
The Agony in the Garden: Visions of the 1904 Revival
John Harvey — 129

Chapter 11
A Hurricane of the Holy Spirit: An Account of the 1904 Revival at Bethesda, based on the Diaries, Letters and Correspondence of the Rev. John Thomas Job

Dafydd M. Job	139
Preparation for Revival	139
The Revival	143
The Fruit of the Revival at Bethesda	146

Chapter 12
The Church in Wales and the Revival of 1904–5

Noel Gibbard	151
Churches	152
Church Pastoral Aid Society (CPAS)	152
Evangelizing	153
Collaborating with Other Denominations	155
Opposition	157

Chapter 13
The Influence of the 1905 Revival Amongst the Merseyside Welsh Community
D. Ben Rees — 159

Chapter 14
Why did the Welsh Revival Stop?

William K. Kay	169
Introduction	169
The Question at Issue	171
Weighing the Answers	173

Conclusion ... 183

Chapter 15
The Impact of the Welsh Revival on Baptist Churches in Scotland
Kenneth Roxburgh ... **185**
Introduction ... 185
Scotland in the Early Twentieth Century ... 188
Welsh Revival ... 189
Scottish Baptists ... 192
Charlotte Chapel, Edinburgh ... 194
Glasgow ... 197
Victoria Place, Glasgow ... 198
Dennistoun ... 198
Partick ... 199
Clydebank ... 199
Lanarkshire ... 199
Bellshill ... 200
Motherwell ... 200
Galashiels: John Shearer ... 200
Hawick ... 201
Aberdeen ... 201
Stirling ... 202
Old Cumnock ... 202
Dundee ... 202
Inverkeithing ... 203
The Role of Women in the Revival ... 203
Modernism ... 204
Kemp and Charlotte Chapel ... 206
Conclusion ... 207

Chapter 16
Scottish Brethren and the Welsh Revival of 1904–5
Neil T. R. Dickson ... **208**

Chapter 17
The Great Awakening of 1905: The Welsh Revival and its Influence on the American Revival
Emmanuel Hooper — 222
Analytical Assessment of the Welsh Revival and its Role in the American Revival — 231

Chapter 18
The Fruit of Revival in Uganda
Tudor Griffiths — 233

Chapter 19
The 1904–5 Welsh Revival and Social and Political Action: A Centenary Perspective
Daniel Boucher — 243
Withdrawal v. Engagement Pre-1904? — 245
Withdrawal v. Engagement 1904– — 251
Future Research — 257

Chapter 20
Revival Movements in the Twentieth Century as an Urgent Task of the International Research Network
Wolfgang Reinhardt — 259
The Deficit — 259
The Effects of the Welsh Revival on Germany — 263
The Task of Future Research — 266
Practical Consequences — 272

Chapter 21
Dream/Vision: A Language of the Soul
Susan Gabriel Talbot — 274

Index — 283

Contributors

Eryn White is a lecturer in the Department of History and Welsh History, Aberystwyth University, and is the author of *Praidd Baich y Bugail Mawr*, the history of the development of the society meetings in the Evangelical Revival in Wales.

David Ceri Jones is a lecturer in the Department of History and Welsh History, Aberystwyth University, with a particular interest in early modern and eighteenth-century Wales.

John Morgan-Guy is the Research Fellow of the 'Imaging the Bible in Wales' project in the University of Wales, Lampeter.

Dyfed Wyn Roberts is a part-time lecturer in church history in the School of Theology and Religious Studies, Bangor University. He obtained his PhD from the University of Wales in 2005.

Mark A. Noll is the Francis A. McAnaney Professor of History in the Department of History, University of Notre Dame, Indiana, USA. Among his publications is *The Civil War as a Theological Crisis*.

David Bebbington is Professor of History at the University of Stirling, Scotland. His recent publications include *The Dominance of Evangelicalism: The Age of Spurgeon and Moody*.

Brian Talbot is Senior Minister of Cumbernauld Baptist Church in Scotland. He obtained his PhD in Scottish Baptist history from the University of Stirling in 1999.

Gaius Davies is Emeritus Consultant Psychiatrist, King's College Hospital. He is the author of *Genius, Grief and Grace*.

Peter Prosser is Professor of Christian History and Doctrine at Regent University, Virginia, USA.

John Harvey is Professor of Fine Art at the School of Art, Aberystwyth University. He is the author of *Image of the Invisible: The Visualization of Religion in the Welsh Nonconformist Tradition*.

Dafydd Job is the Minister of the Welsh Evangelical Church in Bangor, north Wales.

Noel Gibbard was a lecturer at the Evangelical Theological College at Bridgend, south Wales. He is the author of *Fire on the Altar: A History and Evaluation of the 1904–05 Welsh Revival*.

D. Ben Rees is the Minister of the Welsh Presbyterian Church in Heathfield Road, Liverpool, England. He has a particular interest in the contribution of the Welsh community on Merseyside.

William Kay is Director of the Centre for Pentecostal and Charismatic Studies at the School of Theology, Bangor University. He is the author of *Apostolic Networks in Britain: New Ways of Being Church*.

Kenneth Roxburgh is S. Louis and Ann W. Armstrong Professor and Chair of the Department of Religion, Samford University, Birmingham, Alabama, USA. He is the author of *Thomas Gillespie and the Origins of the Relief Church in 18th century Scotland*.

Neil T. R. Dickson is an English teacher at Kilmarnock Academy in Scotland. He is the author of *Brethren in Scotland 1838–2000: A Social Study of an Evangelical Movement*.

Emmanuel Hooper is completing his doctoral thesis on the history of the North American campus revivals of 1905–07 and the student volunteer movement.

Tudor Griffiths is the Rector of Hawarden in north-east Wales. Between 1989 and 1995 he served with the Church Mission Society in Uganda. His PhD thesis was on Bishop Tucker of Uganda.

Dan Boucher is currently the Director of Parliamentary Affairs for CARE, a UK-based Christian charity. His PhD thesis was on the implications of globalization on state sovereignty.

Wolfgang Reinhardt is currently involved with Solace Ministries in Rwanda, working with victims of the genocide.

Susan Gabriel Talbot completed her PhD thesis in 2000. She is a priest and is the foundation sister of an emerging Anglican-based Religious Order in the Manchester Diocese.

Preface

On a damp field by the Loughor Estuary on the south Wales coast, some four hundred Koreans gathered in August 2007 to celebrate the 1904–05 'Welsh Revival'. They had come in part to thank Wales for exporting the revival to their own nation and to worship a God who they believed had transformed lives and communities through the outpouring of his Spirit over a hundred years ago.

This volume is another contribution to those centenary celebrations. The chapters published here were first presented as papers to a conference at the University of Wales, Bangor – a conference held to mark the centenary of what is generally known as the 'Evan Roberts Revival'. The volume can be divided into three parts.

The first has chapters dealing with revivals of a previous age to 1904–05, including a study on the significance of hymnody during the Evangelical Revivals of the eighteenth century by the distinguished American historian, Mark A. Noll. The renowned British historian, David W. Bebbington, also has a chapter in this section on the 1858 revival in the north-east of Scotland.

The second part deals with various aspects of the 1904–05 revival itself. Among these chapters the eminent psychiatrist, Gaius Davies, makes a fascinating study of the young revivalist Evan Roberts's mental health, and William Kay, a historian of Pentecostalism, attempts to answer the question why the revival in Wales stopped. There are other chapters on topics such as Jesse Penn-Lewis and the influence of the revival on the Welsh community living in Merseyside, England.

The third section partly deals with some of the after effects of the revival in Wales and in particular its spread into other nations such as Scotland and Uganda. In this section is to be found the work of the German historian, Wolfgang Reinhardt, urging further research into the history of revivals worldwide.

In Wales today, the churches that were renewed in such a dramatic way in a few short months at the beginning of the twentieth century are in a perilous condition. It is hoped that this volume, as well as making a scholarly contribution to the history of revival, will also encourage the church in Wales to press on in the work she is called to complete.

Acknowledgements

The editor would like to express his gratitude to all the contributors for their willingness to submit their papers for publication. Professor Densil Morgan has as always been an encouragement in the preparation of the work. Most especially, Linda Jones of the College of Arts and Humanities, Bangor University, has worked so hard in providing technical and other support. This volume would not have been finished without her unstinting efforts. Canolfan Bedwyr, the University's Welsh-language support unit, are to be thanked for translating some of the papers from the original Welsh. Finally thanks to the staff of Paternoster Press for their willingness to publish.

Dyfed Wyn Roberts
Bangor University
September 2008

CHAPTER 1

Revival and Renewal Amongst the Eighteenth-Century Welsh Methodists

Eryn White

The revival of 1904 can be considered as the last in a series of periodic revivals in Wales beginning with the Methodist Revival in the mid eighteenth century. The eighteenth-century revival is known as the 'Diwygiad Mawr' or 'Great Awakening', although it could be argued that there were greater revivals, certainly if measured by the number of converts. Evan Roberts is said to have had a vision that a hundred thousand souls would be won over during the revival of 1904–5, and he came close to seeing that vision being substantiated.[1] The number of converts during the early period of the Methodist Revival, between 1737 and 1750, did not come anywhere close to this total. By 1750 about 420 Methodist societies had been established in Wales. On the basis that there were some 20 members on average in each society, it can be estimated that there were between eight and ten thousand Methodists in the country by 1750. It is estimated that the total population of Wales at that time was around 489,000, therefore it is obvious that the Methodists represented a small minority indeed.

That is perhaps not the impression which is conveyed by the name 'The Great Awakening', but it has gained that title mainly as a result of its consequences as it ultimately succeeded in transforming the religious climate of the country by the nineteenth century. During that period, the high noon of Nonconformity, it was natural to extol the effects of the eighteenth-century revival, the revival which was considered to be the heroic starting point of Nonconformist Wales. This tendency can be traced back to William Williams, Pantycelyn, the movement's first historian, who portrayed Wales before the revival as a country in spiritual torpor before the wondrous dawn of the 1730s awoke its people to spiritual enlightenment. More recently Geraint H. Jenkins, in particular, has shown that Methodism grew to some extent out of the

---

[1] R. Tudur Jones, *Ffydd ac Argyfwng Cenedl: Cyfrol II Dryswch a Diwygiad* (Abertawe, 1982), pp. 131, 215.

previous period and the movement undoubtedly drew on the Pietistic influences of the time.[2]

The revival therefore was more limited as regards the number of converts than some of the following revivals and it is also fair to say that the origins of the eighteenth-century revival were more obscure than those of successive revivals. When tracing the origin of the 1859 revival, for example, one can refer to a specific sermon,[3] and to the conferences and early stirrings in Cardiganshire when discussing the start of the 1904 revival.[4] With the Methodist Revival, the tendency is to refer to the conversions of Howel Harris and Daniel Rowland in the early summer of 1735, but there is no one particular occasion of which one can say 'this was the starting point, this is when the revival dawned'. Harris and Rowland started to influence people in their localities gradually from the summer of 1735 onwards. That to a great extent was easier for Rowland as he was curate of the parishes of Llangeitho and Nancwnlle in Cardiganshire, with preaching the Gospel already a part of his vocation. Harris, on the other hand, had to be content to act as an unordained itinerant preacher, a fact which caused him problems throughout his evangelical career. As a result of their efforts, there is no doubt that the Methodist movement was starting to take form by 1737. It was during that year that Harris and Rowland met for the first time and discussed how to co-ordinate the work. From then on the movement continued to expand, with the help of other assistants, most notably Howel Davies and William Williams, Pantycelyn, until regulations and procedures for the movement were established by means of the Association from 1742 onwards. There followed years of growth, until the movement was split in 1750, with Howel Harris being ostracized by the majority of the leaders and exhorters – as the lay preachers were called. This breach was healed in 1763 at a time when a new revival, known as the Llangeitho Revival, was giving substantial impetus to Methodism in Wales.

Naturally, revival was a more novel experience to Welsh people in the 1730s than it was by 1904. In 1904 there were many people who were familiar with the experience of revival, and a number indeed remembered the revival of 1859, but in the 1730s revival was a new phenomenon to the vast majority of the population. Consequently, it was natural perhaps that they were less willing to venture to participate in this novel activity than later generations to whom such an occurrence was familiar, traditional and acceptable. Having said that, revival could not be considered as something completely new even in the eighteenth century, as Griffith Jones had won an enthusiastic response to his ministry in the south-west twenty years before the Methodists ventured out to

---

[2] Geraint H. Jenkins, *Literature, Religion and Society in Wales 1660-1730* (Caerdydd, 1978); idem., '"Peth Erchyll Iawn" oedd Methodistiaeth', *Llên Cymru*, 17 (1993).

[3] Eifion Evans, 'Humphrey Jones: "The youngster who lit the fuse"' in *Fire in the Thatch* (Bridgend, 1996), pp. 186-205.

[4] R. Tudur Jones, *Ffydd ac Argyfwng Cenedl*, II, pp. 122-9.

the fields and byways, and had been subsequently censured by the Bishop of St David's for his conduct. So large were the congregations that came to listen to him that he had to preach in the open as no church could contain them. Indeed, the doors of Llanwenog Church were broken by the pressure of the throng which came to listen to him.[5] However, the leaders of Methodism and their followers had hardly been born when Griffith Jones was making a name for himself as a stimulating preacher and stirring open-air sermons were new and attractive experiences to many of them.

Undoubtedly preaching was a key element in the revival, as the forceful preaching of Daniel Rowland and Howel Harris was the starting point of revival and spiritual renewal for many of the members. If he had not heard the compelling voice of Howel Harris at Talgarth churchyard, it is quite likely that William Williams, Pantycelyn, would have continued his career as a medical student. Both Williams and Howel Davies acknowledged Harris as their spiritual father, as did a number of other Methodists. But preaching alone was not enough to maintain and support the movement through the 1740s and beyond, which is why the society became so important in the movement's history. By gathering members together in the society it was ensured that they would share the company of people who had been through similar experiences so that they could give each other mutual support. In a world which was often hostile towards them, the Methodists gained comfort through the fellowship and support of the society, as well as an opportunity to try to analyse the overwhelming experiences which had befallen them. Williams Pantycelyn in *Drws y Society Profiad* described how members of the society would work on each other:

... fel y mae haearn yn hogi haearn, felly gŵr sydd yn hogi wyneb ei gyfaill. Y mae gan gyfeillach effaith fawr iawn i'n bywiocáu at dda neu at ddrwg, a pha foddion well i fywiogrwydd nag ymgasglu at ein gilydd i gyd-weddio, cyd-ganu, ac adrodd mor dda bu Duw i un a'r llall wedi'r tro diweddaf.[6]

[... as iron sharpeneth iron, so a man sharpeneth the countenance of his friend. Fellowship is very effective in stimulating us to good or evil; and what better means of maintaining liveliness than to gather together to pray together, to sing together and to declare the goodness of God to one another since the last meeting.]

Despite the contribution of the society, the growth of Methodism was not a smooth and inevitable process. It was instead slow, fragmented and spasmodic.

---

[5] Geraint H. Jenkins, 'Hen Filwr dros Grist: Griffith Jones, Llanddowror', in *Cadw Tŷ mewn Cwmwl Tystion* (Llandysul, 1990), p. 160.
[6] G. H. Hughes (ed.), *Gweithiau William Williams Pantycelyn, Cyfrol II* (Caerdydd, 1967), p. 188, English translation from William Williams, *The Experience Meeting*, trans. Mrs Lloyd Jones (Bryntirion, 1973), p. 13.

It was a story of ebb and flow, with gains and losses on the way. The leaders and counsellors knew that it was not always easy to maintain the intensity of the initial conversion over a long period and that there was a danger of backsliding into stagnation and uncertainty. In his *Ateb Philo-Evangelius*, which was written as a result of the revival of 1762, Pantycelyn warned that it should be expected that some who joined during a revival would later turn their backs on their profession of faith, because, as he said,

> ... pan y fo awelon o argyhoeddiad neu ddiddanwch yn disgyn fel glaw ar y gwir dduwiol, mae sŵn y gwynt yn cwrdd â'r rhagrithwyr hefyd, ac yn gweithio rhyw chydig ar eu nwydau naturiol; ac yna y maent fel llong o flaen y gwynt, heb un balast ond tan gyflawn hwyliau, ac mewn perygl o gael ei briwio gan y creigydd, neu ei gyrru i mewn i aberodd amherthnasol.[7]

> [... when breezes of conviction or consolation fall like rain on the truly godly, the sound of the wind meets the hypocrites also, and work a little on their natural passions; and then they are like a ship before the wind, without any ballast but in full sail, and in danger of being damaged on the rocks, or of being driven into irrelevant estuaries.]

Pantycelyn considered the whole history of Christianity as a continuous cycle of renewal and decline. He describes the pattern in *Ateb Philo-Evangelius*, referring to three hundred years of commitment and growth in the Early Church following the first Pentecost. Then, when the Emperor Constantine espoused Christianity, although Christians gained a greater measure of freedom, there followed a period of sluggishness which, in Pantycelyn's view, set the basis for 'all the heresies of the Roman Catholic Church'. During the fifteenth century there was an outpouring of the spirit on individuals, including Wycliff, Hus and the Waldensians, which paved the way for the Protestant Reformation. Again, said Williams, 'after establishing a church, lukewarmness came in like a flood' and, likewise after the Act of Toleration in 1689, apathy appeared hand in hand with religious freedom, until 'around the year 1738 the light broke out like the dawn in many regions of the world'. That revival was again followed by dissension and darkness, namely the Division in Welsh Methodism in 1750. However, writing in 1763, Williams could take heart in a new revival following some years of stagnation. As can be expected this is history written from a Protestant slant, but also emphasized is the belief that apathy seems to follow revival inevitably and that some are fired spiritually during the heat of revival only to cool afterwards. Undoubtedly Pantycelyn had seen this for himself amongst members of the Methodist movement.

Difficulties encountered by some of the members of the societies can be seen in the reports sent to the Association by the local superintendents. The

---

[7] Ibid. p. 15.

Associations from 1743 onwards appointed superintendents for different areas and each had responsibility for between twelve and twenty societies. As the number of societies grew it became increasingly difficult for them to give detailed accounts of the spiritual condition of the individual members under their supervision but, for a time at least, some succeeded in sending reports on each and every member. We know for instance that Mary John, a single woman from the Dyffryn-saith society in south Cardiganshire, was full of the certainty of faith in July 1743 but, two months later in September, she was under dark clouds and battling through storms, according to her superintendent, William Richard.[8] During the same period between July and September 1743 Susannah Rees, from the nearby society of Llwyndafydd, changed from 'teimlo'r hen ddyn yndddi'n gryf' ['feeling the old man strongly within her'] to be described as a 'enaid melys profiadol wedi dod trwy dreialon niferus' ['a sweet experienced soul having come through numerous trials'].[9]

It is impossible not to conclude from these reports that life was not always plain sailing for a number of the members. Bearing this is mind, it is not surprising to learn that the doctrines concerning assurance of faith and salvation proved to be a considerable bone of contention amongst the Methodists.[10] Harris came to believe that those who experienced conversion should feel full certainty of their faith, but Daniel Rowland and William Williams, on the other hand, were concerned that this demanded too much of some of the members, especially the new converts. This difference between them became apparent in a debate in 1742, as Harris recorded in his diary:

> There arose a dispute that held to midnight about our knowing our interest in Christ, between me and Brother Rowland...What I was afraid of in him was his feeding hypocrites; and what he feared in me was my overthrowing weak ones.[11]

Rowland's concerns are reflected in the rules of the societies. When describing the conditions for admitting new members in *Drws y Society Profiad* in 1777, Pantycelyn explained that the same measure of certainty should not be expected from those newly admitted and his opinion was:

> Am hynny nid oes le i gaead allan neb ag sydd tan y caracter o ymofyn, ac o wir ewyllysio cael bywyd tragwyddol, pa mor wan bynnag bydd datguddiedigaethau ac ymweliadau Duw iddynt.[12]

---

[8] National Library of Wales, Archive of the Calvinistic Methodists (CMA), Trefeca MSS 3002, 3004.
[9] Ibid.
[10] See Derec Llwyd Morgan, *Y Diwygiad Mawr* (Llandysul, 1981), pp. 160-4; David Bebbington, *Evangelicalism in Modern Britain: A history from the 1730s to the 1980s* (London, 1989), pp. 6-7, 42-50; Geraint Tudur, *Howell Harris* (Cardiff, 2000), pp. 155-7.
[11] CMA, Howel Harris's Diaries 86, 18 March 1742.

[Therefore, no one in the person of a seeker, and with a true desire for eternal life, should be shut out, however faint may be the revelations and visitations of God to him.]

It was therefore expected that the members would develop and mature in their faith after joining and that that process would not always run smooth.

Entire societies, as well as individuals, went through periods of ebb and flow. From time to time it was noted that there was renewal amongst the members of a particular society at a particular time, for example in the society at Llantrisant in Glamorgan at the end of 1743. On 1 January 1744 the superintendent wrote to the Association to explain that:

Y lle hwn, ag sudd unwaith yn drigfa Dreigiau yn awr yn iraidd. A ffrydia'n torri allan yntho, yma mau'r blaidd yn trigo geda'r ôn ar llewpart yn gorwedd geda'r mun.[13]

[This place, that was once the dwelling place of dragons, is now flourishing. With torrents breaking out, here the wolf dwells with the lamb and the leopard lies down with the kid.]

It appears that the hope was for regular rejuvenation amongst the members. Pantycelyn realized that members of the same society had a great effect either to inspire or oppress each other's spirits. He described the process in his prose works of the 1760s and 1770s, but he had seen the effects at work long before then when he took responsibility for superintending the societies of north Cardiganshire. He sent reports to the Association about them from 1745 onwards, describing their spiritual condition. Throughout this period he had nothing but praise for the members of the society at Lledrod, who 'were keeping in the zeal, fire and first love but increasing remarkably in light and sanctity'; 'like a city on a hill' and 'they do not rest greatly on their own wisdom but they are simple, wanting, honest and easy to handle'.[14] To realize that not all societies were so successful, one only needs to compare this praise regarding Lledrod with Pantycelyn's comments about the society of Tan-yr-allt, near Tregaron, over the same period. In 1745 he noticed that there were twenty members with the women being 'more warm, industrious and increasing than

---

[12] G. H. Hughes (ed.), *Gweithiau*, p. 214, English translation, *The Experience Meeting*, p. 37.

[13] Trefeca MSS 3006. This quotation also, of course, shows how the language of the Bible regularly enriched the Methodists' phraseology, as well as the use of Scriptural images to describe the spiritual condition of the members.

[14] Trefeca 3025, 3078. '... yn cadw yn y sêl, tân a'u cariad cyntaf ond yn rhyfeddol gynhyddu mewn goleini a santeiddrwydd'; 'fel dinas ar fryn'; 'nid ynt yn pwyso fawr iawn ar eu doethineb eu hunain ond y maent yn simil yn eisiau yn onest ag yn hawdd eu trin'.

the men'.[15] By January 1748, he complained that the society was 'very dead and lukewarm and have been thus since I have known them, they have as it were become infatuated with dejection and apathy and their lukewarmness quenches my zeal when I am with them'.[16] Later in the same year he reiterated his sad comments saying that he feared that they were on a 'very rotten foundation'.[17] Despite this, by 1750 he saw a glimmer of hope even for this forlorn society, because he foresaw that the society at Tan-yr-allt was 'pressing bit by bit towards heaven like an ass under its burden'.[18] It is worth remembering that Pantycelyn was well used to trudging, not on an ass but on horseback, over the hills of Carmarthenshire and the Brecon Beacons, and undoubtedly a wealth of experience lie behind this comparison.

Undoubtedly there were other societies like Tan-yr-allt who had to battle hard to gain every inch of ground. Certainly, some societies caused much more problems than others and the exhorters were often concerned that some members were focusing on material and trivial issues. For example, John Richard had difficulty with the society at Cnapllwyd, near Swansea, which was hotly disputing where the society should meet. It is obvious that John Richard lost all patience in the end with this bickering and said, without mincing words, that since he had been appointed to superintend them he therefore expected them to either agree to meet at the place of his choice or to leave the society without further ado.[19] It is not uncommon to see critical comments about a number of the societies and its members, especially from the mid 1740s onwards. By then the early growth had slowed to some extent with many of the Dissenters who were initially attracted to the movement drawing back as disagreements about dogma, and tension concerning the relationship with the Church, led them to turn their backs on the Methodist way. In many reports and letters from this period there is an uneasy feeling that the golden age was drawing to a close with converts lacking their old zeal and commitment. For example, in his report on the societies of south Carmarthenshire and west Glamorganshire in 1745, John Richard complained that they were in the midst of a dark night and that he was earnestly hoping for new life and zeal amongst them.[20] Likewise, Richard Tibbott by October 1746 lamented that there was little growth amongst members of the Montgomeryshire societies and he also expressed the desire for regeneration.[21] His hopes do not appear to have been

---

[15] Trefeca 3025. ' yn fwy gwresog, diwyd, cynyddol na'r gwrwod'.
[16] Trefeca 3049. '... yn farw ac yn glaiar iawn ac fel hyn mae er pan wi yn ei nabod, maent megis wedi rhiw ymwirioni mewn digalondid a marweiddre ag mae eu claiarineb yn diffodd fy zêl inne pan fwi yn eu mysc'.
[17] Trefeca 3058. '... sail bwdr iawn'.
[18] Trefeca 3078. '... yn gwthio gan ei pwyll bach tua'r nefodd fel assen tan ei baich'.
[19] Trefeca 3017.
[20] Trefeca 2945, p. 132.
[21] Trefeca 3035.

fulfilled as he continued to complain about the coldness and stagnation of the members in 1750. Indeed, he had to expel two members of the Llanbryn-mair society for their lassitude.[22] A number of reports from 1745 onwards also draw attention to the fact that the ranks of the societies were no longer being swelled by new members. It appeared that the movement had reached some sort of plateau in its history and, on balance, it appears that there was a decline in its fortunes by the end of the 1740s. By 1748 Howel Davies expressed his concern that the former glory which had surrounded the work had disappeared.[23] It is true to say that similar complaints can be seen throughout the 1740s but, by the second half of the decade, they appeared on a regular basis. This concern was corroborated with statistics from the societies which often showed a decline in numbers after the peak in 1744. As early as the Trefeca Association in February 1745 it was resolved to hold a day of prayer about the general apathy which was plaguing the revival in both Wales and England.[24] Even by this relatively early point in the movement's history, therefore, it had become apparent that some already saw the need for a new visitation to rekindle the flames amongst the current members and to try to attract others to join anew. Some of the Methodists were starting to realize that it was one thing to start a revival and quite another to maintain it.

Despite the difficulties, the way the societies were organized and the supervision over them ensured that there was an awareness of the problems, along with the means of trying to offer help and support. A steward was appointed in every society to lead the discussion and to care for the members. He would then convey any concerns about individual members to the private exhorter who would visit the society regularly. He, in turn, would consult with the superintendent who would visit all the societies allocated to him around once a fortnight. In addition, Howel Harris occasionally visited a number of districts in his capacity as general superintendent of the societies. The purpose of this system was to ensure that members did not feel isolated and lonely and that they did not have to suffer from doubts and fears without support. It is possible that the key relationship was that with the private exhorter as he would be the most regular visitor, as William Williams suggested in one of his reports:

> yr wyf yn dal sulw yn eu plith fel y mae y cynghorwyr private pa un bynag yn fawr mewn ffydd, zel, tan, gwybodeth ie neu clarineb ysowaeth, felly mae y society dan eu llywodraeth.[25]

---

[22] Trefeca 3075.
[23] Trefeca 1760.
[24] Trefeca 2945, p. 144.
[25] Trefeca 3025.

[I notice that however the private exhorters are among them, whether great in faith, zeal, fire, knowledge, or indeed of lukewarmness, so is the society under their government.]

As the private exhorters were the closest link with the societies, it was imperative that they were suitable to shoulder the responsibility. They were criticized by Morgan John Lewis, one of the superintendents, in 1744 for neglecting their duties[26] and Griffith Jones complained to Howel Harris that the lay exhorters were ignorant and unfit for the work.[27] As a result of a suggestion by George Whitefield, during his visit to the Association in 1749, it was resolved to try and ensure that exhorters received lessons in English spelling and grammar. Howel Harris wished to add lessons in logic, geography, history and philosophy to the list, as well as training on how to behave in respectable company and how to use a knife and fork in a genteel manner.[28] Who knows but that this threat of additional lessons for the exhorters may have contributed to their decision to expel Harris the following year!

It is also apparent that a number of the superintendents felt a strong link with the societies, even as the number of societies and members in their care increased. For example, John Richard, expressed his concern to the Association in 1750 that he was not as familiar as he should be with the spiritual condition of the members as he could not visit all the societies as often as he would wish. Consequently, he felt that he should relinquish some of the societies to another superintendent but, he declared:

O'r ochr arall pan y meddylwyf am rhoddi neb ohonynt y fynny byddaf yn teimlo cymmeint o anwyldeb atynt fel nas gallaf mewn modd yn y byd eu gadael.[29]

[On the other hand when I consider giving any of them up I feel such affection for them that I cannot by any means in the world part with them.]

It is therefore obvious that the relationship between the society and its exhorters was of key importance and that regular pastoral care was considered an integral part of the movement.

In addition to this direct support, the members could also call on assistance from the leaders of the movement. Harris's diaries are full of references to members asking him for guidance during his occasional visits to different areas. Some members also took the opportunity to write to him for advice. It must be remembered that this was the generation which received education in Griffith Jones's circulating schools, so amongst them were farmers and craftsmen and their wives and children who were in a position for the first time to

---

[26] Trefeca 1207.
[27] Howel Harris's Diaries, 13 October 1745.
[28] Howel Harris's Diaries 133, 1 February 1749; 134, 14 March 1749.
[29] Trefeca 3081.

communicate by means of the written word. This provided them with a network of support and friendship in addition to that which was available to them through the movement locally. Some members who had never even met Harris ventured to send word to him, secure that they would be welcome to do so as a result of the sense of belonging which was fostered amongst the Methodists. The Methodists were in a stronger position than their predecessors to use the written and printed word to disseminate their message as they were dealing with an increasingly literate audience. This could also facilitate the initiation and maintenance of revivals, as in 1762 when the publication of a volume of hymns by Williams Pantycelyn was one of the prominent features in fanning the flames of the revival.

The sense of belonging and the ability to depend on the support of the wider movement was also a source of comfort at times of difficulties and tribulations. Members were warned constantly not to expect an easy life when joining the movement. The early eighteenth-century Methodists faced substantial enmity from several directions: clerics and gentry who suspected them of wishing to start a revolution, and also family and friends of members who were suspicious of the influence of Methodism on their loved ones. Perhaps the most difficult persecution to suffer was the enmity of relatives and friends who at times threatened to sever all links with individuals if they persisted in attending the societies. It was much easier for later generations who had been brought up within the movement and who were part of an extended family of members. For the first generation of Methodists, it was not always possible to avoid conflict between the family of faith and their natural family. However, in some cases, opposition could serve as a means of strengthening their faith. The leaders offered comfort by reminding members that persecution confirmed that they were on the right path because, according to Pantycelyn 'Persecution is an inheritance which is sure to follow true religion'.[30] In his advice to the societies, which was translated from English in 1740, George Whitefield warned:

Yn ddiweddaf, fy mrodyr, disgwyliwch am rhan fawr o ddirmig; gweision Crist oeddent bob Amser yn Ynfydion y Byd.[31]

[Lastly, my brother, expect a large measure of contempt; the servants of Christ were ever fools in the world.]

In one of his sermons Daniel Rowland maintained that the 'cross is the way to the crown'[32] and Harris, after being mistreated by a hostile mob, took pride in the honour of being beaten for his Lord's sake and like his Lord. When

---

[30] G. Hughes (ed.), *Gweithiau*, p. 29.
[31] George Whitefield, *Llythyr oddiwrth y Parchedig Mr George Whitefield At Societies neu Gymdeithasau Crefyddol a osodwyd yn ddiweddar ar droed mewn amriw Leoedd yng Nghymrua Lloegr* (Pontypool, 1740), p. 25.
[32] Daniel Rowland, *Pum Pregeth* (Carmarthen, 1772), p. 34.

members were severely persecuted they could depend on the movement's support, including practical and financial assistance if there were legal costs. For example, when Morgan Hughes, the exhorter, was imprisoned at Cardigan in 1743 for holding an illegal assembly, Harris worked tirelessly to seek advice from lawyers who were sympathetic towards the movement.[33] A great deal of the appeal of Methodism lay in the ready support which was offered at every level of the movement: by fellow members in the society, by the steward, by the exhorters and by the leaders themselves.

Even during the general feeling of decline at the end of the 1740s, with the tensions which would lead to the Division increasing, there were some amongst the movement who were still full of hope. When writing his report for the Association at Llanidloes in May 1750, the last united association before the split between Rowland's and Harris's supporters, James William described the societies of northern Carmarthenshire as follows:

Y mae llawer yn weinion ag yn llesg, rhai i lawr ag i fyny, megis ar eu traed a'u dwylo yn ymladd a byd, cnawd a diafol, ag yn resolfo i ymladd hyd y diwedd trwy nerth Duw a'n Harglwydd Iesu Grist, nes cael y fuddugolieth yn lân. ... Y mae rhai yn arddel Crist ond nid ŵi yn cael lle i feddwl eu bod nhw yn nabod Crist. ... Y mae rhai gwedy myned i ymresymy ynghylch gwaed y bendicedic Iesu, rhai a hayrant mai trwy waed yr oen, heb rinwedd nag effaith, rhai a fynant mae y rhinwedd ohono a'r olwg arno trwy ffydd a dynodd eu heneidiau ar ol ef.[34]

[Many are weak and feeble, some down and up, as if on their feet and hands fighting with world, flesh and devil, and resolving to fight until the end through the strength of God and our Lord Jesus Christ, until they win a clear victory. ... Some acknowledge Christ but I do not have cause to think that they know Christ. ... Some have gone to reasoning about the blood of the blessed Jesus, some claim that it was through the blood of the lamb, without virtue or effect, some claim that it was the merits of it and the sight of it through faith which drew their souls after him.]

It is obvious from the quotation that James William had a number of problems, including the emphasis on the merits of Christ's blood, which was a sign of the Moravian tendencies which was one of the factors behind the expulsion of Howel Harris. Despite this, he closes the report by maintaining positively: 'Ond yn fyr, y mae yr Arglwydd Iesu yn y seiads bach' ['But in short, the Lord Jesus is in the little societies'].[35] Perhaps James William's attitude is significant in terms of explaining the continuation of Methodism through the following twelve years of division. James William was a farmer from Berws, Llanddewibrefi, and not especially wealthy according to his will. There is no evidence that he received much education, and it does not appear

---

[33] Trefeca 817, Howel Harris's Diaries 98, 25 March 1743.
[34] Trefeca 3074.
[35] Ibid.

that he was proficient at all in English. However, he exhibited the kind of quiet commitment which existed amongst the exhorters to continue to attend to the needs of the 'small societies'; a commitment which was at least partly responsible for the continuation of the movement. The effects of the dissension amongst the leaders were mitigated by the fact that exhorters and superintendents like James William continued to visit the members to try and assuage their fears. In describing the origins of Methodism in England John Walsh suggested that quiet and regular evangelizing work was chiefly responsible for the growth of the movement. 'In England', he said, 'the early extension of evangelicalism was accomplished by gradual, incremental growth rather than by the "big bang" of a Great Awakening.'[36] The same can be said of Wales to a great extent because, despite the importance of revival in creating the movement in the first instance and of subsequent visitations in attracting new members, as in 1762, in essence the movement's success can be attributed to the careful shepherding of the societies through the heady days of the 1740s and through the dire times of the Division in the 1750s. The system and practices established during the 1740s provided a firm foundation which enabled the movement to survive the Division and the period of decline which followed. Methodism continued to exist in Wales, and to flourish in the revival of 1762, because of the support and fellowship which was available in the society and in the wider movement. The future of the revival, therefore, was secured as a result of years of pastoral care and of learning through experience, which surmounted periods when the whole movement appeared to be lumbering along slowly and heavy-laden like an 'ass under its burden'.

---

[36] John Walsh, 'Methodism and the Origins of English-speaking Evangelicalism', *Evangelicalism: comparative studies of popular Protestantism in North America, the British Isles, and beyond 1700-1900* (Oxford, 1994), p. 33.

CHAPTER 2

John Lewis and the Promotion of the International Evangelical Revival, 1735-56

David Ceri Jones

Historical writing about religious revivals has often been content to work within the boundaries of an interpretative structure that introduces a sharp dichotomy between an older providentially-inspired view of revivals and a more modern utilitarian view. Up until about the end of the eighteenth century, evangelicals, it is argued, following the lead given by Jonathan Edwards, believed that religious revivals were 'surprising works of God',[1] the direct result of the outpouring of the Holy Spirit, mirroring what had occurred on the day of Pentecost. However, during the early nineteenth century, a sea-change took place as Charles Grandison Finney transformed spontaneous revivals into events which could be planned and set in motion by the fulfilment of certain conditions.[2] The reality has often been very different. Mid eighteenth-century evangelicals, no less than their nineteenth, twentieth and even twenty-first century counterparts, realized the importance of using 'means' to fan the flames of their awakenings. While there are clearly differences between revivals in different places and at different historical periods, all revivals should, in Susan O'Brien's words, 'take their place on a continuum of Protestant evangelical development'.[3]

---

[1] For Edwards's view of revival see C. C. Goen (ed.), *The Works of Jonathan Edwards, Volume IV: The Great Awakening* (New Haven, 1972), pp. 32-46; George M. Marsden, *Jonathan Edwards: A Life* (New Haven, 2003), pp. 153-63, 172-3, 210-12.

[2] For influential examples of this interpretation see William G. McLoughlin, *Modern Revivalism: Charles Grandison Finney to Billy Graham* (New York, 1959), pp. 1-11; John Kent, *Holding the Fort: Studies in Victorian Revivalism* (London, 1978), pp. 9-37; Michael J. Crawford, *Seasons of Grace: Colonial New England's Revival Tradition in its British Context* (New York, 1991); Iain H. Murray, *Revival and Revivalism: The Making and Marring of American Evangelicalism, 1750-1858* (Edinburgh, 1994).

[3] Susan O'Brien, '"A Transatlantic Community of Saints": The Great Awakening and the First Evangelical Network, 1735-1755', in *American Historical Review*, 91 (1986), 815. For other examples of this modified view see Kathryn Teresa Long, *The Revival of 1857-58: Interpreting an American Religious Awakening* (New York, 1995); Janice Holmes, *Religious Revivals in Britain and Ireland, 1859-1905* (Dublin, 2000), and Kenneth S. Jeffrey, *'When the Lord Walked the Land': The 1858-1862 Revival in the North East of Scotland* (Carlisle, 2002).

Recently, considerable attention has been devoted to some of the ways in which George Whitefield actively promoted and perpetuated his revivals, leading Frank Lambert to suggest that Whitefield, far from holding to an exclusively providential understanding of his revivals, was in fact one of the first proponents of 'modern mass evangelism'.[4] For much of its first decade the Evangelical Revival in England was a maelstrom of competing personalities, ideologies and allegiances all of whom, until early 1740 at least, were contained within the confines of the Fetter Lane Society. Whitefield had been active in London since the summer of 1736 and by early 1739 he had established a network of societies linking together evangelicals in Bristol, Bedfordshire, Yorkshire, Wiltshire and London itself.[5] At this stage, they all, to a greater or lesser degree, shared Whitefield's moderate Calvinism, and his commitment to heart religion. It was not until May 1738, after John Wesley's famous heart-warming experience at Aldersgate Street, that a new element was introduced into the London awakening as the anti-Calvinist rhetoric that Wesley had learned from his mother[6] precipitated the splintering of the English revival into three factions, the Moravians, the Arminians or Wesleyans and the Calvinists or Whitefieldians.[7]

At the same time as he was extending the boundaries of the English revival Whitefield also began to move on a much broader stage. Although the London awakening remained the primary focus for evangelicals everywhere, it quickly became only one facet of an international movement that extended from the American colonies in the west to Ireland, Wales, Scotland, England, many parts of continental Europe, and as far east as Prussia. The one factor that united these otherwise diverse awakenings was the figure of Whitefield himself. His revivals were deeply rooted in the British Atlantic world of the mid eighteenth century. With its tendency to transcend traditional ecclesiastical boundaries, Evangelicalism flourished in those areas that were most free from the

---

[4] Frank Lambert, *'Pedlar in Divinity': George Whitefield and the Transatlantic Revivals* (Princeton, 1994), p. 231. See also Harry S. Stout, *The Divine Dramatist: George Whitefield and the Rise of Modern Evangelicalism* (Grand Rapids, 1991) and Boyd S. Schlenther, 'Religious Faith and Commercial Empire', P. J. Marshall (ed.), in *The Oxford History of the British Empire II: The Eighteenth Century* (Oxford, 1998), pp. 128-50.

[5] Colin Podmore, *The Moravian Church in England 1728–1760* (Oxford, 1998), pp. 34-6.

[6] John A. Newton, *Susanna Wesley and the Puritan Tradition in Methodism* (2nd edn; Peterborough, 2002); Herbert Boyd McGonigle, *'Sufficient Saving Grace': John Wesley's Evangelical Arminianism* (Carlisle, 2001), pp. 73-105.

[7] These divisions are outlined in detail in David Ceri Jones, '"The Lord did give me a particular honour to make [me] a peacemaker": Howel Harris, John Wesley and Methodist Infighting, 1739-1750', *Bulletin of the John Rylands University of Manchester Library* (forthcoming).

institutional control of the established churches.⁸ By appealing to individuals to respond to his message of the new birth on the spot and to take responsibility for their religious lives, Whitefield cannily tapped into the spirit of the age that prized individualism and independence.⁹ Utilizing the marketing techniques that the burgeoning consumer revolution had popularized, Whitefield peddled the gospel as a religious commodity to be purchased by those middling sorts who had gradually also become religious consumers.¹⁰ His strategy was successful because, as Carla Gardina Pestana has shown, the relative dearth of institutional forms in the British Atlantic world tended to favour those faiths that could function well in an institutionally simplified environment.¹¹

The rudimentary spirituality of evangelicalism, eminently adaptable in different cultures and contexts, therefore provided an alternative institutional structure, however basic, that bound evangelicals from diverse backgrounds together into something resembling a coherent evangelical movement. The sinews of this structure were put in place by Whitefield himself who, as soon as he heard about the existence of religious awakenings outside London, set about forging links between them. By first visiting awakenings as they got underway in the later 1730s and then, when that became logistically impossible, creating a network of correspondence that kept the leaders of the awakenings in close contact with one another, Whitefield began to piece together an evangelical movement that had at its core the twin concepts of the new birth and the experience of religious revival – features elastic enough to be interpreted in any number of ways. As the awakenings continued to develop into more established revival movements, these *ad hoc* contacts proved insufficiently flexible to deal with either the amount or sophistication of the information being circulated by letter. Whitefield therefore established more durable forms of communication that included a more complex letter distribution network, co-ordinated from his Tabernacle at Moorfields; an inexpensive weekly religious periodical and an ambitious evangelical publication programme that published both his own books, those of other revivalists and some of the devotional classics written by the Puritans and Pietists.

---

⁸ D. W. Bebbington, *Evangelicalism in Modern Britain: A History from the 1730s to the 1990s* (London, 1989), pp. 26-7.

⁹ See Bruce Hindmarsh, 'Reshaping Individualism: The Private Christian, Eighteenth-Century Religion and the Enlightenment', in Deryck W. Lovegrove (ed.), *The Rise of the Laity in Evangelical Protestantism* (London, 2002), pp. 67-84.

¹⁰ Lambert, *'Pedlar in Divinity'*, pp. 25-36. For the wider context of the transatlantic consumer revolution see Neil McKendrick, 'The Consumer Revolution of Eighteenth-Century England' in Neil McKendrick, John Brewer and J. H. Plumb, *The Birth of a Consumer Society: The Commercialisation of Eighteenth-Century England* (London, 1982), pp. 9-33; John Brewer, *The Pleasures of the Imagination: English Culture in the Eighteenth Century* (London, 1997).

¹¹ Carla Gadina Pestana, 'Religion', in David Armitage and Michael J. Braddick (eds), *The British Atlantic World, 1500-1800* (Houndmills, 2002), p. 74.

Whitefield would not have been able to achieve this without the assistance of a number of loyal and influential printers and booksellers who devoted their professional expertise to overseeing the day-to-day administration of this network from London. Initially, he relied on James Hutton (1715-95), the Moravian bookseller and founding member of the Fetter Lane Society,[12] and William Seward (1711-40), a wealthy former stockbroker, who acted as Whitefield's principal secretary, chief reporter and press agent[13] between 1737 and his untimely death at the hands of a mob at Hay-on-Wye in 1740.[14] By manipulating the media and ensuring that only positive stories about Whitefield's activities appeared in the pages of the most widely read newspapers and periodicals of the day, Seward was able to wield a significant degree of control over Whitefield's public persona, heightening the expectations of people in those areas next on Whitefield's agenda for a visit thereby facilitating the revival's spread from place to place. After Seward's death, Whitefield came to rely on a small group of secretaries, printers and booksellers, that included Hutton, Samuel Mason,[15] John Syms,[16] John Lewis and later Thomas Boddington who combined his duties with the co-leadership of the Tabernacle Society during Whitefield's extended absence in the American colonies.[17] Although none of them accompanied Whitefield on his

---

[12] John A. Vickers (ed.), *A Dictionary of Methodism in Britain and Ireland* (Peterborough, 2000), p. 172; J. E. Hutton, *A History of the Moravian Church* (2nd edn; London, 1909), pp. 283-88.

[13] Lambert, *'Pedlar in Divinity'*, p. 57.

[14] See George L. Fairs, 'Notes on the Death of William Seward at Hay, 1740', in *Journal of the Historical Society of the Presbyterian Church of Wales*, 58, no. 1 (1973), 12-18.

[15] Samuel Mason was originally a butcher at Spitalfields, but after his conversion to Methodism, he opened a bookshop at Love Lane in Wood Street, London. He and his wife Sarah were prominent members of the Tabernacle Society. H. R. Plomer (ed.), *A Dictionary of the Printers and Booksellers who were at work in England, Scotland, and Ireland from 1726 to 1775* (London, 1968), p. 164; Graham C. G. Thomas, 'George Whitefield and Friends: The Correspondence of Some Early Methodists', in *The National Library of Wales Journal*, 26 (1990), 251-64.

[16] John Syms served as Whitefield's secretary during his first visit to the American colonies in 1737-8, taking a particular interest in the Orphan house. He continued as secretary after he and Whitefield had returned to London in 1738. Arnold A. Dallimore, *George Whitefield: The Life and Times of the Great Evangelist of the 18th Century Revival*, I (London, 1970), p. 395; Arnold A. Dallimore, *George Whitefield: The Life and Times of the Great Evangelist of the 18th Century Revival*, II (Edinburgh, 1980), pp. 142, 154, 155, 213.

[17] Thomas Boddington was a London merchant who became the book steward at Whitefield's Tabernacle after John Syms joined the Moravians in 1745. National Library of Wales, Aberystwyth, Calvinist Methodist Archive (Trevecka Group), The Trevecka Letters, 1674, Thomas Boddington to Mrs Doyle (29 June 1747); Lambert, *'Pedlar in Divinity'*, pp. 91-2.

itineraries as Seward had done, they each played an important role at the heart of the revival, co-ordinating the Whitefieldian publicity machine.

None of this group, however, played as significant a role as John Lewis (d. 1756), the London-based printer. Little is known about Lewis's early life or of his activities before he joined the Methodists. We know that he was born in Radnorshire and some have speculated that he may have been the brother of Thomas Lewis, the Breconshire exhorter and later sometime assistant at Whitefield's Tabernacle.[18] He had moved to London by 1728, but when he established his print-works or bookshop at Bartholemew Close is not clear.[19] Neither do we know much about his spiritual pilgrimage. Unusually, he makes no reference to his religious conversion in either his letters or in the pages of his magazine and gives no indication about how or why he had found his way to Fetter Lane in the later 1730s. All that we know for certain is that by 1739, Lewis was a prominent member of the Fetter Lane Society and that he had grown particularly close to Whitefield, a hint perhaps that it had been under Whitefield's preaching that Lewis experienced his spiritual awakening.[20]

In September 1740, Lewis came to greater prominence as the editor of a religious periodical called *The Christian's Amusement*. The repeal of the Licensing Act in 1695 had led to the proliferation of popular and inexpensive newspapers and magazines that flowed from the presses of the hundreds of print shops that had been established in London.[21] Each issue of Lewis's weekly magazine was four pages in length and reflected Lewis's preoccupation with proving the authenticity of the revival. For most of its initial print run Whitefield was absent in the American colonies and his input was therefore negligible. Although it contained accounts of the progress of various awakenings, revival narratives did not figure prominently in its pages at this stage. Instead, Lewis used the magazine to root the revival within a longer Christian tradition by printing pious literature from the past, reprinting letters from prominent ministers in Britain and America and, perhaps most originally of all, including his own narrative history of the Waldenses and Albigenses, radical reform groups from the twelfth century who had attempted to turn-up

---

[18] R. T. Jenkins, 'John Lewis the Printer and his Family', in *Proceedings of the Wesley Historical Society*, 21, no. 5 (1938), 129. For more on Thomas Lewis see J. E. Lloyd and R. T. Jenkins (eds), *Dictionary of Welsh Biography down to 1940* (London, 1959), 561.

[19] Jenkins, 'John Lewis the Printer and his Family', 129.

[20] For more on Lewis's background see M. H. Jones, 'John Lewis, the Printer of *The Weekly History*', in *Journal of the Historical Society of the Presbyterian Church of Wales*, 4, no. 3 (1919), 84-92; M. H. Jones, 'John Lewis, Printer to the Religious Societies', in *Journal of the Historical Society of the Presbyterian Church of Wales*, 5, no. 1 (1920), 6-11.

[21] For the impact of the Act see John Feather, *A History of British Publishing* (New York, 1988), pp. 50-63; Eiluned Rees, 'The Welsh Book-Trade Before 1820', in *Libri Walliae: A Catalogue of Welsh Books and Books Printed in Wales, 1546-1820* (Aberystwyth, 1987), pp. xvii-xxix.

the spiritual temperature of the medieval Catholic church, in much the same way as the Methodists were trying to do. The magazine was printed for seven months, but struggled to win a large enough readership to cover the basic costs of its production throughout its print run. However, it was Lewis's loyalty to Whitefield that had become the biggest hindrance to its success. By 1740 tensions between the followers of Whitefield and those of the Wesley brothers had reached boiling point and Lewis's defence of Whitefield's moderate Calvinism meant that the magazine had become too partisan to be popular with the whole evangelical constituency.[22]

When Whitefield returned to England in March 1740, after almost a year in the American colonies, Lewis was on the verge of abandoning the magazine. Whitefield arrived in London and discovered that his revival was in a sorry state with the Wesley brothers intent, it seemed, on making their Arminianism the dominant expression of the revival in England. Anticipating the impact of imminent controversy with them, Whitefield offered his services to Lewis as both the editor and the source of a regular supply of letters for inclusion in a re-launched evangelical magazine. After little more than a two-week interlude, *The Weekly History* reappeared. Again it was printed weekly, on four folio pages, and quickly established itself as the mouthpiece of all those who sympathized with Whitefield's version of the revival. However, it was very different in tone from Lewis's first magazine. Gone were the lengthy extracts from pious authors, the historical accounts of worthy saints from the past and letters of commendation from prominent ministers. In their place were accounts of Whitefield's itinerancy, news about fresh advances of the revival, conversion narratives and letters addressing some of the problems affecting many of the rank-and-file converts. In Whitefield's hands, *The Weekly History* was transformed into a vibrant and popular means of keeping Calvinist evangelicals in close contact with one another, and of bolstering the position of his awakening at precisely the same time as it appeared that his converts would be swallowed-up by Wesley.[23]

Among the magazine's most enthusiastic supporters were the Methodists in Wales, and perhaps the best way to understand how Lewis's magazine functioned is to examine its role within one particular awakening. The Methodists in Wales had been part of Whitefield's international evangelical network from its inception when Whitefield and Howel Harris first exchanged letters at the beginning of 1739.[24] Whitefield visited Wales on two subsequent occasions, and in April 1739 Harris accompanied him back to London where

---

[22] Trevecka 235, John Lewis to Howel Harris, no date.
[23] Although Susan Durden's, 'A Study of the First Evangelical Magazines, 1740-1748', *Journal of Ecclesiastical History*, 27, no. 3 (1976), 255-75, gives more detail about the role and significance of the magazine, she does analyse its contents in any detail.
[24] Trevecka 133, George Whitefield to Howel Harris, 20 December 1738; and Trevecka 136, Howel Harris to George Whitefield, 8 January 1739.

Whitefield introduced him to the 'ripe saints'[25] at Fetter Lane.[26] It was an exchange of visits that inaugurated the close co-operation of evangelicals in England and Wales. Harris became a frequent sight at Whitefield's Tabernacle, deputizing for him when he was away from London, and Whitefield became the Welsh Methodists' 'Elder brother'[27] who was drafted in to assist when they took decisions that affected the long-term shape of the movement. This relationship was formalized in January 1743 when the first 'Joint Association of English and Welsh Calvinistic Methodism' took place at Watford near Caerphilly. Whitefield was appointed Moderator and Howel Harris was given a roving brief that enabled him to split his time almost equally between England and Wales in the years that followed.[28] It was not until late 1749 when Whitefield attempted to relinquish the leadership of the English Calvinistic revival and Howel Harris was forced to retreat in disgrace to Trefeca that the relationship between the two awakenings atrophied.[29]

Such a brief sketch of the way in which the Welsh and English Calvinistic revivals were drawn together during the 1740s does not do justice to the extent to which there was a free-flow of information, usually in the form of letters, and circulated most effectively in the pages of *The Weekly History*, beneath the level of the level of the pioneer revivalists. In many respects the Welsh Methodists were the mainstay of Whitefield's international communications network and remained some of its most avid readers and frequent contributors. Their letters often sustained the letter-writing network and they were usually among the first to read of the progress of the revival through the pages of John Lewis's magazine. They responded enthusiastically to opportunities to buy and read the latest evangelical literature, and invariably gave sacrificially to support the cause of the Whitefield's Orphan house in Georgia. Much of this activity depended on Howel Harris and he remained, to a significant degree, the main conduit through which the resources of the wider evangelical community reached Wales. Harris committed inordinate amounts of his time to cultivating the relationship between Wales and the wider revival, and it could conceivably be argued that this was one of the main reasons for his commitment to full participation in the London awakening. One of the most fruitful partnerships

---

[25] National Library of Wales, Aberystwyth, Calvinist Methodist Archive, Howel Harris's Diary 43, 25 April 1739.

[26] Geraint Tudur, *Howell Harris: From Conversion to Separation, 1735-50* (Cardiff, 2000), pp. 51-9.

[27] David Ceri Jones, *'A Glorious Work in the World': Welsh Methodism and the International Evangelical Revival, 1735-1750* (Cardiff, 2004).

[28] National Library of Wales, Aberystwyth, Calvinist Methodist Archive (Trevecka Group) 2945, Records of Associations, pp. 5-6.

[29] Boyd Stanley Schlenther, *Queen of the Methodists: The Countess of Huntingdon and the Eighteenth-Century Crisis of Faith and Society* (Durham, 1997), pp. 39-42; Geraint Tudur, 'The King's Daughter: A Reassessment of Anne Harris of Trefeca', *Journal of Welsh Religious History*, 7 (1999), 55-77.

that he enjoyed was with John Lewis, but the extent to which he worked alongside Lewis, providing material for the magazine, seeking out new readers, establishing efficient networks for its circulation, particularly in Wales, and helping Lewis to overcome many of the financial problems that resulted from the undertaking, has not been fully appreciated.

Harris had been an enthusiastic reader of *The Christian's Amusement* and had even offered to be its chief Welsh distributor when its fortunes began to flag early in 1741.[30] Initially, Harris had been cautious about promoting the magazine in Wales because of the obvious language barrier. Most Methodists in Wales were, after all, native Welsh speakers. While some did have an adequate understanding of English, many others had only a rudimentary understanding of the language.[31] To rectify this Harris initially considered launching a Welsh-language version of the magazine, or at least securing the translation of choice passages from the English version, but the logistics of the task quickly put a swift end to his plans.[32] Instead, he used his position at the heart of the English and Welsh awakenings to develop a network of distributors who could receive bundles of the magazine and distribute copies throughout south and west Wales. In 1741, for example, he persuaded Richard Jenkins, an exhorter at Llandinam, to take *The Weekly History* with him as he visited his societies in Montgomeryshire[33] and he similarly urged William Richard to take copies with him as he travelled around south Cardiganshire and western Pembrokeshire.[34] But in south-west Wales more generally, it was Daniel Rowland who acted as the main distributor. In October 1742, for example, he received a large consignment of magazines from Howel Harris, complete with detailed instructions for their wider distribution. Harris instructed him to send copies to Elizabeth Thomas at Longhouse, who would distribute them throughout Pembrokeshire with the help of Howel Davies; and he requested that Rowland forward the remainder to Griffith Jones who, he hoped, would be prepared to take them with him as he travelled around Carmarthenshire.[35]

Precise distribution figures for the magazine in Wales are difficult to ascertain. Frank Lambert has estimated that Whitefield's itinerants delivered at least five hundred copies on their regular circuits throughout England and Wales.[36] By 1747, the minutes of Whitefield's Tabernacle indicate that about four hundred copies were being sent out at any one time and that they were

---

[30] Trevecka 319, Howel Harris to John Lewis (19 March 1741).

[31] Trevecka 235, John Lewis to Howel Harris (no date); Eryn M. White, 'The Established Church, Dissent and the Welsh Language, c.1660-1811', in Geraint H. Jenkins (ed.), *The Welsh Language before the Industrial Revolution* (Cardiff, 1997), pp. 264-5.

[32] Trevecka 319, Howel Harris to John Lewis, 19 March 1741.

[33] Trevecka 372, Howel Harris to Richard Jenkins, 17 August 1741.

[34] Trevecka 668, Howel Harris to William Richard, 29 September 1742.

[35] Trevecka 644, Howel Harris to Daniel Rowland, 14 October 1742.

[36] Lambert, *'Pedlar in Divinity'*, p. 70.

distributed according to the main areas of Calvinistic Methodist strength. By the later 1740s most were sent to the south-west of England, but a significant number were also sent to Gloucester, the Midlands and Essex. There are no concrete figures for Wales, though it would probably be safe to say that circulation figures for 1741 and 1742, when the revival was at its height, would have been far in excess of the four hundred ordered from John Lewis in 1747, when *The Christian History*, as the magazine had then become known,[37] was in its final days. While there is no way of calculating the number of copies that Howel Harris almost always carried back to Wales after his visits to London, we know that substantial numbers of the magazine regularly entered Wales through the endeavours of well-placed Methodist sympathizers in towns on the Welsh border.[38] Demand must have been high at times, particularly when its pages were packed with letters that recounted fresh outbreaks of revival, as happened in Scotland in 1742.[39] In 1743 Harris asked John Lewis to send any spare old issues of *The Weekly History*, which he was confident would be eagerly snapped up by the Welsh Methodists if the price was right![40]

In order to keep circulation figures in Wales buoyant, Harris found innovative ways of circumventing the language barrier, allowing monoglot Welsh speakers to benefit from the contents of the magazine. Where societies possessed a bilingual exhorter letters from the magazine were read aloud with ease by *ad hoc* or précised translations. Issues could also be circulated informally among friends and it is not difficult to imagine society members with some rudimentary understanding of English reading edited highlights to their Welsh-speaking neighbours in more informal settings. There were also others who did not depend on Howel Harris to receive copies of the magazine to quite the same extent. Thomas Bowen established his own links with John Lewis and received regular supplies of *The Weekly History* which he was able to circulate among his friends and fellow society members.[41] Sufficient numbers of Welsh Methodists wrote to either John Lewis or Howel Harris to express their appreciation for the issues of the magazine that they had seen to suggest that this must have been the case.[42]

For those Welsh Methodists who avidly waited for the latest instalment of evangelical news, Lewis's magazine served a number of functions. It quickly became one of the most convenient means to learn about events in some of the

---

[37] Durden, 'A Study of the First Evangelical Magazines', 264-6.
[38] See Trevecka 234, John Lewis to Howel Harris, no date; Trevecka 1288, Joseph Humphreys to Howel Harris, 30 January 1744.
[39] John Lewis (ed.), *The Weekly History*, no. 66, Saturday, 10 July 1742.
[40] Trevecka 853, John Lewis to Howel Harris, 8 April 1743.
[41] Trevecka 816, Thomas Bowen to Howel Harris, 24 March 1743.
[42] Trevecka 504, James Oulton to Howel Harris, 3 March 1742; 'The Copy of a letter from Mrs Anne T__s of Pembrokeshire in Wales to Mr Howel Harris in London (Longhouse, 3 September 1742)', Lewis (ed.), *The Weekly History*, no. 80, Saturday 16 October 1742.

more distant corners of the evangelical world. The letters that they read, and which some of them also wrote, bore ample testimony to their familiarity with the 'glorious work [...] going on in the world'.[43] The revivalists were convinced, echoing the views expressed by Jonathan Edwards, that news of a revival in 'any place, tends greatly to awaken and engage the minds of persons, in other places'.[44] Reading reports about fresh awakenings was designed to concentrate the minds of readers upon the potentially difficult task of emulating what they read about in their own communities, thereby extending the revival into new areas.

The magazine also developed a far more didactic role and became one of the tools that the revivalists used to reinforce their definition of the experience that lay at the heart of the revival – conversion or the new birth. Their stress on the immediate attainability of conversion was a marked departure from the interpretation preferred by most of their Puritan predecessors and, to some extent, reflected the very different priorities of the Age of Enlightenment.[45] John Lewis filled the magazine with case studies of conversions, intended to direct readers towards a correct understanding of the new birth and to help those who had recently passed through such an emotionally demanding experience interpret it correctly.[46] For many of those who had found the magazine to be an indispensable guide through the minefield of the conversion process, there was no logical reason why it could not also be put to other more sophisticated uses. For some it almost became a primitive self-help forum, in which converts wrote letters, usually to one of the revivalists, outlining their problems. These letters were often printed in the magazine, as were replies outlining the advice one or other of the revivalists thought necessary to solve the particular difficulty in question.[47] For many evangelicals aligning themselves with the revival often entailed considerable personal sacrifice.

---

[43] Trevecka 708, Howel Harris to Marmaduke Gwynne, 22 October 1742.

[44] Quoted in Durden, 'A Study of the First Evangelical Magazines', 257.

[45] For more on the relationship between Evangelicalism and the Enlightenment see, D. W. Bebbington, 'Revival and Enlightenment in Eighteenth-Century England', Edith L. Blumhofer and Randall Balmer (eds), *Modern Christian Revivals* (Urbana, 1993), pp. 17-41.

[46] For examples of these model conversion narratives see 'The Copy of a Letter from a Friend in the Country (26 April 1742)', Lewis (ed.), *The Weekly History*, no. 57 (Saturday, 8 May 1742); Trevecka 983, Ann Harry to Howel Harris, 15 September 1743. For further analysis of the Methodist conversion narrative tradition see D. Bruce Hindmarsh, '"My chains fell off, my heart was free": Early Methodist Conversion Narrative in England', in *Church History: Studies in Christianity and Culture*, 68, no. 4 (1999), 910-29.

[47] See, for example, Trevecka 797, Howel Harris to Elizabeth Thomas, 10 February 1743; 'A letter from Mr Howel Harris to a sister under trials', Lewis (ed.), *The Weekly History*, no. 53, Saturday, 10 April 1742; Trevecka 827, Howel Harris to Jane Godwin, 25 March 1743.

Some endured the disapproval of family members, and had to live with the suspicion of husbands, wives, parents or children. But first-generation evangelicals also lived in tense times politically and fears that their enthusiasm was a reversion to the worst excesses of the mid-seventeenth century were widespread. The Jacobite threat in the mid 1740s forced them to reiterate their loyalty to the Hanoverians and to the Church of England and Lewis's magazine became one of the most convenient public forums in which they could do so.[48]

The magazine also served an array of more practical purposes. The new friends and contacts to which it introduced many evangelicals were a source of great consolation to those who had endured the hardship of losing the support of friends and family. A select few were even lucky enough to find their marriage partners through the network.[49] John Lewis had also attempted to create a genuine spiritual community in which members were encouraged to share any practical gifts and services that they had to offer. It was through responding to advertisements in the magazine that many evangelicals in Wales, as well as in London, looked after some of their more practical needs. By drumming up business in its pages, others were able to rescue their businesses from ruin on account of their new evangelical associations.[50] But for many in Wales, the pages of the magazine became the main source of information concerning one of the causes closest to their hearts – Whitefield's Orphan house at Bethesda in the recently founded colony of Georgia. By contributing generously to this philanthropic venture, many of the rank-and-file Welsh evangelicals claimed a tangible stake in the worldwide extension of their evangelical faith. The receipt of up-to-date information concerning some of the ways in which their contributions were being used, regularly repaid their financial sacrifices.

Despite playing such a valuable role in the English and Welsh Calvinistic revivals throughout its eight years in print, John Lewis's magazine was never wholly free from uncertainties regarding its long-term viability. Part of the problem undoubtedly stemmed from the transitory nature of the revival and the magazine's symbiotic relationship to it. When things were going well, the

---

[48] 'From Mr Howel Harris, at Trevecca, near the Hay, in Breconshire, South Wales to Mr Thomas Adams, at the Tabernacle House, near Moorfields, London', John Lewis (ed.), in *The Christian History; or a General Account of the Progress of the Gospel in England, Wales, Scotland and America: So far as the Rev. Mr Whitefield, his Fellow Labourers, and Assistants are Concerned* (1747), 21-3.

[49] For the marriage of Elizabeth James to George Whitefield in 1741 see, Roger Lee Brown, 'The Marriage of George Whitefield at Caerphilly', *Journal of the Historical Society of the Presbyterian Church of Wales*, 7 (1983), 24-30. For the case of Sarah Gwynne, who married Charles Wesley see Frederick C. Gill, *Charles Wesley: the First Methodist* (London, 1963), pp. 125-42; Richard P. Heitzenrater, *Wesley and the People Called Methodists* (Nashville, 1995), p. 172.

[50] 'Editorial Comments', John Lewis (ed.), in *The Christian's Amusement: Containing Letters Concerning the Progress of the Gospel both at Home and Abroad*, no. 12.

magazine prospered, news was plentiful and exciting and circulation figures constantly remained healthy. But when the revival appeared to be foundering, particularly after the divisions of 1740 and 1741 and then again in 1745, the magazine struggled to maintain its place in the regular reading habits of many Methodists. Lewis therefore had to develop a number of innovative marketing techniques to maintain the popularity of the magazine and stave off his own bankruptcy. The magazine had first changed its title in 1741, but it ran into difficulties again two years later. This time Lewis proposed changing its format entirely, printing it in a neat pocket-sized edition, less frequently and with the more cumbersome title, *An Account of the Most Remarkable Particulars Relating to the Present Progress of the Gospel*. By once again lowering its price and offering to deliver it to addresses in London free of charge, Lewis hoped to arrest its flagging fortunes. But within two years he was again wondering whether the magazine was viable and despite Harris's promise to do all he could to support it,[51] he had even at one stage suggested setting-up a fund in order to distribute the magazine to the poor,[52] Lewis's pessimism remained.[53]

By the mid 1740s the Calvinistic awakening was also facing severe problems. Whitefield had sailed for the colonies in 1744 and did not return for another four years, leaving the Tabernacle society bereft of the one factor that could unify its many competing factions. In his absence many of the rivalries within the Tabernacle society that had been suppressed came to the surface and it was decimated by a series of secessions, the most damaging of which witnessed John Cennick's departure for the Moravians along with 400 supporters at the end of 1745.[54] Faced with such a threat to its long-term sustainability, English Calvinistic Methodism turned in upon itself and there seemed little chance of its members supplying Lewis exciting new accounts of the latest successes of the revival.

But perhaps the most significant reason for its difficulties was bound up with John Lewis's own troubled relationship with Calvinistic Methodism. In a sense, Lewis's story is indicative of many of the problems inherent in the revival. Evangelicalism was a highly emotive religion. Its emphasis on the immediacy and ecstatic nature of spiritual experience often placed an acute psychological burden on its most committed members, and it is hardly surprising that some of them eventually found it difficult to maintain the necessary level of spiritual intensity.[55] Maintaining the magazine had brought Lewis to the brink of

---

[51] Trevecka 1368, Howel Harris to John Lewis, 5 November 1745.
[52] Trevecka 602, Howel Harris to John Cennick, 17 August 1742.
[53] Trevecka 1364, John Lewis to Howel Harris, 21 October 1745.
[54] Podmore, *The Moravian Church in England*, pp. 89-95.
[55] For the burden which evangelical and enthusiastic expressions of Christianity placed on their followers see, Ronald A. Knox, *Enthusiasm: A Chapter in the History of Religion with Special Reference to the XVII and XVIII Centuries* (Oxford, 1950); Jon Mee, *Romanticism, Enthusiasm, and Regulation: Poetics and the Policing of Culture in*

financial collapse. In a letter to Howel Harris in 1743 he complained that he had lost all of his 'business among worldly people'[56] on account of his association with the Methodists. But it also appears that neither Whitefield nor John Cennick, who by this point was in charge of the Tabernacle Society, were prepared to give Lewis regular work, because they felt that what he was producing was not of a sufficiently high standard. Despite halving the price of the magazine in response to its dwindling sales figures, matters did not improve and Lewis's debts continued to mount. Coupled with financial difficulties, Lewis was also facing problems at home. His eleven-year old son was, he said, 'given to constant stealing'[57] and Lewis's wife and daughter had recently defected to the Moravians.

However, these difficulties were as nothing compared to where Lewis turned for solace. In June 1745 he admitted to Howel Harris that he had become intimate 'in a religious conscientious way'[58] with a young woman at the Tabernacle Society, out of a desire to help her spiritually. The relationship seems to have quickly become intense and when Lewis tried to end it the woman had threatened to show Thomas Adams and Herbert Jenkins, two of the many itinerants that were based at the Tabernacle, a number of incriminating letters that he had written to her. But his sexual misdemeanours did not end there! He admitted that during the previous six months he had sinned with a 'lustful woman' – conveniently lodged a few doors away from his shop so that he could visit her between 3 and 4 in the morning.[59] He also admitted to having done so on at least four separate occasions before finally repenting. Unwilling to wait for the condemnation and probably expulsion from the Tabernacle society, Lewis took himself off to join his wife and the Moravians at Fetter Lane.[60]

Subsequently, Lewis seems to have practically disappeared from the Methodist scene. By the end of 1745 he had signalled to Howel Harris that he wished to pull out of the printing of the Methodist magazine altogether.[61] Yet in 1747 he was still involved, but by this stage the magazine had been renamed once again; this time as *The Christian History*, and by this stage it only appeared at irregular intervals. The numbers circulated were also far less. Members of the Tabernacle still took their monthly quota of four hundred copies, but the remainder were put on public sale in Lewis's shop. Lewis had

---

the Romantic Period (Oxford, 2003), pp. 24-81 passim; W. Stephen Gunter, *The Limits of 'Love Divine': John Wesley's Response to Antinomianism and Enthusiasm* (Nashville, 1989).

[56] Trevecka 853, John Lewis to Howel Harris, 8 April 1743.
[57] Ibid.
[58] Trevecka 1330, John Lewis to Howel Harris, 15 June 1745.
[59] Ibid.
[60] Ibid.
[61] Trevecka 1368, Howel Harris to John Lewis, 5 November 1743.

also been ousted as editor-in-chief by Thomas Boddington. According to Boddington, Lewis had become unsuitable because of his many 'blunders [...] in composing'[62] the magazine, a reference to complaints that had been periodically made about the number of printing errors that had begun to appear in its pages. The last issue of *The Christian History* rolled from John Lewis's presses in June 1748 and after this date Lewis's name no longer appears in the records of Calvinistic Methodism entirely. There is evidence from some of the Moravian archives that his bookshop was still being patronized by them in 1752,[63] but within a few years a broken and disgraced Lewis had died. He left his wife and children penniless, and in their desperation they were forced to turn to a similarly disgraced Howel Harris for financial support in November 1756.[64] Subsequently their link with the revival became much more tenuous. Lewis's eldest daughter Catherine was estranged from the Moravians for many years until she married a Moravian brother in 1762, shortly before her untimely death in 1767.[65] Lewis's wife, Mary, also strayed from the Moravians for a number of years before she eventually returned in 1766, remaining in faithful membership until her death in 1791.[66]

For almost eight years, John Lewis's Methodist magazine had been the mouthpiece of English and Welsh Calvinistic Methodism. Its contents provide historians with an unrivalled insight into the spirituality of early Calvinistic Methodism, a fact that has only recently begun to be appreciated.[67] But the magazine also functioned at a much deeper level and it demonstrates how the early Methodist revivalists were not averse to cannily utilizing all the means that the rapidly expanding English-Atlantic commercial world placed at their disposal. Whitefield's reliance on individuals such as John Lewis betrays the extent to which the Calvinistic Methodists shrewdly promoted their awakenings and used 'means' to sustain their vibrancy, conscious throughout that they occupied a prominent place at the vanguard of the Kingdom of God.

---

[62] Trevecka 1699, Thomas Boddington to Howel Harris, 29 September 1747.

[63] Daniel Benham, *Memoirs of James Hutton; Comprising the Annals of his Life and Connection with the United Brethren* (London, 1856), p. 265.

[64] Trevecka 2190, James Pritchard and Evan Roberts to Howel Harris, November 1756.

[65] Jenkins, 'John Lewis the Printer and his Family', 130.

[66] Ibid.

[67] Jones, *A Glorious Work in the World*; David Ceri Jones, 'Transcripts of my Heart: Welsh Methodists, Popular Piety and the International Evangelical Revival, 1738-50', Joan and Richard Allen (eds), *'Faith of Our Fathers': Six Centuries of Popular Belief in England, Ireland and Wales* (Cardiff, forthcoming).

CHAPTER 3

'Tinkers and other vermin': Methodists and the Established Church in Wales, 1735–1800

John Morgan Guy

In May of the year 1763 the Revd William Miles, Vicar of Llanblethian and Cowbridge in the vale of Glamorgan, replied to the questionnaire sent out to his clergy by Bishop John Ewer of Llandaff in preparation for his Primary Visitation scheduled for the coming June.[1] Miles was in his fifteenth year as vicar of the thriving little market town at the heart of the Vale. He was a graduate of Jesus College, Oxford, and the latest representative of an established Glamorgan clerical 'dynasty' drawn from the minor gentry. His father and namesake had been vicar of St Lythans,[2] Pendoylan and Llantwit Major,[3] and a chaplain to the Lord Chancellor, Lord Talbot, whose influence was probably responsible for his nomination in 1741 to a prebendal stall in Salisbury Cathedral. Miles's grandfather, John, had been rector of Porthkerry and vicar of St Lythans. John's sister had married Edward Powell of Llysworney, and their son Robert was successively a Fellow of Jesus College, Master of the Cowbridge Free School[4] and Vicar of Llantwit Major. In 1763 William Miles of Cowbridge was forty-four years of age, an established figure in Vale of Glamorgan society, and whose family's influence in the church had obtained for him – at the age of twenty-nine – the important living of Llanblethian, 'coming ashore' after six years as a chaplain in the Royal Navy.[5] Then in 1748 he had succeeded on his father's death to his Salisbury prebend.[6]

Bishop Ewer's first question concerned the presence and numerical strength of dissent in the parish. William Miles's reply, at first reading, verged on the

---

[1] For the Returns see John R. Guy, *The Diocese of Llandaff in 1763* (Cardiff, 1991).
[2] Where he succeeded his father, John, in 1721.
[3] Where his cousin Robert Powell had been vicar before him from 1721 to 1731.
[4] Founded by Sir Leoline Jenkins, the mastership was in the gift of Jesus College. Both Robert Powell and his immediate successor, the Revd Daniel Durel were Fellows of the College at the time of their nomination. See Iolo Davies, *'A Certaine Schoole'. A History of Cowbridge Grammar School* (Cowbridge, 1967).
[5] His father's hand can be detected here. The patrons of Cowbridge were the Dean and Chapter of Gloucester Cathedral, who were also patrons of his own living of Llantwit Major.
[6] Warminster II. He held it until his death.

intemperate. 'No dissenters unless the strolling Methodists may be deemed as such. There is a Methodist meeting house at Aburthyn in this parish. Methodists of all trades and denominations, tinkers, thatchers, weavers and other vermin.'[7] The reply, by far the most hostile to Methodism in the entire corpus of Returns to that Visitation, has become something of a bye-word for the attitude of the clergy of the Established Church towards the movement. But such a judgement is too superficial, it is also facile. Questions need to be asked of this reply, not the least, why should Miles have risked the disapprobation of his new bishop, with whose views he was almost certainly unfamiliar, by putting on record such an uncharitable and intolerant opinion of those who, however much their views and opinions differed from his own, were not dissenters but members still of the Established Church? In fact, the true understanding of his position depends upon the interpretation of the epithet 'vermin'.

That understanding comes not so much from any dictionary definition as from the writings of Jonathan Swift, and the philosophical 'world-view' which Miles evidently shared with the Dean of St Patrick's. The key text is Swift's *Gulliver's Travels*, the first parts of which were published in 1726, and in particular Gulliver's visit to Brobdingnag, which forms Book II. It is here that we find what David Nokes called one of the 'great set pieces' of Swift's satire, the king of Brobdingnag's stinging *riposte* to Gulliver's encomium on European (and, particularly, English) civilized society.[8] In Book I, Gulliver had found himself shipwrecked in the land of Lilliput, where he was a giant in a country whose inhabitants were little more than six inches high. In Book II, Gulliver's situation is reversed. In Brobdingnag, whose inhabitants are giants, he is the Lilliputian, and here he muses 'Undoubtedly philosophers are in the right when they tell us, that nothing is great or little, otherwise than by comparison'. He is inconsiderable, or, to quote the psalmist, 'small and of no reputation'.[9] If we are to understand William Miles, then we must examine the Brobdingnagian 'world-view'.

Whatever else he may have been, Jonathan Swift was a loyal and convinced supporter of the Established Church. He wrote, as Warren Montag expressed it, 'from within the ideological framework of the Church of England'.[10] He sincerely believed the doctrinal position of that church to be the best possible expression of Christian orthodoxy, and that dissent from its teachings was not only erroneous but intolerable. He further believed that a stratified and

---

[7] Guy, *The Diocese of Llandaff*, p. 34.

[8] David Nokes, *Raillery and Rage: A Study of Eighteenth Century Satire* (Brighton, 1987), p. 196.

[9] Jonathan Swift, *Gulliver's Travels* (London, Everyman edition, 1940) p. 89. Psalm 119:141.

[10] Warren Montag, *The Unthinkable Swift: The Spontaneous Philosophy of a Church of England Man* (London, 1994), p. 126.

differentiated society, with unequal ranks, was both natural, original, and in harmony with the Divine plan. It was the duty of every citizen to endeavour to maintain the balance between what Montag called 'the one, the few, and the many'[11] and thus further the common *weal*, co-operating for the common good. Over a century later Mrs C. F. Alexander was to express a similar sentiment in her popular hymn 'All things bright and beautiful': *The rich man in his castle, the poor man at his gate; God made them high and lowly, and ordered their estate.* To move from such a society would be to subvert God's providential design, and if such moves came from those Swift would have designated the 'lower orders' within it, then the result could only be chaos and social disintegration. Again, as Montag summarized it, 'Swift [was] more concerned with the disorder that rises from below than that which descends from above, from the desire for an inappropriate social mobility that dissolves the natural bonds of society ...'[12] It was not only social and ecclesial structures that would thus be threatened, but the very stability of society itself, with the erosion of a true sense of community. Inappropriate 'upward' social mobility would result in rampant individualism. Humanity would be 'disaggregated ... not a community but reduced to solitary individuals, the association of which [would] become increasingly difficult to conceive, and possessed of no other end but that of the gratification of seemingly incompatible appetites and lusts'.[13] Mankind would be reduced to the level of brute beasts, indeed to Yahoos, as Swift so forcefully reminds his readers in Book IV of the *Travels*.

This concern for what Philip Pinkus calls 'the traditional hierarchy of being'[14] and its potential destruction was by no means original to Swift. For example, the poet-Dean of St Paul's, John Donne, had expressed it more than a century earlier, but given it a wider, indeed cosmic, dimension, in his *Anatomie of the World*. Taking as his starting point the Fall, and the entry into the world of sin, Donne in this poem descants upon disharmony, decay and corruption in the created order. 'Then, as mankinde, so is the world's whole frame / Quite out of joint ... The world did in her cradle take a fall ... wronging each joynt of the universall frame. / The noblest part, man, felt it first; and then / Both beasts and plants, curst in the curse of man.'[15] Behind this expression of Donne's sense of dislocation is, of course, the apostle Paul's cry 'the whole creation groaneth and travaileth in pain together until now' as the result of 'the bondage of corruption'.[16] What Donne expresses, and Swift takes up, is 'the doctrine of decay'; man, in his fallen state, paradoxically through his much-vaunted sense

---

[11] Montag, *The Unthinkable Swift*, p. 52.
[12] Montag, *The Unthinkable Swift*, pp. 147-8.
[13] Montag, *The Unthinkable Swift*, p. 127.
[14] Philip Pinkus, *Swift's Vision of Evil. Volume 2. Gulliver's Travels* (University of Victoria, Canada, English Literary Studies, Monograph series No. 4, 1975), p. 16.
[15] Quoted in Pinkus, *Swift's Vision of Evil*, p. 11.
[16] Romans 8:22, 21.

of scientific 'progress' and a pride in autonomous human 'reason', contributes only to his own self-belittlement. He believes he is Brobdingnagian; he is only Lilliputian. Worse, he reveals his Yahoo nature. It was the nineteenth century philosopher Friedrich Nietzsche who, perhaps, expressed it best: 'Alas, the faith in the dignity and uniqueness of man, in his irreplaceability in the great chain of being, is a thing of the past – man has become an *animal* ...'[17] It is in the nature of fallen man to reach 'above himself', but in so doing he diminishes himself.

This is the background to, and context of, Gulliver's celebrated paean on European civilization before the king of Brobdingnag. Swift with great skill draws for us the picture of the tiny Gulliver, somewhat pompously and definitely lengthily, expounding the merits of British political and social structures, the judiciary, the church and the armed forces. Even today it is next to impossible to read chapter VI of Book II without laughing out loud. Swift is consummate in his irony. As we read Gulliver's words, we become more and more aware of the faults and failings of the society he describes. Little Gulliver presumes to lecture the giant-king, but it is the stability and order of the Brobdingnagian state that is the true model for imitation. And, as Warren Montag perceived, what is true of the state is also true of the church. Order and stability are prejudiced when the small presume to stand up and lecture the great – or when the lower orders take upon themselves a status and a role in church and society which it is not theirs to claim or to occupy.[18]

To the king of Brobdingnag, Gulliver is an insect, with an insect's-eye view of the world, and in that sense, he can be classed as 'vermin'. I would suggest at this point that William Miles's use of the word 'vermin' is becoming clearer. His is the Olympian, Brobdingnagian, view. Like Swift before him, he was profoundly disturbed by what he perceived as the subversion of the natural, true, indeed divinely-ordained, structures of church and society by those within his parish who were, by setting up at Aberthyn a rival pulpit. These were the 'tinkers, thatchers and weavers', the 'lower orders' of society who by their actions were threatening to overthrow the 'just balance between the one, the few, and the many'.[19] They were 'side-show freaks'[20] mimicking their betters. What Miles feared was that the new Methodism within the church heralded the imminent dissolution or disaggregation of the social and religious order he was committed to support and uphold.

In his response to Bishop Ewer, Miles used the significant phrase 'strolling Methodists'. It is a very precise use of language; strollers were those who went from place to place giving performances – the sense survives in the description 'strolling players'. Also significantly, the three trades he instances in his reply,

---

[17] Pinkus, *Swift's Vision of Evil*, p. 20, quoting Nietzsche, *Genealogy of Morals*, III, 25, in Walter Kaufman (ed. and trans.), *Basic Writings of Nietzsche* (New York, 1968).
[18] Montag, *The Unthinkable Swift*, p. 147.
[19] Montag, *The Unthinkable Swift*, p. 52.
[20] Montag, *The Unthinkable Swift*, p. 48.

tinkers, thatchers and weavers, were all, to a greater or lesser extent, associated with itinerancy. Thus, economically, he defines the Methodists of Aberthyn; they were representatives of the 'lower orders'; they moved from place to place (a characteristic of Methodist adherents was that they would travel, sometimes quite long distances, to hear sermons or particular preachers); and their ministers too were largely itinerant – or as Miles would have it, 'strolled' from place to place, giving – sometimes dramatic – performances in their sermons. Because of this precise use of language, in addition to the Brobdingnagian perspective we have already discerned his final descriptive epithet of the Methodists as 'vermin' requires very careful examination, and cannot be simply dismissed as an insult.

The king of Brobdingnag's judgement upon Gulliver's encomium of the kingdom of England was incisive and damning. 'By what I have gathered from your own relation ... I cannot but conclude the bulk of your natives, to be the most pernicious race of little odious vermin that nature ever suffered to crawl upon the surface of the earth'.[21] 'Names and the act of naming,' Marilyn Francus has reminded us, 'are perhaps the most common assignments of meaning ...'[22] As with Miles nearly forty years later, Swift's use of 'vermin' in *Gulliver's Travels* is both precise and evocative. Vermin (ultimately deriving from the Latin *vermis*, worm) were those creatures that were injurious to cultivated crops or domesticated animals, noxious insects or parasites. All of these shades of meaning are significant; disorder and disease, harmful, that which is living in or on something else. The king of Brobdingnag's verdict is descriptive of a society that is self-seeking, and by being so destructive of harmony, balance and the divinely-ordained natural order. And vermin are small, busy and mobile. Their natural habitat is dirt. Swift, in a passage laden with disgust, makes this connection, when he has Gulliver describe the beggars who haunt the streets of Brobdingnag's principal city, Lorbrulgrud. The lice which infest their filthy clothes he calls vermin.[23]

Neither Swift nor Miles were unacquainted with vermin. Swift, the city-dweller in London and Dublin, and Miles, who had spent five years and more in cramped quarters on board naval warships, would have been all-too-familiar with them, and would have known, from first-hand experience, the association between vermin and dirt. The two words were virtually synonymous. And here we come to a further layer of meaning in Miles's use of this epithet to describe the local Methodists of Aberthyn. To elucidate this, we need to turn to the

---

[21] Swift, *Gulliver's Travels*, p. 140.
[22] Marilyn Francus, *The Converting Imagination. Linguistic Theory and Swift's Satiric Prose* (Carbondale and Edwardsville, 1994), p. 62.
[23] Swift, *Gulliver's Travels*, pp. 117-18.

anthropologist Mary Douglas, and her classic work *Purity and Danger*.²⁴ Douglas recalls 'the old definition of dirt as matter out of place'.²⁵ In a passage which, I would suggest, throws a great deal of light on Miles's use of the term 'vermin', she says, 'We can recognize in our own notions of dirt that we are using a kind of omnibus compendium which includes all the rejected elements of ordered systems. It is a relative idea. Shoes are not dirty in themselves, but it is dirty to place them on the dining table ... similarly ... out-door things indoors, upstairs things downstairs; under-clothing appearing where over-clothing should be. ... In short, our pollution behaviour is a reaction which condemns any object or idea likely to confuse or contradict cherished classifications.'²⁶ Further, she adds, 'uncleanness or dirt is that which must not be included if a pattern is to be maintained'.²⁷

Miles's description of the Methodists can now be seen as a crescendo. The 'tinkers, thatchers, weavers' were presumptuous in taking upon themselves roles that were not rightly theirs; in doing so, they were 'getting above themselves', rejecting the regulated and ordered 'systems' of the church; and the outcome would be disorder, dis-ease in both church and state. Perhaps even worse, they were parasitic, battening upon the established social and ecclesial structures to achieve their ends. In this sense, they were 'dirt' – matter out of place – thus 'vermin'. For Swift, critics were 'the parasites and scavengers of the literary world. Critics', he believed, 'swarm about the best writers like rats about the best cheese or wasps about the best fruit.'²⁸ He would have said the same thing about dissenters. The Church of England was the 'best cheese ... the best fruit' of Christianity. Its health and safety, security and stability, were endangered by parasites, rats, wasps, vermin. William Miles clearly agreed with him.

Two questions remain: Firstly, what had all this to do with the philosophical concept 'The Great Chain of Being', and, secondly, why should William Miles have been so concerned by the emergence of Methodism among his parishioners? Both can be quite briefly answered. The genesis of the idea of the Great Chain of Being can, as Arthur Lovejoy comprehensively showed, be found in Greek philosophy, and traced, in its various developments and ramifications, throughout the succeeding centuries at least until the eighteenth

---

²⁴ Mary Douglas, *Purity and Danger: An Analysis of the Concepts of Pollution and Taboo* (London, 1996). I am grateful to my wife, Valerie Morgan-Guy, for bringing Douglas's work to my attention.
²⁵ Douglas, *Purity and Danger*, p. 36.
²⁶ Douglas, *Purity and Danger*, pp. 36-7.
²⁷ Douglas, *Purity and Danger*, p. 41.
²⁸Francus, *The Converting Imagination*, p. 163. The reference is to the 'A digression concerning Criticks', Section III of *A Tale of a Tub* (J. M. Dent, Everyman's Library edition, repr. 1982), p. 63.

of the Christian era.[29] The poet Alexander Pope perhaps provided the most succinct summary of the idea in its mature form:

Vast chain of being! Which from God began,
Natures, aethereal, human, angel, man
Beast, bird, fish, insect, what no eye can see,
No glass can reach; from Infinite to thee,
From thee to nothing. – On superior pow'rs
Were we to press, inferior might on ours;
Or in the full creation leave a void,
Where, one step broken, the great scale's destroy'd;
From Nature's chain whatever link you strike,
Tenth, or ten thousandth, breaks the chain alike.'[30]

As Arthur Lovejoy observes, Pope emphasizes that the elimination of even one link in the series would result in the dissolution of the cosmic order – the world would descend into incoherence.[31] Man occupies a particular place in the chain; for him to attempt to rise above it, or allow himself to sink below it, would break the chain. And, as Nietzsche reminded us earlier, in trying to rise above his place, he in fact belittles himself, and sinks.

It is easy to see how such an entrenched idea could be used to bolster the defence of received social or ecclesial structures, and be used as a weapon against social or religious discontent and dissent. To quote Lovejoy, 'The universe, it was assumed, is the best of systems; any other system is good only in so far as it is constructed upon the same principles; and the object of the Infinite Wisdom which had fashioned it was to attain the maximum of variety by means of inequality. Clearly, then, human society is well constituted only if, within its own limits, it tends to the realization of the same desiderata.'[32] Then, in a very important insight for our discussion, he adds, 'The doctrine of the Chain of Being thus gave a metaphysical sanction to the injunction of the Anglican catechism: each should labour truly "to do his duty in that state of life" – whether in the cosmical or the social scale – "to which it shall please God to call him". To seek to leave one's place in society is ... to invert the laws of Order ... Any demand for equality, in short, is contrary to nature.'[33] The laws of Order are God's immutable laws; to leave one's place in society and in the church is to break the Great Chain of Being. The result, for Tory churchmen like Jonathan Swift and William Miles, was too frightening to contemplate. The Methodists of Aberthyn were, by rebelling against what Soame Jenyns had

---

[29] Arthur O. Lovejoy, *The Great Chain of Being. A Study of the History of an Idea* (New York, 1936, Torchbook ed. 1960) – still the most clear and detailed study of the concept.
[30] From the 'Essay on Man', quoted by Lovejoy, *The Great Chain of Being*, p. 60.
[31] Ibid. p. 60.
[32] Lovejoy, *The Great Chain of Being*, pp. 205-6.
[33] Ibid. p. 206.

described, only six years before William Miles's reply to Bishop Ewer's question had been penned, as their 'just subordination', placing in jeopardy the happiness, the regulation, indeed the 'magnificence' of not only church and state, but, ultimately, of the universe. Such would be the magnitude of the disaster.[34]

It is this analogy between microcosm and macrocosm that brings out, essentially, the fear, even panic, which can be detected in Miles's reply to his bishop. The rise of Methodism, the assumption by the 'tinkers, thatchers, weavers' of roles, it has to be emphasized, that, in his philosophical, social and religious 'world view' were not for them, was for him nothing less than a breaking apart of the Great Chain of Being. No wonder, then, he resorts to the epithet 'vermin'. They were indeed 'matter out of place'.

Miles's anger and anguish, so evident in his reply, is also personal. The rise of Methodism in his parish, the establishment of the Aberthyn Meeting House during his incumbency, was a slight to his personal sense of honour. Honour, as Americo Castro pointed out, 'expresses the relation of the individual with society'.[35] Rowan Williams, in his study of Teresa of Avila, has a valuable commentary on the understanding of honour which Castro explores, and one that is relevant to our discussion. Teresa herself was of noble lineage, but her Christian faith led her to reject received understandings of social status. It is what she rejected that Castro and Williams outline, and their words are worth quoting here: 'The opposite of honour is *infamia*, ill-repute, but this is not simply a matter of having disagreeable things said about you. Certain *kinds* of people are innately without honour: they have no weight or worth in the social hierarchy, and are, in themselves, dispensable. ... To be associated with such people, willing to live at their level, is in some extent to contract their worthlessness, their "vile" or "villain" character. Those who *are* innately honourable because of the position conferred by their ancestry must not allow this honour to be lessened by anything, word or action, which might assimilate them to the worthless. So when an honourable person does something inconsistent with the position he or she occupies, honour is compromised, and when one does not react to any attack or insult that suggests one is behaving inconsistently with one's position, that failure to defend oneself automatically constitutes a loss of honour. To quote Castro, "discordance between the individual and society ... produces *infamia*", and that discordance can be expressed both positively, by an act that is at odds with social expectation, and negatively, by accepting some diminution in one's public standing, some insult

---

[34] Soame Jenyns, *A Free Inquiry into the Nature and Origin of Evil* (1757) quoted in Lovejoy, *The Great Chain of Being*, p. 207.

[35] Americo Castro, 'Algunas observaciones acerca del concepto del honor en los siglos XVI y XVII', *Revista de filologia espanola*, 3 (1916), pp. 1-50, 357-86, quoted by Rowan Williams, *Teresa of Avila* (London, 1991), p. 34.

or offence.'[36] It is easy to see how such an understanding of honour fits the person of William Miles, and contributes to his reaction to the Aberthyn Methodists. Castro and Williams were concerned with sixteenth- and seventeenth-century Spanish society, but their analysis is equally applicable to such an instinctively conservative figure as the vicar of Cowbridge. The existence of Methodism in his parish lessened his sense of honour – it diminished him in his own eyes, if not in the eyes of others. Not to react to what he would have construed as an insult would have been, for him, inconsistent with his position. It was necessary that he defend himself, and he does so by transferring the opprobrium to others.

Was William Miles, then, acting out of arrogance or fear when he described the Methodists as 'vermin'? The title of this chapter posed the question. The answer has to be, primarily, fear, though it was fear shot through with a sense of hurt pride – the two so often go together. By 1763 Miles's views may well have been more than a little old-fashioned, but they were nonetheless still widely shared. It was fear – fear of the snapping of the Great Chain of Being with all that that entailed, which he believed that the rise of Methodism within the church might instigate. And it was fear of *infamia*, that posterity would associate him with contributing to it.

So 'vermin' is not just an insult. Examination of the background to, and context of, the epithet, I would suggest, helps us to understand more fully the reason why the rise of Methodism in the mid-eighteenth century provoked such fear and hostility among many within the Establishment. For some it was not renewal, reform or revival; it was the herald of cosmic disorder.

---

[36] Williams, *Teresa of Avila*, p. 49.

CHAPTER 4

The Effect of Charles Finney's Revivalism on the 1858–60 Awakening in Wales

Dyfed Wyn Roberts

In the last week of June 1858 a young Methodist preacher, Humphrey Jones, returned home to Tre'r Ddôl, by Aberystwyth, after spending time in the midst of the revival that swept North America in the previous year. His aim in returning was to ignite the revival fires in his native Wales. His success was overwhelming, for soon a powerful awakening spread like wildfire throughout the nation. It is estimated that one hundred thousand were converted. Among those converts were men who became outstanding leaders, such as Thomas Charles Edwards, who became principal of Wales's first university at Aberystwyth, and Timothy Richard, a missionary to China. It was a revival that converted individuals, renewed churches, and transformed communities. It touched many other nations, including Canada, the United States of America, Ulster, Scotland and other parts of Europe.

This chapter will attempt to show how crucial the ideas of Charles Finney and revivalism in general were to the revival in Wales. To a great extent, historians have tended to interpret the revival in Calvinistic terms, and have denied any Finneyite or revivalist influence. This interpretation sees only God's hand in the revival, with little room for man or his methods. In his assessment of American revivalism, for example, Iain Murray quotes John Simpson, who was writing in 1862 of the British revival,

> We have not seen, in any of these parts of the world we have named the employment of either professional gentlemen or ladies to get up the awakening, nor anything which characterises revival meetings in general ... The awakening seems to have come upon the churches unawares, to have taken them by surprise. Hence, like the movement across the Atlantic, it was not 'got up'; no revival-mongers were employed.[1]

Murray agrees with this assessment and thus denies that there was any revivalistic influence on Wales in 1858.

---

[1] John Simpson, quoted by Iain H. Murray, *Revival and Revivalism: The Making and Marring of American Evangelicalism, 1750-1858* (Edinburgh, 1994), p. 398.

The revival's main Welsh historian is Eifion Evans. By noting his appraisal of the 1839 awakening in Wales, we can understand his views on Finneyism. It is generally believed that the 1839–43 awakening was sparked by the implementation of Finney's ideas. His volume, *Lectures on Revivals*, was published in Welsh in 1839,[2] and was widely read and accepted.[3] However, Eifion Evans denies that what happened in Wales at that time deserves to be called a true revival. One of the main reasons he gives for this assessment is the influence of Arminianism upon the events.[4] For a revival to be a truly God-given revival, therefore, Evans believes that it must be born out of a Calvinistic and non-revivalist matrix. It would appear that anything that derives from Finneyism or Arminianism must be rejected as true revival. In assessing the 1858–60 revival, Evans notes that the theology of most non-conformists in Wales was Calvinist. 'The churches of the three main denominations,' he says, 'were, by and large, orthodox, and militantly so.'[5] According to Evans, it was within this conservative Calvinist 'orthodoxy' that the revival began, and it is why it can be referred to as a truly Holy Spirit-inspired awakening. The fourth main non-conformist denomination in Wales was the Wesleyan Methodist tradition. They were Arminian in theology, and, if we may infer from the above quote, this made them unorthdox in Evans's view. However, as we shall see, it was precisely within this denomination that the revival did indeed spark, and not only that, but Finneyite influence was heavily involved as well.

Charles Grandison Finney was born to a farming family in Warren, Connecticut in 1792. Having spent two years as a schoolteacher, he then trained as a lawyer in New York. However, his legal career was cut short by a religious conversion in 1821, which set him on a new path. Now his desire was to become a minister of the gospel and he was ordained in 1824. He experienced many revivals and was soon to become known nationally as a powerful revivalist. Many of the revivalist techniques that originated in the camp meetings of the west, such as the anxious seat, were used to great effect by Finney.

His use of these techniques reflected his theology. Although he was nurtured within a Calvinistic Presbyterian denomination, he came to change his theological views. Having once believed in man's inability to reach God because of his absolutely corrupted condition, Finney became convinced that not only did man have the duty to respond to God, but he also had the inherent ability to do so. Man was not as corrupted as the traditional Calvinists made out. Believing that man had this ability, Finney then argued that the church had a duty to do all in her capacity to persuade, if not pressurize, man to use that

---

[2] Charles G. Finney, *Darlithiau ar Adfywiadau Crefyddol* (Swansea, 1839).
[3] Richard Carwardine, 'The Welsh Evangelical Community and "Finney's Revival"', *Journal of Ecclesiastical History*, 29, no. 4 (1978), p. 479.
[4] Eifion Evans, *When He is Come* (Denbigh, 1959), p. 18.
[5] Ibid. p. 19.

ability, and respond to God's call in Jesus. Revivalist techniques, such as protracted meetings, strong appeals, and the anxious seat, should be used. If the church did her duty then God would respond by sending revival. Far from being the unexpected and miraculous events of the past, Finneyite revivals were planned for in advance. His detractors claimed they were no more than man-made and ineffective emotionalism with no lasting impact. However, Finney claimed they were merely the natural consequence of God-ordained techniques. Just as the farmer expected a harvest after planting, so the minister could expect a revival after implementing the revivalist methods. And Finney was adamant that God alone deserved the glory.

How did these ideas gain such a ready reception in Calvinist Wales? The answer lies in the fact that Welsh nonconformist Calvinism had undergone significant changes in the thirty years before Finney's publication, and it would be impossible to understand how his ideas influenced the 1858–60 revival without considering this change.

The first step in this theological development was the introduction of the Wesleyan Methodist denomination into the nation. Thomas Coke, their leader in England, believed in the importance of missionary work through the medium of the indigenous language, and so John Hughes, Brecon, and Owen Davies, Wrexham, embarked on the work in Wales in 1800. Unfortunately, their Welsh was patchy at best, and they made little impact in the early months. But as their influence grew, so did the resistance from the Calvinistic Methodists, as they felt threatened by the new mission. An important part of the Calvinistic response was their attempt at defending their theology against the Arminian ideas. Whilst some, like Thomas Jones, Denbigh, responded without rejecting their own moderate views, others formed a more extreme theology, which developed into hyper-Calvinism. The Baptist John Jenkins, Hengoed, published his volume *Gwelediad y Palas Arian* in 1811. In it he defended such Calvinist doctrines as the sovereignty of God, man's total depravation, and the believer's unconditional election by God. He also included his belief in a limited atonement, that is, Christ had died for the elect alone and not for the whole world. He argued that had Jesus died for all and had only some been saved, then Jesus' ministry would have failed, since not all those who he had died for would have received the benefit. Additionally, he did not believe in preaching the gospel to all unbelievers. Among those who shared these ideas, at least for a time in their careers, were John Elias and Christmas Evans, two highly influential leaders.

Having begun as a debate between Calvinists and Arminians, it soon developed into a dispute within the Calvinist ranks. One whose view had a profound impact upon the moderates was the English Baptist, Andrew Fuller. Fuller had been nurtured under a hyper-Calvinist wing, but became dissatisfied with the system, and as he studied both the Bible and the work of Jonathan Edwards he came to espouse a far more moderate form of Calvinism. Such Welshmen as Edward Williams, Rotherham, and J. P. Davies, Tredegar, took up his views. But the main protagonist of this theology in Wales was the Independent minister, John Roberts, Llanbrynmair. In 1820 Roberts published his defence of the New System, as it was referred to, *Galwad Ddifrifol ar Ymofynwyr am y Gwirionedd*. Others contributed chapters to this volume, and it was highly influential in spreading the moderate views.

It is important to underline that the New System was not Arminianism. Its adherents still held on to the belief in election and in the unconditional perseverance of the saints in grace. But they also insisted that Christ had died for all, and not the elect alone – though it was only the elect who would benefit from the atonement. Another important belief, and central to the present study, was that man had the ability to respond to God. Roberts says,

> There is nothing more clear to me in the holy scriptures than God making a sincere offer of eternal life, through the blood of Jesus, to all men who hear the gospel; and that the only reason that any man is lost is because he has no desire to come to God's Son, to receive life.[6]

In another chapter 'J.B.', Liverpool, said,

> Without doubt they are dead in their transgressions and sins – the children of wrath – without hope, and without God in the world. However, they have not been despoiled of their soulish abilities, and their inherent reason; but they remain the holders of God's moral government, and, as such, are bound to be obedient to the Governor.[7]

This makes it clear their belief in man's ability to respond to God.

The New System became increasingly more popular among Welsh Calvinists. For example, R. Tudur Jones said that the system had become mainstream theology within the Independent churches by the middle of the century.[8] It is into this theological environment that Finney's work was published in Welsh in 1839, an environment in which a significant shift had taken place and which ensured his ideas would be widely accepted. If man had the ability to respond to God, then why not use any means possible of persuading him to make that response? The New System had a profound effect on preaching, for example. A style that consisted only of preaching doctrine changed to being an exhortation to faith and repentance, with a strong appeal to believe the gospel.

The impact of the theological changes on the practice of preaching and ministering leads us to consider three individual church leaders who played crucial roles in the preparation for revival and during the revival itself. Two of

---

[6] John Roberts, *Galwad Ddifrifol ar Ymofynwyr am y Gwirionedd* (Dolgellau, 1820), p. 6.
[7] 'J.B.', *Galwad Ddifrifol*, p. 114.
[8] R. Tudur Jones, *Hanes Annibynwyr Cymru* (Abertawe, 1966), p. 169.

them are well know names to students of this revival, namely Humphrey Jones and Dafydd Morgan. The third is not as well known, but no less important, and it is with Thomas Aubrey that we shall start.

Thomas Aubrey represented the deep desire for revival that was within many leaders in the nation. During the 1850s it is clear that such a desire was growing, and that it was based on a perceived need for God to revive his flagging church. Many leaders believed that the spiritual condition of the nation was at a very low point and that the only answer was revival.

By 1858 Aubrey was superintendent minister of the Wesleyan Methodist Bangor circuit, and the chairman of the North Wales province of the denomination. He was born in Cefncoedycymmer, Merthyr Tydfil, in 1808, and experienced a religious conversion at fourteen. Under the wing of an experienced elder he learned the main doctrines of the faith, as the Arminian Wesleyans interpreted them. Soon he began to preach, and in 1830 he was ordained as a full time minister. During his time in London he came across Finney's work on revival and was convinced by the arguments. His biographer said about him, 'He was taken up by the wonderful spirit which permeated the lectures, as the one thing the churches of the age needed ... He implored others to accept them, and he impressed the practical suggestions upon the churches.'[9] Aubrey oversaw significant growth in the membership of some of the churches in his care. In the Merthyr circuit, for example, between 1846 and 1849, the membership grew from 545 to 839. Whilst it is true that the growth in the town's population and the effect of the cholera epidemic in 1849 undoubtedly contributed to the church growth, there is little doubt that Aubrey's Finneyite methods saw much fruit. He ventured on several revivalist plans. In the Holywell circuit (1855–57) he brought the circuits of Llanfyllin, Llanrhaedr, and Llanfaircaereinion together for a day of prayer and preaching. He asked the elders to give a spiritual account of the churches, and those accounts lead to a prayer for revival. In the same period he organized a series of revival preaching meetings in one church, loosely based on Finney's protracted meetings.[10]

However, it was in Bangor that he saw the greatest success. He was superintendent there from 1857 to 1860. In the third week of February 1858, four months before the start of the revival at Tre'r Ddôl, the Wesleyan church at Llanfairfechan held a series of preaching meetings loosely based on the Finneyite plan. A powerful awakening was felt there, which spread to the rest of the circuit. A large number were converted, including 280 who joined the Wesleyan and Calvinistic Methodist churches in Llanfairfechan itself. This was the first fruit of the general revival, and there is little doubt that Finneyite influence was crucial. Ironically, though Aubrey deserves praise for being the one who sowed so much in preparation for revival, he was not the one who had the privilege of harvesting the fruit. By the summer of 1858 he became ill, and

---

[9] S. Davies, *Cofiant y Parch Thomas Aubrey* (Bangor, 1887), p. 133.
[10] *Cofiant y Parch Thomas Aubrey*, pp. 240-2.

had to take leave from his duties to rest and recuperate, thereby missing the full force of the awakening.

The second figure to have a major influence was Humphrey Jones. It was he who sparked the beginning of the revival at Tre'r Ddôl after he had returned home from America, where he had worked as a missionary and minister. He was born in 1832 in Gwarcwm Bach, near Tre'r Ddôl. When he was fourteen his family emigrated to America, but Humphrey was left with his aunt Sophia who kept the Half Way Inn. At fifteen he experienced a religious conversion and soon after began to preach. For the following six years he was a lay preacher with the Wesleyan Methodists, but his dream was to become a full time minister. When he was refused as a candidate in 1854, apparently because there were enough candidates at the time, he left Wales a disappointed man, and joined his family in America.

There he was accepted as a missionary with the Episcopal Methodists, a denomination with a strong revivalist outlook who made wide use of the various techniques. Organizing revival meetings was a central feature of their mission life, and Jones must have been immersed in it all. As the 1857 revival spread through the country, it is clear that Jones had an important role among the Welsh speakers. Morris Roberts, a minister at Remsen, said of him, 'This brother had been keeping revival meetings among the various denominations in Wisconsin, and many had been converted to religion in those meetings.'[11] By the end of this time Jones was known as 'Humphrey Jones the Revivalist' because of his success. He said of his own work, 'Wherever I would go the most powerful revivals would break out and hundreds would be saved.'[12]

It was Humphrey Jones the Revivalist who returned home to Tre'r Ddôl, and he did so with the expressed hope of igniting the revival fires in his native land.[13] He believed that God had called him to be a revivalist among his fellow Welsh people. Such a comment tells us clearly what he thought of revivals. They were not merely a matter of God moving in a sovereign way, but the fire could be ignited using certain techniques. In one of two letters by him published in a Welsh language weekly newspaper, *Yr Herald Cymraeg*, Jones referred to Finney,[14] thus confirming beyond doubt that he had fully absorbed revivalist ideas and methods. We do not know whether it was while in America that he studied Finney, or whether he had done so before leaving Wales, but between those ideas and his experiences in America Jones was firmly within the revivalist camp by the summer of 1858.

His methods reflect classical revivalism. For a month or so at a time he held revival meetings in various villages. First in Tre'r Ddôl, then moving on to

---

[11] Morris Roberts, *Y Cenhadwr Americanaidd* (1858), p. 193.
[12] J. J. Morgan, *Hanes Dafydd Morgan Ysbyty a Diwygiad 1859* (Yr Wyddgrug, 1906), p. 26.
[13] William Jones, *Y Fwyell*, 1894, p. 61.
[14] Humphrey Jones, *Yr Herald Cymraeg*, 11 September 1858, p. 4.

Ystumtuen, then to Mynydd Bach, and by the end of September he arrived in Pontrhydygroes. The pattern was more or less the same in each location. He would hold an evening meeting each weekday, and then two or three on a Sunday. During the weekdays he would sometimes evangelize from home to home, urging people to come to the evening meeting. The meetings themselves followed a pattern as well. There was the double sermon, that is, there would be a second address at the end of the meeting, and it was during this address that the appeal would be made and potential converts were invited to sit on the anxious bench. This was how the national revival began and many hundreds were converted in those early months alone. Humphrey Jones's desire for seeing the American awakening spread across the Atlantic was fulfilled, and the revivalistic methods were most surely in evidence.

It was at Pontrhydygroes that Humphrey Jones met the third leader who was highly influential, Dafydd Morgan. It is Morgan's name that is most closely associated with the revival. Indeed, it is still commonly known as the 'Dafydd Morgan Revival', and we can be certain when we say that he made the greatest individual contribution during that time as he travelled the length and breadth of Wales preaching in revival meetings.

Morgan was born in 1814 in Cwm Bodcoll, to the east of Aberystwyth. When he was ten the family moved to Pontrhydygroes, where the father built a new water mill, which was to be the family business. It was as 'Dafydd Morgan the Mill' that he was known locally. His parents were faithful members of the local Calvinistic Methodist church at Ysbyty Ystwyth, and at the age of twenty two Dafydd himself was converted. Another five years passed before he began to preach, but he was to have very little impact as a preacher. A certain John Jones, Ysbyty Ystwyth, was recorded as saying, 'It was said of Mr. Morgan that he could have been a good preacher if he had worked harder at it, that there was a lot of ability in him, but that he made very little of it.'[15] Indeed, someone referred to him as 'the weakest preacher in the county'.[16] He was ordained in 1857, but only received a church pastorate in 1868. He was, therefore, a peripatetic preacher during the revival, which allowed him to travel around the country without the worry of caring for a church at home.

Humphrey Jones's sermon at Pontrhydygroes had a significant impact on Morgan. Before then he had been rather disapproving of the revivalist's American methods. But having heard him preach, Morgan was touched deeply and became ashamed of his own lack of zeal. Over the following three or four days the two men spent a great deal of time together as Morgan questioned Humphreys about his methods and techniques. The details of those conversations are not available to us today, but it is clear that Morgan was

---

[15] John Evans, *Byr-gofiant 49 o Weinidogion Sir Aberteifi* (Dolgellau, 1894), p. 122.
[16] J. Hughes, *Bywyd y Parch Isaac Jones, Gweinidog Wesleaidd* (Liverpool, 1898), p. 90.

heavily influenced, since from that time onwards he was to make good use of those methods.

It was not only the revivalist who impressed himself upon Morgan. He also received what may be described as an anointing from God. An immediate effect was seen in his preaching. Far from remaining a poor, ineffective preacher, he now became one whom the crowds were keen to follow. One young man from Aberystwyth wrote about him, saying,

> The verse For my thoughts are not your thoughts ... is very plainly illustrated to us in the choices the Lord has made of workmen on the present occasion ... who would have thought that our chapels would be crammed full to hear them, especially Dd Morgan, think of his drawing people after him from town to Penparciau ... and even some went on Friday last week as far as Tregaron to hear him.[17]

Before this anointing no one would have bothered travelling far to listen to Dafydd Morgan. But he was a changed man, and the effectiveness of his preaching touched a generation. When the revival came to an end, Morgan reverted to being an ordinary preacher.

The revivalistic technique best used by Morgan was the anxious seat. In his diary for 1859 he records a number of examples of the conversations he had with those who had come forward. It is worth quoting in full one exchange he had on Anglesey. He mentions the numerous people who had responded, and continues:

> In their midst there was one called Thomas Williams of Bethlehem. When I started speaking to him, I said, 'What is your name?' 'Thomas.' 'Where from?' 'From Garreglefn.' 'Have you ever been a religious person?' 'I had thought of staying behind in Garreglefn this morning, but Satan took me out.' 'Have you been reading the Bible and praying out loud at home?' 'No, never. We do read the Bible every day.' 'Will you try to pray, Thomas?' 'I have decided to, you see.' 'When do you intended starting?' 'This very minute if you're willing.' 'Now,' I said. 'Yes indeed. I have become very angry at Satan.' Then I informed the congregation about Thomas' desire. 'Why can't Thomas pray right now', I said, 'we will join Thomas on his knees for a while.' Down went Thomas on his knees and he shouted with all his might, 'O Lord, forgive the sins of Anglesey's greatest sinner, Anglesey's greatest sinner.' Six times he shouted this, and then changed his prayer, 'Forgive the sins of my father and mother, Lord.' Another six times untill the congregation was weeping loudly and many were praying with Thomas before he gave up suddenly without saying amen. And he lay quietly on the bench for two or three minutes.[18]

---

[17] Aberystwyth, NLW, CMA 1 12,684.
[18] Aberystwyth, NLW, CMA 1(G) 8,716.

This type of conversation was repeated many times over as Morgan made his appeals up and down the nation. He became a master of the techniques, and he made a detailed note of the number who responded at each meeting. Counting the number of converts was important to him, for accompanying each note of where he preached during 1859 there is also the number of those who came forward. Whatever his concerns about the revivalistic methods espoused by Humphrey Jones at the beginning of the awakening, there is no doubt that Morgan had accepted them fully by the end.

It must be said that there were many more leaders connected to the 1858–60 revival in Wales, but these three deserve special note: Thomas Aubrey as the one who did much to stir up the desire and who sparked the first fruit, Humphrey Jones who was the catalyst to start the revival which spread throughout the nation, and Dafydd Morgan who, by his tireless travelling and preaching throughout the period, helped keep the fire burning. As we have seen, two of the three were Arminians, and the third belonged to a Calvinistic tradition that had changed much by the 1850s. All three had been influenced in some way by Finney's writings, and made full use of some of his methods.

As we consider these facts, therefore, it is difficult to come to any other conclusion than to say that the revivalistic techniques, as taught by Finney and others, were a central feature in the 1858–60 awakening. The fruits of the awakening are obvious to all: transformed lives, renewed churches, and changed communities. We would argue that a revival should be judged by studying the fruit, rather than by focusing on revivalistic methods alone. By these criteria it would be fair to conclude that this revival was indeed God-given but with man having a full partnership in its making.

CHAPTER 5

The Significance of Hymnody in the First Evangelical Revivals, 1730–1760

Mark A. Noll

The Welsh revivals of 1904–5 were marked as *evangelical* revivals in large part because of the singing. When in late 1904 W. T. Stead travelled from London to observe what was going on, his accounts featured 'the all-pervading thrill and throb of a multitude praying, and singing as they prayed'. He reported that 'three-fourth of the meeting consists of singing'. And he asserted that 'the revival is borne along upon billowing waves of sacred song', that 'it is singing, not the preaching, that is the instrument which is most efficacious in striking the hearts of men'.[1] Stead's account of one meeting that featured five Singing Sisters is worth quoting at length because of how substantially his positive assessment of revival occurrences was based on his observation of the singing:

> Repentance, open confession, intercessory prayer, and, above all else, this marvelous musical liturgy – a liturgy unwritten but heartfelt, a mighty chorus rising like the thunder of the surge on a rock-bound shore, ever and anon broken by the flutelike note of the Singing Sisters, whose melody was as sweet and as spontaneous as the music of the throstle in the grove or the lark in the sky. And all this vast quivering, throbbing, singing, praying, exultant multitude intensely conscious of the all-pervading influence of some invisible reality. ... They called it the Spirit of God. Those who have not witnessed it may call it what they will; I am inclined to agree with those on the spot.[2]

But of course it was not just singing itself, but also what was being sung, that marked out the Welsh revival of 1904–5 as evangelical. The remarkable singing drew abundantly from Wales's own rich stock of native hymnody—from William Williams Pantycelyn's 'Guide me, oh, thou great Jehovah, Pilgrim through this barren land' to what more than one commentator has called 'the mighty love-song of the revival,' the hymn by Dr William Rees (Hiraethog), 'Wondrous Love, unbounded Mercy! Vast as oceans in their

---

[1] W. T. Stead, 'The Story of the Awakening', in *The Story of the Welsh Revival* (New York, 1905), pp. 61, 64 (last three quotations).
[2] Stead, 'The Story of the Awakening', p. 66.

flood'³. But the repertoire of hymnody also included an eclectic selection from a wide range of English-language hymn writers, including Isaac Watts's 'When I survey the wondrous cross', John Henry Newman's 'Lead kindly light amid the encircling gloom', Fanny Crosby's 'Pass me not, O gentle Savior', and the American Methodist Louis Hartsough's 'I hear thy welcome voice, That calls me, Lord, to thee.'⁴ What at least one report has called Evan Roberts's favourite hymn was A Welsh translation of eighteenth-century stanzas by the American Presbyterian, Samuel Davies, which begins with themes that were central to the whole revival:

> Great God of wonders! All Thy ways
> Are matchless, Godlike and divine;
> But the fair glories of Thy grace
> More Godlike and unrivall'd shine.
>   Who is a pardoning God like Thee?
>   Or who has grace so rich and free?⁵

To this hymn a Welsh refrain had been added by Davies's eighteenth-century Welsh contemporary, Morgan Rhys: 'Ever praise Him, For remembering dust of earth'⁶. In the words of a modern historian, 'Music seemed the best available vehicle for heartfelt expressions of praise, and old hymns were sung over and over. The consensus was that the singing, more than any preaching, stirred hearts.'⁷

Several prominent features revealed the evangelical character of the disparate hymnody sung in the Welsh revivals: the immediate address to individuals, the concentration on themes of salvation, the focus on the gracious work of God in Christ, and the fact that the hymns sung were written by women as well as men, by laypeople as well as clerics. Although a full discussion of the hymn singing of the Welsh revival would be a most worthy effort in itself, my chapter deals instead with hymns and hymn singing during the first years of the modern evangelical movements in the eighteenth-century. Yet what I hope we can see about that singing, more than a century and a half before Evan Roberts appeared on the scene, is the strength of many characteristics that, when they were revived in Wales during the fall and winter of 1904, were

---

[3] This translation is from H. Elvet Lewis, *Christ Among the Welsh Miners* (Salem, OH, 1987 [reprint 1906]), p. 126 (Appendix: 'Hymns of the Revival', 126-8). For an alternative translation ('Love unfathomed as the ocean, Mercies boundless as the wave!'), see R. Parry, ed., *Hymns of the Welsh Revival* (Wrexham: Hughes & Son, n.d.), p. 26.

[4] Lewis, *Christ Among the Miners*, pp. 72, 73, 55, 36.

[5] James A. Stewart, *Invasion of Wales by the Spirit through Evan Roberts* (Fort Washington, PA, 1963), p. 78.

[6] Lewis, *Christ Among the Miners*, p. 127.

[7] Edith Blumhofer, 'The Welsh Revival: 1904-1905', in *Paraclete*, 20, no. 3 (1986), 2-3.

themselves constitutive of another evangelical revival. The most relevant aspects of hymns and hymn singing during the rise of the eighteenth-century evangelical movement concerned the prominence of singing itself in the early revivals, the innovative character of the hymns that were sung, the egalitarian origins of hymn writers and hymn singers, and the heightened meaning of song in early evangelical movements.

The Prominence of Singing in the Early Revivals

The three main antecedents of evangelicalism – the reformist spirituality of high-church Anglicanism, the biblical Calvinism of seventeenth-century Puritanism, and the revived Reformation religion of continental Pietism – each gave a prominent place to singing. It is, therefore, not surprising that the evangelical movements of the 1730s and succeeding years also witnessed a great outburst of song.[8]

The root of evangelicalism found in the high-church Anglican religious societies, which had begun to proliferate from the 1680s, was characterized by serious attention to the singing of psalms. In the words of the societies' most important contemporary advocate, Josiah Woodward, these religious societies had become effective agents for renewal at least in part through song: 'their zeal hath in many places given new life to the celebration of the *Lord's supper, public prayer, singing of psalms*, and *Christian conference*, duties which were in many places almost disused, or performed in a cool and languishing manner'.[9] Of special significance for later evangelicals in the societies' embrace of singing was their willingness to employ new hymns, in this case the freshly paraphrased psalms by Nahum Tate and Nicholas Brady from 1699, and their corresponding willingness to abandon the tried and true versions of Sternhold and Hopkins. Of even greater significance was the fact that one of Josiah Woodward's most faithful colleagues in supporting the religious societies was the Rev. Samuel Wesley of Epworth who, with his wife Susannah, instructed their large family in singing the new psalm paraphrases.

The Puritan root of evangelicalism had also bestowed special significance on singing the paraphrased psalms. For Puritans, such singing magnified the life-giving message of the Scriptures. As John Cotton, writing from Boston, put it in 1647: 'The end of singing is not only to instruct and admonish and comfort

---

[8] On these three strands, see Mark A. Noll, *The Rise of Evangelicalism: A History of Evangelicalism*, vol. 1: *The Age of Edwards, Whitefield and the Wesleys* (Leicester, UK, and Downers Grove, IL, 2004), chap. 2, 'Antecedents, Stirrings'.

[9] Josiah Woodward, *An Account of the Rise and Progress of the Religious Societies in the City of London* (1698), as quoted in Thomas K. McCart, *The Matter and Manner of Praise: The Controversial Evolution of Hymnody in the Church of England, 1760-1820* (Lanham, MD, 1998), p. 21.

the upright, but also to instruct, convince, and reprove the wicked.'[10] By the 1730s and 1740s, this Puritan root of evangelicalism had of course undergone one critical mutation of immense significance for the new evangelicalism. When in 1707 Isaac Watts published his first edition of *Hymns and Spiritual Songs*, this spiritual grandchild of the Puritans and ecclesiastical son of early Nonconformity, gave the first major jolt that pushed English hymnody out of its thralldom to exclusive psalmody. In so doing, Watts became himself an all-important bridge between the older Puritanism and modern evangelicalism because he demonstrated that a freer, more expressive, more Christ-centred hymnody could actually advance the Puritan desire to secure the truths of the Bible in the minds and hearts of those who sang.

The root of evangelicalism from German Pietism was even more directly supportive of innovative Christian hymnody. It is hardly an exaggeration to claim that for much of the seventeenth century the spiritual life of German Protestant churches had been sustained by hymns proclaiming the gracious mercy of Christ as the only hopeful remedy for the sorrowful realities of human existence. Especially during the gruesome carnage of the Thirty Years' War (1618–1648) hymnody had sustained a living faith through a deadly era. Many hymns from that period were later translated into English, including 'Ah, holy Jesus, how hast thou offended? ... I it was denied thee: I crucified thee', by Johann Heerman (1585–1647); 'If thou but suffer God to guide thee' from Georg Neumark (1621–1681); and by the greatest of these hymn writers, Paul Gerhardt (1607–1676), 'Why should cross and trial grieve me' and his translation from Latin of 'O sacred head, now wounded'. When formally organized Pietist movements later emerged in the work of Philip Jakob Spener, August Hermann Francke, Johann Bengel, and others, so too did direct, simple, but also gospel-centred hymnody revive with a great quantity of new song speaking to, for, through, and in the human spirit of eager lay singers. Through several specific hymns, but even more in the commitment to hymns as a form of spiritual nurture and experience, the continental Pietists blazed a path that English-speaking evangelicals eagerly followed. Most notably, the anticipatory first-fruit of the revival was John Wesley's *Collection of Psalms and Hymns*, which he published at Charleston, South Carolina, in 1737. Its hymns included five of his own translations of Pietist hymns, including his rendition of a hymn by the Moravian leader, Count Ludwig Nicholas von Zinzendorf: 'Jesus to thee my Heart I bow, ... Fairest among Ten Thousand thou.'[11]

The singing that took place in the evangelical revivals from the mid-1730s onwards was, thus, not exactly a completely new thing. Yet the pervasive

---

[10] John Cotton, *The Singing of Psalmes a Gospel Ordinance* (1647), as quoted in Stephen A. Marini, 'Rehearsal for Revival: Sacred Singing and the Great Awakening in America', *JAAR Thematic Studies* 50:1 (1983): 72.

[11] J. R. Watson, *The English Hymn: A Critical and Historical Study* (Oxford, 1997), p. 206.

exuberance with which revived believers took to song – first in England and New England, then in Wales and the southern American colonies, then in most of the rest of the British empire – represented a dramatic leap forward in the history of religious music, as well as in the history of Protestant Christianity. Even in Scotland, where exclusive psalmody was maintained with greatest tenacity, the awakenings inspired a fresh surge of evangelical lyric poetry and an increased use of hymnody outside of church. The musical significance of the early evangelical revivals lay in this full acceptance of what had gone before in British dissenting traditions, in the high-church religious societies, and in continental Pietism, but even more in the extraordinary reach of the revivals' new hymnody, new singers, and new devotion to song.

In the earliest records of the evangelical revivals, it is difficult to discover any significant event, person, or structure that did not involve the singing of hymns.[12] It is likewise difficult to discover any significant experience of singing where the hymns had not been freshly written by the evangelicals themselves (or by Isaac Watts, whose hymns they embraced enthusiastically from the start, or the German Pietists, whose works were being translated from the 1730s).

Venue, time, social location, and place hardly made a difference. Hymn singing, for example, played a critical role during the Moravian revivals in the late 1720s, far in eastern Saxony. Those revivals, the missionary personnel streaming out of Count Zinzendorf's estate, and the hymns that Moravians carried with them around the world would exert the broadest possible influence throughout Britain and North America.[13]

In New England, the progress of evangelical revival, especially as recorded in the defining accounts of Jonathan Edwards, was also a progress in song.[14] Edwards was an early, if moderate, supporter of the reforms that from the early 1720s were replacing New England's 'Usual' singing (psalms lined out and sung haphazardly with great local variation) with 'Regular' singing (psalms and even hymns sung in harmony, sometimes with musical accompaniment). Professor Stephen Marini of Wellesley College has even argued that the fault lines of controversy over these innovations in the 1720s anticipated the broader New England fault lines that appeared in response to revival in the 1730s and

---

[12] The following paragraphs are expanded from Mark A. Noll, 'The Defining Role of Hymns in Early Evangelicalism', in *Wonderful Words of Life: Hymns in American Protestant History and Theology*, ed. Richard J. Mouw and Mark A. Noll (Grand Rapids, 2004), pp. 4-6.

[13] W. R. Ward, *The Protestant Evangelical Awakening* (New York, 1992), p. 127; and, more generally, Colin Podmore, *The Moravian Church in England, 1728-1760* (Oxford, 1998).

[14] On the importance of music for Edwards, as both pastoral practice and theological ideal, see George M. Marsden, *Jonathan Edwards: A Life* (New Haven, 2003), pp. 79, 94, 106, 110, 143-44, 156, 191, 221, 232, 245-, 390, 420, 469, 553n12.

following.[15] A very early note that Edwards wrote about the young Sarah Pierpont, who would later become his wife, recorded the fact that 'she will sometimes go about from place to place, singing sweetly; and seems to be always full of joy and pleasure'.[16] In his earliest account from May 1735 of the awakening that had begun in his Northampton, Massachusetts, parish late the previous year, Edwards reported that 'no part of public worship has commonly [had] such an effect on [the people] as singing God's praises'.[17] Then in the longer version of this report, which he prepared at the request of London ministers Isaac Watts and John Guyse, and which had a riveting effect on readers throughout the English-speaking world, Edwards indicated that, while his congregation was still singing only psalms, they were singing them in the new way and with a new fervour: 'It has been observable that there has been scarce any part of divine worship, wherein good men amongst us have had grace so drawn forth and their hearts so lifted up in the ways of God, as in singing his praises. Our congregation excelled all that ever I knew in the external part of the duty before, generally carrying regularly and well three parts of music, and the women a part by themselves. But now they were evidently wont to sing with unusual elevation of heart and voice, which made the duty pleasant indeed.'[18]

In just a few more years, Edwards's congregation moved from the newer way of singing to the newer hymns as well. In 1744 he reported that two years earlier he had authorized the substitution of a hymn by Isaac Watts for one of the three psalms normally sung in a Northampton service. Edwards began this practice because he 'saw in the people a very general inclination to it', in fact so much so that his congregation would have been willing to shift over entirely to the new hymns. His response was to say that 'I disliked not their making some use of the hymns, but did not like their setting aside the Psalms.' The blended worship that resulted was, in Edwards's report, 'to universal satisfaction'.[19] That same year, 1744, Edwards offered an extended public defence of the new hymnody. Against an objection finding fault 'with the singing that is now practiced ... making use of hymns of human composure', he

---

[15] Marini, 'Rehearsal for Revival', 71-91. Also excellent on how renewal of singing presaged the evangelical awakenings as a whole is Michael J. Crawford, *Seasons of Grace: Colonial New England's Revival Tradition in Its British Context* (New York, 1991), pp. 90-97.

[16] Edwards, 'Apostrophe to Sarah Pierpont (c. 1723)', in *A Jonathan Edwards Reader*, ed. John E. Smith, Harry S. Stout, and Kenneth P. Minkema (New Haven, 1995), p. 281.

[17] Edwards to Benjamin Colman, 30 May 1735, *The Works of Jonathan Edwards, vol. 16: Letters and Personal Writings*, ed. George S. Claghorn (New Haven, 1998), p. 54.

[18] Edwards, *A Faithful Narrative of the Surprizing Work of God in the conversion of Many Hundred Souls in Northampton, and ... New-England* (London, 1737), in *The Works of Jonathan Edwards, vol. 4: The Great Awakening*, ed. C. C. Goen (New Haven, 1972), p. 151.

[19] Edwards to Benjamin Colman, 22 May 1744, in *Works: Letters*, p. 144.

again repeated that he wanted to keep using 'the Book of Psalms ... in the Christian church, to the end of the world'. Yet Edwards also argued that he could find no command in the Bible that prohibited hymns of ordinary human creation any more than it prohibited prayers of ordinary human creation. Positively considered, it was, Edwards felt, 'really needful that we should have some other songs besides the Psalms of David', especially to express directly 'the greatest and most glorious things of the Gospel, that are infinitely the great subjects of her [the church's] praise'. Rather than singing always 'under a veil' where 'the name of our glorious Redeemer' was never mentioned directly, he favoured adding the hymns of Watts to the psalms.[20] Throughout the rest of the British empire, other evangelicals by 1744 were moving even farther and faster than Edwards in exploiting the possibilities of song.

In early English Methodism, hymn singing promoted by leaders like John Wesley, Charles Wesley, John Cennick, and others was even more definitive of the new evangelicalism than in New England. Participants and observers at the time made more of Methodism singing than have historians since. In the words of one American Congregationalist who wanted his colleagues to move more quickly in imitating the Methodists: 'We sacrifice too much to taste. The secret of the Methodists lies in the admirable adaptation of their music and hymns to produce effect; they strike at once at the heart, and the moment we hear their animated, thrilling choruses, we are electrified.'[21] Long before the Wesleys' Methodism reached America, however, hymns had become thoroughly established at the core of the movement.

A forthcoming book on early evangelical conversion narratives by Bruce Hindmarsh of Regent College (Vancouver) spotlights the great importance of hymns in the early movement. Several of the converts whose stories Charles Wesley collected in 1738 and following years ascribed to hymns a critical role in their response to the gospel. Typical was Mary Ramsay who told Wesley that one of his own hymns was instrumental in her conversion: 'Another thing that wirkt in me was some words of that hymn called Christ the friend of Sinners' with the lines 'His bleeding heart will make you room, His open side shall take you in.'[22] And so there came back to Wesley words from the hymn that he had composed immediately upon his own conversion in May 1738:

Where shall my wond'ring soul begin?
How shall I all to heaven aspire?

---

[20] Edwards, *Some Thoughts Concerning the Present Revival of Religion in New-England (1744)*, in *Works: Great Awakening*, pp. 406-7.
[21] Quoted in Leland Howard Scott, 'Methodist Theology in America in the Nineteenth Century' (Ph.D. diss., Yale University, 1954), 132n81.
[22] Correspondence to Charles Wesley, cited in D. Bruce Hindmarsh, *The Evangelical Conversion Narrative: Spiritual Autobiography in Early Modern England* (forthcoming, 2005), MS p. 311.

> A slave redeemed from death and sin,
> A brand plucked from eternal fire.[23]

Singing also transformed the early Methodist class meetings into societies of holiness. As an early convert, Thomas Tennant wrote: 'I was glad indeed when one asked me to go to a meeting of Christian friends; but when I came to the door, and heard them singing, I had such an idea both of their goodness, and of my own unworthiness, that I durst not presume to go in.'[24]

Extraordinary reversals also accompanied the singing of hymns. In Wexford, Ireland, local opponents of the Methodists plotted to disrupt a society meeting by hiding one of their number in a sack in the barn where the Wesleyans gathered. The plan was that, once the gathering was underway, he would exit the sack, open the door to his fellow ruffians, and then together they would carry out their nefarious intents. But as the Methodists raised their voice in song, the would-be rioter was himself struck, he paused to give the Wesleyans time to finish their singing, but then was smitten more deeply, began to weep loudly and to cry out to God. Eventually the Methodists figured out what was causing the commotion and released the repentant malefactor. He ended up, according to an eye witness account, 'confessing his sins, and crying for mercy: which was the beginning of a lasting work in his soul'.[25]

For his part, John Wesley did not approve of all aspects of eighteenth-century musical innovation. What he once wrote after hearing a rendition of Thomas Arne's *Judith* was characteristic of an oft-repeated complaint about Baroque performance:

> Some parts of [the oratorio] were exceeding fine; but there are two things in all modern pieces of music, which I could never reconcile to common sense. One is, singing the same words ten times over; the other, singing different words by different persons, at one and the same time. And this, in the most solemn addresses to God, whether by way of prayer or thanksgiving. This can never be defended by all the musicians in Europe, till reason sis quite out of date.[26]

Yet whatever he felt about sophisticated composition, for the evocative compositions of his brother Charles and the other hymn writers of early Methodism, John Wesley was a complete and unabashed enthusiast.

---

[23] *The Works of John Wesley*, vol. 7: *A Collection of Hymns for the Use of the People Called Methodists* (1780), ed. Franz Hildebrandt and Oliver A. Beckerlegge (Nashville, 1983), p. 116 (# 29).
[24] Quoted in Hindmarsh, *Evangelical Conversion Narrative*, MS p. 314.
[25] Quoted in Hindmarsh, *Evangelical Conversion Narrative*, MS p. 315.
[26] Wesley, 29 February 1764, *The Works of John Wesley*, vol. 21: *Journals and Diaries IV (1755-1765)*, ed. W. Reginald Ward and Richard P. Heitzenrater (Nashville, 1992), p. 444.

Calvinist evangelicals were only a few steps behind the Arminian Wesleys. After George Whitefield had preached to huge crowds in Philadelphia in 1739, Benjamin Franklin noted how 'one could not walk through Philadelphia in the evening without hearing psalms sung in different families of every street'. When in 1740, Whitefield's itinerations took him to Dutch Reformed churches in New Jersey, he took special delight in services where his congregation sang in Dutch while he preached in English. And when Whitefield organized the daily routine for his orphans in Georgia, he included provision for singing psalms or hymns four separate times every day (including Thomas Ken's 'morning hymn' with its last stanza, 'Praise God, from whom all blessings flow').[27] In 1753, Whitefield published his own collection, entitled *Hymns for Social Worship ... Designed for the Use of the Tabernacle Congregation*, which did as much for organizing the chapels springing up in the wake of his ministry as anything administratively he ever accomplished, even as the collection also provided a rich resource of hymns for many who never become part of Whitefield's network.

The musical change that so rapidly overtook Calvinist Dissenters – English Presbyterians, Independents, and Baptists – in their willingness to move from exclusive psalmody to the use of hymns was documented in the early days of the revival by the Philadelphia Baptist Confession of 1742. Like earlier Baptist statements of faith, this one mostly presented a lightly revised version of the Westminster Confession. Yet among its very few additions was a clear statement about hymnody. Citing the injunctions of Acts 16:25, Ephesians 5:19, and Colossians 3:16, as well as the example of Jesus who sang a hymn with his disciples after the Last Supper (Matt. 26:30), the Philadelphia Association Baptists called

> singing the praises of God ... a holy ordinance of Christ ... that is brought under divine institution, it being enjoined on the churches of Christ to sing psalms, hymns, and spiritual songs; and that the whole church in their public assemblies, as well as private Christians, out to (Heb. 2:12, Jam. 5:13) sing God's praises according to the best light they have received.[28]

What the American Baptists proclaimed as principle, evangelicals all throughout the Atlantic world were putting aggressively into practice. In Wales, the circle prompted toward evangelical religion by the itinerant preaching and circulating schools of Griffith Jones was also a circle that took to hymnody as by second nature. After being converted in 1735, Daniel Rowland and Howel Harris promoted gospel singing alongside gospel preaching and the organization of gospel societies. Harris, by early 1736, was noting expressly the

---

[27] Luke Tyerman, *The Life of the Rev. George Whitefield*, 2 vols. (London, 1876), pp. 1:338, 279, 444-5.
[28] Philadelphia Confession (1742), in *Baptist Confessions, Covenants, and Catechisms*, ed. Timothy and Denise George (Nashville, 1996), p. 82.

time he was taking to learn various psalms.²⁹ Nothing, however, meant more for the future of evangelical Christianity in Wales than when in 1737 or 1738 a student at Llwyn-llwyd Academy near Hay-on-Wye in Breconshire responded to an evangelistic appeal from Harris. William Williams Pantycelyn immediately began to put his gifts to use on behalf of revival. Soon he was one of several Welsh converts who were recording their experiences of divine grace in singable verse. Hymns by Harris, Rowland, Morgan Jones, and Herbert Jenkins were included in the manual from 1742 that prepared the way for the Welsh Calvinist Methodist Conference, *The Basis, Aims and Rules of the Societies*.³⁰ Two years later the character of Welsh evangelicalism as a hymn-singing movement was sealed when Pantycelyn published a collection of his own hymns, *Aleluja*, which enabled many from far and wide to join in the great work of revival experience set to music:

> To GOD I'm now a Friend,
>   His *Love* makes me feel good,
> My fears at an end,
>   CHRIST has bought me with his BLOOD.
> Whilst I'm on the earth, I'll make my nest
> In *God's own lap*, eternal rest.³¹

In Scotland it took longer for the new hymn singing to catch on, but not for poets to write verse that for evangelizing the Highlands was almost as important as the hymns of William Williams and his associates were for the spread of Calvinistic Methodism in Wales. Chief among these poets was Dugald Buchanan (1716–1768), who had heard Whitefield preach at Cambuslang in 1742 and who after conversion two years later became an itinerant teacher and exhorter.³² It is reported that shortly before his death Buchanan engaged in conversation with David Hume during which the philosopher opined that a scene from Shakespeare's *Tempest* was the most sublime passage in all of literature. To that claim, Buchanan immediately responded by quoting Revelation 20:11-13: 'And I saw a great white throne, and him that sat on it, from whose face the earth and the heaven fled away; and there was found no place for them. And I saw the dead, small and great, stand

---

[29] Richard Bennett, *The Early Life of Howell Harris* (1909), trans. G. M. Roberts (London, 1962), pp. 79, 199.
[30] Derec Llwyd Morgan, *The Great Awakening in Wales*, trans. Dyfnallt Morgan (London, 1988), p. 131.
[31] Quoted in *The Great Awakening in Wales*, pp. 131-2.
[32] D. E. Meek, 'Dugald Buchanan,' in *The Blackwell Dictionary of Evangelical Biography, 1730-1860*, 2 vols (Oxford, 1995), p. 1:159.

before God. ...'[33] Buchanan's Gaelic verse owed much to Isaac Watts; to his fellow Highlanders it conveyed evangelical realities with startling effect:

> Those on His right He shall address –
>   'Ye who are by My grace prepared,
> Come and the Kingdom now possess,
>   Where endless happiness is shared.
> 'The gate against you locked before,
>   My life and death have burst it wide;
> The spear has made for you a door,
>   A new wide entrance in My side.
> 'Ye now to Paradise shall move,
>   With endless joy and blessings rife,
> And all your sores and wounds shall prove
>   The virtues of the Tree of Life.'[34]

In the words of John MacInnes, historian of Buchanan and the evangelical movement he represented, Highland evangelicalism 'succeeded in moulding the life and character of a whole race, albeit a small one. It was their guide and support during the hard and difficult pilgrimage from medieval ways of thought and life to an outlook more consistent with the world in which they had to live.'[35] In the emergence of that evangelicalism, poetry played a large part.

In America, the writing of hymns to express the new evangelical awareness was pioneered by Samuel Davies of Virginia. Davies was a Welsh-descended Presbyterian who as a twenty-four-year-old itinerant began in 1747 the first serious evangelical efforts in the establishmentarian Anglican colony of Virginia. His efforts were resisted by Anglican officials, but welcomed by the white settlers as well as by Native Americans and African Americans to whom Davies went out of his way to include in his preaching. As he preached he sang the new evangelical hymns, including those of his own composition like 'Great God of wonders'. Davies was the first Anglo-American to write a body of published hymns, eighteen of which are extant, including several that would have been as much at home in the Wales or the Scottish Highlands:

> Lord, I am thine, entirely thine,
> Purchased and saved by blood divine;

---

[33] Lachlan Macbean, *Buchanan, the Sacred Bard of the Scottish Highlands: His Confessions and His Spiritual Songs Rendered into English Verse* (London, 1919), p. 39.
[34] Buchanan, 'The Day of Judgment' (English translation), in Macbean, *Buchanan*, p. 54.
[35] John MacInnes, *The Evangelical Movement in the Highlands of Scotland, 1688 to 1800* (Aberdeen, 1951), p. 1.

With full consent thine would I be,
and own thy sovereign right in me.[36]

The new evangelical hymnody also provided a lifeline during the forced migrations of African-American evangelicals.[37] The remarkable place of hymnody among African Americans is illustrated by the life of David George, who was converted as a slave in South Carolina sometime around 1770, was manumitted by the British liberators during the War for American independence, then moved to Nova Scotia when American patriots regained control of South Carolina, and eventually led a band of black Baptists to settle in Sierra Leone. At an early point in this arduous pilgrimage, the black Baptists began to use for special encouragement *A Select Collection of Hymns, To Be Universally Sung in All the Countess of Huntingdon's Chapels*. Those hymns accompanied George and his associates as they pioneered Christian communities in three widely spaced regions of the Atlantic world.

An indication of how important hymn singing became as a result of evangelical promotion is indicated in modern bibliographies. One of the most extensive and helpful of such guides is *The Hymn Tune Index*, which catalogues the music in published works from the mid-sixteenth century to the early nineteenth. Although other factors were involved in accelerating the rate of tune book publication – like a general upsurge in publishing, the growth of population, and the energetic contributions of American printers – the gross figures are still impressive. From 1701 to 1740, English-language publishers brought out an average of approximately sixty hymn-tune books per decade. From 1741 to 1780, the years when evangelical movements began to emerge, the number per decade doubled to about a hundred and twenty. From 1781 to 1820, when evangelicalism began to exert a pervasive effect on the religious life of England, Wales, Scotland, Ireland, and the new United States, the number of hymn tune books brought out each decade skyrocketed to about three hundred and ten. Such enumerations indicate the shape of a cultural, as well as a religious, revolution.[38]

The Innovative Character of the New Evangelical Hymns

The hymns of the evangelical revival were innovative, not so much because they were new *in toto*, but because they breathed new energy into inherited forms and made new adjustments as they sang. Earlier British hymnody had

---

[36] *The Baptist Hymnal, for Use in the Church and Home*, ed. W. Howard Doane (Philadelphia, 1883), p. 227 (# 443).

[37] This paragraph follows John Saillant, 'Hymnody and the Persistence of an African-American Faith in Sierra Leone', *The Hymn* 48 (January 1997), 8-17.

[38] Nicholas Temperley, *The Hymn Tune Index: A Census of English-Language Hymn Tunes in Printed Sources from 1535 to 1820*, 4 vols (Oxford, 1998), pp. 1:409-57 ('Chronological List of Sources').

been thoroughly biblical, but now the evangelical hymns gained strength by deploying the Bible allusively through evocation instead of directly through paraphrase. Isaac Watts was the pioneer in addressing directly the realities of New Testament soteriology, but now the evangelical hymns transformed Watts's beachhead into a full-scale awakening campaign. These elements – the use of the Bible and the depiction of redemption – can be illustrated succinctly, though each would also be worthy of the most extensive development on its own terms.

The hymnody of the first evangelical revivals was thoroughly permeated by Scripture, but it was a use of Scripture that worked by indirect allusion rather than direct paraphrase. Charles Wesley's hymn, 'Will God Appear to Me?' is representative. Its thirty-two lines contain about fifty scriptural references, either direct or indirect. In the second stanza, as an instance, there are references at least to Philippians 2:7, Job 25:6, and Isaiah 53:3:

Will He forsake his throne above / Himself to worms impart?
Answer thou Man of grief and love, And speak into my heart.[39]

The power that could be communicated by Scripture allusion was extraordinary. So it was with the well-known 'Come, thou fount of every blessing' by the Cambridge Baptist Robert Robinson, who exploited the story of God's protection of Israel against the Philistines, as recorded in I Samuel 7, to make a forceful evangelical statement about the Christian journey:

Here I raise my Ebenezer; / Hither by thy help I'm come;
And I hope, by thy good pleasure, / Safely to arrive at home:
Jesus sought me when a stranger, / Wandering from the fold of God;
He to save my soul from danger, Interposed his precious blood.[40]

But so it also could be as well in verse that was not known as widely. Mary MacPherson (or Mrs Clark, or Bean Torra Dhamh), from Badenoch in the Scottish Highlands, rang the changes on Old Testament messianic images in providing an equally evangelical affirmation about the saving work of Christ:

Lily of the Valley, Sharon's sweet rose,
Lion of Judah, You conquer our foes.
Strong rod of Jesse, in desert you bloom;
Light in the darkness streams through your tomb.
By love you conquered; rising again,
Eden of comfort sprang from your pain.
Lord, you have raised us; break through us to shine
Triumphant glory from your face divine.[41]

---

[39] *Representative Verse of Charles Wesley*, ed. Frank Baker (Nashville, 1962), p. 148 (# 111).
[40] *Baptist Hymnal*, p. 92 (# 177).

In Wales, the scripturalism of the revival was so thorough that it frequently happened that different hymn writers produced, as it were, self-conscious riffs on the same passage. Derec Llwyd Morgan points out how this happened most impressively with Isaiah 63:1 ('Who is this that cometh from Edom?'), which was put into Christian verse numerous times, including these lines by Dafydd William:

> The Mighty Warrior
> From *Edom's* land, his foot is fleet,
> His raiment red, a strong-armed fighter,
> The dragon wounded at his feet.[42]

The broader significance of this allusive use of Scripture lies in the fact that these evangelical hymns are distinctly *revival* hymns. In terms explained by several scholars, notably the missiologists Andrew Walls and the historian David Hempton, evangelical revival takes for granted something in which there had once been life.[43] Thus, evangelical hymns, as well as evangelical Christianity more generally, was in a sense parasitic on the educational, liturgical, sermonic, and general biblical work of the inherited established churches. Evangelicals may have concluded that these churches had grown cold, but in their hymnody evangelicals paid them the highest compliment with the assumption that the people who sang their hymns, though they may have needed to be awakened, did not need to be tutored in basic biblical knowledge. It is for this reason that evangelical hymnody has only sometimes been translated successfully into languages where the people do not enjoy a rich immersion in the phrases of Scripture.

A second innovation of evangelical hymnody was to make the drama of personal salvation palpable in every imaginable way. Here the great early masters were Charles Wesley and William Williams Pantycelyn. Although they were far from alone, Wesley and Pantycelyn both left a huge corpus of the most effecting and effective accounts of what it meant to be a Christian. Of course, both were distinctive in how they presented their accounts. Wesley, for example, was never above a little theological by-play aimed at Calvinistic doctrines, like the definite atonement, that he disliked, as in the opening stanza of the hymn that John Wesley placed second in his 1780 definitive collection:

---

[41] Quoted in Douglas F. Kelly, *New Life in the Wasteland: 2 Corinthians on the cost and Glory of Christian Ministry* (Edinburgh, 2003), p. 158.

[42] Morgan, *Great Awakening in Wales*, pp. 282-3.

[43] See Andrew F. Walls, *The Missionary Movement in Christian History* (Maryknoll, NY, 1996), pp. 79-84; and David Hempton, 'Established churches and the growth of religious pluralism: a case study of Christianization and secularization in England since 1700', in *The Decline of Christendom in Western Europe, 1750-2000*, ed. Hugh McLeod and Werner Ustorf (Cambridge, 2003), pp. 81-98.

Come, sinners, to the gospel feast; / Let every soul be Jesu's guest;
Ye need not one be left behind, / For God hath bidden all mankind.[44]

But mostly Wesley's were hymns of unalloyed unction, reassurance, rescue, and praise:

Arise, my soul, arise,
    Shake off thy guilty fears;
The bleeding Sacrifice
    In my behalf appears;
Before the throne my surety stands;
    My name is written on his hands.[45]

Jesu, Lover of my Soul, / Let me to Thy Bosom fly, ...
Other Refuge have I none, / Hangs my helpless Soul on Thee:
Leave, ah! leave me not alone, / Still support and comfort me.
All my Trust on Thee is stay'd; / All my Help from Thee I bring;
Cover my defenceless Head, / With the Shadow of they Wing.[46]

Long my imprisoned spirit lay,
    Fast bound in sin and nature's night.
Thine eye diffused a quick'ning ray;
    I woke; the dungeon flamed with light.
My chains fell off, my heart was free,
I rose, went forth, and followed thee.[47]

O for a thousand tongues to sing / My dear Redeemer's praise!
The glories of my God and King, / The triumphs of his grace! ...
He breaks the power of cancelled sin, / He sets the prisoner free;
His blood can make the foulest clear—His blood availed for me.[48]

Pantycelyn's hymns are not as well known to the English-speaking world, but they too bequeathed the same rarified evangelical unction, reassurance, rescue, and praise:

O! uplift my fainting spirit,
Truly night is drawing near; ...
O! that some device unfailing
Could be found beneath the sun,
Such that constant, sweet communion,
With Thyself for me were won![49]

---

[44] Wesley, *Collection of Hymns*, p. 81 (# 2).
[45] Wesley, *Collection of Hymns*, p. 324 (# 194).
[46] *Representative Verse of Charles Wesley*, p. 15 (# 15, stanzas 1 and 2).
[47] Wesley, *Collection of Hymns*, p. 323 (# 193, stanza 4).
[48] Wesley, *Collection of Hymns*, p. 80 (# 1, stanzas 1 and 4).

He stretched His pure white hands abroad,
    A crown of thorns He wore,
That so the vilest sinner might
    Be cleansed for evermore.
He rose on high to intercede
    For man, with sin opprest,
My spirit too He soon will draw
    Himself to rest.[50]

I have Heaven's own promise with me / Jesus doth the weak befriend,
From the depths the helpless bringing / Their captivity to end;
Shatter brazen bolts of prisons, / Draw the bars of every door;
Let my soul, the pit escaping, / To thy bosom upward soar.

Onward ride in triumph, Jesus, / Gird Thy sword upon Thy thigh;
Neither Earth nor Hell's own vastness / Can Thy mighty power defy;
In Thy name such glory dwelleth / Every foe withdraws in fear;
All the wide creation trembleth, / Whensoever Thou art near.

Two more examples from a vast library illustrate how wide and deep, how clear and sharp, the notes of the gospel were sung in the early evangelical movement. John Cennick, an early colleague of Whitefield and the Wesleys who eventually became a Moravian, could be nearly as straightforwardly passionate as Pantycelyn:

Jesus, my all, to heaven is gone,
He whom I fix my hopes upon;
His track I see, and I'll pursue
The narrow way, till Him I view.
The way the holy prophets went,
The road that leads from banishment,
The King's highway of holiness,
I'll go, for all His paths are peace.[51]

Joseph Hart, who was won from antinomian Calvinism to holy Calvinism, could be nearly as Christ-centred as Charles Wesley:

Come, ye sinners, poor and needy,
    Weak and wounded, sick and sore,
Jesus ready stands to save you,
    Full of piety, love, and power.

---

[49] Parry, *Hymns of the Welsh Revival*, p. 43 (# 19).

[50] Parry, ed., *Hymns of the Welsh Revival*, p. 51 (# 24. stanzas 3 and 4).

[51] *Baptist Hymnal*, p. 158 (# 307, stanza 1).

> He is able,
> He is willing, doubt no more...
> Lo! the incarnate God, ascended,
> Pleads the merit of his blood;
> Venture on him, venture wholly;
> Let no other trust intrude:
> None but Jesus
> Can do helpless sinners good.[52]

Again, the hymns by Wesley, Pantycelyn, Cennick, Hart, and many others, which by 1745 were being sung in all sorts of private, domestic, and society settings, as well as in a growing number of churches, were not the first in British hymnody to announce the themes of Christ-centred salvation. On these themes, however, they were the most concentrated, the most relentless, the most memorable, and the most effective.

The hymns of the early evangelical revivals constituted for almost all evangelical sub-groupings what John Wesley famously wrote in 1780 about his landmark *Collection of Hymns for the Use of the People Called Methodists* – these hymns were 'in effect a little book of experimental and practical divinity ... [a] distinct and full ... account of scriptural Christianity'.[53]

The hymnody of the evangelical revivals did, in fact, innovate in other matters also. Where the hymns of the Moravians and other German Pietists had featured drama, metrical variety, colour, passion, and psychological daring, now hymnody in English indigenized these 'foreign' elements directly as they forged a dramatic and enduring engine of evangelical faith in their native tongues.[54] Not surprisingly, innovation in metaphor, meter, and psychological fire encountered stiff opposition, some for scriptural reasons, some out of class resentment, and some because of what was perceived to be unacceptable style. For example, William Parker, a nervous English rector, worried in 1753 about the sacred musician's susceptibility to corruption by musical passion: 'Let him carefully decline the introduction of all such addresses to the passions in his notes, all such complications of sounds, as, having once been connected with words of levity, may naturally recall into light minds the remembrance of words or their ideas again.'[55] Parker was expressing a legitimately concern, but the tide of evangelical innovation would not be reversed so easily.

---

[52] *Baptist Hymnal*, p. 142 (# 273, stanzas 1 and 4).

[53] Wesley, *Collection of Hymns*, p. 74.

[54] On these elements of the new evangelical hymnody, there are outstanding accounts in Morgan, *Great Awakening in Wales,* pp. 267-97; and Watson, *English Hymn*, pp. 230-64.

[55] Parker quoted in Nicholas Temperley, *The Music of the English Parish Church*, 2 vols (Cambridge, 1979), 1:210.

Hymns as Agents of Egalitarianism

If hymn singing was one of the strongest trans-Atlantic evangelical activities, it also provided one of the few bridges between the classes and the races. Samuel Davies in America, for example, took a particular pleasure from the fact that converted African Americans and Indians became adept at singing his and other hymns of the evangelical revival. In 1756, he informed a British correspondent that, after the welcome reception of some hymnals sent by the Wesleys from England, 'Sundry of them ['the *poor Slaves*'] have lodged all night in my kitchen; and, sometimes, when I have awaked about two or three o-clock in the morning, a torrent of sacred harmony poured into my chamber, and carried my mind away to Heaven. In this seraphic exercise, some of them spend almost the whole night.'[56]

Hymns were also one of the few means open to women for the public expression of their faith. Although there were not too many women hymn writers in early evangelicalism, the English Baptist Ann Steele (1716–1779) and the Welsh Calvinist Methodist, Ann Griffiths (1776–1805), were forerunners of what later became a long line of productive author-composers.

Ann Steele was permanently injured by a fall from a horse when she was just a teenager, and thereafter enjoyed anything but an easy life.[57] Yet she wrote steadily about Christian confidence in God and eventually published three volumes of sacred poetry. Her most poignant verses were occasioned by the tragic drowning of her fiancée only hours before their wedding:

> Father, whate'er of earthly bliss / Thy sovereign will denies,
> Accepted at thy throne of grace, / Let this petition rise:—
> Give me a calm, a thankful heart, / From every murmur free;
> The blessings of thy grace impart, / And make me live to thee.[58]

Ann Griffiths, whose memory for Scripture and sermons was phenomenal, composed hymns that she recited to her household. After she died giving birth to her first child, one of her servants repeated those hymns to her husband, who wrote them down and saw them published. They made unusually full use of biblical imagery, as in these verses describing Jesus and his work in terms of the 'tent of meeting' and the 'Presence' of God taken from the history of ancient Israel:

---

[56] From *Letters from the Rev. Samuel Davies, etc. Shewing the State of Religion in Virginia, Particularly among the Negroes* (London, 1757), p. 16, as quoted by George William Pilcher, 'Samuel Davies and the Instruction of Negroes in Virginia,' *Virginia Magazine of Biography and History* 74 (July 1966): 298.

[57] See Virginia Hampton Wright, 'Anne Steele', *Christian History*, no. 31 ('The Golden Age of Hymns') (1991), 22.

[58] *Baptist Hymnal*, p. 194 (# 374, stanzas 1 and 2).

Sinner is my name and nature,
Fouler none on earth can be;
In the Presence here—O wonder!—
God receive me tranquilly;
See him there, his law fulfilling,
For his foes a banquet laid,
God and man 'Enough!' proclaiming
Through the offering he has made.

Boldly I will venture forward;
See the golden sceptre shine;
Pointing straight towards the sinner;
All may enter by that sign.
On I'll press, beseeching pardon,
On, till at his feet I fell,
Cry for pardon, cry for washing
In the blood which cleanses all.[59]

The Heightened Meaning of Song in Early Evangelical Movements

Hymns were so very important in early evangelical movements because, in the first instance, they were so filled with real life. J. R. Watson, for example, has described evocatively the physicality of Charles Wesley's hymns: they 'are forceful because they contain so many words which are physical; for him the life of a Christian was to be experienced in the body as well as the soul. ... There are physical images everywhere in the hymns: thirst, hunger, fullness, strength, rising up, standing fast, melting down, fighting, shouting, singing.'[60]

But the hymns and the hymn singing also clearly offered what Jim Obelkevich once described as the special gift of music:

> Through music, we come alive, we are made whole again, body and soul reunited; and at the same time we are freed from the constraints of society as it actually exists and taken outside ourselves into a kind of ideal realm – into what might once have been called a state of grace. Music, then, does more than delight us. It prefigures an alternative world, a higher order of human existence, a paradise temporarily regained; that makes it the most prophetic, even eschatological, of the arts.[61]

---

[59] A. M. Allchin, *Songs to Her God: Spirituality of Ann Griffiths* (Cambridge, MA, 1987), pp. 100-1.
[60] Watson, *English Hymn*, 261.
[61] Jim Obelkevich, 'Music and Religion in the Nineteenth Century', in *Disciplines of Faith: Studies in Religion, Politics and Patriarchy,* ed. Obelkevich, Lyndal Roper, and Raphael Samuel (London, 1987), p. 564.

The alternative word that hymnody created for the early evangelicals has been well described by Joel Carpenter: 'Few human acts can so powerfully fuse heads, hearts, hands, and voices like singing.' For evangelicals, 'hymn singing is nearly sacramental; it also can be political. Hymn singing expresses theological ideas, challenges common wisdom, defines and enacts community, and roots the gospel in culture.' It shows the 'powerful effects of ordinary people singing praise to God'.[62] Carpenter's reference to hymn singing as 'nearly sacramental' is apropos, for it was the one physical activity that all evangelicals shared, and it was the one experience that bound them most closely together with each other.

In light of the nearly sacramental character of early evangelical hymnody, words that Philip Doddridge once wrote to Isaac Watts take on new meaning. Doddridge while conducting a mid-week service in humble quarters for humble people was struck by how moved his little congregation was when they sang Watts's hymn:

> Give me the wings of faith to rise / Within the veil, and see
> The saints above, how great their joys, / How bright their glories be.

Then Doddridge went on:

> These were mostly of them poor people who work for their living. On the mention of your name, I found they had read several of your books with great delight, and that your hymns and psalms were almost their daily entertainments. And when one of the company said, 'What if Dr. Watts should come down to Northampton?' another replied, with a remarkable warmth, 'The very sight of him would be like an ordinance to me!'[63]

For evangelicals who took lightly to the forms of inherited church structure, including the sacraments, hymn singing took on special force. So it was when evangelical movements first arose in the middle of the eighteenth century, so it was in Wales in 1904–5, and so it remains in many places around the world to this day.

---

[62] Joel Carpenter, jacket copy, *Wonderful Words of Life*.

[63] Doddridge quoted in E. Paxton Hood, *Isaac Watts: His Life and Writings, His Homes and Friends* (London), p. 165. The letter is referenced in the Doddridge calendar of correspondence.

CHAPTER 6

Revival and the Clash of Cultures: Ferryden, Forfarshire, in 1859

D. W. Bebbington

Revivalism, according to a jaundiced correspondent of the *Montrose Review* in 1859, was 'a vortex of mad excitement', usually 'the result of mental derangement'.[1] Revivals are often thought to be irrational affairs, hysterical outbursts of unleashed emotion that are devoid of intellectual content. Consequently they are often dismissed by historians as hardly worth examination. Two recent works, however, go a long way towards showing how misconceived is the historical neglect and the disdainful estimate on which it is based. In an examination of the awakenings of the period 1858–62 in the north-east of Scotland, Ken Jeffrey has shown that revivalism was an internally variegated phenomenon reflecting the work patterns and social structures of different adjacent areas.[2] In a second book Janice Holmes has laid bare how contested were the practices of the Ulster revival of 1859, with some commentators in Britain as well as Ireland condemning what others approved.[3] Revivals, it is clear from these accounts, were complicated happenings which sympathetic Evangelicals assessed in different ways. The present study, which is based on a single revival in the village of Ferryden contemporary with those researched by Jeffrey and Holmes, takes their analysis a step further by exploring the ideas of the people involved in the awakening. It examines the contrasting attitudes of various groups of preachers and converts participating in the events at Ferryden, bringing out their differences of opinion and identifying the roots of their disagreements. It tries to suggest that around a minor episode rival worldviews came into collision. In the microcosm of Ferryden we can witness a clash of some of the cultural forces that competed for the soul of Victorian Britain.

Ferryden is a village near the mouth of the River South Esk facing the port of Montrose on the north bank. The village stands within the parish of Craig

---

[1] *Montrose Review* [hereafter *MR*], 4 November 1859, p. 6.
[2] K. S. Jeffrey, *When the Lord Walked the Land: The 1858-62 Revival in the North East of Scotland* (Carlisle, 2002).
[3] Janice Holmes, *Religious Revivals in Britain and Ireland, 1859-1905* (Dublin, 2000), chaps 1 and 2.

and in the county which in the nineteenth century was called Forfarshire but which is now known as Angus, on the east coast of Scotland about half way between Dundee to the south-west and Aberdeen to the north. Like most other coastal settlements in the region, the village had an economy that was based almost entirely on exploiting the North Sea. The ancestors of the inhabitants had been transferred from further north in the eighteenth century in order to create a fishing community. In 1855 there were sixty-eight boats and a hundred and eighty-six fishermen in a village of about twelve hundred souls, with many of the other men in related work and nearly all the women regularly occupied in baiting lines.[4] The revival there in 1859 was remarkable in several ways. It was the first Scottish awakening to display the physical manifestations that during recent months had marked a revival in northern Ireland. It therefore attracted a huge influx of visitors, eager to see within Britain what had long been publicized in Ireland. The religious stirring made a profound impact on the community, leading, according to a careful estimate, to some two hundred professions of conversion. It was thought to be as deep-seated as the more celebrated awakening at Kilsyth twenty years before. And, with enormous benefit for the historian, a local minister, William Nixon, went round transcribing the experience of twenty-four of the converts from their own lips.[5] Thus, very unusually, we have an insight into the mental world of the converts as well as knowing a good deal about those who preached amongst them. The Ferryden revival is therefore particularly rewarding for careful scrutiny.

It will first be useful to outline the course of events. During October and into November 1859 there was a series of twice-weekly evangelistic meetings run by laymen from Montrose.[6] A few individuals, including two of the cases whose testimony was recorded by Nixon, became anxious about their souls and underwent conversion in their own homes.[7] On Wednesday 9 November a gentleman evangelist who was due to preach in Montrose, Hay Macdowall Grant, visited Ferryden and was pressed to hold a meeting.[8] A former West Indies merchant as well as an Aberdeenshire laird, Grant was used to making precise calculations of the spiritual temperature of a place. He was said to have 'computed the influence of the Holy Spirit in fractions'.[9] Recognizing that Ferryden was ripe for significant developments, he visited people in their homes two days later and returned the following evening to preach, warning the

---

[4] P. F. Anson, *Fishing Boats and Fisher Folk on the East Coast of Scotland* (London, 1930), p. 269.
[5] William Nixon, *An Account of the Work of God at Ferryden*, 2nd edn (London, 1860) [hereafter *A*], p. 17.
[6] William Mitchell, *Brief but Bright Wilderness Journey: A Memoir of William Guthrie, to which is prefixed a Narrative of the Great Revival of 1859-60, in Montrose and Neighbourhood, and Ferryden, with Illustrative Cases* (Montrose, 1860), p. 8.
[7] *A*, pp. 18, 25.
[8] *Montrose Standard* [hereafter *MS*], 11 November 1859, p. 5.
[9] Charlotte E. Woods, *Memoirs and Letters of Canon Hay Aitken* (London, 1928), p. 80.

members of the congregation to consider what would be the result of dying that night as unbelievers.[10] While Grant was speaking, five people fell down with prostrations similar to those experienced in Ulster. Crowds thronged to hear another address by Grant on the Sunday evening, and, though there were no prostrations during the sermon, there were more cases at an after meeting for serious enquirers.[11] On the Monday, there was a prayer meeting and, as a convert recalled, 'all the town was in a stir'.[12] On the Tuesday, the Free Church minister, Hugh Mitchell, preached in the evening on the wages of sin and the gift of God. One fisherman found himself 'seized with a terrible shake', sank into a semi-comatose state for a quarter of an hour and felt a great gloom before springing up with thankfulness to God for his goodness.[13] On the following evening during a calm address, when, as it was said, there was 'as little to excite as in the ordinary preachings', men and women were 'overwhelmed, crying out, and falling down'.[14] Subsequently there was less public display but there were intense heart searchings, a continuing series of nightly meetings and many professions of conversion. Sightseers flocked to Ferryden, earnest lay evangelists made a beeline for the village and ministers were drafted in from outside to preach and counsel the anxious. There was scarcely a day without a packed evening meeting down to the end of December.[15] For a few weeks Ferryden was the talk of Scotland.

Despite its high degree of spontaneity, the Ferryden revival was partly the fruit of preceding circumstances. Economic factors have often been proposed as precipitants of awakenings.[16] The fishermen of Ferryden, who were thought assertive and grasping by their neighbours in the next village down the coast, normally enjoyed a good income from their business.[17] There were signs, however, that the autumn of 1859 was a time of relative hardship. The winter distribution of clothes and coal to the poor in the parish of Craig by the largest landowner, William Macdonald of Rossie, was a yearly event and did not necessarily indicate special difficulties.[18] The annual soup kitchen in Montrose, however, opened early that year in view of the volume of disease in the town.[19] More crucially, the summer herring season in 1859 had been unusually bad,

---

[10] Mrs Gordon, *Hay Macdowall Grant of Arndilly* (London, 1876), p. 135. *A Pentecostal Shower: Brief Narrative of the Awakening at Ferryden* (Montrose, 1860), p. 11. *A*, p. 49.
[11] *MS*, 18 November 1859, p. 5.
[12] *Pentecostal Shower*, p. 16. *A*, p. 52.
[13] *A*, p. 43.
[14] *A*, p. 31.
[15] *MS*, 30 December 1859, p. 5.
[16] Advocates of this interpretation are usefully listed by Jeffrey, *When the Lord*, pp. 30-1.
[17] D. H. Edwards, *Among the Fisher Folks of Usan and Ferryden* (Brechin, 1921), p. 8. Andrew Douglas, *History of the Village of Ferryden*, 2nd edn (Montrose, 1857), p. 61.
[18] *MS*, 30 December 1859, p. 5.
[19] *MR*, 18 November 1859, p. 4.

with the catch only around three-quarters of its normal level.[20] Later in the year large shoals of dog-fish were reportedly eating the bait put on the lines to catch saleable fish, so that families were making a loss. By December, furthermore, stormy weather was interfering with the ability of the boats to get out to sea.[21] Although some fishermen were undoubtedly able to ply their trade during the height of the revival in November, the weather may have helped its persistence down to the end of the year by keeping men on land. Thus it was a poor year for the fisherfolk of Ferryden. No converts told Nixon that scarcity had turned their thoughts to questions of eternity, but it may well be that lower incomes than normal did have a tendency in that direction.

It is much more certain that the recent religious and social history of the village had a bearing on the revival. The parish minister from the start of the century had been James Brewster, an able Evangelical who remained in Craig for the whole of his career. Brewster earned the attachment of his congregation by his generosity, allowing himself to be cheated rather than doubting anybody's word.[22] He attracted all but one of the local families of Seceders, Presbyterians who dissented from the establishment, back to the parish church.[23] Recognizing, however, that the church, standing on a hill nearly a mile away from Ferryden, was inconvenient for the fishing population, by 1835 Brewster was holding Sunday evening lectures in the village and in the following decade services in a cottage at its centre. He skilfully adapted his style to the audience, so that the cottage was full and the Ferryden people ingenuously asked why they did not enjoy his sermons so much when he preached in the church as when he spoke there.[24] The popularity of the minister ensured that at the Disruption of 1843, when a majority of the Evangelicals left the established Church of Scotland, most of the people of the parish, especially in Ferryden, followed him into the Free Church. Services were held in the open air, a tent or a barn until a building was erected on the edge of the village and then another actually amongst the houses. The Free Church was therefore the possession of the fishing community, not in the fields but in their own settlement. Before the church was built, boat crews contributed a proportion of the value of each catch towards its cost; and fishermen were appointed elders.[25] Brewster succeeded in rooting the Free Church in the affections of the people.

Closely associated with the church were the schools of the parish. An infant school was started in Ferryden in 1834 and a building erected for it four years later. In 1835 the parish school was supplemented by three other schools. There

---

[20] Jeffrey, *When the Lord*, p. 186.
[21] *MS*, 30 December 1859, p. 5.
[22] Douglas, *Ferryden*, p. 23.
[23] James Brewster, 'Parish of Craig', *The New Statistical Account of Scotland*, Vol. XI (Edinburgh, 1845), pp. 258, 262.
[24] Brewster, 'Parish of Craig', p. 258. Edwards, *Usan and Ferryden*, pp. 160, 179.
[25] Douglas, *Ferryden*, pp. 33-5, 22.

were also evening classes that effectively banished illiteracy, at least so far as reading was concerned.[26] A parish library had been started in 1809, and a smaller collection placed in Ferryden itself from 1827. Books, which were 'principally of a moral and religious description', could be borrowed free.[27] One of Nixon's interviewees had a pile of volumes at her elbow.[28] Before the revival copies of tracts, the *Olney Hymns* by John Newton and William Cowper and John Bunyan's *Pilgrim's Progress* were in circulation.[29] There were regular lectures in Montrose, readily accessible to the people of Ferryden, on topics of improving and useful knowledge. In December 1859, for instance, one of the ministers of the town delivered an address under the auspices of the Young Men's Christian Association on 'Perseverance', selecting the life of the engineer George Stephenson as an example and urging his hearers to 'take a lesson from the experience of that distinguished individual'.[30] Samuel Smiles, who had issued a biography of Stephenson two years before, published his classic text *Self-Help* in the very year of the revival. Self-improvement was in the air. The schoolmaster of Ferryden had mused in 1857 that one day the village might have its own scientific associations and museum.[31] That might have been a pipe-dream, but aspirations to higher standards of civilization were not. The people of Ferryden were open to influences that might transform their lives for the better.

The most obvious avenue to self-improvement in the village was the temperance cause. As in most fishing communities of Scotland, dram drinking was endemic. A couple of glasses of whisky a day were normal and on special occasions liquor flowed freely. A birth, a wedding, a funeral or the launch of a new boat were all times for ceremonies in which drinking played a prominent part.[32] In 1835 there were as many as thirteen licensed premises in the parish. James Brewster, deploring 'this fertile source of corruption', set about combating the social acceptability of over-indulgence in alcohol.[33] He set up a temperance society, persuading many of the people to join in. When, in 1848, Hugh Mitchell succeeded Brewster as Free Church minister, he at first gave no backing to the temperance cause, but, no doubt recognizing the clamant need for breaking the power of whisky, soon came round to supporting it. The enthusiasm for temperance associated with the passing of the Forbes-Mackenzie Act in 1853, which introduced Sunday closing in Scotland, made

---

[26] Brewster, 'Parish of Craig', p. 258. Edwards, *Usan and Ferryden*, pp. 129, 157.
[27] Brewster, 'Parish of Craig', p. 260.
[28] *A*, p. 19.
[29] *A*, p. 13.
[30] *MR*, 9 December 1859, p. 5. The speaker was Henry Marshall of St Peter's English Episcopal Church. The newspaper described the organization as the Young Men's Christian Fellowship.
[31] Douglas, *Ferryden*, p. 63.
[32] P. F. Anson, *Fisher Folk-Lore* (London, 1965), chaps 2, 3, 6, 10.
[33] Brewster, 'Parish of Craig', p. 261.

itself felt in Ferryden. The village policeman enforced the act; James Johnston, the Montrose fish-curer to whom the Ferryden fishermen were increasingly selling their catch, promoted the cause; and in 1853 the leading landowner, William Macdonald, built a coffee and reading room in the village as an alternative to the public houses.[34] In that year one of the seamen of Ferryden who acted as a pilot for vessels coming into the port of Montrose became a total abstainer, thereafter refusing the best spirits and wines from the ships that were standardly offered him as a reward for his services. This was a first step on the path to a more serious way of life. Six years later he was to be one of the converts in the revival.[35] Many others among the more than three hundred people who by 1857 had enrolled as total abstainers must have moved on from respectable sobriety to vital religion.

The revival spirit itself, however, was also behind the outburst of 1859. The Free Church saw itself as the champion of revivals, for Kilsyth, Dundee and elsewhere had been marked by awakenings during the 'Ten Years' Struggle', the period immediately before the Disruption when the new denomination was in gestation. During the last year of James Brewster's life, in the autumn of 1846, there was a movement in the Free Church of Ferryden itself. Andrew Bonar, the biographer of the earlier revivalist Robert Murray McCheyne and an eager participant in awakenings, was summoned to help with counselling the distressed. 'They were so easily moved to tears and sobs', he wrote in a letter, 'though their faces were those of hard rough fisher women.'[36] In September Bonar was aware of thirty who were deeply convicted of sin, and two months later, when he returned to assist Brewster conduct a communion, he discovered that some had 'found rest, though most are still tossed with tempests'.[37] One in this category, a young girl who had been deeply swayed but not transformed by the events of 1846, reached that point as a mother in the revival of 1859. The texts and hymns she had learned in the earlier episode returned to her mind thirteen years on.[38] The precedent of the first awakening smoothed the way for the second. The instance of Ferryden confirms the case made by Richard Carwardine in relation to Wales that a major cause of revival is a previous one in the same area.[39] The village had its own revival cycle.

Revivals elsewhere, however, played an even larger part. In the new village reading room the people found newspaper accounts of the Businessmen's

---

[34] Douglas, *Ferryden*, pp. 52-8.

[35] A, p. 41.

[36] A. A. Bonar to unspecified correspondent, 18 September 1846, quoted in Thomas Brown, *Annals of the Disruption* (Edinburgh, 1893), p. 773.

[37] Diary for 20 November 1846, in Marjory Bonar (ed.), *Andrew A. Bonar, D.D.: Diary and Letters* (London, 1893), p. 99.

[38] A, p. 34.

[39] Richard Carwardine, 'The Welsh Evangelical Community and "Finney's Revival"', *Journal of Ecclesiastical History*, 29 (1978).

Revival of 1858 in America and then of the Ulster revival of 1859.[40] The Ulster awakening was officially commended in a circular read in every Free Church pulpit.[41] On 9 November, the day when Grant arrived in Ferryden, two correspondents of the *Montrose Review* took up their pens to defend revivals against a critic in the newspaper who was at least as convinced as they were that one was coming.[42] On the following day, the Free Church office-bearers of nearby Arbroath met to consider steps for promoting an awakening.[43] Anticipation of revival was in the air. So it is not surprising that the first Ferryden convert interviewed by Nixon explained that her initial experience took place while speaking to her sister about 'what was going on in Ireland'.[44] Crucially, among the Scots who flocked over to witness the scenes in Ulster was the lay secretary of the interdenominational Montrose Home Mission named Mudie and a group of friends from the area. On their return, inspired by what they had seen, Mudie and his party held meetings in Ferryden urging the people to seek salvation and look for revival on the Ulster pattern. The first convert heard an address by Mudie, who also prayed with her. It was Mudie who took Grant on his first visit to Ferryden, forging the link that was to precipitate the first outbreak of religious excitement.[45] There can be no doubt that the Ferryden revival was in large measure inspired by what had happened in northern Ireland.

What, then, were the cultural forces at work in the course of the revival? First there must be some notice of the rough culture that, despite the advances of self-improvement, still held sway in the village. It was different from the respectability of some of those who, like one convert, could be described as previously 'a singularly decent and quiet woman' or the nominal Christian allegiance of those who attended communion without any vivid sense of spiritual reality.[46] There was a pattern of life that was definitely suspicious of organized religion, though not, as we shall see, without a sense of the supernatural. It was associated with the public houses as centres of sociability, and, though it was primarily a male affair, it also drew in some of the women, who were in the habit of dividing the day's earnings between crew members on licensed premises.[47] In these circles oaths came naturally, with some men priding themselves on their swearing ability. Cursing, as one convert confessed, was common at sea.[48] In a land where the churches tried to keep up Sabbath

---

[40] *A*, pp. 13-14.
[41] Holmes, *Religious Revivals*, p. 34.
[42] *MR*, 4 November 1859, p. 6; 11 November 1859, p. 6; 18 November 1859, p. 6.
[43] *MR*, 18 November 1859, p. 5.
[44] *A*, p. 18.
[45] *MR*, 11 November 1859, p. 4. Mitchell, *Wilderness Journey*, pp. 7, 8, 12. Gordon, *Grant*, p. 135.
[46] *A*, pp. 33, 25.
[47] Edwards, *Usan and Ferryden*, p. 206.
[48] *A*, p. 41.

observance, ignoring the prohibitions that fenced around the day was a significant marker of flouting Christian allegiance. Many men particularly enjoyed going for walks to look out for shipping with their cronies.[49] There was also a good deal of theft. One man told Nixon that the fishermen 'were constantly taking fish off each other's lines'.[50] Another reported that articles left outside overnight would have disappeared by morning.[51] The rough culture was inevitably resistant to the awakening. When a woman asked her Sabbath-breaking husband to join her to a revival meeting, his only response was, 'Gang yersel'.[52] In Nixon's booklet, the instances of opposition usually had a happy ending when the critic mellowed and submitted to revival influences, but that was not always the case. One recalcitrant husband, for instance, refused to come to Christ. 'There is reason to fear', remarked Nixon, 'that more or less addictedness to intemperance stands in the way.'[53] There was a traditional way of life that encouraged its adherents to have no truck with evangelistic efforts.

The other types of people involved in the Ferryden revival were all species of Evangelicals who were trying to break down the resistance of the rough culture among the fisherfolk. They can be divided, as we shall see, into very different groups, but initially it is worthwhile to stress that they possessed a great deal in common. Local converts, radicals who brought an intense spirituality into the village from outside, and moderates, both clerical and lay, who fostered a more sober approach all shared the typical characteristics of Evangelicals as a whole. Each group, in the first place, believed in conversion. Although they might formulate the experience in different terms, they all held that it was essential for individuals to turn from what Nixon called 'their lost and ruined condition as sinners' to 'a personal Saviour'.[54] Every one of the twenty-four testimonies Nixon collected in the village except three very brief accounts and those of two individuals who were still unsure of their salvation includes some reference to the change of life that had taken place. Again, all parties emphasized the Bible as the source of divine knowledge. Nixon stressed Bible classes as well as Bible reading in explanation of the revival, one of the visiting radical preachers spent whole days studying nothing but the scriptures and twelve of the converts referred explicitly to the Bible.[55] One of them reported that she 'began to get sweet passages o' the Bible into my mind' and five more unselfconsciously echoed scriptural passages in their testimonies.[56]

---

[49] *A*, p. 39-40.
[50] *A*, p. 41.
[51] *A*, p. 47.
[52] *A*, p. 39.
[53] *A*, p. 34. The word 'intemperance' appears as 'i.........e'.
[54] *A*, pp. 63-4.
[55] *A*., p. 13. Henry Pickering, *Chief Men among the Brethren*, 2nd edn (London, n.d.), p. 68 (Gordon Forlong).
[56] *A*, p. 38.

The cross of Christ was a major theological theme for each of the groups too. One of the mentors of the Ferryden folk urged her protégée 'to ask him to wash you from all your sins in His blood', five of them mentioned the atonement in some guise and Nixon commended the converts' reliance on what he called 'the virtue of His atoning blood'.[57] And each circle held that believers must take up the responsibility of active Christian service. One of the visiting radicals named Gordon Forlong preached on 'Sounding out the Word', telling the fishermen to bear witness faithfully,[58] and the people of Ferryden were not backward in fulfilling this responsibility. 'O Katie, seek Jesus', cried a female convert to a friend as soon as she recovered from a swoon; and a fisherman declared that, 'As far as possible I speak to my neighbours, to lead them in the right way.'[59] The moderate ministers around Nixon warmly approved the vigorous spontaneous evangelism of the revival. So the revival featured on all sides the hallmarks of the entire Evangelical movement, a fourfold emphasis on conversion, Bible, cross and activism.

Furthermore there was other common ground between the various sections of Evangelical opinion. Prayer, which was urged by radicals and moderates alike, was mentioned in as many as thirteen of the testimonies as a preliminary to conversion. A married woman, for instance, described how she was 'again and again on my knees in prayer'.[60] The emphasis on prayer echoes what Linda Wilson has discovered about Evangelical Nonconformist women and men in England during the same period.[61] In two other respects, however, the spirituality of Ferryden contrasts with Wilson's findings. All groups spoke freely of Satan as an active opponent of God's work. A radical visitor to the village declared that 'Satan always takes advantage of weak minds'; and equally Nixon wrote that 'Satan seized on the particular sin ... to keep the subject of it from the Saviour.'[62] One of the female converts described how 'Satan came to me, and began to speak to me.'[63] As many as seven of Nixon's interviewees, all female, referred to Satan by name. Very few, by contrast, of the Nonconformist obituaries studied by Wilson mentioned him, and she notes that most of them came from before 1850.[64] Awareness of Satan was still vivid amongst all the Evangelicals of Ferryden. Likewise in the village all parties talked readily of the Holy Spirit. On the same Sunday evening when Grant was speaking in the village, Nixon addressed his own congregation in Montrose on

---

[57] *A*, pp. 50, 64.
[58] *Reminiscences of the Revival of '59 and the Sixties* (Aberdeen, 1910), p. 80.
[59] *A*, pp. 33, 42.
[60] *A*, p. 36.
[61] Linda Wilson, *Constrained by Zeal: Female Spirituality amongst Nonconformists, 1825-1875* (Carlisle, 2000), pp. 112-13.
[62] *Brechin Advertiser* [hereafter *BA*], 27 December 1859, [p. 3]. *A*, p. 44.
[63] *A*, p. 28.
[64] Wilson, *Constrained by Zeal*, pp. 129, 160-1.

'Necessity of the Saving Work of the Holy Spirit – Encouragement to ask Him to Perform it.'[65] Visiting speakers, whom Nixon condemned as having 'more zeal than knowledge', announced that the moderates were opposing the Spirit.[66] For the converts the Holy Spirit was at work illuminating the Bible, changing people's lives, speaking to individuals and even prostrating them. That was what a fisherman meant when he explained that his father was 'struck by the Spirit of God'.[67] Nine of the testimonies mention the Spirit. Wilson, by contrast, found that only nine per cent of the female English Nonconformist obituaries she examined and twelve per cent of the male equivalents referred to the Holy Spirit, but in the Scottish village the proportion was thirty-seven per cent. Wilson's one class of obituaries that made frequent mention of the Spirit related to male Primitive Methodists, who were often active in revival.[68] It seems likely, therefore, that the common allusions to the Holy Spirit at Ferryden were a consequence of the revival atmosphere. His work seemed too much in evidence for the Spirit to be ignored by any of the groups involved.

Yet the overlap between the worldviews of the various types of Evangelical must not be allowed to obscure the substantial differences between them that heady revival days brought to light. The fishing community, conditioned as it was by the life of the sea, generated a distinctive set of attitudes. Some of the most compelling experiences during the awakening took place in the North Sea. One fisherman, while shooting out a baited line, heard beautiful music that was the prelude to an awareness of Christ in the boat. Another was prostrated at sea, dropping his fishing line while he was overcome.[69] The great waters were also the source of imagery used by fisherfolk to express their experience. A woman under conviction of sin 'could compare herself to naething but a ship in a vasty sea'.[70] Another, in describing her conversion, felt that her sins were forgiven. 'And', she continued, 'looking out from the window there to the ocean, I saw Him take them all from off me, and cast them into the depths of the sea.'[71] The perils threatening seafarers were a significant factor in fostering a sense of ultimate issues. On 1 March 1860, while the revival was still smouldering, Alex Pert, a Ferryden fisherman several miles from land, was knocked overboard by a wave, floated on the surface within sight of his comrades for ten minutes and then disappeared from view.[72] Such drownings were regular occurrences. A Friendly Society had existed for fishermen in Ferryden since 1819 partly to

---

[65] *MR*, 11 November 1859, p. 1.
[66] *A*, p. 44.
[67] *A*, p. 26.
[68] Wilson, *Constrained by Zeal*, pp. 101-3.
[69] *A*, pp. 62, 42.
[70] *A*, p. 39.
[71] *A*, p. 54.
[72] *MS*, 2 March 1860, p. 5.

help with funeral expenses.⁷³ Six of the converts spoke of their thoughts about death as a precipitant of their change of direction. One fisherman, for example, had suffered from a fear of drowning.⁷⁴ Another declared that 'there was always something that stuck in my heart about death and the next world'.⁷⁵ Apprehensions about the future concentrated on death rather than hell, which, like heaven, was mentioned in only two testimonies. According to the stereotypes of revival, the prevailing preoccupation should have been with the terrors of hell, but in reality the risk of death, so much nearer everyday experience, was much more prominent in the Ferryden mind.

The physical constitution of the village also had its effects. As in most small fishing settlements, the houses were huddled together as close to the sea as possible, in part to minimize the distance over which heavy gear had to be carried between home and boat. The houses seldom contained more than two rooms and often only one, which, as one convert confessed, meant that she 'couldna get a place convenient to pray'.⁷⁶ If the lack of privacy was sometimes an obstacle to revival, it was usually far more of an advantage. Neighbours were inevitably thrown together in a tight-knit community life. Everybody knew everybody else's business so that news flew with amazing rapidity from mouth to mouth. Quarrels might fester, and in fact one of the consequences of the revival was a healing of breaches in the community, something recounted by three of the converts. But a spirit of camaraderie predominated. Intermarriage within the community was normal, the schoolmaster remarking that it created the potential risk of idiocy.⁷⁷ So many individuals shared the same surnames that, as in many fishing places, everybody was known by a nickname: Buckie, Straiky, Tarvet's Davie, Whiten Beckie, Drummer Sawie's Jemima and so on.⁷⁸ The crews enjoyed a strong solidarity forged by common ownership of the boats and shared experience of danger at sea. Consequently it is not surprising that one fisherman who had seen his spouse converted 'spoke continually to my neighbours in the boat about what had happened to my wife'.⁷⁹ Others recounted how they had discussed the revival with their male friends.⁸⁰ 'When I saw so many people getting peace', declared another, 'I said, It will be an awful job if I am left alone.'⁸¹ But female sociability was even stronger. One woman was crying at night, as she explained, 'till the neighbours heard me' and some of them came in.⁸² Another, going to call on her sister,

---

⁷³ Brewster, 'Craig', p. 260.
⁷⁴ *A*, p. 43.
⁷⁵ *A*, p. 24.
⁷⁶ Anson, *Fisher Folk-Lore*, pp. 15, 18. *A*, p. 39.
⁷⁷ Douglas, *Ferryden*, pp. 25-6.
⁷⁸ Edwards, *Usan and Ferryden*, p. 8.
⁷⁹ *A*, p. 29.
⁸⁰ *A*, pp. 41, 42.
⁸¹ *A*, p. 40.
⁸² *A*, p. 34.

found her on her knees with a friend. 'The comfort which I saw our neighbour ... had got made me all the more distressed for myself.'[83] Most significantly, the report of the conversion of a young married woman in the early hours of Saturday 12 November brought crowds to her home and helped precipitate the revival excitement from that evening. She was, as Nixon justly remarked, 'the most powerful of all the sermons they heard'.[84] In the setting of Ferryden revival was contagious.

The family structure of the village also affected what happened there. Repeatedly converts declared that they had been swayed by relations. A sister followed her brother in finding peace; that sister was followed in turn by her husband. Another two cases were sisters, with both being counselled by their aunt. Nixon observed that no feature of the awakening was more noticeable than 'the influence which the conversion of one member of a family has exercised in leading other members of it to Christ'.[85] Wives, as he also remarked, gained their husbands as well as husbands their wives. The women in fishing communities played a more prominent part in the household than elsewhere. They were essential to the family's earning power, collecting the mussels used as bait and attaching them to the fishing lines. The women of Ferryden, according to the schoolmaster, were deferred to over money and allowed to dominate in many respects.[86] The commitment of wives to bringing their husbands to Christ shines through some of the narratives. The mind of one turned to her husband even before the climax of her conversion, and, as she put it, 'I thought if he was left out, it would only be half a salvation'.[87] Another, knowing her husband was in Montrose, 'said she could walk across the water to tell him, and he must come to Christ'.[88] As Callum Brown has suggested, women championed Evangelical values in the home and transmitted them to their children.[89] The process is evident at Ferryden, where a mother was 'full of the belief that her children will all be saved' and another, at the crisis of her experience, 'dedicated the infant I had on my knee, as well as myself, to the Lord'.[90] In the later stages of the revival during December it was principally the young who professed conversion.[91] But the zeal of the women did not mean that they had a monopoly on the unusual phenomena of the revival. Although sixteen of the twenty-four cases in Nixon's collection were female, only two of the six prostrations, two of the four visions and one of the four auditory

---

[83] *A*, p. 36.

[84] *A*, p. 16.

[85] *A*, p. 60.

[86] Douglas, *Ferryden*, p. 53.

[87] *A*, p. 27.

[88] *A*, p. 34.

[89] Callum Brown, *The Death of Christian Britain* (London, 2001), pp. 62-4.

[90] *A*, pp. 35, 54.

[91] *MS*, 9 December 1859, p. 5. *BA*, 13 December 1859, [p. 3]. Diary for 19 December 1859, in Bonar (ed.), *Bonar*, p. 160.

experiences were reported by women. It is possible that this distribution is the result of deliberate editing by Nixon, who might not wish to convey an impression of female hysteria, but it remains true that a majority of the recorded strange experiences belonged to men. Revival was not gender-exclusive; it was more a family concern.

The people of Ferryden displayed another characteristic that is highly relevant to the awakening of 1859. Fisherfolk in general were known for their superstition, but this village was still supposed, well into the twentieth century, to have preserved a particular awe for signs and omens. If fishermen walking to their boat saw a pig or a minister, it was a portent of disaster and they would refuse to put to sea. One of their number who dared to whistle at sea might induce the whole fleet to return to shore. When property was supposed to be stolen, a Bible would be opened at random, a key would be dropped on the page and its ends, it was held, would point to the initials of the culprit.[92] In this context it might be significant that shortly before the revival, at the end of October, was Halloween, which was associated in fishing communities with divination and the powers of darkness.[93] Although the *Montrose Review* announced that year that the celebration of Halloween in the town was falling into decay, it may well have been kept up in Ferryden and so increased the sense of a struggle between good and evil.[94] In any case it is clear that the *mentalité* of the fisherfolk expected physical indications of unseen happenings, often those still to come. Buzzing in the ears was a sign of malicious gossip, itching in the eyes a warning of sorrow and tickling on the feet a premonition of a journey. Physical actions, furthermore, could ward off ill luck. If an inauspicious word such as 'pig' was uttered, it could be remedied by touching cold iron. Likewise when milk boiled over the edge of a pot into the fire, salt had to be thrown into the fire.[95] The physical was an expression of a supernatural world, the two having no sharp boundary. Sometimes Nixon's interviewees showed the influence of this way of thinking, demonstrating their meaning by actions. One piled up books and knocked one off the top to illustrate her earlier fear that her sins would fall on her; another, in recalling how she rebuked Satan, 'suited the action to the word'.[96] What was called superstition was often a sense of the unity of the world, seen and unseen, and the power of human actions to express its reality.

The everyday assumptions of the fisherfolk inevitably coloured their conversion narratives. What they *felt* took pride of place as an irruption of the supernatural into their lives. The favourite metaphor to convey their experience was acquiring a sense of peace, the word or its equivalent 'rest' occurring in no

---

[92] Edwards, *Usan and Ferryden*, p. 56. Douglas, *Ferryden*, pp. 16-17.
[93] Anson, *Fisher Folk-Lore*, pp. 54-5, 81.
[94] *MR*, 18 November 1859, p. 4.
[95] Anson, *Fisher Folk-Lore*, pp. 47, 38, 24.
[96] *A*, pp. 19, 37.

fewer than fifteen of the twenty-four reports. To 'get peace' was virtually a technical term for conversion. The immediate consequence of undergoing the new birth was often joy (a word that occurs in four reports) or happiness (which is in five). Thus a woman who had been in despair 'clapped her hands, altered wonderfully her countenance, and expressed in a wonderful manner her joy at having found the Saviour'.[97] The converts generally testified their joy and happiness, a newspaper noted, in singing, which was both very popular and often admired by strangers in the village.[98] All day long on the day of her conversion, one woman recalled, happiness 'flowed into my mind in such a way that I continued to speak and fill the house with my singing'.[99] Another common description of their experience, one reported by eleven of the interviewees, was the sense of a burden weighing them down beforehand but then being carried away. Thus a married woman felt 'dreadfully burdened' but later 'my burden left me'.[100] An observer remarked that many used the word 'heavy'.[101] Perhaps influenced by *Pilgrim's Progress*, this form of language again indicated the sheer *physicality* of the change of life as it was conceptualized by the people of Ferryden. One husband could not get rest, according to his wife, 'to his soul or body'.[102] The two, everybody took for granted, were intimately connected.

That is the context for what outsiders found the strangest aspect of the Ferryden revival, the physical phenomena. Many converts spoke of bodily symptoms, not being able to eat or sleep, a strong pain rising from the feet to the heart or sins coming up the throat to choke them.[103] Commonest was 'a great shaking', which was sometimes the prelude to being stricken by a full prostration.[104] 'The person "struck"', explained the *Montrose Standard*, 'is first seized with violent trembling, accompanied, seemingly, by great bodily and mental agony, in which the body is convulsed, and large drops of perspiration start from every pore, the person affected the while uttering piteous cries for mercy.'[105] There were variations on the theme. One woman 'fell back in a swoon; her pulse appeared to stop, she looked like a thing without life, and she remained in this condition for perhaps five minutes'.[106] A fisherman 'canted awa', as he put it, for fifteen or sixteen minutes at the dinner table.[107] And another man reported being one of the five or six who at an evening meeting

---

[97] A, p. 31.
[98] MS, 25 November 1859, p. 5.
[99] A, p. 28.
[100] A, pp. 36, 37.
[101] BA, 3 January 1860, [p. 3]
[102] A, p. 40.
[103] A, pp. 18, 31, 53.
[104] A, p. 41.
[105] MS, 25 November 1859, p. 5.
[106] A, p. 33.
[107] A, p. 41.

'went off, one after another, like a shot'.[108] Such happenings were by no means unique to Ferryden or even to fishing villages, for they had occurred in abundance in Ireland, they took place in roughly half the Scottish revival centres during 1859–60 and in November 1859, at the time of the events in Ferryden, there was an instance in the city of Dundee.[109] But as many as six of the converts told Nixon about a prostration. Their frequency in the early stages of the awakening at Ferryden bears witness to their congruence with the worldview of the inhabitants. At the supreme crisis of life, the physical gave evidence of the spiritual.

Several of the interviewees also spoke of seeing or hearing strange things. There were four each who had visions and unusual auditory experiences. Thus a woman 'told what she saw in heaven'; and a man declared that during a prostration he heard ethereal singing.[110] Trances, we know from another account, were common.[111] One testimony, however, stands out for its vivid detail and deserves quotation in full. It is the experience of an old man who fell into a trance for an hour:

> I was in a room full of benches, with no chair but the one I occupied. A man came to me with a book in his hand, and a pencil in his mouth, and said three times, Do you believe?... Then five small figures came, the first holding in each hand a large-stalked tumbler, containing what I understood to be wine, and offered it to me to drink; then a larger number of persons made their appearance, and I heard them singing, and the singing seemed to be at once loud, and yet at a great distance. The single man who first appeared stood always looking on me; but he spak naething [sic] to me, nor I to him, till I was just coming out of the room, when he said, It is all done.[112]

This remarkable account is clearly influenced by Bible knowledge: the single man is reminiscent of the guiding angelic figures in Ezekiel and Revelation; the repeated query recalls the threefold question to the apostle Peter at the end of John's gospel; and the final remark that it is all done is like the cry of Christ from the cross in the same book. But there is also extra-biblical imagery. Perhaps the smaller figures represent elders, one of whom proffers communion wine to the subject of the vision; and the singers may stand for the full congregation. On that reading the convert is being received into the fellowship of the true church by the single individual, Christ-like as well as angelic, who possesses something like the Lamb's book of life and a recording pencil.

---

[108] *A*, p. 44.
[109] H. M. MacGill, *On the Present Revival of Religion in Scotland* (London, n. d.), pp. 6, 7. *MR*, 25 November 1859, p. 7.
[110] *A*, pp. 35, 45.
[111] *Pentecostal Shower*, pp. 16-19.
[112] *A*, p. 46.

Dreams were held to be significant, often predictive, in fishing communities.[113] Here was one that conveyed the reality of acceptance by the Saviour in profoundly meaningful terms. It formed a further expression of the cosmology of the converts of Ferryden.

A second group falling under the Evangelical umbrella consisted of the radicals who were specially sympathetic to the excitement among the fisherfolk. They numbered in their ranks Hay Macdowall Grant, the original outside speaker, Mudie, the man who took Grant to Ferryden, and Gordon Forlong, another gentleman evangelist.[114] Forlong, formerly an Aberdeen lawyer and still technically an Episcopalian, was a forthright layman who travelled round Scotland stoking up revival fires. He was already moving towards his eventual allegiance as a leader of the so-called Plymouth Brethren whose work in New Zealand he later pioneered.[115] Another figure edging towards a Brethren position was Donald Ross, an evangelist who may well have visited Ferryden during the revival. As secretary and superintendent of the North-East Coast Mission, founded in the previous year to evangelize fishing communities from Thurso down to Ferryden, Ross had a measure of responsibility for the spiritual welfare of the village. He took great satisfaction in the awakening and probably spoke there.[116] The laymen from Montrose who had witnessed events in Ulster were used to their uninhibited style and so were disinclined to discourage similar happenings in Ferryden. The revival there also attracted eager young men from Aberdeen, where thronged meetings under another gentleman evangelist, Reginald Radcliffe, had been proceeding earlier in the year.[117] A circle of lay outsiders criticized by more sober Evangelicals as 'a few crazy enthusiasts' and 'ignorant expounders' was the core of the radical presence in Ferryden.[118]

The true radicals were laymen, but a number of ministers from outside the area adopted a position that was close to theirs. Although these men co-operated closely with the local ministers around Nixon, their stance was discernibly different. Alexander Moody Stuart, of Free St Luke's, Edinburgh, who was called in to conduct services when Ferryden's minister collapsed under the strain, was the leader of a pietistic group of Free Church clergy whose members were particularly well disposed towards revival. Over the previous couple of years Moody Stuart had opened his pulpit to Macdowall Grant and other lay evangelists, venturing to correct their theological statements but being influenced by them to make his own gospel invitations more full, free and persuasive. There was an absence of doctrinal rigidity about

---

[113] Anson, *Fisher Folk-Lore*, p. 47.
[114] *MR*, 24 February 1860, [p. 4].
[115] Pickering, *Chief Men*, pp. 67-9.
[116] C. W. Ross (ed.), *Donald Ross, 1824-1903* (Glasgow, 1987), pp. 37, 92, 124.
[117] *Reminiscences of the Revival*, pp. 13, 79-81.
[118] *MS*, 2 December 1859, p. 4.

Moody Stuart, who specialized instead in probing subjective experience in his sermons. He had an undenominational streak that subsequently found expression in the Perth Christian conferences for Christian workers of any confession of which he was a leading promoter.[119] Unlike Nixon, who denounced the Arminian beliefs of the Evangelical Union as a deviation from the orthodoxy of the Shorter Catechism,[120] Moody Stuart was prepared to accept a Methodist into his pulpit. Although Moody Stuart was concerned to point the Ferryden people in what he considered the right direction, he was also willing to learn from the fishermen, quoting the spiritual wisdom of one of them in a letter of the following year. Remembering that a dream had precipitated his own conversion, he was less averse to their ways than many other clergy. Moody Stuart had been to Ireland, where he concluded that the physical phenomena were no obstacle to the work of grace.[121] He stayed in Ferryden for just under a week, from Friday 25 November onwards, visiting homes and preaching nightly.[122] The visitor, who believed in pulpit spontaneity, was thought 'rather eccentric' and censured in the press for 'preaching in a manner not calculated to compose the minds of his hearers, as his sermons evinced very little care in their composition, and indeed showed few traces of real preparation'.[123] Moody Stuart arranged for a succession of his intimates to follow him in the Ferryden pulpit during December: James Hood Wilson from Edinburgh, Andrew Bonar from Glasgow and Joseph Wilson from Abernyte near Dundee.[124] Each of them showed affinities for the radical brethren, with Bonar, for example, urging the instant conversion that we are about to encounter.[125] This section of opinion was purveying a different style of spirituality from the usual more rational variety favoured by ministers.

Although, like more moderate Evangelicals, the radicals believed in conversion, their understanding of the experience was different. Their distinctive position was eventually to be crystallized in the motto of the *Northern Intelligencer*, the journal of the organization that Donald Ross was to found as a successor to the North-East Coast Mission:

> Eternal salvation is a free, present, attainable, inalienable, imperishable gift – that is, any man or woman in this world, be he or she the blackest sinner in it, may in one moment be justified for ever from every charge of sin, and may rest as sure of

---

[119] Kenneth Moody Stuart, *Alexander Moody Stuart: A Memoir, partly Autobiographical* (London, 1899), pp. 136-40, 227.
[120] William Nixon, *The Doctrine of Election* (Montrose, 1861), pp. iii-iv.
[121] Moody Stuart, *Moody Stuart*, pp. 140, 142, 212, 13, 138. The Methodist was the American Bishop Taylor.
[122] *BA*, 29 November 1859, [p. 3]
[123] *MS*, 2 December 1859, p. 5. *MR*, 2 December 1859, p. 4.
[124] *MS*, 2 December 1859, p. 5; 30 December 1859, p. 5. Moody Stuart, *Moody Stuart*, pp. 141, 55, 181.
[125] Bonar (ed.), *Bonar*, p. 161.

eternal glory as he is certain that in himself he never had deserved, and never will deserve, anything but eternal damnation.[126]

That was deliberately formulated as a manifesto to challenge existing assumptions in Scottish Evangelical circles. Conversion, it was generally accepted at the time, is commonly a protracted experience, involving much soul agony. Thus one of the observers of the Ferryden revival who had been brought to know the truth twenty years before spoke of having passed through 'a sore struggle'.[127] Likewise the general Evangelical view was that assurance of salvation, though desirable, was not an essential requirement before a person could be pronounced a Christian. A village woman caught up in the revival who did not have the sense of peace that others possessed was nevertheless clearly regarded by Nixon as a person 'in Christ'.[128] On both these points the radicals disagreed with the received opinion. Justification, according to Ross's manifesto, could take place 'in one moment'; and a convert could be 'sure of eternal glory'. Instant conversion and full assurance of faith formed the kernel of the 'artificial, hollow, and distempered piety' that, according to a newspaper correspondent, was being spread about by 'ill-informed, unteachable men'.[129]

Behind the specific beliefs of the radicals was a whole cultural ambience. The conviction that it was possible to choose to enter a relationship with God in a moment was a sign of their high estimate of the powers of the will. Again, their strong doctrine of assurance was an indication of their conviction that human beings could be persistently conscious of the divine. The exalting of the will and the insistence on supernatural awareness were both symptoms of the movement of European thought that was known as Romanticism. Although taking its rise around the opening of the nineteenth century in such works as the poetry of Wordsworth and Coleridge, views moulded by Romanticism were steadily diffusing through the religious world during the later years of the century. There was a consistent downgrading of the powers of reason associated with the preceding Enlightenment and, in its place, a stress on faith and simple obedience. These attitudes were formative of the Brethren movement into which Forlong and Ross were moving.[130] They are also evident, for instance, in Grant's understanding of the correct missionary methods. Preachers of the gospel, he held, should go out two by two in conformity with the instructions of Jesus as recorded in Matthew's gospel, a view advocated by the doyen of Romantic Evangelicals, Edward Irving.[131] There was much more tolerance of emotion in circles affected by the new cultural mood, so that the

---

[126] Ross, *Ross*, p. 146.

[127] *A*, p. 31.

[128] *A*, p. 55.

[129] *MR*, 11 November 1859, p. 6.

[130] D. W. Bebbington, *Evangelicalism in Modern Britain: A History from the 1730s to the 1980s* (London, 1989), chap. 3.

[131] Woods, *Hay Aitken*, p. 82.

radicals were willing to endorse the excitements of the revival at Ferryden. Romantics, furthermore, typically idealized the common people and their folkways, so that physical phenomena posed few problems for them. Knowing that prostrations were often connected with conversions, radicals had no desire to discourage them. On the contrary, visitors of that school accused those who tried to restrain the physical phenomena of having 'quenched the work of the Spirit'.[132] Moved by presumptions drawn from the latest developments in high culture, the radical Evangelicals identified closely with the happenings shaped by popular culture at Ferryden.

The third group of Evangelicals participating in the revival can usefully be called moderates so long as it is appreciated that they had no affinity with the party of that label that had once dominated the Church of Scotland. Those who took a moderate line at Ferryden included in their ranks a large number of clergy. Hugh Mitchell, an amiable bachelor who served as the Free Church minister in the village, was active in counselling converts as well as preaching before he collapsed under the strain after only about a week of revival and was taken to his original home in Aberdeen suffering from stress, what was called at the time 'brain fever'.[133] Mitchell was helped in visitation by his friend Stephen Hislop, an ordained Free Church missionary to India.[134] William Nixon, the man who interviewed the converts, had a long-standing interest in Ferryden because he had preached there at the Disruption.[135] As senior Free Church minister in Montrose and, as we shall see, a man of domineering spirit, he naturally took over the co-ordination of ecclesiastical affairs in the village even before, on 28 November, he was formally appointed moderator of the kirk session to take Mitchell's place during his indisposition.[136] Nixon's colleague John Lister, minister of Free St George's, Montrose, joined him in visitation in Ferryden and preached in the village on the first Sunday morning that Mitchell was ill.[137] The other preacher, apart from Nixon, that day was Henry Marshall, the minister of St Peter's English Episcopal Church in Montrose. Marshall had been appointed in the previous year to St Peter's, a congregation of a body that had seceded from the Scottish Episcopal Church in order to sustain a fervent Evangelical identity. Because he was secured for the church by the Ferryden landowner William Macdonald, one of its managers, Marshall's interest in the village was natural.[138] He preached there frequently on weekday evenings in the

---

[132] *A*, p. 44.
[133] *A*, p. 43. *BA*, 29 November 1859, [p. 3].
[134] *A Brief Memorial of the Rev. Hugh Mitchell, M.A., LL.D.* (Aberdeen, 1896), pp. 20-1.
[135] Douglas, *Ferryden*, p. 33.
[136] *MR*, 2 December 1859, p. 4.
[137] *A*, p. 35. Mitchell, *Wilderness Journey*, p. 10. *MS*, 25 November 1859, p. 5.
[138] Minute Book of St Peter's Episcopal Church, Montrose, 12 November 1858. I am grateful for this reference to Pat Meldrum.

period preceding the revival.[139] There was also sufficient involvement in the revival by Robert Mitchell, no relation of Hugh's, a definite Evangelical who had been parish minister of Craig since the Disruption, to induce him to consider issuing a pamphlet about it.[140] There was a prostration in his congregation on Sunday 20 November, causing 'much excitement' because such things did not normally happen in congregations of the established church.[141] But the last two men were exceptional, for the great bulk of the clerical participation was from the Free Church. Other local ministers of the denomination were drafted in to conduct special services: John Bain from Logiepert and Alexander Foote from Brechin.[142] Overwhelmingly the official Christian presence in the village during the revival was that of the Free Church of Scotland.

The moderate Evangelical position, however, was also upheld by a number of laypeople. A lay missionary named Kerr conducted, with others, an evening meeting on 23 November shortly after Hugh Mitchell's departure. He had been employed by William Macdonald, the landlord, for several years to visit house-to-house in Ferryden under the auspices of the Montrose Home Mission, and, though he had moved on, he was recalled to work in the village during the revival.[143] Miss Petrie, the infant school teacher since Brewster's time, when she had been active in the 1846 revival, once more served in 1859 as a counsellor to anxious souls.[144] She had been responsible in the summer for commencing a regular meeting among the village women to pray for revival.[145] Although she may well have been confined to her house at the start of the revival, she seems to have hosted a small group for Bible reading.[146] A farmer, a substantial employer, fulfilled a similar function as a male member of the congregation, regarding himself as apart from 'the people'.[147] A man of even higher status, one of the other landlords of Craig named Patrick Arkley, who served as a sheriff-substitute in Edinburgh, also acted as a spiritual adviser. The role came naturally, because his wife, Louisa, was the daughter of one of the most warm-hearted Evangelical clergy of the Swiss Reformed Church, César Malan. The family residence outside the village was used by visiting preachers

---

[139] *Pentecostal Shower*, p. 7.

[140] *MS*, 16 March 1860, p. 5.

[141] *BA*, 22 November 1859, [p. 3].

[142] *MS*, 9 December 1859, p. 5.

[143] *MS*, 25 November 1859, p. 5. Douglas, *Ferryden*, pp. 55-6. The former says Kerr returned from Perth.

[144] Douglas, *Ferryden*, p. 22. Brown, *Annals*, p. 773.

[145] Mitchell, *Wilderness Journey*, p. 7.

[146] *A*, pp. 32, 38. Miss Petrie is likely to have been the 'intelligent member of the congregation, who has for years been very useful to many of the rising generation' in the first reference and the 'Miss P.' in the second.

[147] *A*, p. 31.

during the revival.[148] Three of the people interviewed by Nixon also embraced views similar to his own. One, a married woman who seems to have been more well-to-do than most village inhabitants, is described by Nixon as 'a very satisfactory case'.[149] Unlike the others in the village, she deprecated experience, 'what I see and feel', as a source of truth. She assured enquirers that she had nothing new to tell them: 'they have the Gospel', she roundly affirmed, 'and I cannot give them grace'.[150] The other two instances, both married women from the fishing community, received Nixon's approbation – paradoxically – because they could not relate any definite conversion, but had simply become 'more decided' in their religion.[151] That frank confession, contrasting with the transports of delight encouraged by the radicals, Nixon found entirely acceptable. So there were people of moderate opinions among the laity and even among the fisherfolk.

The moderate section of the Evangelical community was still firmly attached to the Calvinism professed by the Free Church. Nixon, who had been taught systematic divinity at Glasgow in the early 1820s by the Evangelical Calvinist Stevenson MacGill, published two years after the revival a very orthodox sermon on *The Doctrine of Election*, expounding Romans 9:11-13.[152] He saw the revival events as a vindication of the doctrine of justification by faith and delightedly reported the converts' affirmation of the perseverance of the saints.[153] Nixon approved of spiritual growth that proceeded gradually rather than taking the form of a sudden leap. The interviewee whom he pronounced a 'very satisfactory case' mentioned that the Spirit had been working in her since infancy, so that it was 'no new-begun thing with me'.[154] Likewise growth in grace continued after conversion. The farmer, described by Nixon as a man of 'thorough good sense', declared that it was a great mistake to believe, with the radicals, that the work of God was done 'when sinners get into Christ'. 'There is then', pointed out the farmer, 'the warfare to begin, with the flesh, with its lusts, with evil tempers, and lots of things'.[155] Nixon also looked ideally for a phase of conviction of sin to precede actual conversion, even imposing that model artificially on the events of the revival in his account. The week from 7 to 12 November, according to Nixon, was one of conviction of sin; the

---

[148] A, p. 55. Edwards, *Usan and Ferryden*, p. 112. Moody Stuart, *Moody Stuart*, p. 141.

[149] William Nixon, *An Account of the Late Work of God at Ferryden* (London, 1860), p. 2. This, the first edition of the pamphlet, is virtually identical to the second edition except for the title, the addition of the experience of case U and the list of contents, from which this description is taken. I am grateful to Neil Dickson for the loan of this pamphlet.

[150] A, p. 60.

[151] Nixon, *Late Work*, p. 2. A, pp. 37-8, 54-5.

[152] William Nixon, *Autobiographical Notes* (Perth, 1929), p. 8; *Doctrine of Election*.

[153] A, pp. 63, 64.

[154] A, p. 58.

[155] A, p. 32.

following week was one of deliverance from sin.[156] That was far too schematic, for we know from the reports of the converts that there were instances of deliverance in the earlier week and of conviction in the later. But the received *ordo salutis* of the Reformed tradition called for conviction first and so that was the pattern that Nixon discerned. The Free Church minister and those who thought like him were champions of the Calvinist inheritance of Scotland.

It is possible, however, to be more precise in defining the theological attitudes that prevailed amongst the moderate majority. In decrying the exaggerated appeal to experience of the radicals, Nixon urged that sinners should be taught not just to love and serve Christ for the comfort that he brought them, but also for '*His own sake*'.[157] Underlying this remark was a substantive point of doctrine that is laid bare in a memorable exchange that Nixon records between himself and a girl who worked as a fish-curer in Montrose but was hurrying home to Ferryden ready for the evening revival meeting:

Q. Well, girl, where are *you* going?
A. To the meeting....
Q. And what think you of this work that is going on? Have you, think you, got any good from it?
A. I have found Christ, sir....
Q. Perhaps you love Jesus merely for your own sake, because of what you think He will do for you, and not because you see in His character that which makes you also love Him for His own excellences and attractions. Suppose now that He would shut you out of heaven, would you still see anything in Him to make you love Him?
A. He'll no do that.[158]

Our natural sympathies for the girl must not obscure the significance of Nixon's sentiments here. He was offering a distant echo of the teaching of the American theologian Samuel Hopkins, who in *An Inquiry into the Nature of True Holiness* (1773) had contended that self-interest, even a desire for personal salvation, must not be the basis of motivation in the regenerate. He went so far as to suggest that penitent sinners should be willing to be damned in order to show that they were truly converted.[159] The fish-curer was being subjected to Hopkins's test of spiritual authenticity, and happily she passed. Nixon was indebted to the tradition of New England theology that included Hopkins, though stemming from Jonathan Edwards and including several other distinguished American theologians of the later eighteenth century. This body

---

[156] A, pp. 14-15.

[157] A, p. 58.

[158] A, pp. 47-8.

[159] P. D. Jauhiainen, 'Samuel Hopkins', in Timothy Larsen (ed.), *Biographical Dictionary of Evangelicals* (Leicester, 2003), p. 310.

of thought was at once broadly loyal to the Reformed doctrinal legacy and in harmony with the chief premises of the Enlightenment. It was rational and imbued with the spirit of investigating the world. This was the theological stance of Thomas Chalmers, the prime mover in the foundation of the Free Church of Scotland, who lauded Edwards but thought that he had not moved far enough in the direction of inductive method.[160] The colossal stature of Chalmers in the Free Church ensured that his doctrinal position was normative in its earlier years. Amongst other places, Ferryden felt the influence of this enlightened version of Calvinism.

There were several symptoms of the acceptance of Chalmers's doctrinal paradigm. Nixon showed a high estimate of the importance of the mind. New converts, he wrote, began to treat their children 'reasonably'; and his highest praise for members of the Ferryden congregation was that they were 'intelligent'.[161] He did not trouble to visit children, those who had not yet attained the full use of their rational powers, and so, although there were reportedly many conversions of boys and girls, there are no accounts of what they had undergone from their own lips.[162] Nixon was, however, concerned to investigate the real experience of adults of all ages, an exercise conducted in a scientific spirit. He possessed the temper of a careful observer, judging only those cases that had come 'under my own notice'.[163] He had once, as a young man, attended Chalmers's *Astronomical Sermons*, a triumphant integration of science into an Evangelical worldview.[164] Hugh Mitchell, Free Church minister in Ferryden, was himself a distinguished amateur geologist, discovering a fossil fish that was named after him and delivering an address to the British Association at Aberdeen on the subject in the very year of the awakening in the village.[165] The brother of James Brewster, Mitchell's predecessor, was Sir David Brewster, one of the foremost physicists of the age, who was inducted as principal of the University of Edinburgh only a fortnight before the outbreak of the revival.[166] These were circles in which the harmony of science and religion could safely be assumed, treating as an aberration the case made out by Charles Darwin in the same year that the universe did not need a divine designer. As two letters in the local press avowed, the moderates believed they could proceed by 'induction' and were familiar with 'mental phenomena' in a way

---

[160] Nixon, *Autobiographical Notes*, pp. 46-52. D. W. Bebbington, 'Remembered around the World: The International Scope of Edwards's Legacy', in D. W. Kling and Douglas Sweeney (eds), *Jonathan Edwards at Home and Abroad: Historical Memories, Cultural Movements, Global Horizons* (Columbia, SC, 2003), pp. 185-7.
[161] A, pp. 9, 30, 32.
[162] A, p. 47.
[163] A, p. 22.
[164] Nixon, *Autobiographical Notes*, p. 25.
[165] *Brief Memorial*, pp. 27-31.
[166] *MR*, 4 November 1859, p. 2.

that the radicals were not.[167] The intellectual expertise of the Scottish Enlightenment was on their side.

It was this scientific perspective that the moderates brought to their understanding of the revival. They assumed a fundamental antithesis between, on the one hand, the mental and spiritual and, on the other, the tangible and physical, which was altogether on a lower plane. Thus the editor of the *Montrose Review*, an intimate of Nixon's, could refer to the 'phenomena, physical and mental' of the revival.[168] Conversion, said a correspondent of the *Montrose Standard*, was 'an inward and spiritual work' having nothing to do with 'outward manifestations'.[169] The prostrations of the awakening therefore posed a particular problem for them. The fits afflicting the people of Ferryden seemed to be connected to real conversions and yet they were irreducibly physical. Hugh Mitchell, according to a biographical sketch, took a 'common-sense view' of them, not dismissing the whole movement because of their occurrence.[170] Nixon tended to be more actively critical, holding that in most instances the 'bodily manifestations' had nothing to do with 'the work of the Spirit'.[171] He saw the fits as pathological, freely using the terminology of medical science in discussing his 'cases': they suffered from a 'malady', might have a 'relapse' and were under the influence of 'infection'.[172] He shared the analogy of illness with a critic who on the eve of the awakening censured the entire business of revivalism as an 'epidemic'.[173] For the opponent of revivalism as a whole, everything about an awakening was symptomatic of illness, but for Nixon and his friends who wanted to defend what was happening at Ferryden the great task was to differentiate the spiritual and mental side of events, which was the authentic work of God, from the physical and debased side, which was something else. The result was a dualistic analysis of the revival that contrasted sharply with the monistic conception of the radicals or of the fisherfolk themselves.

The worldviews of the different groups came into collision over a range of connected issues. In the first place, there was tension over prostrations themselves. At the height of the excitement the people of Ferryden were eager to be 'stricken' as a seal of the reality of conversion.[174] Nixon, however, took a strong line with this aspiration. His comment on the desire of one man to be 'struck' as well as for his heart to be changed was tart: 'It would have been

---

[167] *MR*, 9 December 1859, p. 6. *MS*, 2 December 1859, p. 4. Both quotations come from letters sent to the press.
[168] *MR*, 25 November 1859, p. 4.
[169] *MS*, 2 December 1859, p. 4.
[170] *Brief Memorial*, p. 21.
[171] *A*, p. 20.
[172] *A*, p. 22.
[173] *MR*, 4 November 1859, p. 6.
[174] *A*, pp. 33, 34, 45, 52.

more scriptural, and better for him, to have cherished only the last wish of the two.'[175] Secondly there was the related question of visions. When a visiting minister accompanying Nixon round the village heard an account of the elaborate dream of the old man that has already been recounted, the minister 'from his own experience of similar things when his physical frame is disordered, happily showed how little of the supernatural there was in the vision'.[176] This deflating response allocated the vision to the category of the physical and so, on moderate assumptions, immediately distanced it from the supernatural. In the third place there was disagreement over instant conversion. The people expected that any process of conversion would come to a climax in a felt experience at a particular moment. The moderates accepted that sudden conversion could happen, often encouraging it,[177] but did not regard it as essential. 'Gradually light wore on in my soul', said a man whose experience Nixon approved, 'and still it increases.'[178] It was not always possible, the moderates held, to fix a time when a person passed out of spiritual darkness. And in the fourth place there was conflict over the need for psychological certainty of salvation. The popular quest was for 'peace', a felt sense of assurance. A woman who lacked a sense of peace was on contested ground: her Ferryden friends supposed that, since she had no peace, she was not yet a Christian, but Sheriff Arkley, like Nixon himself, encouraged her to think that she might well be one already.[179] They were adhering to the older Reformed view that assurance was not intrinsic to faith. It was wrong, asserted Nixon, to teach that 'none had grace or faith but such as have assured confidence and unbroken peace'.[180] In each instance of disagreement the problem, in the eyes of the moderates, was that the ordinary people were being carried away by their demand to possess a concrete awareness, a physical sense, of what they believed.

The fault of the radicals, according to Nixon, was to encourage these village sentiments.[181] The Free Church minister was suspicious of laymen preaching at all. In his early ministry, at Hexham in Northumberland during the early 1830s, on one occasion a prominent attender of his Presbyterian congregation preached at a Congregational church. Nixon was horrified by the breach of church order, rebuked him soundly and the man left.[182] Now in Ferryden similar unauthorized laymen were intruding into the work of the ministry. The resulting tension was exacerbated by the growing feeling among those such as

---

[175] *A*, p. 45.
[176] *A*, p. 45.
[177] *Brief Memorial*, p. 18. Bonar (ed.), *Bonar*, p. 161.
[178] *A*, p. 36.
[179] *A*, p. 55.
[180] *A*, p. 56.
[181] *A*, p. 23.
[182] Nixon, *Autobiographical Notes*, pp. 78-9.

Forlong and Ross who were moving in the direction of Brethren principles that clergy were, as Ross put it, 'the greatest hindrance in the country to the people's salvation'.[183] Ministers, in his view, were failing to give adequate spiritual guidance and so would better be abolished. Meanwhile an ongoing local controversy complicated relations between Nixon and a section of those more radical than him. Two years before Nixon had fallen out with a probationer minister named Campbell serving a mission in Montrose attached to his own congregation. The mission congregation rallied to the probationer, it seceded from the Free Church and by 1859 had been received into the United Presbyterian Church. A legal case centring on defamatory remarks said to have been made by Nixon about Campbell was before a secular court at the very time of the revival. The whole business soured relations between the Free Church and the United Presbyterians in Montrose.[184] When the spiritual temperature of the town rose following the return of the lay party from Ulster, two congregations of the United Presbyterians, including that of Nixon's erstwhile assistant, were said to have been most blessed.[185] While in the town, Macdowall Grant spoke at two United Presbyterian congregations but at neither of the Free Churches.[186] He was no doubt scrupulous to avoid endorsing either side in the legal dispute, but Nixon's suspicions of lay preachers would have been reinforced by the company Grant kept. Although the Free Church minister praised Macdowall Grant as an 'excellent and earnest layman from the north', Nixon very much disapproved of how the evangelist operated.[187] On the first Saturday of the revival, Grant held a so-called after-meeting, an innovation drawn from Aberdeen services earlier in the year.[188] The scheme was that when a preaching meeting was concluded, those anxious for their souls were invited to stay behind for prayer and counselling. It was at the after-meetings that most prostrations occurred.[189] So tensions over the role of laymen, including even the highly respectable Macdowall Grant, reinforced the ideological differences between moderates and radicals.

The resulting conflict was played out during the events of the revival. After the intense excitement, with many physical fits, of Wednesday 16 November, Nixon determined that it was time to put a stop to them. On Thursday evening he took charge of the evening meeting, and, although there were two further prostrations during his address,[190] he announced that there would be no after-

---

[183] Ross (ed.), *Ross*, p. 39.

[184] Robert Small, *History of the Congregations of the United Presbyterian Church from 1733 to 1900*, Vol. 1 (Edinburgh, 1904), p. 74.

[185] Mitchell, *Wilderness Journey*, p. 2.

[186] *MR*, 11 November 1859, pp. 1, 4.

[187] *A*, p. 15.

[188] Gordon, *Grant*, p. 136. [Jane] Radcliffe, *Recollections of Reginald Radcliffe* (London, n. d.), p. 81.

[189] *BA*, 22 November 1859, [p. 3].

[190] *BA*, 22 November 1859, [p. 3].

meeting. The attenders should go home, where, he said, 'they could obtain relief from their anxieties as well as in the church'. Yet on both Thursday and Friday some people insisted on remaining to pour out their distress of soul. The three Sunday sermons by different preachers were 'of a soothing nature', and at the evening service Nixon told the congregation there would be no revival service the following evening at all. The radicals were driven to blank resistance. Some 'zealous laymen', with the church closed against them, held a meeting in the infant school instead. In the face of this lay opposition, Nixon reversed his strategy. He decided to take over the evening meetings. On Tuesday 22 November his Free Church colleague John Lister conducted the service in the infant school, announcing that from the following evening meetings would once more be held in the church. Safe men, the former town missionary Kerr and the English Episcopalian Henry Marshall, were put in charge on Wednesday and Thursday evenings.[191] The dampening down worked: over the following week there were no known prostrations.[192] But then Nixon's scheme suffered another setback. Moody Stuart, the minister from Edinburgh with sympathies for the radical approach, arrived for a week, and his preaching was by no means calming. So Nixon played his master-card: on Monday 28 November he persuaded the Free Church presbytery to appoint him moderator of the session at Ferryden during the illness of the minister.[193] That gave Nixon the formal control he needed. He undertook visitation, arguing down converts who put stress on fits or visions.[194] The chief risk now, from his point of view, was that fresh disorder would break out at the approaching communion season, a traditional time among Presbyterians for outbursts of revival. He therefore ensured that he himself conducted the opening Fast Day service of the communion season on Thursday 8 December, with a respected and experienced colleague, Alexander Foote, to conduct the Sunday services.[195] There was more excitement during the week than for a while before, but in general it now seemed 'a great work going on quietly'.[196] Nixon had won the tussle for control of events and the radicals were vanquished.

The struggle over the revival extended to its reporting. Robert Taylor, the editor of the *Montrose Review*, the local newspaper aligned with the Liberals and the Free Church, was close to Nixon, who was his chairman when he addressed the YMCA in January.[197] Taylor, unlike the editor of the rival *Montrose Standard*, the organ of the Conservatives and the Established Church, duly avoided reporting the legal case involving Nixon. Equally he played down

---

[191] *MS*, 25 November 1859, p. 5.
[192] *MS*, 2 December 1859, p. 5.
[193] *MR*, 2 December 1859, p. 4.
[194] *A*, p. 19.
[195] *MS*, 9 December 1859, p. 5.
[196] *BA*, 13 December 1859, [p. 3].
[197] *MR*, 20 January 1860, p. 1.

the revival, recording only a bare minimum of detail and, like Nixon, deploring the tendency for visitors to turn it into a spectacle. It was not desirable, Taylor warned his readers, 'that any energetic or inquisitive persons, however zealous or well-meaning, should visit the scene to engage in active labours'. Outside interference would only stir up further 'undue excitement', which he associated with 'physical manifestations and hysteria'. Before the end of November he was considering a visit to the scene of the awakening in order to publish 'an authorised and minute account'.[198] Because the idea was being hatched in conjunction with clerical friends, this is probably the origin of the account that Nixon was eventually to issue in March. The result is a partial perspective on events. Nixon took down the experience of converts mostly in their own words, and, although he normally modified what he heard by translating their dialect into standard English, he could not leave out their testimonies to physical phenomena.[199] He therefore included a four-page critique, contending that in the cases he had seen there was 'no cause whatever to connect their bodily state with any special work of grace'.[200] Likewise there was a sustained assault on the belief of the radicals that a sense of peace was an essential sign of salvation.[201] None of the radicals is named, not even Macdowall Grant; and they are labelled 'one or two unwise visitors that found their way among the people', a pernicious alien force.[202] There is no mention of the initial role of the party of laymen who had returned from Ireland, for which one has to turn to a subsequent booklet issued by one of their number, a Montrose ship-owner named William Mitchell.[203] Instead Nixon attributes the revival primarily to the regular means of grace, faithfully sustained within the Free Church.[204] As Kathryn Long has shown for the Businessmen's Revival in America, the representation of an awakening could be the result of careful image projection for specific purposes.[205] Nixon's account, which was originally designed to mould revivals in other fishing villages along the Scottish coast,[206] was a further effort to stamp his own moderation on events at Ferryden.

The Ferryden revival was therefore a complex phenomenon. At one level it was a challenge to the rough culture of the village by the combined forces of Evangelical religion reinforced by the social aspirations of the people. In that sense it was an undoubted success, changing the ways of the village, generating

---

[198] *MR*, 25 November 1859, p. 4.

[199] *A*, pp. 38, 17.

[200] *A*, pp. 20-3, quoted at 20.

[201] *A*, pp. 55-8.

[202] *A*, p. 23.

[203] Mitchell, *Wilderness Journey*, pp. 1, 2. Mitchell was associated with the United Presbyterians: *MR*, 25 November 1859, p. 4.

[204] *A*, p. 13.

[205] Kathryn T. Long, *The Revival of 1857-58: Interpreting an American Religious Awakening* (New York, 1998), specif. chap. 1.

[206] Nixon, *Late Work*, p. 2.

capable lay preachers and leading to a further, though lesser, revival in 1883.[207] But at another level it was a struggle for ascendancy between different sections of Evangelical opinion. It was not simply a rivalry between clergy and laity, for, although the legitimacy of lay leadership was at issue, laypeople were found in alliance with the assertors of ministerial authority and a set of ministers had sympathies with the advanced revivalists. Nor was there, as David Clark has portrayed the tensions in a North Yorkshire fishing village in the following century, a division between folk religion and official religion, for the collision was between three parties, not two.[208] The fisherfolk, conditioned by seafaring practices and kinship patterns, were inclined to express their religion in tangible ways, expecting the coming of faith to affect their bodies and so to be something felt. The radical Evangelicals from outside the village, untrammelled by institutional and confessional traditions, looked in particular for instant conversion and full assurance of faith. The moderates, by contrast, insisted on a type of Calvinist theology and a scientific understanding of the world. Here were convictions that diverged in their estimate of human nature: for the fisherfolk, human beings were embodied souls; for the radicals, they were essentially volitional and emotional; for the moderates, they were preponderantly rational. For all their shared ground in the fundamentals of theology, the three groups diverged over the nature of anthropology. They embraced outlooks that, although uniformly Evangelical, were strikingly different.

Consequently the awakening in which all three sections of opinion participated was a contest of ideas. It was not an incomprehensible bout of frenzied irrationalism, but an intellectual disputation between contrasting points of view. Although the battle was fought out in an obscure backwater, major cultural movements came into collision. At Ferryden there was a competition between popular culture, the incoming Romantic influences of the times and the reigning Enlightenment paradigm. Three of the leading worldviews shaping the religion of Victorian Britain were at odds. The radicals, representing the Romantic spirit, were to enjoy greater success in other fishing villages, leading to the creation of a host of non-Presbyterian congregations along the Moray Firth.[209] In Ferryden, however, the moderates marshalled by Nixon were the victors, ensuring that the currents of vigorous spirituality in the village ran into the institutions of the Free Church. No other denomination established a presence there. Within the village, the Enlightenment beat off the Romantic inroads and disciplined the manners of the people. It may be surmised that, since similar forces were at work throughout the Evangelical world, many other

---

[207] Edwards, *Usan and Ferryden*, pp. 11-18. James Wells, *The Life of James Hood Wilson*, 2nd edn (London, 1905), p. 216.
[208] David Clark, *Between Pulpit and Pew: Folk Religion in a North Yorkshire Fishing Village* (Cambridge, 1982), specif. p. viii.
[209] Jeffrey, *When the Lord*, pp. 224-8.

revivals were as ideologically charged as this one. But what is clear is that in 1859 Ferryden in Forfarshire was the setting for a clash of cultures.

CHAPTER 7

'Preserved from Erroneous Views?'[1]: The Contribution of Francis Johnston as a Baptist Voice in the Scottish Evangelical Debate, in the Mid-Nineteenth Century, on the Work of the Holy Spirit

Brian Talbot

The nineteenth century had seen a growing divide between Evangelical Protestants in their understanding of the work of the Holy Spirit. Religious revivals were traditionally seen apparently as largely spontaneous in character and perceived as sovereign acts of God in response to the appeals of God's people.[2] Some of the most recent studies in the nineteenth-century revivals have discovered that these movements are considerably more complex in their origins than had been believed by earlier scholars.[3] Prior to the 1840s a majority of Scottish Evangelicals would have affirmed the definition of revival given by New England minister Solomon Stoddard, as early as 1712, who stated that revival was understood to refer to 'some special seasons wherein God doth in a remarkable manner revive religion among his people'.[4] However, revivals were normally located in local communities in which there was evidence of enthusiastic and deep-rooted practical piety, as in, for example, the

---

[1] A reference to a discussion of Johnston's theological views in Peter Grant to William Grant, 17 November 1846, Grant MS, held in a private collection of Grant papers.
[2] See *The Revivals of Religion Addresses by Scottish Evangelical Leaders delivered in Glasgow in 1840* (Edinburgh, 1984 [1840]).
[3] For example, K. S. Jeffrey, 'Making Sense of the 1859 Revival in the North-East of Scotland', in A. Walker and K. Aune (eds), *On Revival A Critical Examination* (Carlisle, 2003), pp. 105-18. K. S. Jeffrey, *When the Lord Walked the Land: The 1858-62 Revival in the North East of Scotland* (Carlisle, 2002). For a representative earlier view see J. Kent, *Holding the Fort: Studies in Victorian Revivalism* (London, 1978), p. 71 and J. E. Orr, *The Second Evangelical Awakening* (London, 1949), pp. 58-77.
[4] S. Stoddard, 'The Benefit of the Gospel', in *The Efficacy of the Fear of Hell, to Restrain Men from Sin* (Boston, 1713), cited by M. J. Crawford, *Seasons of Grace: Colonial New England's Revival Tradition in Its British Context* (New York, 1991), p. 110.

eighteenth-century New England awakening associated with Jonathan Edwards. These revivals did not normally occur in less fertile religious environments.[5]

A new era in the religious history of Scotland began with the appearance of the publications of American revivalist preacher Charles Finney.[6] His *Lectures on Revivals of Religion* had been published in America in 1835, but was only freely available in Scotland in 1839. John Kirk, who was later one of the most prominent supporters of Finney in Scotland, recalling the revolt there against traditional Calvinism in the 1830s, stated that there were two books that were particularly influential in stimulating this process. The first was Andrew Reed and James Matheson's *Visit to the American Churches*, whose descriptions of revivalist meetings in America led enthusiasts such as Kirk to imitate these practices in Scotland,[7] and of even greater value, Finney's *Lectures on Revivals*, that was both widely circulated and inexpensive to purchase.[8] The standard biography of John Kirk, *Memoirs of Rev. John Kirk D.D.*, noted that:

> This remarkable revival ... was inspired continually from abroad and around. Prof Finney's Oberlin Evangelist was regularly read by many of the leading workers and much influenced their methods and aims. Mr Kirk was then to some extent a pupil of Finney, though they had never met.

Kirk did meet Finney later in 1859. The American Evangelist occupied his pulpit in Edinburgh that year for approximately three months.[9] It is important to state that Charles Finney was the most important outside influence on the growth and development of these newer revivalist ideas in Scotland. The significance of this influence had been often overlooked due to the overshadowing importance of the 1843 Disruption in the Church of Scotland, in which a far greater number of people were involved, though it could be argued

---

[5] This point is discussed in S. Piggin, *Firestorm of the Lord: The History of and Prospects for Revival in the Church and the World* (Carlisle, 2000), pp. 45-9.

[6] The best account of the views of Finney is found in D. L. Weddle, *The Law as Gospel: Revival and Reform in the Theology of Charles G. Finney* (London, 1985).

[7] A. Reed and J. Matheson, *A Narrative of the Visit to the American Churches* (2 vols; London: Jackson and Walford, 1835), Vol. 1, pp. 294-8; Vol. 2, pp. 1-50, 64-78. H. Kirk, *Memoirs of Rev. John Kirk D.D.* (Edinburgh, 1888), pp. 138-54.

[8] *Christian News*, 2 September 1865, cited by R. Carwardine, *Trans-Atlantic Revivalism: Popular Evangelicalism in Britain and America, 1790-1865* (London, 1978), p. 97.

[9] Kirk, *John Kirk*, pp. 154-5, extends this ministry to four months, though this is an exaggeration. G. M. Rosell and R. A. G. Dupois (eds), *The Memoirs of Charles G. Finney* (Zondervan, 1989), p. 591, records that 'Finney commenced preaching on Sunday 21 August and continued to 6 November 1859', E. Finney, 'A Journal Kept by Mrs Elizabeth Ford Atkinson Finney during a Visit to England in 1859-1860', pp. 50-53, ms in the Special Collections, Oberlin College Library, as the source of this reference.

that the effects of Finney's influence on the churches in Scotland had been equally substantial.

One Scottish minister who was greatly indebted to Finney was James Morison.[10] The Kilmarnock minister was so excited about his discoveries that he discussed their importance in a letter to his father Robert Morison, a United Secession Church minister, in 1838. 'I do strenuously advise you to get Finney's lectures on Revivals, and preach like him; I have reaped more benefit from the book than from all other human compositions put together.'[11] James Morison had had a similar doctrinal pilgrimage to Charles Finney. The two men had both been brought up in traditional Calvinistic Presbyterian circles and had begun their ministry believing in the Reformed doctrine of election, before later discarding it.[12] The old ideas associated with the consequences of a belief in the doctrine of original sin were also rejected by both men.[13] Likewise the necessity for a supernatural work of the Spirit in a person's heart before conversion was also rejected.[14] Finney, in his 1835 *Lectures on Revivals of Religion*, declared: 'A revival is not a miracle, nor dependent on a miracle, in any sense. It is a purely philosophical result of the right use of the constituted means.'[15] James Morison had already drawn the attention of his peers to his independent mind when he had chosen to oppose his own denomination's belief in the eternal

---

[10] K. B. E. Roxburgh, 'James Morison (1816-1893)', *Records of the Scottish Church History* Society, 32, pp. 132-3, provides a helpful discussion of some of the similarities and differences between the views of Finney and Morison.

[11] W. Adamson, *The Life of the Rev. James Morison* (London, 1898), p. 55. A contrasting view was presented in the 1840 *Revival of Religion Addresses*, which included these words in the preface: 'It is because our American brethren have so frequently mistaken what is at most only concomitant, or merely adjunct or consequent, for what is essential to conversion, that they have fallen into such multifarious errors and abuses, in their zealous attempts to 'get up' and 'conduct' revivals.', p. xvii.

[12] Adamson, *James Morison*, p. 79. G. W. Gale, *Autobiography of Rev. George Gale* (New York, 1964), pp. 186, 274, cited by K. J. Hardman, *Charles Grandison Finney 1792-1875* (Darlington, 1990 [1987]), p. 52.

[13] Ferguson, *A History of the Evangelical Union* (Glasgow, 1876), p. 63. Hardman, *Charles Grandison Finney*, pp. 15-21. For a fuller explanation of Morison's rejection of this doctrine, see J. Morison, 'Original Sin', *Evangelical Repository*, second series, 1.4 (1859), pp. 270, 272. For Finney see C. G. Finney, *Sermons on Gospel Themes*, ed. R. M. Friedrich (Grand Rapids, 2002 [1876]), pp. 98-111. In the New England context Nathaniel Taylor had prepared the way for this view with his 1818 pamphlet, *Man, a Free Agent Without the Aids of Divine Grace*. This point was noted by N. A. Hardesty, *Your Daughters Shall Prophesy: Revivalism and Feminism in the Age of Finney* (New York, 1991), p. 30, though Finney developed Taylor's position by insisting that the sinner had 'a natural capacity for faith', Weddle, *Law as Gospel*, pp. 188-9. John Kirk also rejected the traditional understanding of this issue, Kirk, *John Kirk*, p. 375.

[14] Ferguson, *Evangelical Union*, p. 61.

[15] C. G. Finney, *Lectures on Revivals of Religion*, ed. W. G. McLoughlin (Cambridge, 1960), p. 13.

Sonship of Christ.[16] These rationalistic influences had also made inroads into Scottish Baptist ranks in this era. An article in the Baptist Union of Scotland periodical *The Evangelist*, in April 1851, also denied the validity of the traditional understanding of this doctrine.[17] Morison denied that regeneration occurs prior to faith and because saving faith is a belief of the truth, the preacher must do everything in his power to present the gospel to the minds of his hearers so that they may understand, believe and be saved.[18] He was a consistent rationalist in his thinking and required doctrinal statements to be both biblical and rational. Although he built upon ideas advanced by the Glasites and Scotch Baptists, and especially Charles Finney,[19] Morison in his own right had a significant influence on fellow Scottish Christians in the nineteenth century.[20]

Another important Scottish theologian who would be influential upon Baptist leader Francis Johnston was John Kirk, minister of Hamilton Independent Church from 1839 to 1845, then an Evangelical Union (EU) minister in Edinburgh from 1845, settling in Broughton EU Chapel, in that city, in 1846 until his retirement in 1876.[21] Johnston had moved to Edinburgh in 1845 to found a new Baptist congregation that would be in sympathy with his views, after his attempts to impose his opinions on his Cupar charge had been without success.[22] The closeness of their geographical location and a similar theological pilgrimage made it inevitable that Johnston and Kirk would at the very least have been aware of the contribution each had been making in the contemporary theological debates. Kirk in the 1840s was a young minister with strong opinions that were very forcefully expressed. His 'new views' caused

---

[16] Adamson, *James Morison*, pp. 41-43.

[17] *The Evangelist*, 6, no. 4 (1851), p. 79.

[18] Morison, *Saving Faith*, pp. 49-50. See also J. Morison, 'Nature of the Holy Spirit's Work: Or are the influences of the Spirit Direct or Mediate', *Evangelical Repository*, 2, no. 6 (1856), pp. 238-58; and 'Does Scripture teach that the Influences of the Holy Spirit are Resistible?', *Evangelical Repository*, 3, no. 10 (1857), pp. 121-34.

[19] C. E. Hambrick-Stowe, *Charles G. Finney and the Spirit of American Evangelicalism*, (Grand Rapids, 1996), pp. 258-9, reveals some differences between Finney and Morison, implying that the latter man employed a more rigorously rational approach to theological issues.

[20] Morison's influence on Francis Johnston and other Scottish Baptists is noted in Roxburgh, *James Morison*, pp. 138-40, and Talbot, *Search for a Common Identity*, pp. 229-76.

[21] N. Needham, 'Kirk, John (1813-86)', in Cameron, *Dictionary of Scottish Church History*, p. 460.

[22] R. B. Hannen, 'Francis Johnston', *Scottish Baptist Magazine*, 66, no. 7 (1940), p. 5. It is probable that a proportion of Johnston's congregation of Morisonian Baptists had previously attended as hearers at Kirk's church due to the lack of a Baptist cause in Edinburgh that espoused this theological perspective. See Kirk, *John Kirk*, p. 226.

considerable unease within the network of Scottish Independent churches.[23] Here the controversy was not directly related to the Atonement debate in the United Secession Church; instead it centred on the extent and nature of the work of the Holy Spirit in conversion. Kirk passionately rejected the distinctive Calvinistic doctrines that were commonly associated with the Independent tradition. By contrast, he focused on the universal love of God, a universal atonement and the influence of the Holy Spirit being brought to bear equally on every person without distinction or exception.[24] It was, though, the publication in 1842 of *The Way of Life Made Plain* that brought Kirk to the attention of his denomination. It must first be stated that this is a popular rather than an academic study of Christian doctrine. The author intended his volume to be suitable for reading in 'family circles' and being 'put into the hands of friends and neighbours' and it was 'to the common people that his heart especially turns'. This work was a compilation of thirteen 'lectures' that were originally distributed as individual tracts in the district where he served as a minister. They were collated into one volume with a view to a wider circulation amongst the general public.[25] It is most probable that this book served as a model for Johnston's most controversial publication, *The Work of God and the Work of Man in Conversion*, published in 1848.[26] Johnston's book was also aimed at the common man rather than the academic community and was a compilation of fourteen 'lectures' on similar themes. Kirk was unafraid of controversy and where it might lead and his Baptist contemporary was a minister with a similar disposition. As a result Kirk within Scottish Independent circles and Johnston in Baptist ranks would cause breaches of fellowship within their constituencies that would take a number of years to heal.

Kirk, like Morison, held to a Sandemanian[27] view of faith. There are a good number of references to 'simple belief' throughout *The Way of Life Made Plain*.[28] In Lecture nine, 'The Holy Spirit alone overcomes man's enmity to the truth of God', Kirk rejects the traditional Reformed view of a supernatural intervention in the human mind and heart by the Holy Spirit to predispose an individual to respond to the gospel proclamation. He declares that 'you can

---

[23] It led to the expulsion of nine ministerial students from their Theological Academy in 1844. They had faced an additional examination in the autumn of 1843 regarding their beliefs, which had been viewed (correctly) as sympathetic to the opinions being promoted by Kirk. See W. Adamson, *The Life of Fergus Ferguson* (Glasgow, 1900), pp. 36-48, and *The Expulsion of Nine Students from the Glasgow Theological Academy*, (Glasgow, 1844).

[24] Adamson, *Fergus Ferguson*, p. 37.

[25] J. Kirk, *The Way of Life Made Plain* (Glasgow, 1842), Preface, pp. v-viii. Kirk, *John Kirk*, pp. 193-202.

[26] F. Johnston, *The Work of God and the Work of Man in Conversion* (Edinburgh, 1848).

[27] D. B. Murray, 'Sandeman, Robert (1718-71)', in N. M. de S. Cameron (ed.), *Dictionary of Scottish Church History and Theology* (Edinburgh, 1993), p. 744.

[28] Kirk, *Way of Life Made Plain*, for example, pp. 24, 32, 73, 74, 95.

undergo no change but in the simple way of believing' and followed it up with a question: 'Why does it require Omnipotence to bring about what is nothing more than the belief of a simple truth?' 'The Spirit's work with the unbeliever must be an 'external work', because until an unbeliever turns from his unbelief 'the Holy Spirit of the Lord is excluded from your mind and his work is necessarily from without.' The question that then arises is this: In what way does God speak to people? The answer given by Kirk is that 'God regards himself as speaking when his word is spoken by man.'[29] The idea of an effectual call from God or any form of irresistible grace was discussed in Lecture ten of his book. Kirk declared:

> You must remember that while his power is unlimited, its exercise is limited by the nature of the mind with which he deals. He has pleased to make man a moral being and not a stone and it is no dishonour to his power to say, that he cannot influence a stone as he influences a mind ... if, after God has brought the utmost amount of motive to bear on man which he is capable of receiving, and still he is unchanged, it is no disparagement to turn and ask, 'What more could I have done?'[30]

Kirk also stated that each person was 'absolutely free' in the choices they could make. Johnston's understanding of this doctrine was the same as that of Kirk. In the Baptist minister's eighth lecture on man's ability to turn to God and believe the gospel there is the following statement. 'You will never get the Holy Spirit till you take Jesus. When you receive the truth of the Spirit, then you receive the Spirit of truth, but not till then. Do not, dear friend, be deluded with the notion that you are as passive as a stone ...'[31] This approach to commending the Christian faith was very attractive to a significant proportion of working-class people attending Scottish churches in the mid nineteenth century who had struggled to comprehend some of the doctrines propounded by preachers holding to the standard Reformed views.

Lecture six in Kirk's book, 'Christ Jesus is, in the same sense, and to the same extent, the propitiation for the sins of the whole of mankind', addresses the issue of the extent of the atonement using I John 2:2 as the basis for his discussion of various biblical texts. The author leaves his readers in no doubt as to where his sympathies lie.

> All the sophistry in earth and hell combined, will never be able to make that 'whole world' anything less than that same 'whole world' which the same Spirit says 'lieth in wickedness'. If, therefore, anyone excludes *you* from 'the whole

---

[29] Kirk, *Way of Life Made Plain*, pp. 68-79, but see also pp. 61-8 where similar points are made on this subject.
[30] Kirk, *Way of Life Made Plain*, pp. 80-6.
[31] Johnston, *Work of God and Work of Man*, p. 123.

world' for which Jesus died, he must also exclude you from that which 'lieth in the wicked one'.[32]

Kirk's motivation for promoting these 'new' ideas in mid-nineteenth-century Scotland was primarily evangelistic. Some proponents of Reformed opinions, in his view, had been reluctant to invite people to respond to the gospel message. The justification for the controversy he and other Morisonians had created was this – the large number of people who had professed faith through hearing this interpretation of the Christian faith.[33] For example, Kirk himself was aware of 'many hundreds' who had 'found peace and a total change of character and experience' through reading the separate 'treatises' that made up this book. He also had another aim in producing this work – to show 'earnest Christians' how to more effective in sharing their faith and 'so be better able to bring it successfully home'.[34] Johnston had used the same reasoning for insisting that the home evangelistic work of his Morisonian Baptist Union must be kept separate from the operations of the BHMS, a society whose leaders and preachers held to an Evangelical Calvinistic interpretation of the Christian faith. He believed that given time it would be self-evident that the new approach to evangelistic work would produce more converts and therefore 'we shall more effectively and rapidly advance the cause of God in the land'.[35] Johnston's confidence was misplaced, but the atmosphere of the mid-1840s following the formation of the Free Church of Scotland through the Disruption of May 1843, together with the genesis of the Evangelical Union and the start of the co-operative meetings of the Churches of Christ, all within a twelve-month period, could only be described as a revolutionary change in the allegiances of a significant number of Scottish Christians.[36]

---

[32] Kirk, *Way of Life Made Plain*, pp. 44-52.
[33] A similar interpretation of the justification for Morisonian theology is given in H. F. Henderson, *The Religious Controversies of Scotland* (Edinburgh, 1905), pp. 182-93.
[34] Kirk, *Way of Life Made Plain*, Preface, pp. vi-viii.
[35] Words taken from a motion agreed by delegates at the Baptist Union of Scotland Annual Meeting in Perth, August 1846, n.p., MS in the possession of Bristo Baptist Church, Edinburgh. More details are given in Talbot, *Search for a Common Identity*, pp. 249-51.
[36] A similar confidence was found in the wider social and political context at that time. In Parliament in the previous two decades there had been the Catholic Emancipation Act of 1829; the Reform Bill of 1832; the Abolition of Slavery in the British Colonies in 1833; the Poor Law of 1834; the restoration of the rights of municipalities in 1835 and the foundation of a system of national education in 1839. Henderson's summary of these social trends was apt; 'Brotherhood, equality, and fair-play were clamouring loudly at every closed door, and refusing to be turned away. A corresponding claim, quite independent of politics, was being made in the name of Christian theology. Here also it was demanded that the doors of privilege be thrown open. The conception of a God who maintained His Church and provided redemption for the favoured few was being declared an intolerable anachronism. Freedom for all, food for all, education for all, and

Johnston's book, *The Work of God and the Work of Man in Conversion*, was produced as a conscious challenge to the existing perceptions of theological orthodoxy on the part of some of his colleagues in Scottish Baptist ranks.[37] It was also no coincidence that this work appeared at the same time as Johnston and some of his colleagues had dramatically reshaped the Baptist Union of Scotland as a militant Morisonian body.[38] Francis Johnston was a complex character who combined zeal for the promotion of the Baptist cause in Scotland with an equal zeal to put right the perceived faults of his fellow Baptists. His conflicts with some of his Scottish colleagues would ensure that attempts to unite Scottish Baptists in the late 1840s and early 1850s would ultimately founder. Peter Grant was an example of one individual who faced censure from Johnston. He was a lawyer and lay-pastor of an 'English' Baptist Church in Stirling. Grant had written a booklet entitled, *A Brief Review of a Recent Publication entitled, 'The Work of God and the Work of Man in Conversion'*, in response to this highly controversial book produced in 1848 by Francis Johnston. The Johnston book attracted criticism from many Scottish Baptists besides Peter Grant, but it is the Stirling pastor to whom Johnston responded in the pages of *The Evangelist*. There were five instalments in successive issues from August to December 1850. Johnston's manuscript would have been published earlier, but the editor of *The Evangelist* who first received it in the spring or summer of 1849, James Taylor, refused to publish it on the grounds that 'enough had been said on that subject'. This was a wise decision. A less discerning editor, Thomas Milner, was willing to publish his pastor's remarks.[39] Peter Grant, together with other Calvinistic Baptists, had been concerned about the spread of new theological ideas in Scotland associated with James Morison and the Evangelical Union. Mainstream evangelical Calvinists like Peter Grant tended to follow Andrew Fuller's line in his debates with Archibald McLean regarding faith and to reject the other newer ideas associated with Morison and his colleagues. In 1827 at the founding of the first Baptist Union of Scotland Scottish Baptists had been in almost total agreement about theological matters, their disagreements being confined to ecclesiological issues. Now it appeared that the very foundational doctrines of the faith were being undermined. In such a context as this it is not surprising that Johnston's book aroused strong responses within the Scottish Baptist constituency.

It is important to be aware that Johnston had completely rejected the Calvinistic understanding of God, humanity and salvation. Some modern writers, unlike his contemporaries, appear to underestimate the significance of

---

salvation for all, were now coming to be the national watchwords.' Henderson, *Religious Controversies*, pp. 182-3.

[37] Johnston, *Work of God and Work of Man*, pp. 3-4.

[38] See Talbot, *Search for a Common Identity*, chapter seven for more details.

[39] *The Evangelist*, 5, no. 8 (August 1850), p. 150.

this development.[40] Johnston in his debate with Peter Grant admits that he is an Arminian and that Grant is a Calvinist and that the traditional differences between these two systems regarding the doctrine of salvation are upheld in their writings.[41] Francis Johnston, however, is unwilling to accept the main charges brought by Grant against him. Grant's fundamental criticism refers to the apparent equality of roles in the process of conversion undertaken by man and God:

> in treating of the glorious work of the new creation, thus to place God and man side by side, and as being, as far as the terms go, compeers, and on a footing, is an exceeding violation of reverence and right feeling towards God ... the doctrine of the lectures indicates views and feelings tending to the utter subversion of the grace of God.[42]

At the heart of the issue is the debate over the manner in which the Holy Spirit brings people to faith in Jesus Christ. Peter Grant assumed that Johnston followed Finney and Morison in denying the supernatural influence of the Holy Spirit in conversion as the determinative factor as to whether a person was brought to faith. The claim was denied by Johnston, though his book appeared to confirm the suspicions of his opponents. He argued that the Holy Spirit inspired the writers of Holy Scripture and they passed on the sacred writings to the members of the church who are commissioned to preach it to the world. 'It is thus that the Holy Spirit is at work for the conversion of man to God.'[43] The idea of the Holy Spirit working directly and actively on a human being in opening the mind and bringing it to respond to the gospel, as understood in Reformed theology, was decisively rejected. The effectual call of the Spirit

> is a doctrine of devils, a doctrine in which Satan and his angels and agents delight, as being so subservient to their hellish purposes in deceiving and destroying millions of souls. It behoves the people of God therefore to set their faces against it as a flint.[44]

Johnston appears to believe, echoing Finney, that if the right human methodology is used that there will be a mass turning of the people in the land to the Christian faith. 'Of one thing the writer is certain, that were the doctrines here stated universally preached, there would be a universal revival of religion

---

[40] For example, D. B. Murray, 'Johnstone, Francis', in D. M. Lewis (ed.), *Dictionary of Evangelical Biography 1730-1860* (2 vols; Oxford, 1995), Vol. 1, p. 616.

[41] F. Johnston, 'Reply to Mr Grant IV', *The Evangelist*, 5, no. 11 (November 1850), p. 221.

[42] *The Primitive Church Magazine* (*PCM*), new series, 6, no. 2 (February 1849), pp. 67-68.

[43] Johnston, *Work of God and Work of Man*, p. 20.

[44] Johnston, *Work of God and Work of Man*, pp. 112-13.

in our churches.'⁴⁵ The notion of one religious prescription to cure all the spiritual ills of Scotland would be challenged by the religious revival of the late 1850s and early 1860s. However, in the 1840s the men of Morisonian opinions were supremely confident that they would win the competition for the spiritual allegiance of a growing proportion of Scottish Christians

Johnston had the opportunity to correct any mistakes in Grant's critique of his book on the work of the Spirit in conversion, but instead appeared to confirm his opponent's position. He admitted that 'Faith is the work of man as well as the gift of God',⁴⁶ and that the working of the Holy Spirit during the ministry of Jesus on earth was solely 'the Father drawing souls simply through Christ's doctrines and miracles. We ask, were not these the means through which God exerted or put forth that influence which alone could bring them to Christ?'⁴⁷ Far from reassuring fellow Baptists by his extended reply to Grant's accusations, Johnston only confirmed the suspicions of many that he had departed from the bounds of Christian orthodoxy. An anonymous article by a Scottish Baptist, in the strict communion periodical the *Primitive Church Magazine*, hinted at the dissension in the ranks of the Baptist Union of Scotland as a result of the publication of Johnston's controversial book.

> All holding evangelical doctrine (and even some who are still of Mr J.[ohnston]'s party) are unanimous in pronouncing his book erroneous, insidious, and of evil tendency ... Most sincerely do we regret the position of the theological tutor of the Baptist Union of Scotland. Some of the best supporters of his theological school, it is said, will support it no more.⁴⁸

This was not a lone voice, other Calvinistic Baptists held similar sentiments, even some people who had long admired Johnston for his vision and evangelistic zeal. Peter Grant, minister of Grantown-on-Spey Baptist Church, had been concerned about the Cupar minister's theology in 1846, long before the damage caused by his 1848 treatise. In a letter to his son William, Peter Grant expresses his hopes and also his fears for Johnston's future:

> If the Lord preserves Johnston from erroneous views you will see that he will be one of the cleverest men of our denomination. I am not sorry that you cultivate acquaintance with him, I hope it will not offend anyone.⁴⁹

Peter Grant was a most perceptive minister who had seen before many of his colleagues the direction in which Johnston was going. Johnston, unfortunately, had surrounded himself with men of like mind and had alienated colleagues

---

⁴⁵ Johnston, *Work of God and Work of Man*, p. 206.
⁴⁶ Johnston, 'Reply to Mr Grant chapter I, *The Evangelist*, 5, no. 8 (1850), p. 152.
⁴⁷ Johnston, 'Reply to Mr Grant chapter IV', pp. 221-2.
⁴⁸ *PCM*, new series, 6, no. 3 (March 1849), pp. 91-2.
⁴⁹ Peter Grant to William Grant, November 17 1846, Grant MS.

who could have helped him focus his gifts and enthusiasm in a more beneficial direction. There was a sense of inevitability about Johnston's resignation from his work in Scotland in January 1856 and the acceptance of a new pastorate in Cambridge. This step closed the door on a painful episode in Scottish Baptist history.

After some time for reflection, a small group of Scottish Baptist leaders began, in September 1856, to search for new ways to build bridges to overcome the old causes of division within their denomination.[50] *The Freeman*, the English Baptist periodical, contained the following comment on the relationships between Baptists in Scotland in 1858. 'We congratulate them on the fact that a more genial and unitive spirit has of late appeared amongst them.'[51] The focus of attention in this denomination, together with other Evangelical Protestants, was now firmly on the revival of religion that had been evident in the USA from 1857[52] and had now been witnessed in northern Ireland and Scotland. It is important to note that this revival was probably the first truly national revival in Scotland,[53] with a corresponding impact on the work of the different churches. As a result of the focus on the revival of spiritual life within the churches, the increasingly sterile debate over the significance of the Holy Spirit's work in the conversion of sinners began to subside, in favour of the proponents of traditional opinions, who had stressed the necessity of an active regenerating work in the human heart prior to conversion. This development was, however, accompanied by the emergence of a more pietistical and less doctrinal form of Evangelicalism, not only within Baptist ranks, but also within the other Protestant denominations in Scotland.[54]

There had been a time of great theological turmoil and conflict in the ranks of Evangelical Protestants during the mid-nineteenth century. James Morison in the United Secession Church, John Kirk amongst the Independent Churches and Francis Johnston from the Baptist Union of Scotland were amongst the most prominent proponents of the newer views in theological circles, with respect to the work of the Holy Spirit. Johnston, the primary focus of this study, was probably the least influential of the three within Scottish Evangelicalism, not least because he was a minister within the ranks of one of the smaller denominations. Johnston had the grace to recognize that in his zeal to promote

---

[50] Talbot, *Search for a Common Identity*, chap. 8.
[51] *The Freeman*, 4 (1 December 1858), p. 731.
[52] J. E. Orr, *The Event of the Century: The 1857-1858 Awakening*, ed. R. O. Roberts, (Wheaton, 1989), pp. 47-67. K. T. Long, *The Revival of 1857-58: Interpreting an American Religious Awakening* (New York, 1998), pp. 12-18. Orr, though, traces the start of the revival earlier than Long and in other urban centres, prior to the start of the Fulton Street Prayer meetings in New York.
[53] Jeffrey, *When the Lord Walked the Land*, p. 2.
[54] Talbot, *Search for a Common Identity*, pp. 291-3. For similar developments on a wider scale, see D. W. Bebbington, *Evangelicalism in Modern Britain* (London, 1989), pp. 151-80.

his cause he had overstepped the mark and alienated colleagues who wished to work with him. Two Baptist colleagues in Scotland, Henry Dickie and James Paterson, spent time with Johnston in 1861 assisting him in reflecting on some key theological issues at the heart of recent debates. In a remarkable transformation of his views Johnston made the following written statement of his new understanding of divine truth. In respect of his controversial book he stated:

> All passages which it is impossible to harmonise with the absolute necessity of the Holy Spirit's work in the faith and regeneration of the sinner, I myself renounce and blot out. This acknowledgement I freely and frankly make, and hope my brethren will accept.[55]

His reconciliation and restoration to service in Scotland was a fitting finale to his career. The last word ought to be given to one of his closest friends, William Landels, who said this of Johnston:

> His faults sprang more from an excessive zeal for what he believed ... His excessive zeal sometimes led him to forget – so engrossed was he in his work – that those who differed from him might not like to have their own beliefs assailed, and that the statement of his views at unsuitable times might justly give offence to those who were possibly as conscientious as himself. This peculiarity roused prejudices against him in the minds of some; but it did not hinder others from catching the infection of his zeal ... He might not always be sound; but he was always clear ...[56]

---

[55] Francis Johnston, to Henry Dickie, 28 August 1860. See also 'Contrasting Interpretations of Baptist Identity in Nineteenth Century Scotland: The Contributions of Rev. Francis Johnston, Rev. Jonathan Watson and Dr James Paterson', unpublished paper delivered at the Third International Conference on Baptist Studies, at the International Baptist Theological Seminary, Prague (2003), pp. 6-12.

[56] W. Landels, 'Denominational Reminiscences by an Old Baptist,' III, *Scottish Baptist Magazine*, 12, no. 10 (October 1886), p. 268.

CHAPTER 8

Evan Roberts: Blessings and Burnout

Gaius Davies

According to the late lamented Dr R. Tudur Jones, once the much loved and admired Principal of a College in Bangor, North Wales, and the best historian I know of the Welsh revival of 1904–5, more has been written about Evan Roberts than any Welshman except perhaps David Lloyd George and King Arthur. His book *Faith and the Crisis of a Nation* (2004) is now available in an English Translation. One important fact underlined by Dr Tudur Jones is that, of the tens of thousands of meetings during the Welsh revival, Evan Roberts appeared in only some two hundred and fifty of these meetings.

Most of what I have read in Welsh is marred by an uncritical adoration of the young hero on the one hand, and a somewhat malicious attitude on the other. Such was the case of J. Vyrnwy Morgan and those who espoused the point of view of Peter Price a Congregational Church minister in Dowlais. Price notoriously wrote to the *Western Mail* – which in one way had created Evan Roberts as a media hero – and said he thought there were two revivals, one genuine and the other false: he accused Evan Roberts of creating a false fire, a 'carnal or human, fleshly fire'[1] instead of the divine fire which had appeared in the first months of 1904. It is a severe criticism, and yet in the later years of his life Roberts himself seems to have come to believe that demonic influences entered the revival and vitiated the whole thing.

It is sad that such standard lives (written both in Welsh and English versions) by the Reverend D. M. Phillips of Tylorstown reads rather like a mediaeval plaster saint's memoir: like much else written at the time, it is hagiography. It was written in 1906 and contains little by way of appraisal of what went on in the revival as attributed to *Evan Roberts The Great Welsh Revivalist and His Work*. Perhaps it was too soon in 1906 for any assessment of value. The last paragraph about Evan Roberts in Phillips's book describes him as being invited by Mrs Penn-Lewis to her home in Leicester in March 1906 for a complete rest. In late April he attended a convention in Bangor, North Wales, and appeared briefly in Porth Rhondda in June. He stayed in Leicester until 1925. When his brother and his father made the difficult journey from Loughor to Leicester they were not allowed even to meet with Evan Roberts.

---

[1] D. J. Roberts, *Cofiant Peter Price* (Abertawe, 1970), p. 99; also J. Vyrnwy Morgan, *The Welsh Religious Revival* (London, 1909).

Perhaps no other revivalist of the time was visited and interviewed by a consultant psychiatrist – in this case, M de Fursac from Paris at the request of the French Home Office. His account of his trip to Wales was published in Paris in 1907 and is translated as *A Contemporary Mystical Movement: The Religious Revival in Wales*. I will consider his opinions in due course: inevitably he might be criticized as something of a French impressionist – how could it be otherwise after a brief visit? Another French visitor wrote what some consider the best books on the revival: he was a Professor from Montauban called Henri Bois.

One of the Welsh poets used the image of Wales as a modern 'burning bush', and saying that Wales, also, was not consumed by the fire. Evan Roberts had a 'complete breakdown in health'[2] in 1906, when he was spirited away to the home of the famous Mrs Jessie Penn-Lewis and her husband in Leicester. My best understanding of the situation is that Evan Roberts suffered so much from the excessive stresses imposed upon him in the two years or so of his revival work, that he himself was in fact badly burned, if not a case of 'burnout'. Though I do not wish to squeeze the remarkable young man into a Procrustean bed of psychiatric diagnosis, what little we know about the suffering of Evan Roberts is very suggestive of what might now be called post-traumatic stress disorder (or PTSD).

Some Burning Questions

I will describe Evan Roberts before the revival, seeking to establish something about his temperament and his character. This may help us to understand his vulnerabilities as well as his special gifts. I would like to describe some of the influences such as those of the revivalist Charles Finney, the Keswick Convention teaching on the Holy Spirit and the 'second blessing'. Finney led him to speak of the conditions of revival. I will discuss Mrs Penn-Lewis and ask whether Evan Roberts was a mystic and if so, did his personal mysticism help or hinder him?

Secondly, I will try to describe some of the ways of working, which give cause for concern to his admiring colleagues at the time, and may alarm us today. We know a great deal about this from newspaper accounts and the many reports in religious periodicals of how he behaved as a Christian leader. It is hard to accept uncritically that such methods were appropriate in his work. How much did Evan Roberts go astray as leader?

Thirdly, I will try to offer an appraisal of the man and his work, and in this I will be guided by two writers Roberts must have read – Ann Griffiths the hymn writer, and William Williams ('Pantycelyn') who had written extensively on the problems of the eighteenth-century revival. Brooding over all my considerations is Jonathan Edwards, the American divine and first President of

---

[2] Mary N. Garrard (ed.), *Mrs Penn-Lewis: A Memoir* (London, 1930), p. 230.

Princeton, whose detailed works on the New England revivals are still among the most penetrating of all. I begin and end with Edwards's view that all revival is a mixture of the true and the false, of the human and the divine, of the spirit and the flesh. In our day we might say that human psychological pressures may be inextricably mixed up with the influences of God's grace and the work of the Holy Spirit. Crowd manipulation and the use of trance states and other techniques by powerful leaders have often masqueraded as true revival.

'A Personal Statement'

Perhaps I should end this introduction by declaring my interest. I am not writing simply because I am a psychiatrist and a Christian, but because I grew up in a village much affected by the revival of 1904–5. The church of which my father was the Literature Secretary was founded by those who 'came out' from other churches as a result of the revival, to follow their vision (the 'Apostolic Vision') of a restored church exhibiting all the gifts listed in the New Testament. Evan Roberts is said by one historian to have anointed its two main leaders (D. P. Williams and his brother W. Jones Williams), as, respectively, apostle and prophet.

Many such people were the children of the revival: they influenced me a good deal, for better or for worse. At the annual international conventions we saw some visiting charismatics who might be described kindly as performance artists. There were also many godly saints (less interested in spectacular phenomena) who were 'normal Christians' who 'adorned the doctrines' that had become vital to them in the revival.

When I grew up, the high tide of charismatic phenomena that our village was reputed to exhibit was receding, and the tide of such remarkable phenomena was going out with Arnold's 'melancholy, long-withdrawing roar'[3] as in his poem *Dover Beach*. It could be argued that those who do not know the history of charismatic revivals are condemned to repeat the mistakes of earlier movements: these may mar the good work, and which often cause much scandal and concern because of the way they bring the Christian Gospel into disrepute and take away from God's glory.

Evan Roberts before the Revival

I realize that some may feel I should heed the words about 'touch not the Lord's anointed' but I trust what follows will be a modest attempt to make sense of the human side of Evan Roberts. He was brought up in the Calvinistic Methodist tradition. I have no doubt that he was a true Christian and a devout one. His excellent Christian character was never in doubt, as far as I can see.

---

[3] Matthew Arnold, 'Dover Beach', in J. Wain (ed.), *The Oxford Library of English Poetry* (Oxford, 1986), p. 167.

He never attracted criticism in his handling of money. His conduct was exemplary from the moral point of view, whatever gossip there may have been about him and the women who accompanied him. His alleged engagement to Miss Annie Davies may have injured his good name but that may have been a lack of tact or social skills on his part more than anything of a morally dubious nature.

Evan Roberts must have known (at some level) from his Bible, his small library of excellent books, and from the hymns he sang so often, that no person may enjoy a faith in Christ without the work of the Holy Spirit. Yet he stated that he had not received the Holy Spirit: this is one thing which I believe reflects how he was influenced by teaching which was 'in the air' about the need for the Baptism of the Spirit as taught by many – and that Evan as a young man came to believe wrongly that he had not received the Spirit. Had he absorbed that teaching which was part of his church's faith – he was after all a Calvinistic Methodist – and understood the wealth of experiential application of this teaching in his hymn book, he would have thought in a more biblical way about the Holy Spirit. When he went to Newcastle Emlyn he seems (at that school for preparing men for the Christian ministry) to have found the work quite a strain on his resources.

Seth Joshua, a hard-working evangelist who had seen splendid fruit in his work, had prayed that God would call someone ('like Elisha') who was an ordinary worker and not an academic or a professional minister of religion to lead the revival. He must have felt his prayers were answered in the calling of Evan Roberts. While not saying he was anti-intellectual, it would seem that Roberts was not really interested in Christian doctrine but much more in experience. Had he chosen the mystic's way of relating to spiritual things and to God? I think he had, and his emphasis on prayer vigils in the night may be part of that. But the hallmark of his mysticism was his emphasis on the Holy Spirit and his belief that he had a special, direct access through what – in the jargon of our day – might be called 'the hot line to God'.

In this connection it is notable that before the revival that when he met a Dr Hughes who was visiting Swansea from his Presbyterian Church near New York, that minister was concerned about Evan Roberts's mental health. He asked the two daughters of Evan Phillips, the godly old sage of Newcastle Emlyn (who had lived through the 1859 revival), to keep a careful eye on Roberts: Dr Hughes feared he might be developing into 'a religious maniac'.[4] At this time, before the experience of Blaenannerch with Seth Joshua and others, there had been months when Evan Roberts was hoping and praying for revival, and that he should have a part in it. It became one of governing thoughts and desires of his mind – what some psychologists would call *an overvalued idea*.

---

[4] R. Tudur Jones, *Faith and the Crisis of a Nation: Wales 1890–1914* (Cardiff, 2004), p. 294.

Was he by this time a mystic, and was he beginning to feel a very special person with a mission and gifts, personal to him, of listening to the guidance of the Holy Spirit? I confess he reminds me of the young George Fox, whom I had to study for a paper published in 1996.[5] They shared somewhat similar visions, and both had a very marked emphasis on what Fox called the inner light, and what Roberts called the Holy Spirit within him. The Quakers, according to one of their historians Professor H. Larry Ingle, author of *First Among Friends*, noted a quip about mysticism in their ranks, which he considers had a ring of truth. The quip consisted of saying that 'mysticism had I in the middle, started in mist and ended in schism'.[6] This is not, of course, to dismiss the real and profound quality of much Christ-centred mysticism in Christian teaching and experience.

What bothers me is that Roberts does not seem to have doubted, later on, that every thought that came to him was of Divine origin and that any such thought must lead to obedience, immediate and complete – as if to God's voice. A little of the gift of discernment might have helped him a great deal, and might have prevented the later practices which we shall now discuss. And, of course, there were many schismatic churches formed after the revival, whether Roberts intended that or not.

Two Contemporary Accounts

I will summarize two accounts, the first from the Rector of Aberporth, which describes a visit by Evan Roberts to Blaenannerch. It is a clear and plain account unlike some of the reports in the newspapers. He describes how the chapel was full in the morning, and Evan Roberts arrived at 3 p.m. He began by describing

> his awesome and dreadful experience: for two minutes my feelings were inexpressible ... if God's dealings with a sinner in His love are so awesome, how much more so the visiting of an unrepentant person in wrath and righteousness? ... He then spoke against people having unloving feelings for each other, and accused someone present of stealing from God's treasury reading Malachi 3:8 (Will a man rob God yet you rob me). ... He grasped the Bible and asked what do we call this? The answer came: God's Word. He announced someone was there who did not believe this and who denied God's word. He called on him three times to confess. He then named him as Thomas Walters aged 33. He walked out and was prayed for in his absence. ... Roberts ran through a gamut of his feelings: shaking, sobbing and silence. He said revival is taking on a new aspect: God wanted to purify his church ... terrible awesome things were to happen ... he then

---

[5] Gaius Davies, 'George Fox: Radical Spirit', in *The Fire Divine: papers read at the 1996 Westminster conference* (Mirfield, 1996).

[6] H. Larry Ingle, *First among friends: George Fox and the creation of Quakerism* (New York, 1994), p. 106.

stopped the singing and said someone was about to give himself to Christ and he appeared content and joyful. He then read the fifth commandment and urged the young people present to honour their father and mother.[7]

The rector expressed his doubts as well as rejoicing in the revival. I believe that Roberts's behaviour shows how the light of God's grace was refracted through his flawed personality. He was often, as in this account, too suggestible and credulous, and trusted too much in his own intuitions believing them always to be the promptings of the Spirit.

The second account in the *Lancet* of 26 November 1904 which many might deem hostile to the revival. The leader writer quotes *The Western Mail* of 19 November 1904 thus:

> His restlessness is marvelous, he is walking about all day with the springiness of a man treading on wires, his arms swaying unceasingly. During a period of 48 hours he has only one hour's sleep. He eats very little food. There has been a suggestion of his being animated by magnetism and he is quoted as saying no watch will keep time with him. At one meeting he fell prostrate and remained with his face on the floor for some time seeming to be in an agony or weeping like a child. He is reported to have said: 'When I go out to the garden I see the devil grinning at me, but I am not afraid of him. I go into the house and when I go out again I see Jesus Christ smiling at me.'

The *Lancet* asks that his friends and any doctors should kindly point out to him the dangers which menace his intellectual equilibrium. It then reminds its readers of the 1859 revival and the fact that one of its leaders, Humphrey Jones, suffered a breakdown in Aberystwyth and had to be admitted to the lunatic asylum in Carmarthen – one knows from other accounts that this is true.

Some reflections based on Ann Griffiths and William Williams (Pantycelyn): Ann Griffiths (1776–1805) was a remarkable young woman whose hymns and letters have been a treasury of wisdom and profound Christian insight for those who know them. Dr E. Wyn James in *Rhyfeddaf Fyth* (Gregynog Press, 1998) has made them available to Welsh readers. Ann has been the subject of praise by poets such as R. S. Thomas and Rowan Williams (who has translated some of her hymns into English). There are English studies of her by A. M. Allchin. What would Ann say to Evan Roberts?

Ann knew much about profound experiences of ecstasy and rapture – being 'lost in wonder, love and praise' – and glorifying God's grace. Yet she knew the dangers of what she called her 'imaginations'. She said she wanted to believe through revelation in Scripture rather than through her imagination. She judged herself for thinking improperly of the Holy Spirit: 'having imaginative

---

[7] Thomas Phillips, 'Ymweliad Mr. Evan Roberts a Blaenannerch', in *Yr Haul* (1905), p. 89.

thought which were misleading about a Divine being'.[8] She wanted to know the true and living God to such a degree that all her imaginations of all kinds would be killed. The contrast between Ann Griffiths and Evan Roberts in terms of mystical experiences could not be more marked. Yet Evan Roberts must have known her hymns well, and must have sung them often. But he danced to a different drum, taught by such people as Finney and influenced by such current trends as those being taught by various kinds of Higher Life movements and the Keswick Convention.

As to Williams, Pantycelyn, one can do no better than refer to Dr Tudur Jones's book quoted in my first paragraph (p. 358). There was 'a mixture of grace and nature, of good and bad ... in the churches upon whom God shines his face'. The 'sound of the wind' touches hypocrites and incites their 'natural passions' and then 'they are like a ship before the wind, without ballast but with their sails fully unfurled, and in danger of being shattered by the rocks, or driven into narrow coves'. Williams, an expert leader of the societies which were such a feature of the eighteenth-century Welsh revival, was in the analytical tradition of Jonathan Edwards, and constantly seeking to help Methodist believers to learn discernment of spirits, and for this wrote among other things his book which in English was published as *The Door to the Experience Meeting*. The lovingly critical spirit shown by Williams was often absent from the revival which Evan Roberts led.

It is a sad fact that many made shipwreck, and that the marked increase of admissions to the psychiatric hospitals of people diagnosed as 'religious mania' cannot be brushed away, but continues to be a standing rebuke to those who will not consider the harmful effects of the later period of the Welsh revival of 1904–5. Some spoke of their experience of 'the hurricane of the spirit' as if it were entirely beneficent: but hurricanes can also be very destructive.

Unanswered Questions

The material available to us poses three questions which may be hard to answer. Firstly, what was his personality like? Secondly, in what way was he ill, and when? Thirdly, what was his complete breakdown to which his later mentor and guardian Mrs Penn-Lewis refers?

I believe that, as a person he was both vulnerable and – most importantly – very suggestible.

Many doctors would I think have called him an hysteric, but I would prefer to describe him as showing many histrionic traits which came out in many well publicized performances. His suggestibility and his histrionic tendencies both made him more liable to what are now called altered states of consciousness, or

---

[8] E. Wyn James (ed.), *Rhyfedaf fyth: Emynau a llythyrau Ann Griffiths ynghyd â'r byrgofiant iddi gan John Hughes Pontrobert, a rhai llythyrau gan gyfeillion* (Y Drenewydd, 1998), p. 60.

trance states. I believe he made too much of his intuitions, lacking Ann Griffiths's self-criticism, and was easily misled and indeed carried away by the winds of doctrine. Thus he talked like Charles Finney about the conditions of revival, and his beliefs about the Holy Spirit were, as I have said, very different from those of his church, its doctrines and its hymns.

To the second question we have already noted that an American visitor, a Dr Hughes who was a church minister, feared religious mania before the revival started. A visiting French psychiatrist saw him in Neath when 'the Spirit had commanded seven days of silence'[9] and thought Roberts both confused and delirious. Henri Bois – like such experienced observers as Elfed – disliked and doubted the value of his 'occult and telepathic utterances'.[10] Four doctors whom he was asked to see in Liverpool diagnosed Evan Roberts as 'mentally and physically quite sound'[11] and advised a period of rest from the overwork that had so affected him.

My view is that he had a mood disorder, and that some of his prolonged night vigils in prayer and revelations might be partly due to his mood disorder, although no one can exclude God's grace using that capacity in Roberts for elation, sadness and anxieties. At times I believe this mood disorder and his personality traits led to his being out of control, and badly affected his judgment. I believe that the stresses and strains that he was under for many long months contributed to his behaving unusually, and showing lack of judgment. It is said, for instance, that the visit to Anglesey and other parts of North Wales that followed the recommended rest of nearly four weeks recommended by the four Liverpool specialists was very different from some earlier campaigns by the revivalist. Summarizing a huge amount of evidence, Dr Tudur Jones describes the work done in Anglesey as 'the most blessed and tranquil of all Evan Roberts' journeys'.[12] How we might wish that more of Evan Roberts's remarkable ministry might have been so blessed.

The Breakdown: Mrs Penn-Lewis and the Long Silence

It is hard to understand how in March 1906 Evan Roberts should be invited to join Mrs Penn-Lewis and her husband in their large home in Leicester, and that he should stay there until 1925, two years before his hostess's death. He was thought to be a kind of prisoner there: visitors were not allowed, and letters to him were not answered or a letter might be signed by Mrs Penn-Lewis, whose memoir (p. 230) speaks of it all thus:

---

[9] R. Tudur Jones, *Faith and the Crisis of a Nation*, p. 351.
[10] Ibid. p. 352.
[11] Ibid. p. 325.
[12] ibid. p. 328.

Through the strain and suffering brought upon him during eight months of daily and continuous meetings in crowded, ill-ventilated chapels, one of the chief figures of the awakening in Wales completely broke down needing rest and recuperation. His recovery, however was slow and intermittent, lasting many months, and during the long periods of convalescence he began to open his mind to his hostess on many experiences of supernatural forces witnessed during the revival.[13]

His time with Mrs Penn-Lewis led to a joint work called *War on the Saints*. But why did he join her, and why did he stay? Two other contributors to these studies have helped to make me understand it a little. Professor Prosser in his study of her says she had 'three months of elation and joy and gladness' after being 'carried up into the bosom of the Father'. Later she had a long period of depression when she 'stayed in the dark night of the soul'. To any doctor these large claims add up to a period of manic depressive disorder in her life. Then there are letters from her to Evan Roberts, printed in *The Western Mail* which indicate her sense of his being a kindred spirit, whom she shadowed and almost stalked, waiting for an opportunity to invite him to her lair and her care. This is one of the sidelights of the study by William Kay. He may have adopted him as the son she was never able to have, but one would like to know much more.

I consider her influence was an unhealthy one. But in what ways was he ill? I believe, like those who had shell-shock in the First World War, or post traumatic stress after the Vietnam War, he was anxious and depressed for a long time. It seems he had no medical help, and perhaps no recognition of what help he needed. He did not return to Wales until 1925 and then lived the life of a lonely bachelor. Anecdotes about his doubts may easily be found, and some of his letters show a warm Christian concern for his friends. In the years to his death in 1951 he never returned fully to the Christian scene, except for some recorded visits to Gorseinon, not far from where he was brought up. The rest is silence.

Forgive Our Foolish Ways

The hymn of Whittier, *Dear Lord and Father of mankind*, is often voted top of the pops. I found it interesting to learn that the Quaker hymn writer wrote this as part of a much larger work *The Brewing of Soma*. What he is attacking is the tent revivalists of North America, whose strong potions of religion he compares to the intoxicating drugs freely available. His 'hymn' is a prayer to be saved from the foolish ways of the tent revivalist. It may serve as a reminder that it has often been the case that the worst enemy of true revival is the revivalist who thinks he can bring revival about, and who sometimes ends up as the sorcerer's apprentice.

---

[13] Mary N. Garrard, *Mrs Penn-Lewis*, pp. 230-1.

CHAPTER 9

Jessie Penn-Lewis

Peter Prosser

Introduction

Jessie Penn-Lewis's influence on Evan Roberts was extremely powerful. Was she a benign helper who meddled too closely in his ministry, effectively closing it down and helping to stop the Welsh revival? Was she a trouble-maker who made it her business to stop what she saw as a demonic attack on the church of Wales by getting to Evan Roberts and neutralizing him as a leader? Or was she someone in between, a motherly type who only wanted to save Evan Roberts from destroying himself by making him rest? The controversy continues today. Let's have a look first at Jessie Penn-Lewis, who she was, what she did, and how her influence grew to be so powerful over Evan Roberts.

Who was Jessie Penn-Lewis?

Jessie Penn-Lewis, nee Jones, was born in July 1861, in Neath, South Wales. Married to William Penn-Lewis at nineteen (by no means too young a woman to be married in those times) she was apparently happy. Even though the doctors pronounced her too frail to have children, she was married for forty-five years to William, and found her substitute family through her extensive writing ministry. She died in 1927. An influential woman for her time, she was actually better known in Western Europe, Russia and Asia, than in her native Great Britain. She was a significant speaker and spiritual writer, affecting both the Keswick movement in England, the Welsh revival, through her apparent domination of Evan Roberts, and the publishing of her book, *War on the Saints* in 1912. She wrote over fifty books and pamphlets, many of which were translated into Russian, Finnish, Swedish, French, Arabic, Chinese and Japanese. On a visit to India she found that some of her books were even translated into Bengali. Although she was physically weak, she was indomitable in personality. She seems to have thrown herself into her work, often going off on missionary journeys for three months at a time every year for several decades, provoking her husband to write plaintive letters asking when he could expect her to come home! It seems to have been a rather strange marriage, and was perhaps emotionally barren. Was this due to lack of family life at home?

Her Self-Commissioning

No woman at that time could be ordained. Few could get a university education and fewer professions were open to women. (This was ironic considering that Queen Victoria was on the throne of the British Empire from 1837 to 1901. Victoria was the most powerful woman in British History and yet no woman could vote!)

Jessie early saw herself called of God. A temperance worker at twelve years old, she apparently attended both the Church of England and the Welsh Calvinist Chapel at the same time. Converted at twenty-one, in 1882, she longed to give both body and soul to the Lord's service. She longed to be delivered of a ruffled temper and from speaking hastily. Two books read by Jessie up to 1888 were Madame Guyon's *Spiritual Torrents* and Andrew Murray's *Spirit of Christ*. She became convinced that she had a ministry: '[I determined] to proclaim the message of the cross, at a time when it had almost ceased to be referred to in the pulpits. I saw that God miraculously opened doors before me proclaim this message, which no man could shut[1] ... God had committed this message to me, and, at whatever cost, I must go forward.'[2]

In 1889, she began to work at the YWCA in Richmond, Surrey. In 1890, she became full-time secretary. At first she was very unsure of herself. She was dissatisfied with her labours among the girls there.

> After a time, I became conscious that the spiritual results were not equivalent to the labour of the work. I began to question whether I knew the fullness of the Holy Spirit ... My weekly Bible Class was a great trouble to me, for I had no power of utterance. Organizing work was much easier, but meetings were a sore trial. Self-consciousness almost paralyzed me ... so all the people I could discover who were filled with the Spirit, I invited to Richmond ... to come and speak to my girls. I was so anxious that they should get this blessing. I settled in my mind that I was not the channel. I was not the one to speak. Until one day the Lord turned on me and said 'Why not yourself?' These people have quite enough to do without coming to do your work! 'Why not you the channel'? But I said, 'I cannot speak! It takes me a whole day to prepare for my class: What can I do? It is impossible!'[3]

She felt encouraged by the Holy Spirit to try to speak herself, without the help of others. She first went through an experience she called 'being broken'. She recounts this in her own words

> He waited until I came to the end of my own energy and strength. 'How I taught' ... 'How full my Bible was of notes, and how carefully I prepared a dish of spiritual food for them.' 'Food' – all obtained second-hand from other books ... But they did not change much in their lives! I thought it was the fault of the girls,

---

[1] Mary Garrard, *Jessie Penn-Lewis: A Memoir*, p. 266.
[2] Garrard, *Jessie Penn-Lewis*, p. 267.
[3] Garrard, *Jessie Penn-Lewis*, pp. 18-19.

until the Lord spoke to me and said, 'it is yourself!' 'But, Lord, I am consecrated! What can it be in me? I give time every morning to read and pray: I have put everything right in my life as far as I know'. But the Lord still said, 'It is you.' And then He began to break me, and there came to me the terrible revelation that every bit of this activity, this energy, this indomitable perseverance was myself after all, though it was hidden under the name of 'consecration'.[4]

Her Experience of Being 'In the Spirit'

She began to depend on God's strength and two years later (1892) said that she came to the 'fullness of the Spirit.' One of her many spiritual experiences, she was on a train from Wimbledon to Richmond, Surrey. Although she did not speak with tongues, she said she did have a mystical experience in the Spirit world. She said that she felt 'caught up into the bosom of the Father'.[5] At that time she called this the 'Baptism of the Holy Ghost'.

Through this experience, she said that she was clearly able to see 'sin standing out' in the world[6] like black specks on a white surface. This presumably enabled her to discover 'what was of the flesh' in a revival and what was of the Spirit. This experience evidently was still not to her satisfaction. She goes on to say that three months later, she was delivered from a 'self-absorbed life'[7] (her own words). She felt that one should *not* rely on spiritual gifts but rely on God himself. (Here, we can begin to see how her spiritual experiences were building up to her disapproval of the Welsh revival.) She began to see all revivals through the prism of her own experience. Jessie again:

> I lived in a very heaven of joy and light and gladness ... Then came the gradual cessation of this heavenly experience, and the time of danger ... I began to dread the loss of my experience, and to seek now the 'experience' that seemed to be slipping from me. At this point, I was shown,[8] by the mercy of God, the path of the cross, and the wisdom of God in withdrawing the gifts of God, for the soul to rest entirely in Him, and not in joy or ecstatic communion, which made me spiritually self-absorbed, and apt to pit (myself against) others not on my plane of spiritual life ... [9]

Unfortunately, this is not true. For the rest of her life she *did* pit herself against others who were not on her spiritual plane! She became like Madame Guyon, explaining that her spiritual experience was the authentic one, and that

---

[4] Garrard, *Jessie Penn-Lewis*, p. 19.
[5] Garrard, *Jessie Penn-Lewis*, pp. 27-8.
[6] Ibid.
[7] Ibid.
[8] She does not explain how she was shown this.
[9] Garrard, *Jessie Penn-Lewis*, p. 28.

other spiritual experiences were either as demonic, or as spiritual childishness. She explains why:

> But when I saw that the loss of this spiritual delight and ecstasy meant fruit, through death and a life in God Himself above His gifts, I gladly chose the path of the Cross and consented to walk in the night of faith to that goal where God would be all in all.[10]

The above quote could have come from Madame Guyon, Saint John of the Cross or Francois Fénelon. This is exactly the same type of experience that John Wesley went through from 1725 to 1738 with the mystic writers, except that he emerged from his dark night of the soul to a solid conversion with the Moravian Brethren at Aldersgate Street, London. In fact, he blamed mysticism for side tracking him all those years, saying 'I almost foundered on the spiritual rock of mysticism.'

After these experiences, she resigned from Richmond, and began to be invited to speak at various conferences in Great Britain in 1893 and 1895. Denounced for daring to be a woman speaker at Keswick in 1895, she became very despondent. Andrew Murray came to her defence, saying that she should be allowed to at least speak to the women in attendance. This she was allowed to do, but controversy would follow Jessie all of her life. She went on to speak in Dublin and Belfast in Ireland, and then, in 1896, in an extraordinary turn of events, was invited to speak in Sweden and Finland, to members of the royal family. This led to a return invitation to Sweden in 1898, and through the Scandinavian royal families, to an invitation to Russia to speak in private gatherings of Russian nobility, which was inter-married with Danish royalty.

In Russia, 1898

She had, by this time become a famous Christian writer and teacher. In 1898, she travelled to the Russian court in Saint Petersburg, where she was able to instruct the Empress of Russia, her children, and other members of the royal family and the court in the ways of prayer.[11] It was to be a fateful meeting. In 1918, the Danish-born Empress, her husband and all of her five children would be murdered by the new Soviet government. She went on to revisit Scandinavia, Canada, the USA, Egypt, and India. By 1904, she had launched her own Christian newspaper to propagate her beliefs and teaching, called *The Overcomer*. She organized a soul clinic for weary missionaries and ministers, instructed and corresponded with Christian workers around the world, including Watchman Nee in China. She was a popular speaker (though controversial) in the Keswick Movement in England. She organized her own

---

[10] Garrard, *Jessie Penn-Lewis*, p. 28.
[11] Garrard, *Jessie Penn-Lewis*, pp. 147-8.

conventions for converts, set up a prayer sanctuary and a Christian book room filled with her own writings and those of others who agreed with her version of the spiritual life, discipleship and the doctrine of tripartite Christianity. All of this, and yet she suffered lung damage from tuberculosis, a common, but serious malady at the time!

She was a tireless supporter and promoter of women's ministry worldwide, and felt that women should have a strong influence in revivals. In spite, or perhaps because of her extensive and tireless labours, Jessie had continual bouts of physical, spiritual, and emotional illness, such as deep depression lasting a year at a time, as Brynmor Jones points out in his extensive study on her life.[12]

Jessie Penn-Lewis and the Tripartite Nature of Human-Kind

After establishing her periodical *The Overcomer*, Penn-Lewis began to teach the tripartite nature, using I Thessalonians 5:23. She taught that the Christian could adjust and control his or her spiritual nature by letting the Holy Spirit dominate the soul and body. I quote:

> 'The God of peace sanctify you ... spirit, soul and body ...' God (is) in the spirit sanctifying the soul, controlling and dominating the body.
>
> Fausset – a commentator of authority – says that in the threefold division of man's being – body, soul, and spirit – the due state in God's design is, that the spirit which is the recipient of the Holy Spirit, uniting man to God, should be first and rule the soul, which stands intermediate between body and spirit. From this clear statement you will understand that the spirit must be first, and dominate the soul and through the soul, control the body.[13]

This rather odd teaching of Fausset seems to have been taken to the extreme by Penn-Lewis where she believed that the spirit of man could be *ordered* to dominate the soul and body through an act of will. The believer, when they received the Holy Spirit in the part of the person called 'the spirit' was not filled in the body and soul! This left the soul to be filled with demons if the person attended an emotional revival service and left themselves open to demonic powers! One can easily understand, then, how Penn-Lewis could be profoundly frightened and suspicious of the Welsh revival!

War on the Saints

In her book published in 1912, and supposedly read and supported by Evan Roberts, she felt that the emotion stirred up in the revival left persons open to

---

[12] Brynmor P. Jones, *The Trials and the Triumphs of Mrs. Jessie Penn-Lewis* (New Brunswick, NJ, 1997).

[13] www.tripartiteman.org/historical/penn-lewis.html

reception of demon spirits through giving 'ground'[14] to evil powers. She explains in her book that 'giving ground' meant opening up oneself to demonic manifestation through deception of the mind.[15] This would include accepting demonic thoughts,[16] wrong conceptions,[17] wrong interpretations, believing lies,[18] and being passive in spirit, body, or soul. She believed that being passive in prayer during the revival was actually a sin which led many to accept counterfeit spirits (that is, evil spirits counterfeiting the real Holy Spirit).[19]

Thus, her doctrine of the tripartite nature, her own experience of having the fullness of the spirit (the railway carriage experience in 1892), and the subsequent turning away from this experience three months later (her 'death' to spiritual experiences and her embrace of the cross) led her to believe that the Welsh revival would lead many believers away into the spiritual deception of the devil. She even accused the Welsh revival of being involved in clairvoyance and witchcraft.

The unfortunate result of all this was her gaining control over Evan Roberts, her virtual 'imprisonment' of him in her home for seven years, and the making of Roberts into a virtual spiritual recluse. Penn-Lewis evidently (for this is what *War on the Saints* teaches) set out for Roberts how he had opened himself to deception in wanting the Welsh revival in the first place, and then working himself into an emotional fever pitch where demons were controlling the revival. He had 'given ground' to the devil to take it over. The only way to get it back was to get *out* of the revival, stop praying for it (!) and give up the wish for revival. In this, she was entirely successful. He virtually never preached again!

This essentially meant that he (and all the others who were deceived) had to revoke consent in wanting the Holy Spirit's experience,[20] persistently refuse spiritual experiences and turn away from them,[21] and claim Romans chapter 6

---

[14] Jessie Penn-Lewis, *War on the Saints* (World Wide Web edition, originally published in 1912), p. 192. Further references are to this edition (abbreviated as *WoS*).
[15] *WoS*, p. 199.
[16] *WoS*, pp. 69, 155, 156.
[17] *WoS*, p. 160.
[18] *WoS*, pp. 94, 175, 176.
[19] *WoS*, pp. 70, 72, 86, 118, 122, 149.
[20] *WoS*, pp. 190, 193, 198.
[21] *WoS*, p. 193.

for deliverance.[22] She further taught that if the believer renounced these things, evil spirits would lose 'ground' and depart from the believer.[23]

The key to the 'reception' of these demonic powers was passivity, she felt.[24] This meant that prayer meetings where believers were 'tarrying' or waiting on God in prayer were 'ground' for Satan to come in. Those 'waiting' on the Lord for revival (and Roberts had prayed that way for eleven years before the revival) and giving themselves over to spiritual experiences were opening themselves to the demonic. This resulted in an extreme fear of all spiritual experiences on the behalf of Penn-Lewis, which she passed on to Evan.

The extensive re-education of Roberts through *War on the Saints* (during his almost eight-year 'silent' period 1905–12) led to giving up 'waiting on God' passively.[25] (This would presumably include meditation.) The believer had to face the fact that the devil had entered in through giving 'ground'.[26] And at all points where deception had entered in, through emotionalism, beliefs, thoughts, etc., these deceptions had to be given up and never returned to. Already exhausted from at least three nervous breakdowns, Penn-Lewis's teaching caused Roberts to believe that there had been no revival, and that he had been a spiritual dupe, and perhaps even that he had been opened to mediumistic spirits.[27] This belief of deception became so extreme that Penn-Lewis listed in her book a whole group of experiences as being demonic, including day-dreaming in a religious service[28], weakness[29], fear[30], cravings[31], passivity[32], burdens[33], insanity[34], talkativeness[35], and impatience,[36] among others. One can

---

[22] *WoS*, p. 95. She taught that, by claiming Romans chap. 6, believers would reckon themselves dead to sin and alive to Christ. This would mean also turning away from emotional experiences, since emotions were in the area of the soul, which the Spirit did not fill.

[23] *WoS*, p. 111: She taught that the problem of the Welsh Revival was passivity, which enabled demons to enter, 'What is true surrender to God? You surrender sin by dropping it. Yield actively to God.'

[24] *WoS*, pp. 190, 193.

[25] *WoS*, p. 93.

[26] *WoS*, p. 183.

[27] *WoS*, pp. 115, 116.

[28] *WoS*, p. 158.

[29] *WoS*, p. 91. She explained 'Weakness is not given by spirits, but produced by them.'

[30] *WoS*, p. 112.

[31] *WoS*, p. 145. This included cravings for drink in the body, and in the soul, cravings for love, fellowship, affection etc. She emphatically stated, are *not* from God!

[32] *WoS*, p. 86.

[33] *WoS*, p. 280.

[34] *WoS*, p. 173.

[35] *WoS*, p. 165.

[36] *WoS*, pp. 158, 159.

easily see that such teaching, coupled with the suggestibility of Roberts's nature, would cause him to renounce the revival.

Roberts's Breakdowns

What happened to Evan Roberts for him to be taken in (and perhaps taken over) by Penn-Lewis?

Roberts was a solitary man, easily moved to tears,[37] who was involved, once the revival began, in non-stop meetings. They would run seven days a week, lasting eight to ten hours a day. Evan would try to attend them all and would depend on the Holy Spirit for his sermon preparation.[38] There are reports of him falling to the floor and remaining there, prostrate for hours.[39]

'Manifestations' of the Holy Spirit were, if not encouraged, at least not stopped, except loud shrieking and wild gestures.[40] Roberts did not believe in standing in the way of the Spirit and wanted to stand humbly aside and let God work. This all lead to an imbalance or void in leadership. Roberts was criticized for the shallowness of his Bible exposition and his allowance of emotion.[41] Others felt that his willingness to step aside and let the Spirit lead brought honour to God.[42]

He was criticized from within and outside the ministry, but probably his worst enemy was himself. What do I mean by that? Simply that his fear of getting in the way of the Spirit, his fear of hindering revival, led him to nervous collapse. Authors have noted that he had suffered nervous breakdowns on at least two occasions, maybe more.[43] After a major breakdown in February 1905 he took a week-long 'sabbatical'. Later, when questioned by loving friends concerning the principle object of 'the silence' (the seven-day rest) he remarked 'It was not for the sake of my mind or my body to have a rest, but for a sign. When I asked the Lord what was the object of the seven days of silence, he (the Lord) distinctly said, "As thy tongue was tied for seven days, so shall Satan be bound seven times."'[44] Clearly Roberts did not understand the concept of taking a rest. He waited for God to tell him to take one, and when God did not tell him, he would not rest. This led to more breakdowns in health.

---

[37] T. E. Prosser, *Notes on Church History: The Welsh Revival* (Virginia Beach, 1996), p. 85.
[38] Gordon Lindsay, *They Saw it Happen* (Dallas, 1983), p. 21.
[39] Vinson Synan, *The Century of the Holy Spirit* (Nashville, TN, 2001), p. 42.
[40] Kathie Walters, 'Welsh Revival', in http://www.goodnews.netministries.org, April 2004.
[41] Robert Bradshaw, 'Bending the Church to Save the World: The Welsh Revival of 1904', http://www.sendrevival.com/history/welshrevival/bending_save_the_world_bradshaw.htm .
[42] *The Watchword*, vol. 25 (26 February 2004).
[43] James Stewart, *Invasion of Wales by the Spirit* (Fort Washington, PA, n.d.), p. 41.
[44] Ibid.

It is certainly true that Evan Roberts was overworking himself. He was following, true to form, many other evangelists who felt that they could take no rest in case the revival stopped. Many of these also suffered emotional and nervous breakdowns because of lack of rest and adequate food and sleep.[45] His behaviour began to become bizarre. In January 1905, at the Aberdafne meeting, just before his nervous breakdown, Roberts suddenly jumped up, demanded total silence, and then began to accuse the congregation of hypocrisy.[46]

After this outburst, Peter Price, a Cambridge graduate and pastor, accused Roberts of spoiling a genuine revival by bringing an imitation enthusiasm. His article was published in the Western Mail, a local newspaper.[47] Roberts became odder in his behaviour. At Ogmore Chapel, Roberts again attacked the congregation. He announced that the Spirit had fled because people had begun to expect the Spirit to be there, over-confidently. He had begun to criticize people who even smiled in his services (but then so did John Calvin). Something was wrong. He was heading for nervous collapse, which certainly happened on 23 February. After a short rest, he gave away all his money and determined to live in poverty. He purposed to go to Liverpool in April 1905. Upon his arrival there, he became angry when he found that the local churches, cashing in on the Welsh revival, had strongly advertised his services. A mob scene ensued. People began to climb over the railings to try to force their way in. The hall was vastly overcrowded and police had to intervene to save some who were suffocating on the ground, trodden on by gate-crashers. Over six thousand were crowded into Sun Hall. Roberts began to act oddly, announcing that God had locked up heaven due to five persons present who were hindering revival.[48] (There had apparently been a church split.) The following day, after the Lord Mayor's reception, he denounced certain people and left the packed Sun Hall without preaching. On Tuesday 11 April he denounced the Welsh Wesleyan Chapel. On Friday 14 April, after sitting silently for two hours in the hall, he was challenged about his offensive behaviour. Instead of speaking and acknowledging anything, Roberts got up and walked out without a word. On Sunday 16 April, Roberts came back to the meeting, asking forgiveness of those he had wronged, on his knees. He then left for Wales, never coming back to Liverpool again.[49]

---

[45] Among these were: John Alexander Dowie of Zion City, near Chicago, at the same time as Evan Roberts, William Branham, Kathryn Kuhlman, and others.
[46] Kathie Walters, 'Welsh Revival', p. 4.
[47] Walters, 'Welsh Revival', p. 5.
[48] Walters, 'Welsh Revival', p. 10.
[49] Ibid.

Last Services, 1905 and Enter Penn-Lewis

Roberts went back to North Wales, having some of the largest services of his short career. Six thousand attended his services in Llangefni, nine thousand in Holyhead, and ten thousand at Caernarfon's Eisteddfod in July. At Bala, Jessie Penn-Lewis stepped in. She volunteered to help Roberts, but was accused of interfering with Roberts's ministry. Hurt by this accusation, Penn-Lewis went back to England to her home at Woodlands in Leicestershire. There she continued to write to Roberts, imploring him to come to her home for a complete rest.

Penn-Lewis could certainly see that Roberts was near collapse and was obviously trying to help him. Roberts had broken down in February and was out of his depth in dealing with religious leaders. After Bala, Roberts broke down again, this time much more seriously.[50] After receiving five letters of invitation, Roberts acquiesced and agreed to go to the Penn-Lewis's home at Woodlands for a complete rest. He moved into her home and under her protection. She wrote to Rev. R. B. Jones of Porth explaining this. She and her husband apparently then took Roberts off to Switzerland for convalescence. It was at that time, that Penn-Lewis introduced the idea that Roberts had been misled over the emotional happenings of the revival.

She promised that Roberts's healing would benefit the church greatly. He was going to gain in discernment also. She wrote: 'I see in the peaceful interval we are having that we (note: not Evan, but 'we') are being specially trained for special work. I do not wonder that the adversary has raged. I knew that God was going to equip Evan here, so no wonder the enemy sought to hinder ...'[51]

Returning from Switzerland, Roberts was supposedly so ill that he could not walk for a year. Physicians who examined him told him never to preach again. This was extremely puzzling to his followers. Why was Penn-Lewis guarding him like this? Roberts remained at the Penn-Lewis home, refusing to see his family, or allowing them to visit. Some years later, he finally broke silence by writing an article in Penn-Lewis's *Overcomer* magazine in December 1913.

> Nearly eight years ago I was invited to Leicester (Woodlands) by Mr. and Mrs. Penn-Lewis. [This was after his nervous collapse after Bala-PEP.] The church of God acknowledges this servant of God's, Mrs. Penn-Lewis as one 'sent by God.' During the revival in Wales, I in my ignorance, did not escape the wiles of the enemy ... Then seeing what I was not, understanding what had as yet not been broken on my spiritual vision, Mrs. Penn-Lewis wrote me a very reasonable and spiritual letter asking me to come and stay at her home in Leicester. The last seven years of seclusion are ... hidden and not public ... I make no apology whatsoever for my conduct these last seven years. There is nothing to apologize for; there is none to apologize to. God is my master, what he bids, I do. Where he commands,

---

[50] Walters, 'Welsh Revival', p. 11.
[51] Ibid.

there shall I stay. Should I deviate from my course of life and work because men fail to understand me? I will not do so.[52]

But where was this rested champion, promised by Mrs Penn-Lewis, who had grown in discernment and strength? He would not even see his family, saying he had a higher calling and was obliged to forget blood ties to his own family![53] During these silent years, until 1912–13, Penn-Lewis encouraged him to look at his revelations and visions as being a demonic deception, albeit an innocent one. Even after seven to eight years of indoctrination by Penn-Lewis, Roberts announced suddenly that the Lord was going to come back in 1913! This caused a sensation and Jessie put him back into seclusion to check his revelations. Roberts grew to believe that his breakdowns, depression, and spiritual struggle had been the result of deception from Satan. The result of this was that Roberts then began to believe that most of the Welsh revival had been a spiritual deception. These ideas are written into *War on the Saints*. He grew deeply disillusioned and suffered more depression for the rest of his life. He was never really well for the rest of his life, and he continued as a recluse even after Mrs Penn-Lewis died in 1927. Roberts died in January 1951 aged seventy-two. Apart from some poems, Roberts had become a shadow of himself. Even people who knew him did not realize that he was still alive. He rarely went out and only with reluctance spoke at the funeral of his father.[54] He no longer even attended church.

Matthews, in speaking of Roberts's turning against the Welsh revival, states

> It was a gratuitous denial of the reality of much of the finest work done by the revival while it proceeded on its irresistible course. How anyone who had witnessed the miracles of grace wrought during this wonderful manifestation could possibly ascribe so much of it to Satanic influences poses a conundrum.[55]

Toward the end of his life, Roberts had become extremely unsure of himself. A man had written to him in 1942 asking for advice and guidance. Roberts told him to 'use your common sense, revelation only seems to undermine it. Harness your intellectual powers and drive hard.'[56] Nothing about prayer, nothing about the Bible. But, for all of that, Roberts seems to have come to some peace of mind. His last poem displays his thoughts: 'Thanks be to God! His love is mine. Heaven's dazzling rays around me shine, freed through the cross, the night is over. Take, Lord, the glory evermore.'[57]

---

[52] Evan Roberts, in a letter written to *The Overcomer* (December 1913).

[53] Roberts, in *The Overcomer* (December 1913), p. 12.

[54] 'Perspectives on Revival: The Welsh Revival', *The Way Christian Ministries Magazine*, 1999.

[55] David Mathews, *I Saw the Welsh Revival* (Chicago, IL, 1951), p. 124.

[56] Walters, 'Welsh Revival', p. 14.

[57] Walters, 'Welsh Revival', p. 15.

Conclusion

In this chapter I've tried to explore some of the life of Penn-Lewis where it intertwines with Evan Roberts. It is complex indeed, but some of the conclusions I have come to are as follows:

1. Penn-Lewis herself had some kind of transcendent experience in the railway carriage in 1892. This experience stayed with her for several months, before she turned her back on it.
2. She also saw herself called by God to speak. Although she published a disclaimer in *War on the Saints* saying that no woman should be allowed to teach or usurp authority over men, but to be silent (I Tim. 2:12), she apparently believed that a woman should be free to exhort and expound the Word of God, since Priscilla did this in Acts 18:26.[58] She also believed that the Bible did not forbid a man from privately soliciting a woman's opinion in any matter.[59] Although she did not believe in the charisma of prophecy, she believed in 'Women prophets as part of the spiritual economy of the New Testament'.[60] Besides this, the editors of the Web edition of *War on the Saints* say that because Mrs Penn-Lewis had died in 1927, she is not in any position to usurp authority over any man.[61] Curiously, they claim that her book is so important that even if it was proven that Mrs Penn-Lewis should not as a woman have presumed to write such a book as *War on the Saints* that it is 'still the best book about how to recognize and escape the great dangers in the modern trend to replace faith with spiritual immediacy'.[62] The editors of the Web edition classify the book as 'Post-canonical!'[63] They also admit that Evan Roberts 'hopefully' had contributed to Penn-Lewis's book but that how much he 'had to do with composing "War on the Saints"' is not known.
3. She went through some kind of 'dark night of the soul' experience akin to the mystic writers such as Madame Guyon and Francois Fénelon.
4. She 'heard' God's voice speaking to her all of her life.
5. She saw things in literal black and white after a spiritual experience where sin stood out as black specks on a white background. She was thereafter able to discern the demonic spirit from the Holy Spirit.
6. She established herself as a spiritual writer and leader through *The Overcomer* magazine and through the writing of *War on the Saints* in 1912. This influence extended through the Keswick conferences and the Welsh revival to Watchman Nee's movement in China.

---

[58] *WoS*, disclaimer.
[59] *WoS*, foreword disclaimer.
[60] Ibid.
[61] Ibid.
[62] Ibid.
[63] Ibid.

7. Through her own 'death' to spiritual experiences, she felt the need to 'save' Evan Roberts from himself, and the need to extensively reeducate Roberts to the reality of his self-opening to demonic spirits.
8. This naturally led to her labelling the Welsh revival as a spurious, counterfeit emotional experience akin to clairvoyance and witchcraft.

So was she a saint, a devil, a messenger of God? All of these terms were used of her. Much maligned and the subject of ugly accusation, Penn-Lewis was probably guilty of dominating Evan Roberts, but that was probably more in the sense of mothering him, trying to save him from himself and trying to straighten him out. There does not seem to have been a romantic involvement, although she seems to have had a strange, emotionless marriage to William. In being so involved with Roberts, she caused him to turn away from the revival and permanently side-lined him for the rest of his life. Her own prior spiritual experiences and emotional depressions caused her to see the same in Evan Roberts, and the rest is history.

CHAPTER 10

The Agony in the Garden: Visions of the 1904 Revival

John Harvey

Visions have been a characteristic of every revival. During the New England awakening in the eighteenth century, visions, trances, dreams, and revelations were a common occurrence, according to the American Congregational clergyman and anti-revivalist Charles Chauncey (1705–87). Witnesses testified to seeing angels, being transported (spiritually) from earth to heaven, and receiving visions of Christ.[1] The latter experience, the Scottish minister James Robe (1688–1753) deduced, 'was owing only to the strength of their imagination, to the disorder of their head, and of the humours of their body at that time';[2] the visions were neither real nor divine significations. In old England, John Wesley (1703–91) while believing that these phenomena were likewise often manifestations of mental confusion and devilish counterfeit also conceded that, on occasions, they had been genuine – given by God 'to strengthen and encourage them that believed, and to make his work more apparent'.[3] Visions were one of the most conspicuous and problematic features of the 1904 revival. The phenomenon represented a tendency 'to make [God's] work more apparent' unprecedented in the history of the Calvinist denominations in Wales. They were a feature in the ministry of Evan Roberts (1878–1950), in the anticipation and furtherance of the revival itself, and provided emblems of the common people's religious experience.

Visions were among several supernatural occurrences recorded during the revival, including Pentecostal dancing and tongues-speaking, and what was called 'the singing in the air' (auditions of angelic choirs),[4] and one of three categories of visualization which mediated the consequences and character of

---

[1] Ann Tave, *Fits, Trances, and Visions: Experiencing Religion and Explaining Experience from Wesley to James* (Princeton, NJ, 1999), p. 22.
[2] James Robe, *Narratives of the Extraordinary Work of the Holy Spirit of God, at Cambuslang, Etc., Begun 1742* (Glasgow, 1790), pp. 200–1.
[3] John Wesley, *The Works of John Wesley*, Oxford Edition of the Works of John Wesley, xxi (Oxford, 1975), p. 234.
[4] *Aberdare Leader*, 19 November 1904, 4; *North Wales Chronicle*, 31 December 1904, 7; *South Wales Daily News* [hereafter *SWDN*], 26 November 1904, 6; *SWDN*, 3 December 1904, 3; *SWDN*, 14 February 1905, 6.

the revival. The first of these are the journalistic images reproduced in the national newspapers of Wales depicting the salutary effects of the awakening. Many of them illustrate the repentance and new found piety of the formerly dissolute coalminers (who made up the vast majority of revival converts).[5] Others in this category show the cost of the revival for the professions which had either provided for or prohibited the miners' prior dissipations, while yet others depict the extraordinary vitality of the religious enthusiasm. The second category comprises photographs and drawings showing the revival's human intermediaries. Portraits of Roberts combine expressions of earnest piety with scholarly intensity and youthful zeal with confidence and determination. He is also represented in the company of Welsh worthies and his assistant revivalists, and as an emblem of and missionary to the revival. The third category of visualization, the visions, received no tangible illustration. They exist, now as then, in the form of secondary verbal descriptions of the witnesses' primary perceptual experience. Roberts's visions were invisible and transcendental images (internal icons) which sought to convey the revival's divine causation and spiritual underpinning.

Many Nonconformists believed that they fulfilled Joel's prediction: 'I will pour out my spirit upon all flesh ... and your young men shall see visions' (Joel 2:28).[6] That God had done so was evident from the many thousands who were being converted; therefore, Roberts reasoned, the prophecy was a direct reference to the present revival. In this way, the revival also bolstered the conceit that the Welsh were, like the Jews, the object of God's special mercy and, moreover, that Wales at the beginning of the twentieth century was the context for the consummation of biblical history. Significantly, Roberts claimed that in one vision he saw Wales being lifted upward to heaven. In this example, he inverts and transposes John the Divine's vision of the new Jerusalem coming down out of heaven (Revelation 21:2). The influence of biblical visions and the confluence of the biblical and everyday worlds typified the iconography, typology, and ethos of Roberts's other visions too. For some Nonconformists, the visions' connotation of and resemblance to those of the Old and New Testaments authenticated their divine origin and inspiration.[7] Roberts's visions have in common with those of Ezekiel and John images, themes, development, and style of description. Sun, moon, and stars undergo a supernatural metamorphosis to become vehicles of awful spiritual significance. Many of the revival visions were traditionally biblical, inasmuch as their imagery was derived from Scripture rather than being innovative. However, biblical imagery

---

[5] John Harvey, *Image of the Invisible: The Visualization of Religious Concepts in the Welsh Nonconformist Tradition* (Cardiff, 1999), pp. 26-58, 119-39.

[6] D. M. Phillips, *Evan Roberts the Great Welsh Revivalist and His Work*, 2nd edn (London, 1906), p. 164.

[7] D. M. Phillips, *Evan Roberts a'i Waith*, 212; Awstin, 'The Religious Revival in Wales', *Western Mail*, pamphlet no. 5 (1905), 3-8.

was adapted to circumstances familiar to the visionary. For example, two horses, one red and the other white, are seen galloping together in a vision at Loughor (his home village). They represent the most direct reference to Johnine apocalyptic imagery (Revelation 6:2, 4).[8] However, in Roberts's vision the horses appear pulling a contemporary carriage.[9]

Other visions involved creative syntheses of biblical imagery. On a Sunday afternoon in October or November 1904, Roberts, filled with despair over the state of the church, walked in the garden, where:

> in the hedge on his left, he saw a face full of scorn, hatred and derision, and heard a laugh as of defiance. It was the Prince of this World who exulted in his despondency.
>
> Then there suddenly appeared another figure, gloriously arrayed in white bearing in hand a flaming sword borne aloft. The sword fell athwart the first figure and it instantly disappeared. He could not see the face of the sword bearer.[10]

The vision sets up a contrast by juxtaposing two opposing figures. The story of the temptation of Christ provides the only biblical precedent for such a confrontation, although the Gospel narrative gives no indication that the devil took on physical form. In the temptation, Christ wields against the adversary 'the sword of the Spirit, which is the word of God' (Ephesians 6:17). Roberts depicted Christ with a literal sword, possibly also an allusion to the flaming sword God placed east of Eden (Genesis 3:24). In the context of his vision, the sword does not read as a deterrent, but as the power of God wielded against the enemy of the church. Roberts's 'art', therefore, consisted in creating new conjunctions of images drawn from the Bible. These in turn generate fresh symbolic readings expressing his own ideas. Visions of Christ and the devil, perceived either together or independently, were by far the most common experienced by Roberts and others. Such visions objectified the twin spiritual forces that fought for the soul. As in the case of Roberts's vision in the garden, the figures often played out personal religious crises.

Hymns, too, exerted a considerable influence on the iconography and mode of the visions in general, and of those depicting Christ in particular. For example, the conversion experience was figuratively visualized by Daniel P. Williams (1882–1947), the founder of Pentecostalism in Wales. The vision came to him at a revival meeting. He was awaking from a blackout brought on by Evan Roberts having 'laid hands' upon him. The attendant circumstances had a bearing on the vision's imagery:

---

[8] Phillips, *Great Welsh Revivalist*, pp. 237-8.
[9] Phillips, *Great Welsh Revivalist*, p. 219. Roberts also fused the spiritual and the mundane in his choice of illustrations for public speaking (Awstin, 'The Religious Revival in Wales', in *Western Mail*, pamphlet no. 4 (1905), 10).
[10] *SWDN*, 19 November 1904, 6.

As he regained consciousness, Williams heard a woman singing a line from a hymn: 'The gates of heaven opened wide, I see a sea of blood'. It was then that Williams had a vision of Jesus on the cross, his body streaming with blood, and underneath it a sinner's head. As the blood fell on the sinner's head, it became white – like snow. The sinner, Williams realized, was himself.[11]

The hymn's metaphor of the sea of blood triggered the visualization of the stream of blood which poured from Christ's body. A verse from a popular hymn of the time by William Cowper (1731–68) almost certainly exerted a direct influence on Williams's emblem for forgiveness:

There is a fountain filled with blood
Drawn from Immanuel's veins;
And sinners, plunged beneath that flood,
Lose all their guilty stains.[12]

From the seventeenth century, hymns often enjoined worshippers to 'see', 'view', 'gaze upon', 'survey', or 'behold' Christ crucified. 'Looking' was generally conceived in the figurative sense of comprehending with the eye of faith the death and atoning work of Christ as, for example, in the lines from Isaac Watts's hymn 'When I survey the wondrous cross'. Such sentiments did not encourage a vivid mental conception of the crucifixion. However, in William How's (1823–97) 'It is a thing most wonderful' (a hymn popular among Nonconformists in the nineteenth century), the spectacle of Christ's suffering is described more literally – 'seeing', as in the visionary's experience, is a contemplative and conscious act of mental visualization:

I sometimes think about the cross,
And shut my eyes, and try to see
The cruel nails and crown of thorns,
And Jesus crucified for me.[13]

In How's hymn, the focus of meditation is upon the instruments of Christ's torture. It was so too in many revival visions of the afflicted Christ. In a preamble to an address about Christ's suffering, Roberts recalled a vision in which he had seen a Roman soldier in the act of nailing Jesus to the Cross: 'I could see him kneeling on his arm; see the nails being driven in; see the hammer falling.'[14] Rather like the salutary images showing the wounds and

---

[11] G. G. Johnson, 'A Centenary Celebration for Pastor Daniel Powell Williams 1882–1982', in *Riches of Grace*, 6, no. 51 (May 1982), 68-9 (69).

[12] William Cowper, 'There is a fountain filled with blood', *Olney Hymns*, new edn (London, 1797), no. 79.

[13] William W. How, 'It is a thing most wonderful', *Children's Hymn Book* (London, [n.d.]), no. 161.

[14] Awstin, 'The Religious Revival in Wales', *Western Mail*, pamphlet no. 2 (1905), 19.

nails of Christ once used in Roman Catholic contemplation, such visions focused the believer's attention on the intensity of Christ's suffering, and thereby stimulated their will and affections to holy living. Visions of the crucifixion were a notable if ephemeral transgression of Calvinist principles. Pictures depicting the crucifixion were rarely set up on the walls of either the chapels or homes for fear of idolatry, though a few engravings of the scene were included in illustrated family Bibles.

Roberts's visions demonstrate a figurative attitude to religious concepts. In this sense, comparisons can be drawn with the series of allegorical scenes that John Bunyan's (1628–88) Christian is shown at Interpreter's House, in *The Pilgrim's Progress* (1678). Both are revelations in the form of spiritual similitudes, identified by interpretation, and designed either to cheer or to warn the spectator. In one scene, Interpreter shows Christian 'a place where was a fire burning against a wall'. The devil cast water upon the fire while, at the back of the wall, another figure, identified as Christ, poured on oil. The emblematic representation of Christ and the devil in an adversarial relationship is a likely progenitor of the revivalists' visions of the same.[15]

Many of Roberts's visions could be described as emblematic in that they represent symbolic objects that, individually or together, convey a spiritual message. One cannot be sure that Roberts, like Bunyan, was familiar with emblem books, though it is not unlikely. At least thirty editions of Francis Quarles's (1592–1644) *Emblemes* (1635) were published in the nineteenth century alone.[16] The hymnist Augustus Toplady (1740–78) considered the book to convey spiritual lessons 'in the most pleasant and interesting manner – by hieroglyphics, or figurative signs and symbols, of divine, sacred, and supernatural things'.[17] The term 'hieroglyphic' could apply to Roberts's visions which comprise a single element or a conjunction of static elements – for example his vision of a key, signifying that God had given him the ability to open the hearts of men.[18] There are specific iconographic similarities between the visions and emblems. Roberts's visionary confrontation with Christ and Satan in his garden recalls Quarles's emblem of the 'just man' confronted by an angel holding an olive branch and the devil holding a feather. In this context, they personify virtue and temptation. Roberts received a vision of a candle and the sun, in which the light from the latter outshines that of the former. Quarles depicts Cupid about to 'snuf and trim' a burning candle set upon an orb; to the right of the orb a boy blasts at the sun with a bellows. In Roberts's vision, the

---

[15] There was a steady demand for the book in Wales from 1688, fours years after its original publication, when it was first published in Welsh ('*Pilgrim's Progress*, Welsh and English', *Baptist Quarterly*, 1 (1922–3), 39-42, (39)).

[16] Karl Josef Höltgen, *Aspects of the Emblem: Studies in the English Emblem Tradition and the European Context*, Problemata Semiotica 2 (Kassel, 1986), p. 164.

[17] Francis Quarles, *Emblems, Divine and Moral*, new edn (London, 1834), p. iii.

[18] Phillips, *Evan Roberts a'i Waith*, p. 220.

contrast of these two lights indicated that the success of the revival in its latter days would greatly exceed that of its beginning.[19]

The sun and other celestial bodies, airborne phenomena, and dazzling lights were a stock-in-trade of visions experienced by Roberts and others. When on his way to Aberdare, in November 1904, Roberts saw black elongated balls rolling out of the sun. 'The balls were enormous, rolling out with strength and speed ... The kingdom of light casting out the kingdom of darkness was what the vision suggested to him.'[20] A similar anomaly is sometimes experienced by sufferers from cataracts or retinal damage. There may have been other physiological triggers for the visions too. Newspaper accounts of the revival include several references to Roberts having had a spasmodic heavy cold during the revival. The sustained pressure of his itinerary and public expectation no doubt taxed not only his spiritual but also his constitutional reserves, increasing his susceptibility to illness. In the nineteenth and early twentieth centuries, cold medicines and painkillers often contained laudanum – a hydro-alcoholic tincture containing ten per cent opium. It was prescribed for everything from headaches to tuberculosis, and beloved by of Romantic poets especially. Its hallucinogenic side effects were well documented and exploited. Given Roberts's manic disposition (he was renowned for rapidly oscillating between bouts of tears and laughter), laudanum may have contributed to his flights of exalted imagination.

Other visions involving heavenly and aerial objects feature in the account of a pastor who saw a ball of fire descending from heaven on the church in South Wales; and, in February 1905, in a vision witnessed by a group of people which took the form of a star that increased in brightness, lowered from the sky, and came to rest above a building. They claimed that within the star was the cross with Christ upon it, his arms outstretched – beckoning.[21] A star features in a most extraordinary vision witnessed by Mary Jones and numerous others. She was a Primitive Methodist and farm woman who had lived all her life on the west Wales seaboard at Dyffryn, halfway between the towns of Barmouth and Harlech. She described herself as the female counterpart of Roberts, a prophetess, and the recipient of figural and abstract visions. The latter included an encounter with strange lights and a brilliant star.

The vision of the star took place at the mid point of the revival, in February 1904. (More paranormal activity was reported during that month than at any time during the two years of the awakening. The daily newspapers carried accounts of not only visions but also numerous sightings of ghosts.[22]) The first

---

[19] Phillips, *Great Welsh Revivalist*, pp. 237-8.

[20] Phillips, *Evan Roberts a'i Waith*, p. 220.

[21] *SWDN*, 3 February 1905, 6; *SWDN*, 6 February 1905, 6; *SWDN*, 21 February 1905, 6.

[22] *SWDN*, 26 November 1904), 6; *SWDN*, 10 December 1904, 4; *SWDN*, 9 February 1905), 4; *SWDN*, 14 February 1905, 5; *SWDN*, 21 February 1905, 6; *North Wales Chronicle*, 18 February 1905, 1.

appearance of the star was preceded by another vision. It was of a luminous arch, like a misty rainbow, one end resting on the sea, the other on the mountain top, bathing in soft effulgence the roof of the little chapel where she preached. The star, which was of unusual brilliance and magnitude, and could travel at great speed, emitted dazzling sparks, like flashing rays from a diamond. It appeared in the southern sky and would vanish with the appearance of 'the lights' so-called which preceded or followed her, illuminating the roads that lead to the chapel. Similar lights had been seen in the locality two hundred and fifty years earlier. The Welsh antiquarian Thomas Pennant (1726–98) described what were called *tan dyeithr* (angelic strange fires), which moved in the sky over Cardigan Bay.[23]

Jones's visions represent a confluence of unusual natural phenomena with biblical motifs, such as the star that preceded the Magi to Bethlehem and stood in the sky over the stable. Today, the luminescences would be interpreted as an electromagnetic discharge, sometimes known as earth lights. In 1904 they signified heavenly approbation of her mission, divine guidance, and further evidence of God's particular regard for the land of Wales. One of the most often sung hymns of the revival was John Henry Newman's 'Lead Kindly Light'.[24] After Jones's visions were made public, the sentiment must have assumed an unusual poignancy.

Bizarre accounts of this nature had an extraordinary hold on the congregations' imagination for several reasons. First, from the eighteenth to the mid nineteenth century sermons (along with hymns) had provided a ready supply of emblems symbolizing common ideals like the prosperity of the church, the victory of Christ, and the vanquishing of the devil. However, by the end of the nineteenth century Welsh preachers were deemed to have lost the ability to use concrete, easily understood, and arresting images. Roberts's visions, in part, supplied that want. Secondly, the concept of visionary revelation would have been an attractive doctrine to the working class, who made up the greater proportion of the revival congregations. For here was a form of religious experience that was as accessible to an illiterate person as to the greatest theologian or biblical scholar.[25] Thirdly, visions were also a mode of religious experience which was accessible to women. The revival gave prominence to women, and several of them accompanied Roberts on his mission to provide impassioned solos and conversion testimonies. The spontaneous and non-hierarchical structure of the services also allowed female members of the congregation to articulate their experience openly in song, prayer, frenzied gesticulations, and recounts of visions – signifying that not

---

[23] *Evening Express* (9 February 1905), 3; *North Wales Chronicle* (28 January 1905), 5.
[24] Appropriately, the hymn was sung by coalminers at underground colliery services during the revival, *SWDN*, 5 March 1905, 6.
[25] Hugh McLeod, 'Religion and the Working Class in Nineteenth-Century Britain', in *Studies in Economic and Social History* (London, 1984), 27.

only men were the conduit for new revelations. Even when these revelations proved to be spurious, many believers in the congregations were reluctant to criticize the visions publicly. This may have reflected their desire to use to them to provide evidence for the supernatural, miraculous, and revelatory nature of Christianity. Belief in these doctrines had been severely undermined by late-nineteenth-century liberal and higher-critical theology.

The Roman Catholic Church had appealed to miraculous relics and religious visions to the same ends and also to encourage the faithful. The Church's most remarkable relic, the Turin Shroud, was placed on public exhibition six years before the revival, in 1898. In that year the shroud was photographed for the first time. The photograph provided a token of the original which could be reproduced and disseminated widely as a means of inspiring faith. Possibly for the same reason, and in order to publicize their significance, Roberts wanted to illustrate several of his visions in the form of picture postcards.[26] The popularity of postcards showing the revival's mediators and message (see above) would have convinced him that this was a sound strategy. However, this resolve, like his visions, never materialized. During the subsequent four years the shroud's photograph gave rise to a heated scientific investigation into the relic's authenticity. The shroud represented, putatively, the burial cloth of Jesus and, thus, empirical evidence for his existence, death, and appearance. Unlike a vision of Christ, this miraculous self-portrait was tangible and permanent.

Photography was a means of objectifying and securing another manifestation of spiritual phenomenon prevalent at that time – ghosts. Since the 1860s psychic photographers claimed to portray an 'extra', so-called. This was a supernatural form which, while invisible when the photograph was taken, developed on the photographic plate alongside the image of the ostensible (living) subject. The countenance of the 'extra' often resembled that of a departed relative. Such appearances posed to same veridical and ontological problems as religious visionaries had had to ponder. Were apparitions of Christ, the Virgin Mary, and holy persons the actual supernatural presence of the person or merely representations of them? In the case of 'extras', were they the disincarnate spirits of the dead (thus providing evidence of post-mortem survival), or just simulacra made and sent by the spirits or some other intelligence? Like spirit photographs, visions certified the existence of a reality beyond common sense. However, for Roberts and other Nonconformists it was more important to believe that visions of Christ, the devil, and biblical figures were genuinely spiritual phenomenon than it was to distinguish between degrees of actuality. For, as in the tradition of emblems, it was the verbal message rather than the visual medium that mattered most. Consequently, Roberts always recounted a description of his visionary experience accompanied by a homiletic or prophetic interpretation.

---

[26] Phillips, *Great Welsh Revivalist*, p. 198; Phillips, *Evan Roberts a'i Waith*, pp. 266-9.

In the Roman Catholic tradition, visions are often mute. A silent apparition appeared outside the gable end of the local church in Knock in the county of Mayo, Ireland twenty-five years before the Welsh revival, in 1879.[27] It lasted for about three hours, was seen by many villagers of different ages simultaneously, and took the form of three iridescent figures – Mary, Joseph, and the Apostle John – accompanied by a lamb upon an altar and angels. The compositions and motifs derive from early Renaissance art. Indeed, as a matter of rule, Roman Catholic visions tend to follow a prescribed iconography or an established visual code embodied in the fine art tradition (to which believers are habitually exposed in churches and religious books).

The Calvinistic branch of Protestantism, having largely rejected iconic representations and the use of images in places of worship, based its meagre tradition of visions upon literary imagery derived from the Bible, hymns, and devotional literature for the most part. Hence, Roberts's visions adopt and adapt modes, patterns, and symbolism based upon the raw materials provided by these sources, sources which were very familiar to the Nonconformist congregations and which, in the absence of a significant fine art tradition, supplied a cultural lexicon for interpreting the visions' appearance and meaning. Welsh Nonconformity's paucity of fine art influences is evident in relation to, for example, Roberts's vision of a Roman soldier in the act of nailing Jesus to the cross (see above). Roberts remarked on the unusualness of the vision, for he had never seen a picture of this aspect of the crucifixion. However, several well-known Victorian painters had pictorialized the scene prior to 1904. James Tissot's (1836–1902) painting *The First Nail* (1899) was a popular magic lantern slide at the time.

Roman Catholic visions, while no less ephemeral than those experienced by Nonconformists during the revival, were made permanent in illustrations. The most frequently illustrated vision by far was that of the Virgin Mary, received by Bernadette Soubirous (1844–79) in the hollow of a rock near Lourdes nearly forty years earlier, in 1858. Pictures of visions conditioned the faith community's way of seeing and expectations regarding the visual character of holy persons and symbols in visions. The absence of tangible and enduring images of the revival visions may have severely limited the development of a continuity or tradition of visionary experience, and of a consensual agreement among Nonconformists regarding how holy persons should be visualized and identified.

Soubirous received a further eighteen visits by the same apparition in the same place. Later, a spring emerged from the rock whose waters it was claimed had miraculous properties capable of healing the sick and lame. The Virgin also commissioned the construction of a shrine on the site which has been a place of pilgrimage ever since. In contrast, Roberts received many different types of

---

[27] A vision of the Virgin Mary was supposed to have appeared at Llanthony Abbey a year later, in 1880 (*SWDN*, 31 August 1905, 7).

vision in a variety of places. Moriah Calvinistic Methodist chapel is the only religious site associated with Roberts's visions. It was here that he received the one depicting red and white horses (see above). More significantly, Moriah was Roberts's home church, the chapel where he first preached, and the launch pad of his evangelistic journeys. While curative efficacy was never been associated with the building, it has (in a far more modest way) become a place of pilgrimage for those who look back nostalgically to 1904 and await another renaissance of the same order.

No vision of the future was given to Bernadette. However, the visions Roberts received were often predictive in nature, signifying the course and success of the present revival and the immediate prosperity of the church. One of his visions proved to be uncannily prophetic of events beyond the period of the revival. Early on in the awakening he had a vision of darkness perceived during a period of confinement to bed due to an illness. It happened at the lightest part of the day. The room began to darken until it was as dark as night. The meaning of *this* vision eluded him. Fifty years later, the light of Christianity in Wales was to be almost extinguished.

CHAPTER 11

A Hurricane of the Holy Spirit:
An Account of the 1904 Revival at Bethesda, based on the Diaries, Letters and Correspondence of the Rev. John Thomas Job

Dafydd M. Job

Although the 1904 revival, to many people, is mainly associated with the name of Evan Roberts, the young man from Loughor in South Wales, the story of what happened must take account of many others who became in various ways affected by what happened in Wales during the years of 1904 and 1905. The revival took hold in many places which Evan Roberts did not visit, and there were spiritual movements which preceded his involvement and were carried on independently of his involvement. He himself was present in only about two hundred and fifty meetings, when the estimated number of meetings was over ten thousand. Therefore to understand what happened, we need to consider other factors, and other people who were affected in some way by the happenings of those years.

One of the lesser known stories maybe is that of Bethesda in North Wales. The pastor there at the time, the Reverend John Thomas Job, kept diaries and notes of some of the events. These have recently come to light, together with letters sent to him during this time. This account therefore may help us to understand what happened.

Preparation for Revival

The Church believes in a Sovereign God, whose right and privilege it is to bless those whom he wishes to bless, and to move in a totally sovereign way. However, although revival is often spoken of as being unexpected – we hear of the Holy Spirit coming suddenly upon people – yet generally speaking, on looking back there are certain factors which have been at work which prepares the people for the blessing. In scriptural terms, John the Baptist was sent to prepare the way of the Lord. It is not surprising that it was upon the apostles that the Holy Spirit fell at Pentecost – they had been prepared by the Lord. It is not surprising either that Cornelius was the gentile who received the words of life from Peter – he had been spiritually exercised for some time[1].

And so we ask, why did revival take hold in such a powerful way at Bethesda? It was a sprawling village a few miles outside Bangor in North Wales – with most of the population being poor slate quarry workers. There was nothing special about the area, and yet the revival took hold there in such a way as to make it a centre from which the fire spread to the surrounding area. Why? We need to go back in time.

Bethesda was a religious village – it got its name from the Congregationalists' chapel, but there were other chapels there – at the beginning of the nineteenth century there was one small Calvinistic Methodist cause there, and during the nineteenth century that one cause planted no less than seven daughter churches in the area. Most of the population were church members of one sort or another. They had known revival during the century – very notably in 1859. And the hundreds of people who lived there were cultured – there were choirs; there were good theologians among the elders of the churches; they were people who prayed, and in 1898 they called a pastor to Carneddi Calvinistic Methodist chapel, who was himself becoming a national figure. The Reverend John Thomas Job, minister of Nazareth, Aberdare had won the chair – one of the most prized competitions – in the National Eisteddfod in 1897, and in 1900 he would win the crown in the National Eisteddfod with a long poem (of over 1200 lines) on Williams Pantycelyn. In 1903 he would win the chair for the second time. Indeed the preachers, and especially the poet/preachers, were the idols of their time. He was on good terms with and sharing correspondence with the leading politicians, academics and religious leaders of the age. Such a man was their minister. Surely religion was in a fine state in Bethesda.

However there is a scriptural principle that 'God resists the proud, but gives grace to the humble.'[2] The people of Bethesda were to learn something of their own frailty in the first years of the twentieth century.

Conditions in the area were dire. Lord Penrhyn, who owned the quarry, lived in resplendent luxury. The quarry built up by his father, exported slate around the world. The profits rolled in – but he paid the workers a pittance. When the slate industry took a downturn, he merely withheld the pay of the workers. There was extreme poverty, illness and harsh conditions for all but the few. So they called a strike – it was a long strike which lasted three years. Many families were divided – about a thousand men had to go to South Wales, leaving their wives, mothers, children whilst they went to look for work in the coal mines. Others emigrated overseas. Some decided to break the strike and Lord Penrhyn rewarded them by building better houses for them – houses still known today in the village as Tai Bradwyr (*Traitor's Houses*). People were set

---

[1] Mark 1:2-4; Acts 1:8; Acts 10.
[2] James 4:6.

against each other – family against family, street against street. Children died of disease – tuberculosis was rife. At Christmas time in 1901 there were riots, with windows of the traitor's houses broken. Lord Penrhyn even called the military in to deal with the strikers.

And the feelings entered the chapels; Job would speak of one man – a wonderful man on his knees in prayer, who could bring heaven down – but had he been asked to take part publicly, the whole congregation would have walked out – he was a 'traitor'[3]. Now the real traitor was Lord Penrhyn – with one word he could have brought the suffering to an end. But the leaders of the churches talked in their reports of the disease and the curse of the strike. These people found that their so-called Christianity could not deal with the intense hatred that lurked in their hearts. They were brought low. They were humbled.

And their Pastor – the man who was becoming a national figure – what of him? He saw his people suffer, yes, but there was more. In 1894 he had married a beautiful and godly wife – Etta Davies. They had three children – but because of the disease that was rife in Bethesda, they lost first one daughter, then the second daughter. Then Etta herself died, leaving him to care for the surviving baby, Aneurin who was desperately ill. The diary for April/May 1902 has an entry over and over again – '*nyrsio Aneurin bach*' (nursing little Aneurin), and before long he had passed from this world also. Within two years he had lost his wife and children, and what use was national acclaim in the face of such loss.

The people of the area and their pastor were all brought low indeed as they were emptied of all pride and self-sufficiency. In such a way the people seemed to be prepared for that which was to come. This seems to be one reason why the revival found such fruitful ground there.

Secondly – let us ask the question – in these difficulties that they experienced as a people and as a pastor – why did they look to God to send a revival? Many people, facing difficulties, turn away from God, and their hearts are filled with bitterness. But here they sought God, for example these words come from Job's diary the day after his second daughter died:

> This has been the darkest week of my life. I have been forced into terrible depths! I called on God 'Spare her!' But that was not His will! I am like a vessel in the tempest – at the mercy of the waves. Etta is away, and I have to bury sweet Non without her mother seeing her! Yet He must have a glorious reason for all of this, or else I must throw my Bible overboard. But I'd rather drown with the Bible in my hand, than live without it. O Lord! Keep dear Etta![4]

And again at the end of 1902 – the year after the last of his children died

---

[3] Personal conversation with E. M. Job, son of the Rev. J. T. Job.

[4] J. T. Job Diary, Monday 14 January, 1902.

> Thus another year full of mercies has passed.... Etta, Olwen, Non and little Aneurin are in your own heaven. Guide me to them to the quiet haven in your own good time.[5]

This is not a bitter man. This is a man looking to God – but why, when God had allowed him to suffer such heavy blows?

Part of the answer lies with his parents. Job was brought up in the little village of Llandebie, outside Ammanford. His parents were godly people and many preachers stayed with them whilst preaching in the chapel where his father was an elder. His mother in particular was a godly woman – her text books were: The Bible, the hymn book, James Hughes's *Commentary* (a sort of Welsh Mathew Henry) and volumes of the sermons of David Charles, Carmarthen, John Jones Talysarn, and Islwyn. Her last words on her deathbed were, 'Draw me, and I will run after Thee.'[6] An uncle, Thomas Job Conwil, a godly preacher from Carmarthenshire, also had a profound influence on him. Surely under these influences he could not but have seen God as someone to turn to in adversity.

And in Bethesda – in a report on the situation in the churches in 1903, the church secretary writes –

> We are longing very much for a dawn on the slate industry; but whilst waiting for that, let us not forget to look to the God of all grace for a powerful visitation from on high: only the latter can transform the fabric of the community.[7]

The churches kept alive the memory of past revivals. There were people there who had been alive in 1859 when the power of God had been felt very much. In their praying the people heard more than the memory of the great 'Quaking of the Revival'. In particular they spoke of one Sunday known as *Sul Mawr Evan William* (Evan William's Great Sunday), when sixty-nine adults and twenty-two children were brought to faith and into the church. Just as Joshua brought stones from the Jordan when they crossed into Canaan, so that 'When your children ask in time to come, "What do those stones mean to you?"[7] then you shall tell them that the waters of the Jordan were cut off before the ark of the covenant of the LORD. When it passed over the Jordan, the waters of the Jordan were cut off. So these stones shall be to the people of Israel a memorial forever.'[8] So these kept alive memories of what God had done in their midst.

As well as the memory of God's dealings with them, another factor influenced the people there. Job's wife, Etta, came from New Quay in

---

[5] J. T. Job Diary, 1902.
[6] J. T. Job, 'Marw Goffa Mrs. Mary Job' (Obituary of Mrs Mary Job), in *Y Goleuad* (4 May 1898), p. 12.
[7] Handwritten document among papers of J. T. Job.
[8] Joshua 4:6, 7.

Cardiganshire. The man who officiated at their wedding was Joseph Jenkins – the minister who was the guiding light to young people in the area. In early 1904 there was a powerful spiritual movement at New Quay, generally regarded as the beginning of the 1904–5 revival. In May the late Etta's father wrote to Job:

> My dear Son in Law,
> I have been thinking for days and weeks of writing you a letter, to break on this silence, and to give you some news of the revival which has broken out here, especially amongst the young people, although its gentle effects are felt amongst the middle aged and old people.

Florrie Evans, the first to be brought under the influences of the revival, lived two doors away from Etta's father. The letter was an inspiring report of God moving there.

> The place was last night over packed. Old drunkards are coming in and in the prayer meeting, shouting out for prayer, and praising God before leaving.
> Yes, this is how things are here now, I hope it will last. It is easy to preach and pray here now.[9]

Undoubtedly Job shared this with the prayer meeting at his church and with leaders in the other churches. Later on he could say – 'there has been a quiet pleading amongst the people of God for some months'.[10] During the summer months he visited New Quay himself, preaching there on 28 August, seeing the work first hand. In October he visited the South again to preach, and stayed with two fellow ministers – Twynog and D. Cunllo Davies, who would both be heavily influenced by the revival. No doubt their conversation would have turned to what was happening in Cardiganshire. So the story of what was happening elsewhere was itself a means of raising longing and even hopes that God might do something in Bethesda.

The Revival

The free churches decided to do something – they organized a series of meetings in November. They came to Jerusalem, the most central Chapel in the village, and invited the Reverend Hugh Hughes, a Methodist minister, to preach for four nights. On Monday evening 21 November he preached, and then on the Tuesday afternoon they opened the vestry for the women of the area to come to pray. Over two hundred turned up, and an awesome time was had as a spirit of prayer descended upon the place. That evening, Hugh Hughes preached and God's presence was apparent. The words in Job's diary are 'Mae'r Diwygiad

---

[9] E. Davies; Personal letter to J. T. Job; 5 May, 1904.
[10] J. T. Job in E. E. Evans, *Y Diwygiad a'r Diwygwyr* (Dolgellau, 1906), p. 144.

wedi dod yma! Diolch byth!' – (The revival has arrived here. Everlasting thanks!)

On Wednesday over five hundred turned up to the prayer meeting in the afternoon. The people gathered for prayer for an hour before Hugh Hughes preached. He preached and then the young people had a meeting for three hours, where they were aware of God's presence. This was repeated on Thursday. Friday and Saturday were given to Prayer meetings. The following week Hugh Hughes returned to preach three nights, and another preacher came for Thursday and Friday. It was a remarkable two weeks, with people – in the words of my grandfather – 'conquered by the death of the cross'. Only church members were affected – the world would be moved later. But each afternoon for months the women were to gather to pray in their hundreds. Most evenings there would be either prayer meetings or somebody preaching. And in my grandfather's diary what do we read? 'Jesus is here.' And yet – this was only seen as the first wave, or the beginnings – they anticipated more. And more came.

Three weeks later Joseph Jenkins was in the north. It was natural that he should come to help his friend at Bethesda, and he arrived there with two of the New Quay girls – Florrie Evans and Maude Davies – and three girls who had been set aflame in Talysarn, a village where Jenkins was preaching before coming to Bethesda. They held a meeting on Wednesday night, 21 December, which was remarkable. Joseph Jenkins spoke for about twenty minutes on a phrase someone had uttered in the prayer meeting – 'As you will, so let it be', saying that we must allow God to do His will amongst his people. However, on the following night we have one of the clearest descriptions of what was happening. It was Thursday 22 December. Job describes the meeting as a *Hurricane* of the Holy Spirit. His understanding of what happened is helpful in explaining the experience.

The meeting was preceded by prayer, and following an hour and a quarter of prayer, Joseph Jenkins preached from Philippians 2:12-13 'Work out your own salvation with fear and trembling. For it is God which worketh in you both to will and to do of *his* good pleasure.' His theme was God's work in us – not God working in us and then we work it out – rather it is God who does it all, from the new birth to the glorification. God taking hold of man's will, making him captive to Christ: the Holy Spirit turning man's nature as the tide of the sea towards holiness. The sermon is described as full of fiery bolts fired from heaven through the fiery heart of the preacher himself. The people listened in silence as God spoke to their hearts. After twenty minutes the whole place was awash with tears. Someone could not stand it any more – he shouted out – his memory of his father on his knees praying for him overcame him. Another gave out a hymn – 'Y Gŵr a fu gynt o dan hoelion dros ddyn pechadurus fel fi' (The Man who once suffered the nails for a wretched old sinner like me). It seemed like another Pentecost.

What really happened there? Job himself tries to describe the essence of the experience:

> I felt the Holy Spirit as a deluge of light causing my whole nature to quake; I saw Jesus Christ – and my nature turned to liquid at his feet; and I saw myself – and I abhorred! And what more can I say? I can only hope that I am not deceiving myself. But Oh! The Love of God in the death of the Cross is wonderfully powerful![11]

His understanding was that the Holy Spirit, the Third Person of the Trinity, came to glorify Christ, the Second Person of the Trinity, and to bring people face to face with him. And in coming like this, they could only flee to the cross. They were brought to that point where it didn't matter who else was present – all that counted was that they were standing before Christ, naked unless He gave them clothing, condemned unless forgiveness was found in Him.

The people there were as far as can be ascertained, all professing Christians – and yet they came to a deeper understanding than ever before of the reality of their own sinfulness. Job himself had no doubt been a Christian for many years, and a faithful minister of the gospel – but he writes in his diary – 'Is this the great night of my salvation?' It is not that he wasn't a Christian before, but the veil seemed to be pulled back, and he became aware of a reality which he hadn't known before; an assurance that he had not previously experienced.

Note – this was work that was going on within the Christian Church – not yet deeply affecting the world. The church itself had much that needed to be dealt with. Firstly there were professing Christians who realized that their religion up to now had been a formal, outward one, not a religion of the heart. They asked that they might renew their membership vows, as they didn't really mean much the first time. Then there were broken relationships which had to be healed – the strike had caused so much ill feeling. Mothers who had lost their little ones forgave those whose husbands had been 'traitors'. There was much confession of sins.

Added to this, among the quarrymen returning home for Christmas from the south were some who had caught the fire there. Among them, one William Hughes, who was brought under conviction in one of Dan Roberts's meetings (Dan was the brother of Evan Roberts). He experienced bitter remorse for his sins, and wanted to find somewhere to be alone with God. In the end, the only place he could find was down on the coal face during one of his shifts, and there, he entered the man-hole – the miner's place of refuge from the coal trucks passing – and he felt the air thick with the memories and guilt of days of cursing. He shouted with all his might a prayer for God's mercy and help. And he felt as if a physical burden was being lifted off him. Tears came, but the bitterness was gone and amidst those tears, songs of rejoicing and triumph in

---

[11] J. T. Job in E. E. Evans, *Y Diwygiad a'r Diwygwyr*, p. 217.

Christ. Of course, when he came home for Christmas, he added his own testimony to the work of God there. A scene from one prayer meeting has William Hughes being greeted from the other side of the room by two of his former drinking partners – 'William Hughes – we have been in Satan's service for long enough now.' 'Yes, but we've turned to a better Master now, Bob', he answered. 'And what a lovely rest home he has prepared for us – we'll never go back to the old master', says the third.

The prayer meetings continued – in the afternoon for the women, and in the evening for the young people – and a meeting was started for children, with over fifty children between the age of four and thirteen singing with all their might to Jesus Christ. These effects lasted not days, but months. Evan Roberts paid a surprise visit to the place at Easter 1905, and saw that God was still at work in a mighty way.

The Fruit of the Revival at Bethesda

Zechariah is told by God that in a Time of Blessing God will come (chapter 12:10)

> And I will pour out on the house of David and the inhabitants of Jerusalem a spirit of grace and pleas for mercy, so that, when they look on me, on him whom they have pierced, they shall mourn for him, as one mourns for an only child, and weep bitterly over him, as one weeps over a firstborn.

This spirit of supplications was prominent in Bethesda. People would seek the lonely places to seek the Lord. One mother got up early one morning to find her nine year-old daughter already up, singing 'Ar Ei ben bo'r goron' (May the crown be on His head), and wanting her mother to pray with her. The old 59ers had been recognizable because of the way they prayed, and the spirit of prayer filled the area. The women in the afternoons, the quarrymen, drunkards brought home to their Father, the young people into the early hours of the morning. Heaven had come close, and there was a reality in prayer that had not been known before. Men found themselves seeking God on the lonely paths in the mountains. Women prayed for their sons who were down in South Wales. They also prayed for other regions. A postcard arrived for Job from Edinburgh seeking prayer for there, and for Calabhar and Syria. And this was acted upon immediately.

It Produced a Living Vital Christianity

If you look at the figures, then not so many were added to the churches in the area, when you compare with some parts of the country. During the first two months of the revival only about a hundred and forty were added to the churches – a relatively small number when compared with some areas. But it was an area where nearly everyone was already a church member. However, many realized that their religion had been a formal outward religion – not that of the heart. In a report to the *British Weekly*, Job wrote:

> The Revival has been the means of infusing *A New Spirit* – a spirit of consecration in the service of Christ – into the churches of the district. It is felt already as a Breath of love from on High amongst us – real and divine, and among its results, the spirit of enmity between workmen and families, gives way. O! the grandeur, the gentleness, yea the sweet reasonableness of Divine Love! Verily, it is a pleasure to live here now; the 'Society' in each Church is blossoming as a rose under the Breath of a Heavenly Spring. Truly Christ is to His garden once more come among us. The vast majority of our people are church going and are with only a few exceptions enrolled members already. Hence we cannot expect very many new members here. Still about 50 have joined the churches already. A scene was witnessed in Carneddi Church the other night – when a young man of about 32 got up, and said he desired to give himself anew as a member. The love of Christ constrained him to do so, he said, although he already enjoyed that privilege. What is this, I asked, but a true revival within the church itself? – And when Zion itself puts on 'her beautiful garments', the unbelief of the world will soon vanish away. We still expect greater things. The Death of the Cross is gradually conquering the young people of the district; they already in hundreds put forth wings and rush like eagles to bask in the divine sunshine.

And with this vital Christianity came holiness of life – Drunkards gave up their reverie. The taverns over Christmas were empty. The quarrymen, rather than spending what little they had on drink, took their wages home to their families. At one point the police had nothing better to do than form a choir, to go round the churches singing!

It Produced Great Evangelistic Activity

When Andrew first came to a realization of who Jesus was, he immediately went to find his brother, Simon, and bring him to the Messiah.[12] So also when the people of Bethesda felt the work of the Holy Spirit amongst them, they had to tell others. By the time Joseph Jenkins came to preach, there were students there from Bangor, and men and women from surrounding villages. The prayer meetings were full of supplication for family members – some for the boys 'in that terrible place – South Wales' with all its evil influences. Others for husbands long held under by the power of drink. And then within three days of the Hurricane of the Holy Spirit, Job went to Betws y Coed to preach on Christmas Day, taking with him some who had been set alight by the heavenly fire to give their testimony. By the end of the day, revival had reached Betws y Coed. The activity was intense: in January 1905 Job preached twenty-eight

---

[12] John 1:41.

times, held open air meetings in Llangefni and other places; lectured on Williams Pantycelyn twice, led forty-three prayer meetings, and four Seiadau (spiritual societies). He visited Capel Curig, Abergwyngregyn, Penygroes, Niwbwrch, Colwyn Bay, Glan Conwy, Aberffraw, Rhosgoch, Garreglefn, Llangwyllog, Caeathro, Deganwy, and Dinorwig. And this intense activity would continue without much abatement for several months. He received a postcard from Joseph Jenkins in March,

> 'Voice has gone. The nervous system is protesting. I must be quiet for a while. It's hard. I've never had such a fever of a passion for preaching before. What a pity that twenty years of sleeping have passed.

Job also had to rest up – with the flu in March – but he was preaching again as soon as he could, and whilst there was much work to be done in Bethesda – whenever he was there he was leading frequent prayer meetings – he was away frequently right through to the summer months and beyond.

HIS METHOD

Since much is made of the methods used by Evan Roberts and others, it is interesting to note how Job went about the work. He would take some with him, to take part – some to sing godly songs, others to give their testimony. But he also took a care to emphasize the place of preaching the Word. He expected the people to respond to the truth preached. There were times when the Spirit overcame everything. The last Sunday in April he could not get further than giving out the text; the place was awash with repentant tears and people being brought through the valley of conviction of sin, to a place of praise.[13] At another Presbytery meeting, where he had spoken on a theological matter, he was asked to sing – he had a beautiful voice and he sang one of the revival songs – a song about the people whom Jesus called, with the refrain, 'Call me also, Sweetest Jesus, to follow Thee'. The place became a sea of tears.

But these were the exceptions. So whilst there were others who were denigrating preaching, saying that singing and praying were to carry the day, Job believed that preaching would last throughout the days of this world. And the message preached should be Christ and the cross – 'This is the gospel that still wins souls for the Son of God, and builds up the saints.'

He travelled much in North Wales especially, and was the instrument of bringing revival to a number of places, but it was through preaching the word of God that he did this. He believed that the Spirit has ordained the use of means, and Job insisted that the preaching of the word had to remain central.

He also wrote about what was happening, and when some demanded royalties for their accounts, he made a point of freely sharing what God had

---

[13] J. T. Job Diary, 30 April 1905.

done. The letter he received in May 1904 from his father-in-law had been instrumental in helping him, so he wanted to encourage others.

It Encountered Resistance

The work of revival often finds resistance from unexpected quarters. One of the most difficult aspects of the work at Bethesda for Job was the way some resisted the influences of the work that was happening there. We have already mentioned the strike. Job had terrible trouble with some church members – they refused to come to the revival prayer meetings, or preaching meetings. They knew that if they came, they would have to forgive. They would have to confess the hate they felt towards the strike breakers. They had lost loved ones. They had had families breaking up. They felt they were justified in holding a grudge. They did not want to forgive or forget. So they refused to come and resisted the influences of the revival.

It gave a Thirst for the Felt Presence of God

The work could only be furthered through the power of the Holy Spirit. So we read in the diaries, time and time again, after noting what the meeting was – Preaching in _____; or Prayer meeting for the women, Prayer meeting for the young people, etc. Then we have an assessment: 'Great anointing'; 'Great light'; 'Jesus is here'. At other times you get a sense of disappointment: 'Not much light tonight'; 'Felt great hardness'. They sensed the difference between man-made blessing and God's presence. There was a thirst to share the genuine. Job travelled to Liverpool to hear Evan Roberts, having heard so much about the blessing upon the man – but even there he noted differences between one meeting: 'Great anointing', and another, 'not so powerful'.

The letter he received in May 1904 from New Quay had been a means of quickening his own desire for God to work, so he went to various places to share what God was doing, and was sometimes disappointed in the lack of reaction. 'Great hardness in this place' – but then he would write in his diary, 'Things are beginning to warm up', and then, 'The fire is breaking through'. What lasting effects the revival had is difficult to assess. Church membership did not keep up during the following years, and the reason for this may be manifold. Many families left the area to find work because of the downturn in the slate industry. Many others within ten years were sent to the trenches in the First World War, and never came back.

Within ten years, Job himself had re-married and moved away to Pembrokeshire to minister in Fishguard. But his testimony was that in the 1904–5 revival something happened which left its effect on him for the rest of his life. Although well known as a hymn writer, he did not compose much during the heat of the revival. Years later however he wrote hymns which have an intensely personal nature, and show that his experience then of God was something which stayed with him throughout his years.

And he held to the belief that the gospel of Christ crucified was the only hope for the Welsh nation. A number of his hymns contain confession for national sins of pride and unbelief. In 1918 he again won the chair in the National Eisteddfod, this time for a long poem in strict metre, where he traced the story of Christianity through the history of the Welsh nation, and to him the only path to offer any hope for the future was the one leading to the cross of Christ. In a day when many turned from the Calvinist traditions of their denominations, for him, the revival had reinforced the message of Christ crucified, and the effect lasted throughout his life until he died in 1938.

CHAPTER 12

The Church in Wales and the Revival of 1904-5

Noel Gibbard

Discussing the relationship of the Church in Wales to the revival of 1904–5 is a topic which has been neglected. Almost a century ago J. Vyrnwy Morgan[1] drew attention to the influence of the spiritual awakening on the Church. And, more recently, David Jenkins,[2] Roger Brown[3] and R. Tudur Jones have drawn attention to this neglect and noted some facts to explain the relationship.[4] There is plenty of room to expand.

Before the revival Dean Howell expressed his heart's desire to see a revival in the land. He welcomed the intention to hold the Keswick conference at Llandrindod, and Anglicans were on the stage during the 1903 and 1904 meetings.[5] Societies and unions were formed to pray specifically for the Church's spiritual needs and these were attended by both clerics and lay people. The Daily Prayer Union was instituted in Britain and other countries, with the Bishop of Durham as its patron and the Bishop of Liverpool its president. When the revival came it was welcomed by the Bishop of St David's and other leader of the Church in Wales. In general, the revival was welcomed within the Church – sometimes warmly and more warily in other cases. There were, however, some instances of opposition to it.[6]

---

[1] J. Vyrnwy Morgan, *The Welsh Religious Revival 1904-5* (London, 1909), p. 113.
[2] David Jenkins, 'The Religious Revival of 1904-1905', *Agricultural community in south-west Wales at the turn of the twentieth century* (Cardiff, 1971).
[3] Roger L. Brown, *The Welsh Evangelicals* (Cardiff, 1986).
[4] R. Tudur Jones, *Ffydd ac Argyfwng Cenedl*, vol. 2, (Abertawe, 1982), pp. 123, 147, 152, 201.
[5] 'Cymanfa Llandrindod Er dyfnhau Bywyd Ysbrydol', *Y Tyst*, 29 July 1903, 9; ibid. 18 February 1904, 5; 'Convention at Llandrindod Wells', *The Radnorshire Express*, 13 August 1903, 5; Brynmor Pierce Jones, *Spiritual History of Keswick in Wales, 1903-1983* (Cwmbrân, 1989); Jessie Penn-Lewis, *The Awakening in Wales* (Overcomer, n.d.), 25-7.
[6] For example, *St David's Diocesan Gazette*, January-April, August 1905; *Royal Commission on the Church in Wales*, 1911, vol.2, book 1, pp. 3572-4.

Churches

Some individual churches felt the effects of the revival. A number of churches on Anglesey were stirred, especially in Holyhead.[7] Particular examples are the events which occurred in the churches of the Deanery of Arllechwedd. Even before November 1904, the parish churches were filled with a desire to deepen and intensify their spiritual lives. Their wish was fulfilled during the revival as can be seen in the Deanery records: 'Comments on the course that the revival had taken showed that the churchmen of Arllechwedd had not only come to terms with it, but had welcomed it and profited by it'.[8]

Church Pastoral Aid Society (CPAS)

Many churches were supported by the 'Church Pastoral Aid Society'.[9] This trust's aim was to provide support for evangelical incumbents and churches and also financial aid to the churches. The revival was welcomed by a substantial number of these churches. In the Diocese of Llandaf one can name the churches of Rhymney, Taff Vale, Blaenavon, Caerphilly, Ferndale, Treherbert, Tylorstown and Ystradyfodwg. One of the most enthusiastic was the Vicar of Rhymney. Here is his testimony:

> When I was going round the congregation to see if any prodigal had returned, old people over sixty years of age were weeping like little children, on their knees. When the Revival commenced in the West, I called the parishioners together for prayer on Monday, November 21, and on the following Saturday we had hundreds of people in the church. We continued the meetings every evening for the following fortnight, and God blessed us in a special way, for we have received seventy-one names to join the Church, all adults and over sixteen years; out of these about thirty-three have never been confirmed.[10]

The first week of 1905 was set aside for prayer. In the Diocese of St David's the effects of the revival were felt at Pen-bre, Brynaman, Cwmaman and Swansea. The Vicar of Cwmaman used to give the congregation an opportunity to confess Christ as their Saviour. He asked all who wished to confess to stand up and, on one occasion, ten strapping young men got to their feet:

> They were now beckoned to and invited to come forward, which they did – walking through the midst of the large congregation to a place reserved in front of

---

[7] 'The Church of England thoroughly Aroused, *The British Weekly*, 2 February 1905, 448.

[8] 'The Rural Deanery of Arllechwedd', *Cylchgrawn Llyfrgell Genedlaethol Cymru*, 18 (1973), 163.

[9] For information on the Society's work see Brown, *The Welsh Evangelicals*, chap. 4.

[10] 'The Revival in Wales', *Church and People,* February 1905; ibid. 'Notes of the Month'.

the pulpit. At further weekly and Sunday services similar results followed – though in smaller numbers.[11]

Two full of enthusiasm were Cecil Lillingston, vicar of Sketty (1903–8)[12] and Talbot Rice, vicar of Swansea (1902–9).[13] Sketty was formerly a high church parish but it was transformed under Cecil Lillingston's guidance. He emphasized the value of studying the Bible and organized regular prayer meetings. He also arranged a weekly Communion service and a church meeting on Wednesday. Talbot Rice was a devotional man, a careful pastor with a missionary zeal. He used to hold open air meetings in his parish. The work of these two men, and support from the CPAS, turned Swansea into one of the most evangelical centres of the Established Church. Both welcomed the revival without any reservations.

Evangelizing

One way of promoting the revival was evangelizing. The Church in Wales had a home missionary in the diocese of St David's before 1904, Canon Camber Williams. A native of Llanystumdwy, the Canon was a priest, missionary, lecturer and editor.[14] His campaigns were characterized by personal enquiry and he emphasized the importance of prayer and reading the Bible. This was the case with the meetings held at Nevern during October 1904, with one of the Bowens of Llwyn-gwair – a descendant of the family which had welcomed John Wesley on his journey through the west[15] – at the organ. The Canon used a hymn book most appropriate for evangelizing work: *Hymn Book for Missions & Sunday Schools, also suitable for Advent and Lent, together with forms of worship* (*Hymnal of the parochial mission*). He liked the revival hymns and one of his favourites was 'Y Gŵr wrth ffynnon Jacob', on the tune 'Bryniau Cassia'. Another favourite was 'Beth yw'r udgorn glywai'n seinio?' At St David's Church, Maesteg, the Canon sang the first four lines of the first two verses, and the congregation the last four lines. Camber Williams sang the

---

[11] 'The Revival in Wales. What our clergy say', *Church and People*, February 1905.

[12] F. G. Cowley, *A History of St Paul's Church Sketty* (St Paul's, 2001), pp. 22-4.

[13] Roger L. Brown, 'A Man in a Hurry: Talbot Rice: Vicar of Swansea', *Minerva*, 4 (1996) (Journal of the Royal Institute South Wales, Swansea).

[14] He was born in 1860 and educated at Keble College, Oxford. He served in several parishes before being appointed lecturer at Lampeter. He was chosen to serve a home missionary in 1899, and appointed Canon of St David's in 1908. One of the staunchest defenders of the Established Church, he died at Llandudno in 1924. Information received from Huw Tegid Roberts, Bangor.

[15] 'Nevern', *The Cardigan and Tivyside Advertiser*, 30 September 1904.

question in the third verse with the congregation answering. The Canon joined with the congregation in singing the last four lines.[16]

In Loughor and the surrounding area, Canon Williams arrived to fan the flames because the fire was already burning there. Meetings were held in the Parish Church and in the National School (where Evan Roberts had been a pupil). One of the two Mary Davieses and her family were faithful church members. The Rector tried to lead the meetings in accordance with the usual practice but, by 20 December 1904, all formality had been set aside. The speaker was the Vicar of Swansea, Talbot Rice, and the congregation was overcome with feelings and emotions. The meeting was held in English but, suddenly, the Welsh speakers broke out in praise of God.[17] Camber Williams and five other clerics joined in assisting with the work. The people flocked to the meetings and then returned to their own communities to spread the revival, and it is said: 'The experience at Loughor was repeated in parish after parish as the revival spread.'[18]

At Loughor and, after moving to Cocket, Swansea, Camber Williams's message remained the same. His central emphasis was on prayer and he used to urge the congregation to pray to God to reveal His will for them personally. Whilst the congregation was singing the last hymn (usually the favourite 'Y Gŵr wrth ffynnon Jacob'), Canon Williams and his assistant, James Jones, used to distribute cards from seat to seat. On these were printed a number of questions:[19]

'Have I given myself to God?'
'Do I read some portion of the bible every day?'
'Do I hold family prayer at home?'
'Do I pray for others?'
'What am I doing to bring those around me to God?'

The congregation was pressed upon to earnestly consider these questions.

The Rev. Mr Jones, Solva, was the missionary at Llantrisant. During his sermon in one meeting the congregation started singing 'Throw out the lifeline'. The preacher left his pulpit and walked down the church; he then went down on his knees in prayer and the congregation did likewise. The old Welsh hymns were sung and, at the end of the service, the missionary announced that there would be an opportunity for people to give their personal testimony in another service during the week.[20]

---

[16] 'Maesteg Aroused', *The Evening Express*, 7 December 1904, 4; 'Canon's Revival in Maesteg', *South Wales Daily Press*, 7 December 1904.

[17] Brown, *Welsh Evangelicals*, p. 154;'The Welsh Revival', *South Wales Daily News*, 14 December 1904.

[18] *St David's Diocesan Gazette*, December 1904, 4.

[19] 'South Wales Revival Fever', *South Wales Daily Post*, 15 December 1904, 14.

[20] *Church and People*, 1905, 250-1.

Zealous evangelizing took place in the Diocese of Llandaf. Six missionaries were charged with evangelizing in Cardiff. A campaign had been organized before the revival but, according the Vicar of Canton, the revival gave the campaign a particular impetus. At a quarter past seven every evening, the Church members, including the choir in their surplices, marched along the streets. Revival hymns were sung in the meetings.[21]

Collaborating with Other Denominations

What about joint meetings with other denominations? There is enough evidence available for these meetings as well. This is surprising perhaps, because this was the period of heated debate concerning the Education Act of 1902. According to this Act nonconformists were expected to provide financial support for Church schools. This led to tensions, and even bitterness, in several circles. But the Holy Spirit demanded its place as well. There was collaboration in Loughor and the surrounding area, the home territory of Evan Roberts himself. As has already been mentioned Mary Davies, the soloist, and her father – who used to attend revival meetings with his daughter – were Church members. Mary Davies, Gorseinon, and Annie Davies, Maesteg, were invited to Llandilo Tal-y-bont Church (which is now at St Fagans). The Vicar preached on Luke 2:20 (Mary's song) and urged the congregation to praise God. The two sisters sang 'Ni fuasai gennyf obaith am ddim ond fflamau syth', and afterwards the Vicar continued to preach. The girls sang once again whilst the Vicar walked down the Church, and the congregation joined in the singing. The Vicar returned to the altar and the girls sang once more. The collection was completely forgotten.[22] The same was the story at Pontarddulais and Llanedi.[23]

The collaboration continued in South Cardiganshire, at New Quay, Cilcennin and Abermeurig, and within the Diocese at Nevern and Pencader. The Vicar of Abermeurig used to attend the Nonconformists' meetings, and invited them in turn to the Church. He experienced the phenomenon of hearing singing in the air, as had happened during the Beddgelert revival in 1817 and the revival of 1859.[24] The Rector of Aberporth attended Evan Roberts's meeting at Blaenannerch on 14 March 1905. It was at that meeting that he said that there was an impediment in the congregation and referred to one person by

---

[21] 'Mission at Canton', *The Evening Express*, 25 February 1905, 3; 'Cardiff Church Mission', *The Christian Herald*, 16 March 1905; *Royal Commission on the Church in Wales, 1911*, vol. 2, book 1, pp. 12310-1.

[22] 'Revival Outburst at Church', *The Welshman*, 30 December 1904; 'Sparks from the Great fire', *South Wales Daily Post*, 5 January 1905.

[23] Ibid. 'Church and Revival', 8 December 1904.

[24] *Y Diwygiad a'r Diwygwyr*, p. 326.

name. In the Rector's opinion Evan Roberts looked tired although this was straight after a period of recuperation at Neath.[25]

The Vicar, E. D. Glanley, was at the fore with the unified meetings at Ystradgynlais. At a unified meeting it was agreed that the denominations would hold separate meetings initially, and then come together for a unified service. That meeting, held at the Church, was attended by eight hundred people. A sermon was delivered by Owen Prys (Calvinistic Methodist), and other Nonconformist ministers took part in the meeting. The Vicar testified to the healing influence of the revival.[26]

In the north a prominent place was given to collaboration at Rhosllannerchrugog and Pwllheli. In both places the Holy Spirit swept tens of people into Christ's kingdom. This was a cause for great joy for the Vicar of Rhos, Thomas Prichard.[27] He greatly enjoyed praising God with the Nonconformists and was completely at ease with the miners, with their black faces but clean hearts. He invited a Nonconformist minister and Maud Davies to the Sunday school and then went with them to the Sunday school at Capel Mawr, where he delivered a sobering address. This was what he wrote at the end of January 1905:

> The result in my own mission of our Welsh church is the addition of thirty to this church. Most emphatically the great bulk exhibit signs of true conversion in word and deed, in attendance at services, mission work, institution of family prayer. The mass of our people are (sic) appreciative and sympathetic. The Welsh wholly so. The Revival is pronouncedly Welsh, Rhos being a Gibraltar of Welsh on the border. Of course the human touches everything in church and chapels, but were there not cartloads of men in cold, formal services?[28]

When Evan Roberts reached Liverpool the Vicar went there to listen to him and was greatly pleased.

Thomas Prichard travelled to various places to preach. Strong spiritual influences were felt under his ministry at Chirk. He also ventured further afield to Pwllheli where the revival flames burned strongly. There he joined the parish Vicar and two clerics from Merionethshire. Unified meetings were held there under the guidance of Henry Rees (Baptist) and Canon Davies. The other three clerics had come to assist. Meetings were held at St Peter's Church and at the Town Hall. In one meeting Thomas Prichard gave an 'excellent address'.[29]

---

[25] NLW 15668B; David Jenkins, 'The Religious Revival of 1904-1905', *Agricultural community*.

[26] 'Every barrier down', *South Wales Daily Post*, 21 December 1904; *Church and People*, February 1905.

[27] 'The Vicar of Rhos's Sympathy', *The North Wales Guardian*, 27 January 1905; *Church and People*, 1905.

[28] 'Rhos and Ponkey', *The Wrexham Advertiser*, 1 April 1905.

[29] 'Pwllheli', *Yr Udgorn*, 15, 22, March 1905.

Opposition

The revival within the Church was not without its critics. Several churches commented from a distance. They feared an overflow of emotion and believed that many of the revival meetings lacked dignity. It was also difficult to forget the controversies relating to the Education Act of 1902. At Llanllwch, Glan-y-fferi and Llansadwrn in Carmarthenshire the Church refused to collaborate with the other denominations, and churchgoers in Wrexham and Llanelli kept their distance and looked at the revival from afar so to speak.[30]

There is therefore enough evidence of the revivalist surge within the Church in Wales. The churches were revitalized spiritually. There was much better attendance at services, families started to worship at home in some cases and a missionary zeal was fostered. There was also a pronounced increase in the number of communicants.[31]

Figures of Easter Communicants:

1905	134,234
1906	135,234
1907	138,172
1908	144, 411
1909	146,407
1910	155,191

A steady increase is therefore apparent for the years 1905 until 1912. Undoubtedly the revival was one of the main reasons for this increase. It is possible that there were other influences, such as social considerations and the personal influence of particular incumbents or bishops.

The Church in Wales succeeded surprisingly in tasting the revival and safeguarding its own identity at the same time. It was possible to sing Church hymns and the new revival hymns, have personal testimonies and the 'Te Deum'. At least two authors have suggested that we can speak of two revivals, one amongst the Nonconformists and the other within the Church in Wales.[32] The former was characterized by profound feelings, extreme at times, whereas the characteristics of the latter were good order and teaching. It is very doubtful that this view can be accepted as it oversimplifies the issue. Teaching was not a prominent feature in a number of Church meetings. They were often overwhelmed by feeling, exactly as was the case in the Nonconformist

---

[30] *Royal Commission on the Church of England, 1911*, vol. 2, book 1, 3572-4, 2484; vol. 4, book 3, p. 48494.

[31] John Williams, *Digest of Welsh Historical Studies* (Cardiff, Pontypool, 1985), p. 257.

[32] William K. Kay, *Pentecostals in Britain* (Paternoster, 2000), p. 9; Brown, *Welsh Evangelicals*, p. 155.

meetings. On the one hand R. B. Jones, Joseph Jenkins and J. T. Job placed an emphasis on preaching, but Camber Williams gave a place to the sermon as well. It is true that the Church safeguarded its own characteristics but this was not because the revival within it was different in essence to the revival in other denominations. It was merely channelled differently. One of the differences between the Churches and the other denominations was the liturgical and sacerdotal emphasis. In the missions especially, Communion was held early in the morning. Camber Williams used to do this regularly. As the correspondent of *The Church Times* said when referring to Evan Roberts 'The work of sacramental energy is not dwelt upon, and here we part company.'[33] However, sacerdotal grace was not elevated above evangelical grace conveyed through God's word. Consequently, an emphasis was placed on personal conversion. The two aspects, the sacerdotal and evangelical, were combined. Howell Harris would have been much pleased with this emphasis.

Both Camber Williams and Thomas Prichard gave an assessment of the revival.[34] Both agreed that its stirrings were God's work and, despite some weaknesses, the also believed that Evan Roberts was a man of God. Both believed that the revival had shaken the country from its slumber and they said harsh things about the spiritual condition of Wales prior to 1904, noting amongst other things, that there was too much organization, formality and frostiness. During the revival a new life was breathed through the churches and feeling in religion was given its appropriate place. There was a dire need to release the feelings. Camber Williams welcomed 'enthusiasm' but he was suspicious and wary of 'excitement'.

It was a source of joy to both to see so many converts with the fruits of grace so apparent in their lives. More respect was shown to the Bible and more faithfulness towards Communion, and more families conducted worship at home. The revival was the people's movement and the Church was forced to think anew about the place of lay members in its worship and activities. They believed that the revival would promote the influence of the Church in Wales.

Neither of them was blind to the dangers of the revival. Camber Williams referred to superficial feeling. They clearly maintained that 'excitement is not conversion', a message very similar to that which Keri Evans regularly proclaimed, namely that 'conviction is not conversion'.[35] The answer was to teach the converts about dogma, the sacraments and the practical, personal life. Also, according to Thomas Prichard, the Church should work on a social and personal basis as well spiritually. There was a need for better houses for the workers and more just laws, especially to control the sale of alcohol.[36]

---

[33] Quoted from Phillips, *Evan Roberts*, p. 333.
[34] Camber Williams: *St David's Diocesan Gazette*, Jan-April, 1905; Thomas Prichard: *An After Reflection on the late Great Revival in Wales* (1908).
[35] *St David's Diocesan Gazette*, Jan-April, 38.
[36] Prichard, *An After Reflection*, p. 8.

CHAPTER 13

The Influence of the 1905 Revival Amongst the Merseyside Welsh Community

D. Ben Rees

Liverpool and its satellite towns like Bootle and Crosby had a large Welsh-speaking population at the beginning of the twentieth century.[1] It had a larger Welsh-speaking presence than Cardiff or Swansea, Wrexham or Newport. Indeed it had some of the largest Welsh Nonconformist chapels anywhere in the United Kingdom. At Princes Road Presbyterian Church of Wales in Toxteth it had a large congregation as members and adherents and in the person of the Reverend Dr John Williams, one of the most powerful preachers of his era. He was also a great propagator of the revival. One of his contemporaries in Liverpool aptly described him, as one who had thrown himself 'body, soul and spirit into the activities of the Welsh religious revival'.[2]

John Williams was the instigator of the revival amongst the Welsh of Liverpool. He and two of his fellow Welsh Presbyterian ministers in south Liverpool had arranged in the autumn of 1904 a gathering in preparation for a revival.[3] This meeting which catered mainly for young people had soon spread its influence into other Welsh Presbyterian chapels. It spread also into the activities and meetings of a new sect which had arisen amongst the Welsh of Liverpool, in the clash of personalities and an accusation of secret alcoholic drinking and flirting with loose women that took place between the Minister of the Chatham Street Welsh Presbyterian Chapel, Reverend W. O. Jones and some of his elders. The conflict escalated when the Liverpool Presbytery became involved as well as the North Wales Association. W. O. Jones decided to leave the Connexion and began his own section, known as *Eglwys Rydd y Cymry* (The Welsh Free Church), an organization which soon attracted a sizeable number of dissatisfied Welsh Presbyterians on 20 November 1904 in one of the Welsh Free Church chapels in Donaldson Street, Liverpool, during a

---

[1] W. H. Parry maintained in 1867 that Liverpool had a population of 520,000. Of these 120,000 had been born in Ireland, 80,000 in Wales, 40,000 in Scotland and 5,000 in the Isle of Man: 245,000 Celts. See W. H. Parry, *Y Cymry yn Liverpool eu Manteision a'u Hanfanteision* (Liverpool, 1868), p. 45.

[2] R. R. Hughes, *Y Parchedig John Williams, DD, Brynsiencyn* (Caernarfon, 1929), p. 156.

[3] Ibid.

lively debate on the merits of preaching or congregational singing the Holy Spirit came on ninety per cent of those gathered for the occasion.[4]

One must emphasize also the close connection of the Liverpool Welsh community with some of the early pioneers of the revival. Reverend Joseph Jenkins of New Quay in south Cardiganshire had been a minister in an English-speaking Welsh Presbyterian church in Anfield and the saintly Anglican, Reverend David Howell (Llawdden), had a son as a priest in St Bees Church, Toxteth.[5] The two American evangelists Reuben A. Torrey and Charles Alexander arranged a huge crusade over Christmas 1904 and the New Year in a huge pavilion which seated eleven thousand opposite the Edge Lane Presbyterian Church of Wales, a chapel which experienced the revival. On the platform Charles Alexander arranged a choir of three thousand to bring a special atmosphere to the meetings and amongst the choristers there was a sizeable section from the Liverpool Welsh community. They were thrilled at the opportunity.

The Welsh revival had become a reality in that period to the Reverend W. O. Jones himself.[6] He took part in the Preaching Services of a nondenominational Nonconformist chapel known as Sutton Oak Welsh Chapel, which is situated between the town of St Helens and its neighbouring settlement of St Helens Junction. This event was held on Boxing Day 1904. The preaching service became a revivalist meeting. W. O. Jones had an extremely high regard of the young revivalist, Evan John Roberts. Indeed some of the most fair-minded appraisals of Evan Roberts came from the pen of W. O. Jones in the monthly magazine of his new religious organization, *Llais Rhyddid* (The Voice of Freedom). Evan Roberts, according to the appraisal of W. O. Jones, inspired everyone of Welsh extraction of all age groups. He said: 'Yn sicr, nid oes yr un esboniad yn bosibl arno ef, ac ar ei waith, heblaw y goruwchnaturiol. Rhaid mai offeryn ydyw yn llaw Duw.' (Surely there is no possible explanation for him, or his work, except the supernatural. He must be a vehicle in the hand of God.)

Evan Roberts was in Jones's opinion a master communicator. W. O. Jones with one of his lay leaders travelled all the way from Liverpool by train to

---

[4] 'Y Diwygiad', *Llais Rhyddid*, Cyf III, Rhif 9, 1904, p. 202.

[5] There were Welsh-speaking ministers within travelling distance of Liverpool who had been prominent in the Keswick Movement. Take Rev. John Rhys Davies (1855–1926), a native of New Quay where Joseph Jenkins ministered and who became a Baptist minister in Southport in 1902. They had been praying for a revival in Wales since 1896. M. N. Garrard, *Mrs Penn-Lewis, A Memoir* (London, 1930), p.221. Another of the Keswick supporters was the Rev. D. Wynne Evans (1861–1927) a minister with the Congregationalists in Chester since 1902. He wrote in Welsh an important book on the phenomenon of the Revival, *Yr Ysbryd Glân a Diweddar-Wlaw y Diwygiad* ('The Holy Spirit and the Latter Rain of the Revival') (Chester, 1906).

[6] 'Y Diwygiad', p. 214; and 'Nodiadau Misol', *Llais Rhyddid*, vol. 3, no. 10.

Swansea to see the revivalist at his task of winning souls.[7] He wrote of his experience: 'Ar ôl ei weled a'i glywed, gellir ffurfio dirnadaeth fwy clir am broffwydi yr Hen Destament ac Apostolion y Testament Newydd. Diolch i Dduw am un arall o broffwydi Cymru.'(After seeing and hearing him, one can form a clearer appreciation of the prophets of the Old Testament and the Apostles of the New Testament. Thanks be to God for another prophet of Wales.)[8]

The tragedy of the Evan Roberts crusade in Liverpool was this: that one of his most sincere supporters, W. O. Jones was forced to change his initial opinions of the revivalist and that Evan Roberts was dragged into the bitter conflict between the Welsh Presbyterians and those who had left Presbyterianism for a new spiritual home on Merseyside.

Evan Roberts had his reservations on the proposed visit to the thriving Welsh-language community of Merseyside. He spent a whole week at Neath in total silence before travelling to his preparatory college at Newcastle Emlyn and south Cardiganshire. Evan Roberts then went home to Loughor where he decided to give away every penny that he possessed, most of it I presume had been his savings and gifts from his zealous evangelical well wishers. Roberts gave £200 to clear the debt on the small building known as Pisgah, Bwlchymynydd where he had been a Sunday school teacher and then a superintendent and £150 towards the funds of Moriah, Welsh Presbyterian Chapel, Loughor, the chapel where he and his parents were members and which had a financial burden to shoulder. There he gave £10 to a fellow student at the Academy in Newcastle Emlyn, David Williams of Llansamlet. This was a great deal of money, comparable in our day to some £36,000. Then on the railway station at Loughor he realized that he had some money in his suit which he gave to his brother Dan Roberts to hand over to an elderly and poor female who lived in the village, so that he could arrive at Lime Street Railway Station in Liverpool without a penny.[9] He caught the train to Cardiff and then joined with his sister Mary Roberts, the soloist Annie Davies of Nantyffyllon, Maesteg, Reverend D. M. Phillips, Tylorstown and his niece Miss Edith Jones Phillips.[10] D. M. Phillips, Tylorstown and his great friend, Evan Roberts stayed at 1 Ducie Street with Mrs Edwards but his enthusiastic supporters soon came to know of his whereabouts within a few hours. Ducie Street had a large crowd waiting for a glimpse of the Welsh revivalist.

The crusade in Liverpool and Merseyside was so different to anything that Evan Roberts had experienced in the valleys of South Wales. There he had moved on his own initiative as led by the Holy Spirit from one village to

---

[7] Ionawr 1905, p.238; W. O. Jones, 'Evan Roberts y Diwygiwr', *Llais Rhyddid*, vol. 3, no. 2 (1905), p. 245.
[8] 'Nodiadau Misol', *Llais Rhyddid*, vol. 3, no. 12 (Mawrth 1905), p. 263.
[9] D. M. Phillips, *Evan Roberts a'i waith* (Dolgellau, 1912), p. 335.
[10] Ibid.

another, and from one valley to another, but his campaign in Liverpool had been thoroughly prepared by the Liverpool Welsh Free Church Council. The Council had been extremely thorough, canvassing through the members of the various chapels of every denomination, all the houses in Liverpool and Garston as well as Bootle and Birkenhead and had discovered thirty thousand Welsh speakers. Amongst this large community there were at least four thousand who had no chapel or church allegiance.[11] Seventeen meetings were to be arranged for him in centres in south Liverpool, central Liverpool, Bootle, Seacombe and Birkenhead. This was to be a concentrated effort and there were so many Welsh communities denied a visit, like the towns of St Helens, Southport, Wigan, Ashton-in-Makerfield, Warrington, Runcorn and Ellesmere Port.

The campaign began in Liverpool at the large cathedral-like chapel of Princes Road on Wednesday 29 March 1905.[12] The end result was that there were more people outside the chapel than were inside. This became the pattern for the Merseyside campaign. The largest Welsh as well as the English Nonconformist chapels on Merseyside were packed, even the large Sun Hall in Kensington which catered for a congregation of six thousand. Posters of Evan Roberts were to be seen in hundreds of shop windows and in the homes of the welcoming Welsh exiles. The Welsh community was making an impact in the city of Liverpool, and the leading ministers of the Protestant faith were also attending the meetings.

But the campaign was beset from the beginning by the festering disagreement amongst the religious adherents. Hundreds of Welsh Presbyterians had left their chapels to form the new chapels and many of the leading ministers, such as the Reverend Griffiths Ellis of Bootle, had been deeply hurt. Griffith Ellis had laboured all his life at Bootle. A student of Balliol College, Oxford he had given of his utmost to Stanley Road Presbyterian Church of Wales. He admitted that he had experienced a worst bereavement in the loss of a hundred and sixty members who had left to start a Welsh chapel 400 yards from his citadel than in the death of his eldest daughter, Leta.[13] By the third meeting on 31 March in Birkenhead the confrontation had again shown its ugly head. Evan Roberts went so far as to claim that the chapel had to be cleansed as there were people present who could not forgive each other.[14] A young member of Eglwys Rydd y Cymry stood on

---

[11] Phillips, *Evan Roberts a'i waith*, p. 337.

[12] R. Tudur Jones, *Ffydd ac Argyfwng Cenedl: Hanes Crefydd yng Nghymru 1890-1914 Cyfrol 2: Dryswch a Diwygiad* (Abertawe, 1982), p. 168.

[13] John Owen, *Cofiant y Parch Griffith Ellis, MA, Bootle* (Liverpool, 1923), pp. 55-6. Leta Eleanor Ellis died 6 May 1897, before her twentieth birthday.

[14] 'Nodiadau', *Llais Rhyddid*, vol. 3, no. 11 (1905), p. 279. Many felt that in the atmosphere of the revival the time was ripe for them to shake hands and to be friends and the Central Committee of the Eglwys Rydd y Cymry sent a pleading letter to the Council of the Welsh Free Churches of Liverpool for reconciliation. The response

his feet and prayed with fervour on God to bend the people to work together in the Welsh Nonconformist vineyard on Merseyside. But Evan Roberts was not exhibiting the wisdom that W. O. Jones expected of him, he insisted that the Holy Spirit was being challenged and a large number of Welsh Christians were stubbornly refusing to forgive one another in the forgiveness of the Gospel. The following day, on 1 April, in the Wesleyan Welsh Methodist Chapel in Shaw Street he announced suddenly that the Holy Spirit had left them as orphans as there were five leaders present, three of them ministers of religion who were extremely jealous of the successful work carried out by him through the power of the resurrection.[15] The congregation was somewhat startled by his boast and by his accusation. The Reverend John Williams who knew the Liverpool Welsh better than the young twenty-six year-old revivalist made a valid effort to soothe the worshippers. He suggested that the meeting should be brought to a close.[16] His younger colleague Evan Roberts disagreed. The powerful and experienced John Williams had to acknowledge the impossible situation. For Evan Roberts could be extremely difficult within the confines of a huge meeting in particular to be persuaded to listen to anyone else. April 6 and 7 1905 were difficult days in his campaign. On 6 April he had gone to visit Hilbre Island to be with the Welsh-speaking lighthouse keeper, Lewis Jones known by his bardic name of Ynyswr (Islander). The press published an account of an accident which could have proved fatal that had occurred to him, and years later in his autobiography Lewis Jones claimed that there was no truth whatsoever in the story.[17] One has to remember that the press was very well represented in the Merseyside campaign. Reporters from the national press, *Daily Mail, Daily Dispatch* were present, as well as journalists from the Welsh dailies, *Western Mail, Liverpool Daily Post*, the Welsh-language press, *Yr Herald Gymraeg*, and the local press, like the *Liverpool Courier*. Many of these hacks were creating news, often exaggerating, enlarging it, suggesting that the Merseyside campaign was not as successful as the South Wales meetings had been with regard to the number of converts.

On 7 April the leading lights of the organizing committee, in particular the Secretary, Councillor Henry Jones, and Chairman, William Evans, who had served on the City Council had persuaded the Lord Mayor of Liverpool, Councillor John Lea to prepare a reception for the young revivalist at the Mansion House. Councillor John Lea was a coal magnate and a staunch

---

according to *Llais Rhyddid* was disappointing for the letter was brushed aside. A golden opportunity had been lost.

[15] R. Tudur Jones, *Ffydd ac Argyfwng Cenedl*, p. 168.

[16] Ibid.

[17] Lewis Jones, *Atgofion Ynyswr* (Lerpwl, 1939), p. 61. 'Ynyswr' or Lewis Jones states that 'the story was a big lie from beginning to end.' But the accident is recorded as a true account by the journalist Gwilym Hughes and the friend of Evan Roberts, Rev. Dr D. M. Phillips, Tylorstown, who wrote him a substantial biography in Welsh and English.

Protestant.[18] The Reverend John Williams presented Evan Roberts, who had spent most of his life as a miner in the Welsh Glamorganshire coalfield to the colliery owner of great wealth, 'Allow me, Lord Mayor to present to you Mr Evan Roberts, servant of the Lord Jesus Christ.'

The top table had been kept for five – Evan Roberts, the Reverend J. A. Kempthorne, Rector of Liverpool, the Reverend Dr John Watson, the Reverend John Williams and the Lord Mayor. It was an entirely new experience for Evan Roberts. Surrounded by the elite of the Liverpool political and religious life the young miner cum revivalist was completely lost. He refused to say a word at the reception to the dismay of the guests. However, the Reverend C. F. Aked, the radical minister of Pembroke Place Baptist Chapel, responded to the challenge, thanking the authorities and praising the young working-class hero. For Aked was an enthusiastic socialist.[19] The Reverend D. M. Phillips maintains that since their arrival in Liverpool Evan Roberts had received hundreds of letters and many of them were anonymous, extremely critical and some downright rude. According to his ministerial friend from the Rhondda it did not affect him.[20] I do not believe it. That night in Sun Hall before a large audience of at least six thousand he overstepped the mark from the beginning of the meeting to its end. He was nervous, grumpy and extremely irritable. Roberts was responsible for one confrontation after another. The first confrontation was to do with the effort of a person in the vast Hall to hypnotize him. Then he delivered a strange and completely uncharacteristic statement: 'Mae rhai ohonoch yn gweddïo ar yr Arglwydd i achub y person hwn. Ni allaf fi wneud hynny. Gallaf weddïo am ei symud oddi ar wyneb y ddaear, ond ni allaf ofyn i'r Arglwydd ei achub.' (Do not pray for him. I cannot do that. I can pray to remove him from the face of the earth, but I cannot ask the Lord to convert him.)[21]

Then Roberts attacked verbally an individual in the congregation who was in his opinion a negative critic. He had a message for him from the Holy Spirit: 'Os na chyffeswch, peidiwch â rhyfeddu os na fedrwch godi'ch llaw ar ôl heno. Yna byddai'n rhaid i chwi gario'r arwydd hyd eich bedd.' (If you do not

---

[18] John Lea (1850–1920) held a passionate Protestant ideology. He owned collieries in Lancashire and had been a Liberal Councillor on the City Council since 1890. A member of the Presbyterian Church of Scotland Lea was a strong supporter of the temperance movement. He was criticized by the Welsh bohemian artist, Augustus John, as a philistine. P. J. Waller, *Democracy and Sectarianism: a political and social history of Liverpool 1868-1939* (Liverpool, 1981), p. 498.

[19] Liverpool in all its history had few radical ministers of his calibre, and his campaigning efforts have been noted by Jan Sillers, *Salute to Pembroke: The Story of the Rise, Progress, Decline and Fall of a most remarkable, dissenting congregation, Pembroke Chapel, Liverpool 1838–1931* (Alsager, 1960), pp. 12-24.

[20] Phillips, *Evan Roberts a'i waith*, p. 337.

[21] R. Tudur Jones, *Ffydd ac Argyfwng Cenedl*, p. 170.

confess, do not be surprised if you cannot raise your hand after tonight. You will have to carry that sign with you to you grave.)[22]

Then the revivalist disturbed the large congregation by stating that this individual was a minister of religion. Two local Welsh Nonconformist ministers were greatly upset. One was the Welsh Baptist minister in Edge Lane, Hugh R. Roberts, and the other was the Welsh Independent Minister in Belmont Road on the border of Anfield and Newsham Park, the Reverend O. L. Roberts, one of the six from Liverpool who had travelled to Dowlais, near Merthyr Tydfil to persuade the revivalist to visit the Seaport to win souls for Christ. The congregation took the side of Evan Roberts, and the words 'cywilydd, cywilydd' (shame, shame) were uttered when the two ministers stood up for an explanation from the revivalist. John Williams intervened to bring the meeting to a dignified close, and Evan Roberts and his two female colleagues escaped from the Hall. The following day a well known hypnotist, Dr Walford Bodie who worked in the Lyric Theatre, admitted that he had sent his deputy along to hypnotize Evan Roberts.[23] The revivalist soon recovered his integrity and even George Wise, the militant Protestant, commentated publicly on the revivalist.[24] He was above everything else, admitted Wise, a ripe study for a psychologist. So was George Wise if he could admit it! Then on 10 April, at the English Congregationalist Chapel of Westminster Road, W. O. Jones took part in prayer, pleading for reconciliation. Evan Roberts was moved to tears. The following evening at the Welsh Wesleyan Methodist Chapel of Mynydd Seion in Princes Road, Evan Roberts made a critical appraisal in the name of God of Eglwys Rydd y Cymry: 'Rhoddodd Duw y neges honno imi ... Y mae a wnelo'r neges ag Eglwys Rydd y Cymry. Mae'r neges uniongyrchol oddi wrth Dduw – "Nid yw sylfeini'r eglwys honno ar y Graig". Dyna'r neges.' (God has given me this direct message ... The message has to do with the Free Church of the Welsh. It is a direct message from God – 'The foundation of this Church is not on the Rock'. That is the message.)[25]

The journalists were delighted. They went immediately to the home of the Reverend W. O. Jones in Percy Street and Gwilym Hughes was given the opportunity of interviewing him. No one in Welsh Nonconformist circles, besides D. M. Phillips and John Williams, had praised Evan Roberts like W. O. Jones. The pulpit giants of his day, in his opinion, could not be compared with the young revivalist: 'Ym mhob oedfa y mae'r effeithiau yn annisgrifiadwy a'r

---

[22] *Y Cymro* (13 April 1905), pp. 2-3, 5.

[23] R. Tudur Jones, *Ffydd ac Argyfwng Cenedl*, p. 170.

[24] Pastor George Wise (1856–1917) moved from London to Liverpool in 1888, and became an important figure in the sectarian conflict between Catholics and Protestants in the Everton/Scotland Road area. He was a militant Protestant leader, see P. J. Waller, *Democracy and Sectarianism*, pp. 117-18, 140, 166, 174-6, 188-9, 191-2, 198-206, 227-8, 230-2, 237-41, 244-47, 150-1, 257, 260, 265, 303, 313, 427, 429, 451, 517.

[25] R. Tudur Jones, *Ffydd ac Argyfwng Cenedl*, p. 170.

cynulleidfaoedd mawrion fel cŵyr toddedig yn ei ddwylaw.' (In every service the effects are indescribable, and the large congregations like melting wax in his hands.)[26] Consider also this opinion of Evan Roberts from the pen of W. O. Jones: 'Llefara yntau ar bob pwynt, fel un ag awdurdod ganddo; braidd na theimlech ambell funyd ei fod yn hawlio anffaeledigrwydd, fel genau i'r Ysbryd Glân.' (He speaks on every point, as one who has authority, you felt for some moments as if he claims infallibility as a spokesman of the Holy Spirit).[27]

But Evan Roberts had deliberately snubbed W. O. Jones. The leader of a new sect in Liverpool naturally changed his opinion of him. He became a dangerous critic of Evan Roberts and claimed that he was inspired by the occult in Liverpool, and that he had never before seen anyone pursuing occultism 'for the propagation of the Christian Religion'.[28] But if such a criticism was damaging, worse conflict was on the horizon, especially in the meeting arranged at Chatham Street where the devastating show-down between the Welsh Free Church and the Welsh Presbyterians began in 1900. This meeting was for men only and everything went well under the guidance of the Reverend Richard Humphreys who addressed the revivalist with these words and with anger in his voice: 'A wyt ti wedi dy gymodi â'th frawd cyn dod i'r cyfarfod heno? Pam wyt ti'n chwarae â phethau sanctaidd fel hyn.' (Have you been reconciled with your brother before coming here this evening? Why are you playing with holy things in this way?)[29]

The Reverend Daniel Hughes of Chester was referring to the relationship between Evan Roberts and W. O. Jones. He was not a man to be silenced and his latest biographer, Ivor T. Rees has called him The Sledgehammer Pastor.[30] A vigorous debate ensued between the evangelist and the ministers in the *sêt fawr* (big seat) of Chatham Street Chapel.

Daniel Hughes had a supporter in the person of a Presbyterian minister of Rhydlydan, near Pentrefoelas, the Reverend H. M. Roberts. He stood up and stated dogmatically, 'Nid gwaith yr Ysbryd Glân yw hwn ond gwaith athrylith dyn. Ffug yw popeth a ddigwyddodd yma heno.' (This is not the work of the Holy Spirit but the work of a man of genius. Fantasy is everything that has happened here tonight.)[31]

It was time to bring the service to an end. That night there was great excitement in Percy Street, the home of W. O. Jones, where Daniel Hughes stayed and within a few months he had moved to Liverpool as pastor of a

---

[26] W. O. Jones, *Evan Roberts y Diwygiwr*, p. 243.

[27] W. O. Jones, *Evan Roberts y Diwygiwr*, p. 246.

[28] *Llais Rhyddid*, vol. 4, 30-7, pp. 49-56.

[29] *Y Cymro*, 20 April 1905, p. 3.

[30] Ivor T. Rees, 'Sledgehammer Daniel Hughes, The Sledgehammer Pastor, 1875-1972', *Cylchgrawn Llyfrgell Genedlaethol Cymru*, vol. 32, no. 2 (2001), pp. 147-75.

[31] Rees, 'Sledgehammer Pastor', p. 149.

chapel belonging to the Disciples of Christ.[32] The following day, 15 April, a letter appeared in the *Liverpool Courier*, a bitter attack on Evan Roberts by Hughes.[33] He claimed that the revivalist belonged to the world of the occult and telepathy, and that he would like to follow him around and lecture on the subject *Evan Roberts, explained and exposed.*

What had happened in Chatham Street had become the talk of Liverpool. That day, he had more exposure and he was criticized by the cotton broker, Thomas Davies, at the opening of another chapel belonging to Eglwys Rydd y Cymry.[34] The Reverend John Williams had arranged for him to be examined by four medical men in 88 Rodney Street. The verdict of James Barr, William Williams, Thomas H. Bickerton and William MaAfee was hopeful: 'We find him mentally and physically quite sound. He is suffering from the effects of overwork and we consider it advisable that he should have a period of rest.'

There were two more meetings that required his presence. The Reverend H. M. Roberts had by the second meeting on 17 April repented of his criticism, and now claimed that Evan Roberts was the nearest human being to Jesus, and resembled him more than any other religious leader. Evan Roberts however did not receive such an apology from Daniel Hughes. But he was leaving Liverpool as he came, a celebrity of the first order. He left Lime Street in style on 18 April for the Royal Hotel in Capel Curig where he was to stay till 16 May for a deserved rest. He left behind on Merseyside:

i   A strong temperance witness which was praised by the Chief Constable of Liverpool;
ii.   At least the building of one new chapel, which is Salem Presbyterian Church of Wales, Laird Street, Birkenhead;[35]
iii.   A stronger Sunday school through the medium of the Welsh language. The Calvinistic Methodists or the Presbyterian Church of Wales Sunday School on

---

[32] Rees, 'Sledgehammer Pastor', pp. 149-50. This is the denomination that Ronald Regan, future President of the United States of America, was nurtured in and owed a great debt to it. See Ronald Regan, *American Dream* (Norwalk, 1990), p. 32.

[33] Gwilym Hughes, pp. 87-89. This is part of the letter: 'Brother Evan Roberts look to yourself and pray for forgiveness, confess the bitter injustice you have perpetrated. Seek the Rev. W. O. Jones, fall on his neck and weep, he will be ready to forgive; see that, before you speak in the name of God again, you are right with your brother in the ministry.' Daniel Hughes was willing to call Evan Roberts a genius but his letter is dynamite for a sensitive soul such as Evan Roberts.

[34] 'Gosod Ceryg Sylfan Capel Newydd Upper Canning Street', *Llais Rhyddid*, vol. 4, no. 2 (1905), pp. 271-280.

[35] W. Henry, 'Anerchiad at yr Eglwysi', *Ystadegau Eglwysi y Methodistaid Calfinaidd am y flwyddyn 1904* (Liverpool, 1905), p. 1.

Merseyside gained in that year of 1905 606 new scholars as the result of his visit.[36]

The biggest failure was the sniping and the confrontation between him and a number of Welsh Nonconformist ministers. The biographer of the pulpit giant, John Williams, the Reverend R. H. Hughes, places the blame on the minister of Princes Road Chapel.[37] So does Alderman Joseph Harrison Jones (an elder at Princes Road Chapel since 1877). He claimed that his minister had lost his usual diplomacy and had spoilt the Evan Roberts visit by pursuing with him the *Eglwys Rydd y Cymry* controversy.[38] John Williams decided the following year to return to his native Anglesey, and admitted that his own chapel of Princes Road had not benefited as it should from the 1905 revival.[39] But if the best man, W. O. Jones, at the wedding of his friend John Williams to a daughter of a Liverpool Welsh builder in May 1899 had not been expelled from the Connexion in 1901, one could argue that the Evan Roberts visit would have been conducted against a completely different background. W. O. Jones was a controversial individual and his presence was very evident throughout the crusade. Evan Roberts was a sincere revivalist who had been converted on the Damascus road and had experienced the Baptism of the Holy Spirit. It was this experience that dominated his whole campaign, as he himself admitted in a meeting at the Wesleyan Methodist Chapel in Shaw Street, Liverpool: 'Mae dyn wedi ei achub am achub pawb, fel un wedi dianc o wreck, am achub y gweddill.' (A man who has been saved wants to save everybody else, like a person who has escaped from a shipwreck wants to save the rest of the crew and passengers.)[40]

---

[36] R. Aethwy Jones, 'Anerchiad at yr Eglwysi', *Ystadegau Eglwysi y Methodistiaid Calfinaidd am y flwyddyn 1905*, (Liverpool, 1906), p.1. Dr D. M. Phillips states that 750 new members joined the Welsh Nonconformist chapel. D. M. Phillips, *Evan Roberts a'i waith*, p. 337.

[37] R. R. Hughes, *John Williams*, p. 158.

[38] Ibid.

[39] R. R. Hughes, *John Williams*, pp. 162-3. Also D. Ben Rees, 'Welsh Calvinistic Methodists and Independents in Toxteth Park, Liverpool', *The Journal of Welsh Religious History*, 3 (2003), pp. 78-93.

[40] D. M. Phillips, *Evan Roberts a'i waith*, p. 339.

CHAPTER 14

Why did the Welsh Revival Stop?

William K. Kay

Introduction

We rightly celebrate the revival that began in 1904. Although it was a major event in the life of Wales, its influence was strongly felt in many parts of the world. Other writers have been concerned with the origins[1], nature[2], and course[3] of the revival; I want to ask why it stopped.

The story of the revival has been variously told, and the account that is, to my mind, most persuasive is that offered by R. Tudur Jones[4] whose synthesis of numerous sources, balance and clarity is masterly. His account recognizes the contribution of Evan Roberts without presuming, as tended to be the case in popular imagination, that the revival was only due to Roberts and without him there would have been nothing. In this respect, the revival was unlike an evangelistic crusade dependent upon Billy Graham or D. L. Moody. The revival began well before Roberts started his ministry and continued, albeit in a diminished form, slightly after his public life petered out.

---

[1] J. Penn-Lewis, *The Awakening in Wales: and some of the hidden springs* (The Revival Library, King's Christian Centre, CD-Rom, 1905).

[2] J. Vyrnwy Morgan, *The Welsh Religious Revival, 1904-5: A retrospect and a criticism* (The Revival Library, King's Christian Centre, CD-Rom.1909); S. B. Shaw *The Great Revival in Wales* (The Revival Library, King's Christian Centre, CD-Rom, nd); W. T. Stead, *The Revival in the West: A narrative of facts* (The Revival Library, King's Christian Centre, CD-Rom,1905).

[3] Awstin [T. Awstin Davies], *The Religious Revival in Wales* (Western Mail, supplements 1 and 2, The Revival Library, King's Christian Centre, CD-Rom,1904); ibid. (supplements 3, 4, 5 and 6, 1905); A. G. Goodrich, G. Campbell Morgan, W. T. Stead, W. W. Moore, E. Evan Hopkins and others, *The Story of the Welsh Revival: As told by eyewitnesses together with a sketch of Evan Roberts and his message to the world to which is added a number of incidents of this most remarkable movement* (The Revival Library, King's Christian Centre, CD-Rom,1905); E. Evans, *The Welsh Revival of 1904* (Bridgend, 1987); H. E. Lewis, *With Christ Among the Miners* (The Revival Library, King's Christian Centre, CD-Rom, 1906); D. Matthews, *I Saw the Welsh Revival* (The Revival Library, King's Christian Centre, CD-Rom, 1951).

[4] R. Tudur Jones, ed. R Pope, trans. S. Prys-Jones, *Faith and the Crisis of a Nation: Wales 1890-1914* (Cardiff, 2004).

Prayer for revival took place in 1901 at St Asaph. There was a Keswick-type convention in August 1903 at Llandrindod and, as a further evidence of spiritual life, there were conversions under Seth Joshua's ministry all that year. Meetings held by W. W. Lewis of Carmarthen before Christmas 1903 aroused emotion among young people but Joseph Jenkins of the Calvinistic Methodists in New Quay reckoned that the revival proper started in February 1904. This was when his own congregation caught fire and it was just after this date that Congregationalists in Maesteg and Baptists in Aberdare also began to experience revival enthusiasm. Wesleyans saw fresh converts in April 1904 in Rhos during a conference on 'The Holy Spirit and His work'. Revivalistic outbreaks in Blaenannerch, the Rhondda, Ponciau, Cardiff and Noddfa all took place before the summer. That autumn, on 29 September 1904, Evan Roberts was present at a meet where Seth Joshua was the main preacher. Roberts responded to the evangelist's prayer, 'Humble us, O Lord' and slumped forward in his seat. From that time onward he found it impossible to continue his studies for the Calvinistic Methodist ministry and, by 31 October, was conducting his own meetings, first in his home chapel at Loughor and later elsewhere. He was twenty-six years old.

Thereafter, the events that constituted the revival began to overlap with each other. Roberts was often at the centre of them and he, unlike many other ministers, was itinerant. He travelled to places where the revival had not started in order to spread the spiritual fire or, alternatively, he visited places where revival had already taken hold and incited further intensity. In essence he remained in South Wales until the end of March 1905. Meanwhile, partly because press reports fanned the flames, revival took hold in North Wales during interdenominational prayer meetings, preaching campaigns or among the working men in the period between shifts. Roberts was the target of criticism when the Reverend Peter Price of Dowlais wrote to *The Western Mail* (31 January 1905) accusing him of perpetrating a 'sham revival, a mockery, a blasphemous travesty of the real thing'. After resting for a few days, Roberts worked in the Maesteg area in February and then spent a week in complete silence at the end of that month in Neath. Meanwhile in Anglesey, Bangor and other parts of the north, including Bala and Pwllheli, the revival continued its life-giving course.

Roberts visited Liverpool until the middle of April 1905 and, though there were joyful meetings of many thousands of people, there were also contentious incidents when Roberts collapsed in tears or rebuked the congregation or implied that some of the ministers present were hindering the revival through envy or unforgiveness. His oracular pronouncements were taken to be revelations from the Holy Spirit or, by his critics, as examples of occult powers or mesmeric tricks. In response to the furore Roberts underwent a medical examination that concluded he was mentally stable but in need of rest. So, from 19 April until 16 May 1905, he stayed in a hotel in Snowdonia before beginning a successful campaign in Anglesey, one that found him willing to play down emotionalism. A visit to the students at Bala took place on 5 July 1905 and the students were warned of the difficulty of distinguishing between God and the devil.

> The higher you ascend in the spiritual life the harder the conflict becomes – and the more difficult it will be to distinguish between the devil's voice and that of God. That is my difficulty at present. If there be a rule to determine the difference I know not of it as yet, the devil is able to mimic the voice of God wonderfully at times.[5]

Roberts went home, attended a singing festival at Mountain Ash in October and in November went to Bridgend, Pencoed, Kenfig Hill, Tylorstown, Trecynon and Bristol. In December he went to Pwllheli and by now he was beginning to preach about the cross.[6] Early in 1906 he retreated to the home of Mr and Mrs Penn-Lewis where he lived until 1925. He spoke infrequently at public meetings until he attended the convention at Llandrindod Wells in August 1906 in the company of Mrs Penn-Lewis. Although there were sporadic signs of exceptional spiritual life in Wales up to about April 1906, the revival was over and Roberts, the one man who might have rekindled it, remained in reclusive invisibility till his death in 1951.

The Question at Issue

The analysis of historical events is notoriously difficult. Numerous interpretations of the same historical documents can be constructed. These difficulties are multiplied in relation to the concept of causation: among the multiplicity of events and actions carried out at any one point in time it is well-nigh impossible to show conclusively that one act or one event led inexorably to another act or another event later in time. Yet, these provisos aside, we normally think in terms of cause and effect in relation to the natural world and it seems faintly absurd to suspend these categories in relation to human history.

In relation to the revival we could argue that the metaphor of fire provides an answer to the eventual cessation of the exceptional religious phenomena. The fire burns up everything that can be burned and eventually burns out. If we change the metaphor to one of rain, the same kind of notion of a cycle pertains.

---

[5] Unknown Student, *Evan Roberts visit to Bala College* (The Revival Library, CD-Rom).

[6] I take this to be indicative of Mrs Penn-Lewis's influence since she had begun to develop teaching about the cross that required identification with Christ's sufferings leading to the extinction of sin. See B. P. Jones *An Instrument of Revival: The complete life of Evan Roberts 1878-1951* (South Plainfield, NJ, 1995), p. 160; M. N. Garrard, *Mrs Penn-Lewis: A memoir* (Leicester, 1930), p. 151f; O. Stockmayer, 'Victory over Satan', in *The Word of the Cross*, 20, 6 (1911).

There is a period of drought and then the rain falls and saturates the parched land. But the rain is not a perpetual condition of nature.

We could argue that the revival is the result of bigger historical or social forces. Such an analysis deliberately sidesteps the issue of divine causation of human events. It presumes that the great events of history are at the mercy of indistinct large-scale causes that cannot be identified precisely. This analysis is secular in tone and may derive its coherence from philosophical presumptions like those that infuse Marxism.

Alternatively, the answer could be located within the churches since these are the agencies through which revival began and by which it was spread and maintained. If the revival begins in the churches, it must end there also; if the revival begins because the churches change, it must end because the churches change back to the way they were before.

Alternatively again, we can place the course of large events within the hands of individuals. We can assume that, just as individuals have an impact upon their immediate circle of friends or colleagues, so they may also have an effect upon their localities or their country. This theory of history, mocked by Tolstoy[7] and more scientifically minded historians, is one that appeals because of its simplicity and directness.

So in answer to the question 'why did the revival end when it did?' we can at least begin to offer a series of answers. These answers can be put under three main headings: the theological, the collective, and the personal.

Theological

1. The revival began and ended because it was the will of God that it should do so, and no other explanation is necessary.

Collective

2. The revival ended simply because it had nowhere else to go – there was no one else to be converted. Exhaustion brought the revival to a halt.
3. There were political or social factors behind the stoppage.
4. The churches were at fault in being unwilling or unable to accommodate the new converts.

Personal

5. Roberts was the cause of the revival's decline by unpredictable behaviour and eventual retirement from the public scene.
6. Mrs Penn-Lewis damaged the revival by her influence over Roberts and the doctrines into which she inducted him.

---

[7] I. Berlin, *The Hedgehog and the Fox: An essay on Tolstoy's view of history* (London, 1979), p. 25f.

Weighing the Answers

Theological

THE REVIVAL BEGAN AND ENDED BECAUSE OF THE INSCRUTABLE WILL OF GOD

The theological explanation comes from a strong Calvinistic tradition which emphasizes the sovereignty of God. Although this explanation has validity, particularly when drawn from an examination of the history of Israel or the passages dealing with the temporal activity of God that are found in the epistle to the Romans, the difficulty with this position is that *every* event may be credited to an all-powerful God. By putting every atom of causation into the divine category, the human category is reduced to zero. History becomes a series of the divine actions over which humans appear to have no control and for which they appear to have no responsibility. Such an account can hardly be defended theologically, especially since a strong view of the sovereignty of God, even in the writings of Luther and Calvin, is tempered by the need for the church to preach the Word of God while offering the other means of grace. In other words, in the writings of the Reformers, there is an assumption that human beings have the capacity to increase the likelihood, though the church, that God will or will not act in human affairs.

Collective

THE REVIVAL HAD NOWHERE ELSE TO GO

If we assume that the revival begins by revitalizing the church and that, because of this, members of the congregation go out into the community or, conversely, the members of the community attend the church, there are likely to be conversions, additions to the membership of the church. There must be a theoretical limit to this process as the church grows and fewer and fewer people are left outside it.

If we assume that revival is the revitalization of the church through expressions of emotion and by the re-apprehension of the reality of the spiritual realm, there must come a point when each congregation has been fully renewed. Each member has received fresh spiritual experience, each member has repented of his or her sins and has made a new consecration to Christ. So, again, there will be a theoretical limit to this process. It cannot be repeated endlessly and, if attempts are made to re-consecrate the already consecrated or to discover fresh sin when sin has already been forgiven, then the revival will take a forced and harsh course: greater and greater manifestations of extreme behaviour will be demanded on the assumption that only they function as an index of interior spiritual life.

Perhaps the nearest parallel to the 1904 revival is to be found in the 1859 revival. In 1859 the chapels and churches of Wales were revived through combined prayer meetings where the reconsecration of members began, and the effects then spread out into the community.[8] People changed their lifestyles and the pattern of their leisure activities. Theological quarrels abated and crime and drunkenness dropped and this brought what was happening in churches and chapels to further public attention. Yet, eventually, after church membership rolls had increased dramatically, church life settled down to the normal round of services. The slow relapse to normality was not accompanied by the retirement of a leading revivalist who faded into the background. Nor were there obvious divisions within the Christian community that brought an end to spiritual harmony.

The cyclical nature of the process may not have been obvious to its participants. Moreover many of them were equipped with a theology that discouraged them from looking for natural causes even if, by theological reflection, they might reach out for spiritualized explanations. In particular the Calvinistic Methodists did not wish to attribute conversion to human effort. For this reason they saw the revival as being an altogether divinely inspired occasion that arrived in answer to prayer by mysterious divine agency and, equally, departed when the divine agency inscrutably decided that this should be so.

They spoke of a 'visitation', the unexpected arrival of a person, of 'strange' and 'powerful' experiences that lead to unrestrainable singing, of men being 'overpowered' in church. The result is that in some communities, for example Cwmcamlais near Brecon, 'all the inhabitants have now turned to the Lord'.[9]

The 1859 pattern fits the 1904 revival well. Although the population of Wales had grown and moved in the intervening years, the advent of the railway (by 1871, 15,736 miles of track had been laid[10]) allowed twentieth-century preachers and missioners to move rapidly around the whole country. All the large urban centres had been visited if not converted in 1904–5 and the small rural communities where older members of population continued to live – and where memories of the previous rival were freshest – had also been influenced. It makes sense therefore to suggest that the 1904 revival ran its course in the same way that the 1859 one did.

THERE WERE POLITICAL AND SOCIAL FACTORS BEHIND THE STOPPAGE

By the end of the nineteenth century Wales had been industrialized. By 1880 'between a quarter and a third of the male labour force of Wales worked in the coal industry' and this number rose to about a half of those working if the railways and docks were added in. Unionism grew. From the same date

---

[8] J. E. Orr, *The Second Evangelical Awakening in Britain* (London, 1949).

[9] T. Phillips, *The Welsh Revival: Its origins and development* (Edinburgh, 1860 [Reprinted 1998]), p. 37.

[10] P. J. Cain, 'Railways 1870-1914: the maturity of the private system', in Michael J. Freeman and Derek H. Aldcroft (eds), *Transport in Victorian Britain* (Manchester, 1988), p. 92.

national identity was fostered and produced a pressure for home rule, disestablishment of the Anglican Church and for increased use of the Welsh language.[11] Preaching could be turned to political ends with the result that popular sentiments could be aroused by passionate public speaking on disputed issues – as they were by Lloyd George on education in 1902 – because a London government imposed a policy designed for urban England on rural Wales. Education had been a sensitive issue ever since 1847 when the Reports of the Commissioners of Enquiry into the State of Education in Wales were published. The commissioners painted an unflattering picture of Welsh schooling. Resistance to the 1902 Education Act had had the effect of increasing the value of Sunday school attendance since primary education was only available in the churches in cases where schools were denied their grants.[12]

This combination between social change and national struggle focused attention on national identity. Indeed Henri Bois considered 'there was a close link between the revival and Wales's national identity'.[13] This explanation, while it may have merit, is difficult to generalize to other cultures and, more to the point, cannot show why this particular revival eventually came to stop. Was national identity established? Was sufficient emotion released? The questions are unanswerable and, moreover, they ignore the conversion accounts of the participants themselves which are, by any historical canons, primary data from which a proper explanation must be constructed; no convert said, 'now I feel more Welsh' or 'now I feel more placid'.

Other explanations might take account of the role of the mass media, the newspapers, in the spread of the revival and the assumption that what was increased by media attention might also be decreased by media inattention. Yet this explanation does not convince. There was no obvious media storm of criticism against revival. And, while it is true that the general election took precedence in the newspapers in January 1906, this hardly shows why the fervour of the chapels and churches declined so rapidly. In the long term, perhaps, the drift of the nonconformist chapels towards political causes distracted Welsh Christianity from its primary evangelical concerns. The movement to disestablish the Anglican Church[14] and the internal swirl of debate brought about by the linkage between trade unionism and socialism arrived at a time when traditional Christian doctrine was being questioned. By 1912 Keir

---

[11] J. Davies, *A History of Wales* (Harmondsworth, 1994), pp. 468, 473.

[12] Tudur Jones, *Faith and Crisis*, p. 87. A convention in October 1904 'was held in Cardiff at which the local authorities and the Free Churches of Wales were represented. The decision of that conference was that ... nonconformist parents of children at non-provided schools would then withdraw them and they would be educated out of voluntary effort, in chapels and vestries'. See also, G. E. Jones, *The Education of a Nation* (Cardiff, 1997), p. 86f.

[13] Tudur Jones, *Faith and Crisis*, chapter 14; H. Bois, *Le Réveil au Pays de Galles* (Toulouse, 1905).

[14] D. D. Morgan, *The Span of the Cross* (Cardiff, 1999), p. 33.

Hardie could preach a Christ who looked more like a social radical challenging the Roman empire on behalf of the working man than the redeeming Son of God.[15] In the short term, however, it is hard to say that the revival came to a halt just because politics suddenly replaced religion in the minds of Welsh people.[16]

Equally, industrial relations did not impinge upon the revival – if anything the opposite. The revival helped to sweeten industrial relations within Wales so that unionized and non-unionized men would work together and conciliation between employers and employees would be encouraged.[17] There was, it is true, some sarcasm to be found among the middle classes. When Mr Charles Taylor reported,

> this week, very reluctantly, I have had to dispense with the services of one of my servants for this very reason. She found it impossible to become sufficiently 'revived' in two-and-any-half hours nightly; invariably coming home an hour or so late. My friends tell me they have the same thing to face.[18]

The disdainful curling lip is almost visible upon the page. The servants were out enjoying themselves and the gentry did not like it. Yet even this was hardly likely to bring the revival to a halt. The gentry, after all, did not act in a concerted fashion.

So was there a demographic dimension to the revival? Can the explanation be found by an imbalance of power between the generations such that, when the young people had been converted and empowered within the churches to make their wishes felt, there was no further need for spiritual experience? The problem here is that the revival appeared to reach all age groups and, though it was popular among the young, was not confined to them and there appears to be no real criticism of the participation of young people in the revival meetings. Admittedly, the 'girls' in the company of Evan Roberts were singled out for scorn by Peter Price in his complaining letter to the newspaper but there was never a youth movement separate from the main phenomena of revival. The demographic explanation of stoppage does not begin to work.

THE CHURCHES WERE UNABLE TO ADJUST

The churches may have failed to adjust either by their lack of welcome and care for the new converts or else by falling out with each other. Jones provides evidence suggesting that the customs and structures of church life rapidly reasserted themselves shortly after the revival was over.[19] In at least one

---

[15] H. Davies, *The English Free Churches* (London, 1963), p. 183; Tudur Jones, *Faith and Crisis*, p. 401f., 409.

[16] A suggestion tentatively offered to me by David Bebbington.

[17] Jones, *An Instrument of Revival*, p. 214.

[18] Jones, *An Instrument of Revival*, p. 248.

[19] Jones, *An Instrument of Revival*, p. 271.

instance women were no longer allowed to take part in the weeknight meetings because the deacons forbade them. Similarly, processions of children and gospel singers were also discouraged. The congregational vitality and spontaneity of the revival meetings could quickly slip back into the deadening control of the professional clergy and their assistants.

So we can envisage the churches filling up and then gradually, as the revival meetings ebbed, the fervour and excitement that had originally attracted converts being edged out until the converts themselves felt that they were unwelcome. This picture of a kind of counter-revolution against the new converts may explain why some congregations rapidly lost the members they had so recently gained but it cannot explain why the revival as a whole slowed down and stopped. For there were congregations that made room for the converts and inducted them into church life in a sane and sensible way. In addition, as Morgan points out, 'the proliferation of independent evangelistic halls in industrial South Wales was one result of the 1904–5 revival'.[20] Where the converts found themselves unwelcome, they went elsewhere.

Nor is there any evidence that the churches themselves destroyed the revival by denominational bickering. The revival had brought them together, either in united prayer meetings or in much larger gatherings, and their doctrinal differences did not suddenly break into public view. If there were disputes between ministers, these were over the validity of phenomena within the revival itself. But such differences did not fall along denominational lines as the letters for and against Evan Roberts in the *Western Mail* after Price's attack demonstrated.

Personal

ROBERTS WAS THE CAUSE OF THE REVIVAL'S DECLINE BY HIS UNPREDICTABLE BEHAVIOUR AND EVENTUAL RETIREMENT FROM THE PUBLIC SCENE

It may seem absurd and abstruse to criticize Evan Roberts for his contribution to the revival. He can hardly be blamed if his ministry was not that of an organizing Wesley or an evangelistic Whitfield. Yet, whether he wanted to or not, he had become the leading figure in the revival and it is worth considering whether, with the gifts that he had, he might have ensured the continuation of the revival beyond 1906 and, indeed, might have strengthened the church within the big urban centres where it was weakest.

His own ministry was unique and there was nothing like it until the kind of gatherings ministered to by Pentecostal and charismatic figures in the late twentieth century. We could not call Roberts an expository preacher. Nor was he an evangelist. But he did tell people how the Christian faith might be worked out or what they needed to do to find God. The meetings he conducted were

---

[20] Morgan, *The Span of the Cross*, p. 13.

uninhibited and full of congregational participation, and he had no theological scruples about allowing women or children to pray publicly. In some of his early meetings he came out of the pulpit to walk among the congregation addressing individuals directly during the meeting. Sometimes he walked out of the meeting to speak to people in the street and then walked back in again. He was not worried about when meetings ended. Although he did not include the laying-on of hands as a regular part of his meetings, several witnesses certainly felt that he had imparted something to them physically by his touch.[21]

One first-hand account of the way that Roberts conducted himself said,

> Evan Roberts tests a meeting before he begins to speak. What is most provoking to many of his hearers seems to me the clearest human explanation of his success in bringing each meeting to a dramatic and sensational climax. His apparent indifference and immobility for an hour or so before he says anything breaks up all the composure an audience of human beings can command. Add to this his habit of transfixing each and every person present with his, not unpleasant, but homage-compelling gaze. For a long time he reviews methodically the rows upon rows of faces. It is the gaze of the practised physician. By the time he gets up to speak he has made a mental report or census of his audience. He knows what souls are ill at ease. He predicts conversions, and he detects hindrances. He is doubtless a man of faith relying on the promptings of the Holy Spirit, but is not a man who neglects picking up all the data available by human beings concerning the condition of his audience.
>
> His 'break-downs', or what some of his unsympathetic critics call 'contortions', must be taken into account. In three out of five meetings I witnessed three of his nervous collapses, and I was on each occasion near enough to him to render first-aid if necessary. I could not believe that he was shamming. He would cry 'his heart out', his tears and sobs affecting the most callous present... but though no 'shamming', the 'collapse' was most effective in evoking whatever sympathy the audience had hitherto withheld. There was in each case a burst of prayer throughout the building when the revivalist was in such distress. And as he had a way of recovering suddenly, there was a burst of praise the moment he stood up again.[22]

This account, written in May 1905, outlines the rapport Roberts built up with his congregations. It also shows how he, perhaps unintentionally, validated publicly embarrassing behaviour. If Roberts could weep in public, then the socially constrained Christian could make an open declaration of his or her faith. And, if one man was willing to confess his shortcomings in front of the whole congregation, others would feel an ability to follow suit. We could see this as an exercise in crowd psychology but that hardly does justice to the occasion. Undoubtedly, in the early phases of the revival, Roberts wanted to

---

[21] G. Weeks, *Chapter Thirty-Two: Part of a history of the Apostolic Church 1900-2000* (Barnsley, 2003), p. 13.
[22] J. U., *Nantymoel* (The Revival Library, CD-Rom).

break through the 'Sunday best' façade of church order and he would do whatever was necessary to ensure this happened. He needed both a sense of awe in the presence of God and a sense of emotional intimacy. Tudur Jones points out that the revival was one of love and grace rather than of judgement.[23] This may help to explain why the Welsh language was 'indispensable' (J. U.'s word, though not quote above) to the meetings: this was the language of home and hearth.

I want to argue that if Roberts had had a more fully developed theology of charismata he might have understood his own ministry better, or at least have been able to sustain it longer. As it is, Roberts found himself being criticized, on the one hand, for claiming direct contact with God through the Holy Spirit (Price's criticism) and, on the other, for convening disorderly meetings that kept young people out later than was good for their morals.[24] More damagingly, Roberts was accused of making outrageous theological statements about the withdrawal or departure of the Holy Spirit in the face of recalcitrant individuals or places.[25] Worse, he was said to have threatened such individuals with damnation.[26]

In the midst of this theological deep water it is hardly surprising that Roberts found himself unable to distinguish between what he took to be the voice of God and the voice of the devil, as his answers to the students at Bala show. Even during his week of silence he was concerned to 'differentiate Thy voice from the cunning of the Evil One'.[27]

We could hardly blame Roberts for failing to utilize a theology that had yet to be developed. Pentecostal and charismatic theology of spiritual gifts developed by a consideration of the New Testament as a whole but particularly out of the relevant passages in 1 Corinthians.[28] Many Pentecostal commentators accept that spiritual gifts may operate in an intuitive way such that natural and spiritual faculties may function almost in unison. Certainly the idea that spiritual gifts are perpetually being challenged by demonic counterfeits within the life and ministry of a single person are ruled out by a robust sense of salvation and sanctification. Moreover, spiritual gifts are normally seen as functioning in a coordinated fashion building up an individual congregation or supplementing evangelistic activity. The 'word of knowledge' described in 1 Corinthians 12:8 occurs within a general framework where spiritual gifts may be tested (1 Corinthians 14:29), which implies that they may be fallible, partial or immature *without being demonically false*.

---

[23] Tudur Jones, *Faith and Crisis*, p. 19.
[24] Jones, *An Instrument of Revival*, p. 260.
[25] Vyrnwy Morgan, *The Welsh Religious Revival*, p. 68.
[26] Vyrnwy Morgan, *The Welsh Religious Revival*, chapter 4.
[27] Awstin, *The Western Mail*, 3 March 1905.
[28] W. K. Kay, *Pentecostals in Britain* (Carlisle, 2000); W. K. Kay, and A. E. Dyer (eds), *Pentecostal and Charismatic Studies: A reader* (London, 2004).

So did the revival come to a halt because Roberts withdrew from it? No, here the evidence must be in Roberts's favour. The revival was beginning to slow down by the autumn of 1905 but Roberts continued his ministry during that period. It is more interesting to speculate on what would have happened if Roberts had returned with renewed vigour after the general election of January 1906. On balance, it is probable that Roberts *could* have prolonged the revival or, perhaps, turned its energies towards large urban congregations along the south coast. Yet this was not to be, and the reason for this lies wrapped up in the controversial figure of Mrs Jessie Penn-Lewis.

MRS PENN-LEWIS DAMAGED THE REVIVAL BY HER INFLUENCE OVER ROBERTS AND THE DOCTRINES INTO WHICH SHE INDUCTED HIM

Mrs Penn-Lewis was born into a Calvinistic Methodist family in 1861, in Neath, the grand-daughter of one of their eminent ministers and the daughter of a mining engineer. At nineteen she married a man who was later to become the borough treasurer for the city of Leicester, and this gave her financial stability and a comfortable home for the rest of her life. She underwent evangelical conversion at the age of twenty-one and felt herself to have been baptized in the Holy Spirit ten years later.[29] She became known for her work with the YWCA (despite her disputes with its leadership) and travelled widely, including trips to Russia, India and the United States, in the years following. She was involved with Keswick conventions from 1899, wrote books and booklets that were widely distributed and helped initiate the Llandrindod Wells conventions beginning in August 1903.

Mrs Penn-Lewis wrote six letters to Evan Roberts that were published in the *Western Mail* some time in or after 1906.[30] The first of these was sent from Neath and fits the occasion in February 1905 when Roberts spent a week in silence.[31] In it she writes, 'I have much on my heart from the Lord, and I believe He means me to have time to speak with you on things of God. He will tell you this.'

In the second dated 31 August 1905, she wrote, 'This is just a note to tell you I shall not get home to Great Glen, near Leicester, until 2 September, but if my husband has returned home, and if you should wish to see him he will give you a glad welcome'.

---

[29] Garrad, *Mrs Penn-Lewis*, p. ix. Garrard's book is largely compiled from diaries and notes written by Jessie Penn-Lewis in preparation for writing her biography.

[30] I have a press cutting of the letters but, unfortunately, the date of the newspaper's publication is not visible. The sixth letter is dated 27 July without giving a year. From its tone and content it appears to belong to 1905 but the newspaper prints it after the letter of 14 September 1905 and before the letter of 1906. In Awstin's report in the *Western Mail* (17 November 1913) there is a suggestion that Roberts's family published the letters to indicate the 'kind of subtle influences that had been brought to bear on him'.

[31] This is also the view of the introductory commentary in the newspaper.

This suggests that she has already spoken to Roberts about going to Leicester. The letter goes on, 'It is strongly upon me to say to you to be very careful to test your guidance in regard to this matter. I mean that the adversary will use every possible means to prevent any converse between us ... the adversary works through the "natural" fallen life, whilst the Holy Ghost works through the new imparted life of Jesus.'

Which is a line of thought that would help lever Roberts away from his family. She goes on, 'I cannot but feel deeply, in view of what I see the Lord preparing for you, that to have further time for converse over these things would hasten His, or rather ripen more quickly[,] His purpose.'

And, then drawing Roberts further into her secret negotiations while still needing to get him to come to her home as soon as possible, she writes, 'Should you need to wire me or my husband, the initial R or X will be sufficient to let us know the sender ... I am here till Saturday morning. You could go through London if you preferred.'

The third letter is dated the following day, 1 September 1905. In it she passes on a letter from a third party that has been lost. Her prose is colourful and has a Mills & Boon feel to it. 'As I read a burning heat seems to run through my whole being ... I cannot get you out of my prayers night and day ... I see you with a trumpet to cry to the whole world ... I have no rest in my spirit in crying for you ... Oh! How my whole being is quivering in this fright, throbbing with the certainty of the coming victory.'

And then she concludes triumphantly, 'God will bring you to Glen. It will be your Bethany ... God bids me tell you that it can be your Bethany when you want to get away from the world ... feel free to come, even if only for a few days'.

The fourth letter is dated 14 September 1905. It shows her persistence. Roberts had decided after all not to visit her, but she puts this down to devilish opposition while also realizing that he may have very practical misgivings about going to stay with strangers.

> I see that you are now in Swansea with Mr Lloyd, so you have not felt led to come here. When you replied to my husband that you saw the path open it seemed to me that the Lord had given you light as to His will, but after I left Llandrindod the impression grew strongly that the adversary would hinder your coming ... I saw afterwards that we were practically strangers to you after the flesh, and that you knew nothing of our exterior lives ... you needed to know more of our home arrangements ere you could be sure that this would be the right place for you.

After outlining the domestic arrangements – the house is situated outside the city, there is only a secretary to help Mrs Penn-Lewis, Mr Penn-Lewis goes to work every day and he has sacrificed 'all social claims for the Lord's sake', which seems to mean that none of his friends visits the home – she reverts to spiritual language. 'I see God opening to you this sanctuary' and her own forgetfulness in outlining the comforts she is offering is because 'the subtlety of the adversary is terrible'. Of course, if Roberts wishes to pop back to Wales from time to time, that is easy because she herself makes the journey often. And then she returns to her spiritual sympathy for him, 'I have been in a sea of conflict, sometimes hand to hand with the adversary himself, and it has been mainly over the consciousness that all the hosts of hell were round about you ... because I had the impression that your coming here at this time meant great consequences to God.'

In the light of her subsequent writing about the cunning of the devil, her breath-taking assumptions that she knows what God wants while having been 'hand to hand' with Satan is extraordinary. On 19 February 1906 she is confident that at last Roberts will accede to her requests, 'I am waiting for the Lord to show you His will and His time for coming here [because] He is pouring into my heart so much for you.'

She has put all her persuasiveness into these letters by appealing to his spirituality and his natural desire for rest. God is going to help Roberts through her. God is going to give Roberts free and comfortable accommodation through her hospitality. God is going to take Roberts out of the battle for a while. She is a co-worker with him and understands his problems perfectly. Everything she is doing is in the full confidence she knows the will of God. Her certainties contrast very obviously with his uncertainties.

So, Roberts went to live with the Penn-Lewises in their spacious house near Leicester at the end of March 1906[32] and travelled to his remaining preaching engagements from there. She had been corresponding with him since early in 1905 when the revival was in full swing.[33] She had pestered him throughout the summer and must only have added to his sense of spiritual conflict. She must have underlined his worries about the cunning machinations of the devil and her one aim appears to have been to get him away from Wales and the heat of revival into her own circle of influence where she could share with him what was 'on her heart from the Lord'. Nothing she says in these letters encourages him to carry on with the meetings that had made him world famous, and there appears to be little concern for the state of the unconverted in Wales or for the Welsh chapels and churches if they are deprived of an emerging national leader.

During Evan Roberts's stay in Leicester, he received numerous invitations to preach elsewhere. Eventually there were criticisms of Mrs Lewis that she had managed to keep Roberts against his will. His family was concerned about his mental state. There were accusations that she was making money out of him. As result Awstin of the *Western Mail* (17 November 1913) went with Roberts's

---

[32] Date given by Tudur Jones, *Faith and Crisis*, chapter 14; Evans suggests February 1906, see *The Welsh revival of 1904*, p. 178.

[33] *The Overcomer* says that she invited him to her own home in August 1905. It also says that 'she met Mr Roberts on several occasions'. Presumably these meetings were as unsettling as her letters.

brother, Dan, up to Leicester to speak with him and to attempt to persuade him to return to Wales.

The visit was a failure. Although Roberts appeared for tea and spoke with Awstin and appeared to be perfectly level-headed and claimed that he had a message for the world concerning the imminent return of Christ, he absolutely refused to return home or to spend time with his family. Mrs Penn-Lewis seems to have cooperated fully with a visit and even to have added her voice to the chorus asking him to return home. It was to no avail.

In 1913 a report appeared in *The Overcomer* (Mrs Penn-Lewis's newspaper) saying that Roberts had been invited only for a fortnight but that he had stayed longer because his recovery was so slow.[34] Instead 'he recognised that the hand of God had led him into an environment in which he could exercise the highest spiritual faculties with the most far-reaching results'.

Mrs Penn-Lewis asserted that Roberts was engaged upon important Christian work while he was in her home. He was praying and he was writing a book. The book, *War on the Saints*, took six years to complete and was published as being by Mrs Penn-Lewis 'in collaboration with Evan Roberts'. It repeated many of the things that she already said in *The Warfare with Satan and the Way of Victory* (1906). It was, in essence, an attack on revivalism and, although it did not rule out the possibility of a direct link between individuals and the Holy Spirit, it presumes that, at the same time that individuals were in touch with the Holy Spirit, they were particularly vulnerable to the onslaughts of demons. As a consequence access to the Holy Spirit was clouded by demonic influences. All this was set within an eschatological framework that prioritized evil and deception. The upshot of this was that much of the extraordinary power of Roberts's ministry and the meetings over which he presided were called into question. If anything was a repudiation of his ministry, this book was. And, extrapolating from this repudiation, it is evident that the book was an attack on the emerging force of Pentecostalism that Mrs Penn-Lewis took it upon herself to oppose.

Conclusion

Leaving aside the theological explanation because it does not rule out the importance of free human action, I conclude that the revival was brought to a halt for two reasons. First, because it had run its natural course and that everybody who was likely to be converted had been converted. In some places literally everybody had been converted and in others the social climate had changed in a way that suggested a permanent influence on Welsh life had been achieved. Following on from this, but not connected with its cessation, the inability of the churches to cope with new converts in some districts and the

---

[34] J. C. Williams, 'Mr Evan Roberts seclusion', in *The Overcomer* (November, 1913), The Revival Library, King's Christian Centre, CD-Rom.

reassertion of pre-revival norms, led to a more rapid falling away of new converts than was the case after 1859.

Second, the influence of Jesse Penn-Lewis on Roberts is likely to have been detrimental not only to his health but also to his interpretation of spiritual phenomena.[35] Although this conclusion may appear to be harsh, in the light of subsequent suggestions that he suffered from a heart condition, it is improbable that someone with 'a weak heart'[36] would have lived for forty more years. With a better theological understanding of his own charismatic gifts, he would have been fortified to continue his ministry for many years. He would have had an appreciation that charismatic gifts must be judged because they are fallible and would not have attributed every failing and every mistake to demonic power. But this was not to be. In my judgement, Mrs Penn-Lewis did more than any other person to ensure that, when the first phase of the revival was over, no second phase followed.

---

[35] Jones interprets events differently, *An Instrument of Revival*, p. 160. Roberts was in the throes of one or more nervous breakdowns and Mrs Penn-Lewis helped to 'save Evan from total abandonment of his service to the Lord'.

[36] Awstin [T. Awstin Davies], 'Mr Evan Roberts Interviewed', in *Western Mail*, 17 November 1913.

CHAPTER 15

The Impact of the Welsh Revival on Baptist Churches in Scotland

Kenneth Roxburgh

Introduction

The revival tradition in Scotland was one which was intimately woven into the experience and expectation of Christians in Scotland. Accounts of the Scottish Reformation under John Knox, as well as later spiritual awakenings in Stewarton and Irvine in 1625 and Kirk of Shotts in 1630[1] were often recalled with nostalgia as evidences of God's blessing on the nation.[2] Recurring periods of spiritual awakening affected the religious life of the Scottish church, often bringing surges of emotional intensity, popular interest and renewal to the life of the nation.[3] The phenomenon of revival, as it affected Scotland, was not, however, uniform in its appearance. During the seventeenth and eighteenth centuries, revival affected parishes within the Church of Scotland, often during communion seasons when the preaching of the crucified Christ, linked to the visible signs of the sacrament, often led to these occasions becoming converting ordinances. Many people who flocked to these corporate expressions of their faith[4] experienced personal renewal of their individual lives and encountered immediacy in their experience of the presence of God. In

---

[1] Accounts of the earlier Scottish revivals can be found in R. Fleming, *The Fulfilling of Scripture* (Edinburgh, 1850), Vol. 2, pp. 95-99. See also W. J. Cooper, *Scottish Revivals* (Dundee, 1918), pp. 26-39.

[2] Ian Muirhead comments that 'revivals occurred frequently throughout a period of more than 150 years of Scottish church history, were widespread across the country, and were of significance as the continuing source of much that was effective in the life of the Scottish church'. See Ian A. Muirhead, 'The revival as a dimension of Scottish church history', in *Scottish Church History Society Records*, XX (1980), p. 179.

[3] These included an awakening in Moulin, near Pitlochry in 1798, Arran in 1804, Skye in 1812 and the Isle of Lewis between 1824 and 1835.

[4] M. J. Crawford comments that 'the celebration of the Lord's supper ... was a revivalist ritual that served as a conduit for the outpouring of grace'. *Seasons of Grace: Colonial New England's Revival Tradition in its British Context* (Oxford, 1991), p. 219. Alexander Whyte spoke of how the Lord's Supper 'has been made a converting ordinance to many in all ages of the Church'. Cited in W. J. Couper, *Scotland Saw His Glory* (Wheaton, 1995), p. 326.

1839, a revival associated with the preaching of William Chalmers Burns in several cities in the Scottish Lowlands, encouraged the hope that the experience of revival could once again influence the religious life of the country. It was not, however, until 1859 that the national movement impacted the country as a whole, as Scotland shared in an awakening with truly international proportions, affecting different parts of Great Britain as well as the United States.

In the nineteenth century, awakenings began to be associated with significant preachers such as D. L. Moody, whose appearance in the cities of Edinburgh and Glasgow in the 1870s brought many people to faith in Christ. John Coffey[5] has demonstrated that Moody went out of his way to reach men and women who had little contact with the church, holding his meetings in agricultural and city halls rather than churches and chapels, thereby distancing himself from traditional, institutional religion. His simple use of language[6] appealed to ordinary people and drew them in their thousands to his meetings.[7] Moody's message stressed a theology of the love of God demonstrated at Calvary and was warm and moving in its appeal, an indication of a 'growing shift in Scottish Presbyterianism towards a more Arminian perception of Salvation'.[8]

Moody's mission in Scotland was endorsed by several eminent ministers from various denominations.[9] Moody's message was favourably received in cities such as Glasgow where his mission lasted for over three months.[10] C. H. Spurgeon spoke of the 'gracious visitation that has come upon Edinburgh ...

---

[5] Historians have often considered Moody's evangelistic ministry as failing to reach the unchurched and the working classes. See W. G. McLoughlin, who speaks of Moody's work as a 'failure', *Revivals, Awakenings and Reform* (Chicago, 1978), p. 143; John Coffey, 'Democracy and popular religion: Moody and Sankey's mission to Britain, 1873-1875', in *Citizenship and Community*, ed. Eugenio F. Biagini (Cambridge, 1996), pp. 93-119.

[6] W. G. Blaikie said that 'Moody's sermons were certainly not intellectual, and those who went to his meetings in hopes of hearing something original and brilliant were doomed to disappointment. They were plain, honest, somewhat blunt appeals, but wonderfully brightened and made telling by a copious supply of illustrations, anecdotes and personal reminiscences.' Cited in Couper, *Scotland saw his Glory*, p. 319.

[7] Ken Jeffrey speaks of how Moody 'succeeded in reaching the urban masses', *When the Lord Walked the Land: The 1858-62 Revival in the North-East of Scotland* (Carlisle, 2002), p. 18. However Couper states that 'at the concluding meeting for converts in Edinburgh 'not fewer than 1,700 were present, young men and women of all social grades, but mainly belonging, it has been ascertained, to the families of Christian professors', *Scotland*, p. 322.

[8] Holmes, *Religious Revivals in Britain and Ireland 1859-1905* (Dublin, 2000), p. 72.

[9] John Kennedy, from Dingwall cast aspersions on Moody's character and business dealings, as well as his theological views. These were countered by a fellow minister of the Free Church of Scotland, Horatius Bonar.

[10] 8 February to 17 May 1874.

such as was probably never known before within the memory of man ... the hand of God [is] in the matter'.[11]

One other major influence on revival thinking in Scotland was that of Charles G. Finney. His basic premise concerning a 'Revival' was that it 'is not a miracle or dependent on a miracle. It is a purely philosophical result of the right use of the constituted means.'[12] Finney argued that Christians could influence the work of the Spirit and promote a work of revival through prayer and action. This view stood opposed to the older view of Jonathan Edwards that revival was a 'surprising work of the Spirit of God'. Finney's influence on Scottish Christianity was seen in the life and ministry of someone like James Morison whose popular theological writings eventually led to 'the end of the Calvinist ascendancy and the beginning of an era in which evangelical Arminianism would predominate'.[13]

---

[11] Cited by Couper, *Scotland*, p. 324.

[12] Cited by McLoughlin, ibid., p. x. Elsewhere in his writings, Finney spoke of the Confession as 'a paper pope' and argued 'That the instrument framed by that assembly should in the nineteenth century be recognized as the standard of the church, or of any intelligent branch of it, is not only amazing, but I must say that it is highly ridiculous. It is as absurd in theology as it would be in any other branch of science'. Charles Finney, *Systematic Theology* (Minneapolis, 1976), author's preface, xii.

[13] See Brian Talbot, *The Origins of the Baptist Union of Scotland 1800-1870*, PhD, Stirling, 1999, pp. 396 and 400. Morison was not the only voice to speak of the universal nature of God's love but his influence permeated to preachers and people in various sections of the Scottish church and the *Christian News* was undoubtedly correct in saying that no one 'had done more ... to mould the theological mind of Scotland of the present day and to liberalise the churches of Scotland' than James Morison. *Christian News*, 5 October 1889. Cited in Morison's *Jubilee*, p. 95. Although Morison welcomed accounts of conversions and crowded prayer meetings he was critical of excesses associated with the movement. He questioned the validity of a revival when society itself was not changed and cited the way in which there had been a 'steady increase of crime in America during the period of the revival'. See James Morison, Book Review in *Evangelical Repository*, 2nd series, VI (December, 1859), p. 110. He was scathing in his denouncement of what he considered 'a very large infusion of what is merely human'. See James Morison, Book Review in *Evangelical Repository*, 2nd series, VII (March, 1860), p. 190. In particular he questioned the way in which physical disorders were equated with the work of the Spirit. He questioned if it was right 'to ascribe the physical manifestations connected with the revival movement in Ireland to the direct interposition of God'. See James Morison, Book Review in *Evangelical Repository*, 2nd series, VI (December, 1859), p. 122. The result, he commented 'has been an inundation of hysterical, mesmerical, and other mystic influences, that have injured health, dishonoured modesty, fostered fanaticism, and issued in drivelling trances, visions and dreams'. See ibid., p. 130.

Through the efforts of Moody and Sankey in the 1870s, and the plethora of evangelistic enterprises during the latter half of the nineteenth century,[14] evangelical Christianity reached the zenith of its influence and has been described as the 'evangelical moment'.[15] Revival, as a phenomenon, however, had virtually disappeared from the religious life of Scotland by the turn of the twentieth century.

Scotland in the Early Twentieth Century

Scotland experienced major changes during the latter half of the nineteenth century, and into the early years of the twentieth-century, which altered the structure and character of Scottish society. Industrial development brought about a change in work and the movement of population to Clydeside in Glasgow and the growing industries in Lanarkshire. Social transformation of industrial towns and cities produced a working class that was often housed in degrading living conditions. In 1901 it was estimated that around a half of the total population lived in two-room or single-roomed houses.[16] J. T. Forbes, minister of the influential Hillhead Baptist Church, one of the largest in the country, addressed the Baptist World Congress in London in 1905 on *The Attitude of the Baptists to the Working Classes*. Forbes argued that changes in society confronted Baptists with fresh opportunities and challenges, although he confessed that 'in many places we have not a great hold on the working man – the artisan and the labourer'.[17] Forbes was expressing the fear felt by many, that the institutional church was becoming alienated from the working classes.

It was, however, a period that was generally marked by religious growth. Church attendance as a whole continued to rise from a figure of 48 per cent of the population in 1890 to a peak of 50 per cent in 1905,[18] a period when Baptist churches in various parts of Scotland flourished.[19] Yet, despite encouraging statistics, there was a 'widespread feeling of despair among the British evangelical community' as they saw the influence of 'social amusements, and a

---

[14] Callum Brown speaks of how 'from 1796 to 1914, Britain was immersed in the greatest exercise in Christian proselytism this country has ever seen. ... the salvation industry was a vast and inescapable facet of nineteenth- and early twentieth-century Britain.' *The Death of Christian Britain* (London, 2001), pp. 39, 56.

[15] John Coffey, 'Democracy and popular religion', p. 119.

[16] T. C. Smout, *A Century of the Scottish People, 1830-1950* (Glasgow, 1986), p. 58.

[17] *Proceedings of Baptist World Congress*, London July 11-19, 1905 (London, 1905). p. 266.

[18] See Callum G. Brown, *Religion and Society in Scotland since 1707* (Edinburgh, 1997), p. 147.

[19] During the ten years between 1891 and 1900, Baptists in Edinburgh and Lothian experienced a 95 per cent increase in church membership, much greater than the growth of the population which was only 4 per cent.

growing disregard for religious ordinances' within society as a whole.[20] In this context, many church leaders believed that only a fresh spiritual awakening could curb the tide of evil being unleashed on the country. John McLean expressed his hope that 'if a God-sent revival would sweep over Scotland, our churches would increase by leaps and bounds, for Baptists were born in a revival, and in revivals they have been born again down through the centuries ... we can by prayer, holy living, earnest consecration and aggressive effort, create such a warm, spiritual atmosphere in our churches, that conversions will take place continuously'.[21] This note of confidence that encouraged a desire for and expectancy of revival in the churches, created a spirit of prayer in the lives of many Scottish Baptists.[22]

Welsh Revival

When the Welsh revival occurred in 1904, it was 'totally unexpected'.[23] Indeed, as far as Baptists in Wales were concerned, the work of Home Mission, founded in 1895, had to stop in 1904 because of lack of funds. However, by October of 1904, the revival movement was affecting several Baptist congregations in Wales, although the work of Evan Roberts, the acknowledged leader of the movement, did not begin until November of 1904. By January 1905 some 3,000 new members had been added to Baptist churches in the

---

[20] Janice Holmes, *Religious Revivals*, p. 167.
[21] McLean, *Our Witness as Baptists and how to maintain it*. Scottish Baptist Year Book 1907, p. 22
[22] The Twentieth century fund, organized by Scottish Baptists, made it possible for the Baptist Union of Scotland to support church extension work. During the 1905 Baptist World Congress, two prominent British Baptist leaders, Alexander McLaren and F. B. Meyer, in keynote speeches, sounded a confident note in the hope that revival would touch the heart of the nation. In his Presidential address, McLaren spoke of the 'touch of the fiery Spirit, the Spirit of burning and the Spirit of holiness' and of how 'we are all crying out for revival'. Near the end of the Congress, Meyer stated that Baptists are 'optimists; the future is with us. I do not believe that the world has got to get worse before it gets better. I dare not believe it. The law of evolution is carrying us up and onwards towards the goal.' *Proceedings of the Baptist World Congress*, pp. 20 and 306.
[23] T. M. Bassett, *The Welsh Baptists* (Swansea, 1977), p. 377. W. T. Stead, editor of the British review of Reviews, commented that 'never in the history of Revival has there been any Revival more spontaneous than this'. 'Mr Evan Roberts', in *The Story of the Welsh Revival* (New York, 1905), p. 54. Stead was a friend of William Booth and an active spiritualist who supported the Welsh revival because of its impact on social reform and wrote three articles on the movement. Like another person involved in the revival, John Harper, he died on the Titanic's maiden voyage across the Atlantic. See Brynmor P. Jones, *Voices from the Welsh Revival* (Bridgend, 1995), p. 155. Basil Hall says that 'its unordered spontaneity, so frequently commented on by observers, makes it unique in the history of revivals'. 'The Welsh Revival: 1904-5: A Critique', in *Popular Belief and Practice* (Cambridge, 1972), p. 295.

Rhondda Valley with similar numbers being seen in other Baptist Associations.[24]

Some connection has been made between the revival in Wales and the influence of the Keswick Convention where many miners had gone in 1904.[25] Furthermore, a number of ministers who had experienced renewal of personal life at Keswick became leaders of the revival movement in Wales. One of the strong elements of the Keswick movement that undoubtedly influenced the revival movement was the connection made by leaders at Keswick and Wales between the necessities of seeking personal holiness of life before a revival could ever take place. For Evan Roberts the churches needed to 'learn the great lesson of obedience to the voice of the Spirit' and then 'the world' would be upon 'the threshold of a great religious revival'.[26] Campbell Morgan, in a similar vein, spoke of the three principles he had learned from the revival movement 'listening to the Spirit, confessing Christ openly; absolutely at his disposal'.[27] Conversely, the revival leaders were convinced that worldliness and sin could hinder or quench the work of the Spirit. To A. T. Pierson 'hugging the world' or a 'doubtful indulgence' such as 'smoking a cigar' could resist the work of the Spirit.[28]

It was a movement that was characterized by the involvement of laity, especially young men and women and even children, the absence of preaching and prolonged meetings that were taken up with singing, prayer, testimony, exhortations and the free expression of human emotions. It was an expression of popular religion, unregulated by ordained clergy. Campbell Morgan, minister of Westminster Chapel in London, visited the scene of the revival and commented that 'there is no preaching, no order, no hymnbooks, no choirs, no organs, no collections, and finally no advertising ... everybody is preaching ... they abandon themselves to their singing ... a praying remnant have been agonizing before God ... and it is through that the answer of fire has come'.[29]

---

[24] See Bassett, *Welsh Baptists*, p. 378.

[25] See Charles Price and Ian Randall, *Transforming Keswick: The Keswick Convention Past, Present and Future* (Carlisle, 2000), p. 168.

[26] Evan Roberts, 'A Message to the World', in *the Story of the Welsh Revival*, p. 6.

[27] G. Campbell Morgan, 'The Lesson of the Revival', in *The Story of the Welsh Revival*, p. 51.

[28] A. T. Pierson, 'Resisting the Holy Ghost', in *Keswick Week, 1905*, pp. 58, 60, 61.

[29] G. Campbell Morgan, 'The Lesson of the Revival', in *The Story of the Welsh Revival*, pp. 42-44. '[S]ong and prayer and testimony and conversion and confession of sin by leading church members publicly, and the putting of it away. And all the while no human leader, no one indicating the next thing to do, no checking the spontaneous movement.' G. Campbell Morgan, 'The Revival: Its source and Power', in *Glory Filled the Land: A Trilogy on the Welsh revival of 1904-1905*, ed. Richard Owen Roberts (Wheaton, 1989), p. 171. Although Campbell Morgan was profoundly moved by the revival and said that 'the whole thing is of God; it is a visitation in which he is making man conscious of Himself without any human agency ... God has given Wales in these

The chief characteristic of the message of the revival was the person and work of Christ,[30] 'the joys of heaven here on earth rather than the terrors of hell hereafter'.[31] When Evan Roberts preached, reporters spoke of how 'he frequently dwells on the Passion of our Lord, often breaks into tears as he describes the Divine suffering ... and instead of directly attacking secular amusements ... seeks to draw man from bondage to the world by the superior love of Christ'.[32] D. M. Phillips described his 'preaching' as being 'extremely simple; with a great deal of action, always expressive' but with 'no attempt at oratory ... just a few remarks thrown in as occasion arises'.[33] The effectiveness of the message came, however, not through the spoken word, but 'upon the billowing waves of sacred song. ... It is in the singing, not the preaching, which is most efficacious in striking the hearts of men.'[34]

One of the striking features of the Welsh revival was the public involvement of women, as singers and preachers,[35] a feature of earlier revivals in the nineteenth century,[36] and one which offered the freedom of expressing spiritual

---

days a new conviction and consciousness of Himself' ('The Revival', p. 177) and 'I have never seen anything, like it in my life' ('The Lesson of the Revival', p. 39), there is no mention of the awakening in his biography or the volume of autobiographical letters edited by his daughter.

[30] E. Cynolwyn Pugh, *The Welsh Revival of 1904-1905*, p. 232.

[31] D. M. Phillips, *Evan Roberts, the Great Welsh Revivalist and His Work* (London, 1906), p. 333. Roberts stated that he was 'merely trying to show people the love of Christ as I have experienced it'. Arthur Goldrich, 'The Story of the Welsh Revival', in *The Welsh Revival*, p. 15.

[32] A. T. Fryer, 'The Revival in Wales', *East and West: A Quarterly Review for the Study of Missions* (April 1905), p. 181.

[33] Phillips, *Evan Roberts*, p. 333.

[34] Phillips, *Evan Roberts*, p. 302. The *Western Mail* commented that 'Mr. Roberts did not preach a sermon' although 'the congregational singing was at times very effective, but the "sermon" contained in that pathetic hymn caught the congregation and swayed it considerably with emotion'. *Western Mail*, 21 November 1904.

[35] Calum Brown speaks of how 'from the standpoint of women's history, British religiosity became highly feminised, and evangelicalism created a vital side for the discourse on women's identity and role'. *The Death of Christian Britain* (London, 2001), p. 59.

[36] Jeffrey, *When the Lord Walked the Land*, p. 12. Janice Holmes argues that 'female participation in public preaching was a regular feature of revival activity, even in the later stages of the Victorian period and among denominations ... who had formally prohibited such female endeavour. ... Leading revival meetings gave women an opportunity to fill personal spiritual gifts as well as leadership aspirations. ... Rather than viewing the phenomenon from the perspective of decline, female preaching should be seen as adapting and taking on new forms in response to a changing social and religious environment. Although marginalized in the face of growing denominational institutionalization female preaching continued to exist throughout the nineteenth century, in areas which remained favourable to popular revivalism'. *Religious Revivals*

gifts in the public arena. The *Western Mail* reported that 'Miss A. M. Rees was, as usual, particularly energetic in all her evangelistic work, and her quiet conversations with dozens of young men were remarkable in every aspect.'[37] Roberts surrounded himself with several young women[38] who took a lead in the singing of hymns and spiritual songs during the revival meetings. One of the young women, Annie Davies, who took a prominent role, was eighteen when the revival broke out and travelled to all Roberts's meetings during his final three journeys and then was involved in other missions in London and different areas of Scotland[39] when 'the audiences were enraptured by her signing'.[40] One description of her role in the meetings commented that 'Miss Davies had started a hymn, in the midst of which she broke into tearful, beseeching prayer, that Evan Roberts stood up and exercised his almost uncanny power.'[41]

Scottish Baptists

The Welsh revival received many visitors from different parts of the world, including significant leaders such as F. B. Meyer, G. Campbell Morgan, General William Booth and Gypsy Rodney Smith. Included in their number, numerous Scottish Baptist ministers travelled south to experience the movement for themselves and returned to encourage an expectation that the awakening could also affect Scotland.

The first notice of the Welsh revival took place in an editorial within the *Scottish Baptist Magazine* for January 1905.

> An extraordinary revival of religion has visited Wales ... the meetings [are] emphatically prayer meetings ... earnest, brief, personal and urgent ... the people do not engage in prayer, but pray with all their hearts, as those who desire a blessing, and will not rest until their obtain it. Men, women and children have been taking part in the Welsh revival meetings, many of which are prolonged for hours, without weariness and with comparatively little excitement. In many cases the meetings have no leader, but they have nevertheless proceeded with perfect order ... short exhortations, professions of faith, hymns and prayers alternating without restraint, but with an absence of confusion. There are hundreds; we might without exaggeration say thousands of professed conversions. Ministers testify that their membership is increasing at a rate that has scarcely ever been known

---

in Britain and Ireland, p. xviii, 108. She also mentions a Miss Graham of Edinburgh who attracted huge audiences of the curious in Peterhead in 1863, p. 123.

[37] *Western Mail*, 8 December 1904.

[38] Phillips says that there were five 'singing sisters', although one 'Madam Morgan Llewelyn, who was a professional singer – are as conspicuous in the movement as Evan Roberts himself'. *Evan Roberts*, p. 304.

[39] Miss Davies visited Coldstream for a five week mission in 1907 with Rev. F. Clarke and both were described as Welsh evangelists. *Charlotte Chapel Record*, April 1907,

[40] Phillips, *Evan Roberts*, p. 265.

[41] Phillips, *Evan Roberts*, p. 403.

before ... and the people of Wales are manifesting the keenest interest in the present and eternal welfare of their friends and neighbours ... this movement is seizing and reforming the indifferent multitudes where regular and evangelical efforts have failed. ... Will it visit us? Yes; if we are prepared to use the means – to pray, not in a perfunctory and matter of custom way; but with earnestness and sincerity, that God would send us the blessing.[42]

In his presidential address to the Baptist Union Assembly in 1906, John McLean reflected, not only on the statistics of the revival which were impressive but on its significance for Baptists in Scotland.

From all parts of Wales, our sister churches report abnormal progress because they received an abnormal blessing during the recent revival. The number of baptisms is far beyond anything recorded in previous years: viz. 24,651 as compared with 5746 from the previous year, and 5874 two years ago. ... If a God-sent revival were to sweep over Scotland, our churches would increase by leaps and bounds, for Baptists were born in a revival, and in revivals they have been born again down through the centuries. It is not in our power to command revivals...for revivals come down from heaven, and are not got up by men. But we can, by prayer, holy living, earnest consecration and aggressive effort, create such a warm, spiritual atmosphere in our churches, that conversions will take place continuously.[43]

In March 1905, the editor of the magazine returned to the subject of revival and spoke of how

The desire for a deep and widespread revival of religion has been growing in connection with our churches and throughout Scotland generally. Everywhere an impression prevails that a revival of no ordinary kind is coming; and this feeling has of late been much accentuated by the remarkable success that has attended the movement in Wales. ... We have now arrived at a stage when even worldly people look upon a revival as a thing to be expected.

Responding to the criticism that the revival in Wales was characterized by emotionalism due to the character of the Welsh people and that the 'Scotch, on the other hand, and especially the educated among us, set much value of a certain cold stolidity', he argued that

the thing to be aimed at is a legitimate and wise self-control; but self-management does not necessitate the locking-up of the fountains of our emotions ... we conduct

---

[42] The magazine also gave a description of the Welsh revival in a separate article on p. 9 describing the ministry of Evan Roberts and his success in different parts of South Wales. The *Revival Times* noted 'much blessing in connection with evangelistic services in different parts of Scotland – a new interest ... a greater readiness ... to respond' and particular mentioned meetings in Glasgow, Motherwell and Forfar. 15 May 1905.
[43] Scottish Baptist Year Book 1907, p. 22.

ourselves best when we allow just that amount of play to our emotions that is justified by the circumstances in which we are placed. To repress emotion when it ought to be expressed is to do violence to our nature.

He concluded his editorial by assuring his readers throughout Scotland that

the revival has begun in many of our Churches ... our own Baptist ministers are in fullest accord with the movement, and prepared to do their utmost to speed its progress ... [during] our Union quarterly meetings ... on two occasions ... our ministers engaged in special prayer for personal quickening and revival in the churches. The prayers were brief, pointed, and earnest to a degree – expressive of the burden of their hearts – showing with what intense anxiety they are seeking the effectual operation of the Holy Spirit.[44]

Charlotte Chapel, Edinburgh

In the many Scottish communities where congregations were enjoying, as well as eagerly expecting and praying for a copious outpouring of the Spirit, none was more dramatic than Charlotte Baptist Chapel in the West End of Edinburgh.[45] The revival as the church experienced it was a close reflection of what had occurred in Wales.

In February 1902, when Joseph Kemp accepted the invitation to become the new pastor of Charlotte Chapel, membership of the congregation numbered 100, but only 35 were active in attendance. Three years later 347 new members had been added to the church and the congregation continued to grow in succeeding years, becoming the largest Baptist church in Scotland.[46]

Kemp avidly read the accounts of revival in George Whitfield's life and was influenced in his thinking on the work of revival by the writings of Charles Finney. During a period of recuperation in the south of England in January 1905, Kemp heard of the revival in Wales and spent two weeks 'watching, experiencing, drinking in, having my own heart searched ... then I returned to

---

[44] *Scottish Baptist Magazine*, March 1905, pp. 41-42.

[45] The Chapel was founded in 1808. In 1956 Gerald B. Griffiths commented that 'it was the experience of revival which rescued the church from the fate of being sold as a city warehouse for one the Princes Street shops, and transformed it into a centre of exultant evangelism'. See Preface to I. D. E. Thomas, *God's Harvest: The Nature of True Revival* (Bryntirion, 1997), rev. edn, p. 7.

[46] Kemp had studied for two years in the Bible Training Institute in Glasgow and worked with the Ayrshire Christian Union as an evangelist. He pastured two churches in the Borders, Kelso and Hawick where he stressed the importance of revival and imminence of the second coming of Christ. 'He took great delight in the doctrine of the Lord's Second Coming ... and prepared a chart to illustrate ... the progress from chaos to cosmos' as 'he reviewed the different dispensations.'

my people Edinburgh to tell them what I had seen'.[47] J. J. Thomas returned from Wales with him and on Saturday 22 January they held a conference on revival that lasted from 3.30 p.m. until midnight. It was to be the first of innumerably prolonged meetings over the coming weeks and months. One of the chief characteristics of these meetings, following the experience of Wales, was that of prayer, testimony and singing. Even on Sunday services there were occasions when Kemp found it difficult to preach because of the audible prayers of the congregation. The Chapel held 750 people but was often crowded with every nook and cranny being utilized by young and old, including many children. In 1905 around 1,000 were converted and 203 new members were added to the church, bringing the membership at the end of 1905 to 520. Following a period of relative quietness, a Sunday evening service at the end of 1906 brought a fresh sense of God's presence and 'the fire fell ... quite suddenly, upon one and another, came an overwhelming sense of the reality and awfulness of His presence and of eternal things ... prayer and weeping began and gained in intensity every moment ... prayer broke out, waves and waves of prayer', and when meetings were held on 1 January 1907 at 11, 3 and 6.30 the pattern of 'prayer, confession, testimony and praise' once again characterized the spiritual awakening.[48]

One of the features of this period of revival was that 'there has been very little or no preaching'.[49] Although the movement in 1906 was a 'year of advance', Kemp commented that it was not to the same extent as 1905.[50] By February 1907 the church realized that the dramatic events of the previous two years had finally come to an end and they began to 'reorganize the work in the Chapel on generally accepted Church lines', although conversions were experienced throughout the rest of the year. Indeed later that year Kemp commented that 'office bearers and church members' were often to be found 'sitting in other churches while their seats in their own church are vacant', a fact that he found 'disquieting and discouraging'.[51] In April 1907, Kemp once again delivered his lecture on the Welsh revival in the Tent Hall, Glasgow, the *Record* commenting that the 'recital made us long for a return of the movement'.[52]

Kemp believed that the characteristics of the revival that they experienced in Edinburgh was marked by three features: firstly, of a 'deep conviction of sin' when even 'many things thought to be right have been seen to be wrong and sinful ... a thing which may have been in itself perfectly lawful, has been abandoned because it stood in the way of full surrender' – as an example Kemp

---

[47] Kemp, *Joseph Kemp*, p. 29.
[48] Charlotte Chapel Record for December 1908, pp 20-21.
[49] Charlotte Chapel Record for December 1908, p. 22.
[50] The Chapel had 130 baptisms in 1905 and 102 in 1906.
[51] Charlotte Chapel Record.
[52] Charlotte Chapel Record, April 1907, p. 1.

recalled the way in which 'many testified to victory over novel reading, dancing, theatre going etc';[53] secondly, he identified 'prolonged intercession, sometimes for hours ... here we have learned something of what Wales experienced'; thirdly, a 'new spontaneity and power of the Prayer meetings ... the stream of prayer flows on unhindered'.[54]

Kemp himself began to widen his sphere of influence both in Scotland and America. In Scotland, he was a frequent speaker at various churches, giving his 'lamp light lecture on "The Welsh Revival"' in a variety of Baptist churches. On some occasions, such a visit to Aberdeen, the congregation of six hundred continued 'in prayer and waited on the Lord till nearly midnight'.[55] In 1912, the *Life of Faith* began a weekly Bible Correspondence course 'Back to the Bible' which had an initial membership of 2,200 that soon increased to 2,500. He would later preach at the Keswick Convention.[56] His revival experience drew several invitations to the United States where he came into contact with many American proto-fundamentalists. One of these contacts, A. C. Dixon[57] considered 'Mr. Kemp's work in Charlotte Chapel, Edinburgh, to be more lasting and further reaching than the Welsh Revival'. Kemp preached in the Moody Church of Chicago in July 1907 when Dixon was minister. Kemp also made contact with James M. Gray, Dean of Moody Bible Institute in Chicago[58] and invited him to conduct summer Bible Schools in Charlotte Chapel.

---

[53] Charlotte Chapel Record, December 1908, p. 22.
[54] Charlotte Chapel Record, March 1907, p. 1.
[55] Charlotte Chapel Record, June 1907. Kemp also was a speaker in Ayr, Maybole, Stirling and Abbeyhill, Edinburgh and at a conference on revival in Glasgow.
[56] In July 1926.
[57] Kemp, *Joseph W. Kemp*, p. 84. In 1901 Dixon became pastor of Ruggles Street Baptist Church, Roxbury, Massachusetts, a Boston suburb. Here Dixon taught at the Gordon Bible and Missionary Training School and wrote his famous *Evangelism Old and New*, an attack on the Social Gospel movement. In 1906 he accepted the pulpit of the Chicago Avenue Church (Moody Memorial Church), and he spent the war years ministering at Spurgeon's Tabernacle in London. During these years he was conspicuous at Fundamentalist gatherings.
[58] James M. Gray (1851–1935), born in New York City and reared in the Episcopalian Church. For sixteen years he pastored the First Reformed Episcopal Church in Boston. He was a Professor of what later came to be known as Gordon College. Founded in 1889 as a missionary training institute the school was named for its founder, the Rev. Dr. A. J. Gordon, a prominent Boston clergyman of the late 1800s. Dr Gray was involved at Moody Bible Institute for forty-three years as a summer guest lecturer, dean, executive secretary, editor of *Moody Monthly* and president from 1925 to 1934. He authored twenty-five books and booklets and served as one of the seven editors of the first Scofield Reference Bible.

Glasgow

During the nineteenth century Glasgow was at the peak of its self-confidence, referring to itself as the 'second city of the Empire'. Its cultural life was vibrant, reflected in fine classical buildings and its University was attracting scholars of international distinction. By 1870 more than half of the British shipbuilding workforce was based on the Clyde. One of the areas of Glasgow where work was booming was Govan with a population that grew from 9,000 in 1864 to more than 90,000 by 1914. Yet, despite its exceptional economic growth, everyday life for the majority of its population was one of poverty, overcrowded housing and sickness,[59] a city of contrasts, filled with challenges for the church at the turn of the twentieth century.

In 1895 the Baptist Union of Scotland supported the work of a young evangelist called John Harper, from Paisley Road, Govan and a church was constituted with 25 members in September 1897. In 1901, when the church had grown to 230 members, a hall with seating for 600 was built and over the following four years its membership grew to 445, the most vibrant period being September 1904 to October 1905 when 232 converts were baptized on profession of faith.[60]

The story of the church is one of active evangelism with over a thousand homes being visited on a yearly basis, with tracts and copies of Spurgeon's sermons being distributed. It ministered in an area of social need and Church Meeting minutes mention the 'great evil they had to contend against was strong drink as many homes were being ruined by it'.[61] In 1903 the Sunday school had 368 children on the roll with an average attendance of 246.

In the latter part of 1904 John Harper, assisted by Mr Dunn, held meetings every night for several weeks. The crowds were so large that in addition to nightly meetings in the Baptist church, the congregation took over the White Memorial Free Church and both buildings were full for several weeks of nightly meetings.[62] In April 1905 the *Scottish Baptist Magazine* reported that since December 1904 over 700 people had professed conversion with 100 being added to the church membership. In October 1905 the membership stood at 507. By August 1906 there were indications that the revival was ebbing and the church minutes complain that 'had it not been for the spiritual declension which has been quite manifest in our midst the number of conversions would have been very much larger' although 'the majority of the members are praying for a

---

[59] A School Board survey of 1906 indicated that a fourteen year-old living in a poor area of Glasgow was, on average, some four inches shorter in height than another child from the prosperous West End. A national survey of 1902 revealed that Glasgow was the most overcrowded city in Britain.

[60] *John Harper 1872-1912* (Harper memorial Baptist Church, May 1972).

[61] Members meeting Minutes from November 1901 to 1913. See minutes of meeting held on 8 October 1903.

[62] *Scottish Baptist Magazine*, February 1905, pp. 42-3.

great revival which will surely be given'.[63] In the summer of 1905 Harper's health broke and in January 1906 his wife died leaving him a baby girl. In 1910 he left to go to London and spent three months in the Moody Church in Chicago and a further movement of revival was experienced in the United States. Following a visit to Britain, he sailed back to America to spend three more months in Chicago but died on the Titanic on 10 April 1912. The church in Glasgow renamed its building Harper memorial Baptist Church.[64]

Victoria Place, Glasgow

The church was located in the Govanhill areas of the city, and John McLean was appointed as minister in 1889.[65] For twenty-nine years he exercised a strong evangelistic ministry and the church grew from 150 members to 450 in 1906. McLean became the convener of the Baptist Evangelistic Committee in 1904, and then President of the Baptist Union of Scotland in 1906. He preached 'the old evangelical truths of the Gospel with such fervour and sincerity, and with such an insight into, and knowledge of, the human heart, that the pews in the new building quickly filled and Victoria Place Church became a centre of light and leading in the district'.[66]

In May 1905 the church reported that it was in the fourth week of a special mission. Miss Maggie Condie, whom McLean had met on a visit to Wales, was acting as an evangelist and her 'sweet, simple, spiritual singing and testimony' was effective in winning many people to Christ. McLean commented that she was booked to conduct meetings in a number of Baptist churches in Scotland 'and a blessing is sure to attend her consecrated services wherever she goes'.[67]

Dennistoun

When news of the Welsh revival came to the Dennistoun church in Glasgow, the congregation committed themselves to intense prayer, holding meetings

---

[63] Minutes of Church meeting in August 1906.

[64] The new building was opened in 1922 by his daughter.

[65] Brought up in the Free Church in Argyllshire, McLean moved to Stirling, was converted and became a Coast Missionary in Eyemouth in 1879. Two years later he changed his views on baptism, returned to Stirling and was baptized through the ministry of George Yuille. Yuille was minister of Stirling Baptist Church from 1870 to 1913 and then became Secretary of the Baptist Union of Scotland. He edited the *History of Baptists in Scotland* (Glasgow, 1926). In 1883 McLean received a call to the pastorate in Dumbarton and during the next six years he not only attended classes at Glasgow University and the Free Church College but also founded congregations in Alexandria and Clydebank.

[66] See 'In Memoriam for John MacLean', *Scottish Baptist Magazine*, February 1923, pp 20-1.

[67] *Scottish Baptist Magazine*, May 1905, p. 87.

every evening for six weeks. During the last two weeks some visitors from Wales conducted a mission and a 'great number of people were brought to the great decision'.[68]

Partick

The Partick church was founded in 1904 as a church plant from Hillhead Baptist Church. During the early years of the century it engaged in energetic evangelistic outreach. In 1903 it reported that '134 kitchen meetings had been held with cheering soul-saving results' with 57 new members (taking the total membership to 212). Although their morning services averaged congregations of 300, the evening services had between 500 and 600 attending, with many conversions taking place. In 1905 over 120 conversions took place in a mission at which Miss Clark from Wales took part.[69] This growth continued and in 1907 a further 51 members were added to the church.[70]

Clydebank

In the middle of April 1905 the church presented the pastor with 11 guineas, three Sunday's leave of absence to visit the scene of the revival in Wales. On his return, the church held a conference on revival, which proved to be an inspiration and a success. The report indicated that times of revival did not stop the church being 'hampered' during the winter 'by the defective heating of the church on cold days'.[71]

Lanarkshire

The industrial growth in coal, steel, engineering and related industries brought growth to Lanarkshire during the latter part of the nineteenth century. The number of collieries grew from 151 in 1881 to 257 in 1895, with population growth continuing apace. Motherwell grew from a village of just over 9,000 inhabitants in 1871 to a large town of over 49,000 by 1921, a period of time that saw significant growth for Baptist churches in the area.

---

[68] *The Venture: Magazine of the Dennistoun Baptist Church, Glasgow*, no. 153, October 1951.
[69] *Scottish Baptist Magazine*, June 1905, p. 105.
[70] Scottish Baptist Year Book 1904, p. 96 and Charlotte Chapel Record, March 1908, p. 42.
[71] Scottish Baptist Year Book 1906, p. 66.

Bellshill

The Rev. George Harper, brother of John Harper of Govan, was inducted into the Pastorate in 1900 and during his ministry the building had to be considerably enlarged. A special mission in 1905 was instrumental in the conversion of many, the majority of whom ultimately became members, the membership almost doubling itself.[72] Harper reported that the 'town and community has been stirred as never before ... scores have had to be turned away from our Chapel unable to get near the door ... boys and girls are a marvel in their power of prayer and testimony'.[73] He attributed the beginning of the movement to a series of prayer meetings held at the beginning of January, lasting for three to four hours and which continued in the following months.

Motherwell

Joseph Burns came to Motherwell in 1898 and his long pastorate of seventeen years saw the Church grow into one of the strongest of the Lanarkshire congregations. During his ministry a wave of revival swept over the town and as astonishing increase in the numbers. The membership increased from 80 in 1898 to 290 by 1906. In 1898 the church had been in debt after the building of the church in 1895 and Burns came in on a supported ministry by the Baptist Union. In 1906 this debt was cleared and the ministry was self-supporting.[74] Mr Thomas from Wales came to conduct a mission in 1905 although the church reported that the mission had 'practically no speaking – praise and prayer taking up the whole time'. The church was attempting to capture something, not only of the spirit of the revival in Wales, but its very substance.

Galashiels: John Shearer

One of the most formative experiences of Shearer's life was his visit to the scene of the Welsh revival in 1905. During a church business meeting, Shearer 'earnestly pleaded for a more prayerful spirit being evidenced in order that we might share in the great work of revival Wales was presently experiencing'.[75] Shearer spent a week in Wales[76] attending meetings which he described as 'strangely solemn, yet ineffably joyous'. He spoke of the 'great waves of unseen power' which evoked 'prayer like a torrent. ... God is felt to be very near, and hot tears tell of deep repentance and reawakened love ... strong men [are] broken down in an agony of remorse'. Shearer met Evan Roberts whom he described as combining 'manly courage with womanly gentleness ... modest

---

[72] Yuille, *Baptists*, p. 216.
[73] *Scottish Baptist Magazine*, April 1905, p. 67.
[74] Yuille, p. 221 and an e-mail from the minister, Derek Watson, on 13 May 2003.
[75] *Scottish Baptist Magazine*, March 1905, p. 58.
[76] See *The Revival in Wales* reported in *Scottish Baptist Magazine*, April 1905, pp. 67-9.

and brotherly ... a man of God, possessed by the Holy Spirit'.[77] He returned to the Scottish Borders 'with a new heart and a new bible',[78] and 'much blessing followed' as the church held nightly meetings from 3 April to 8 July 1905, with over a 120 conversions recorded.[79] The longing for revival continued into 1906 when Shearer 'expressed a desire for the spread of prayer' during a Deacon's meeting 'and at the end of the meeting all the brethren present engaged in prayer, especially for revival'.[80] Although the numbers added to the church in Galashiels were not significant (membership rising from 244 in 1904 to 269 in 1906), this occurred during a period of time when trade depression hit the Border's area and affected all the churches in the area.[81]

Hawick

One other church in the Scottish Borders, Hawick, encouraged their pastor, D. McNicol to visit the revival in Wales and a meeting in the town hall the Sunday after his return drew 1,500 people. J. J. Thomas from Maesteg, South Wales held a mission and during a meeting when J. W. Kemp spoke of his experiences of revival, 'the soiree became a prayer meeting – just as much a miracle to some as water becoming wine'.[82]

Aberdeen

Gilcomston Park Baptist Church was founded in 1886 and in October 1902 A. Grant Gibb was inducted as the new pastor. Following his study of divinity at New College, Edinburgh he went to Limerick the way 'many testified to victory over novel reading, dancing, theatre going etc', and in Ireland he had a successful ministry and served as president of the Baptist union of Ireland. In 1905 he visited Wales and when he returned to report his experience 'the church betook itself to prayer, and ere long a gracious wave of revival swept over us ... there was a continual stream of additions to the fellowship which in 1908 reached its highest figure of 355'.[83] During his ministry of thirty-four

---

[77] *Scottish Baptist Magazine*, April 1905, p. 68.

[78] Comment in memorandum notebook.

[79] Shearer reported in the *Scottish Baptist Magazine* for June 1905, that 120 had been converted. Stirling Street had 37 Baptisms in 1905. The revival affected other Baptist churches in Scotland with John Harper, minister of Paisley Road, Glasgow (later Harper Memorial) reporting 700 conversions and over 100 added to their membership. See reports in *Scottish Baptist Magazine* for April, May and June 1905.

[80] Minutes of Deacon's Meeting, Stirling Street Baptist Church, 26 January, 1906.

[81] See Bebbington, *The Baptists in Scotland*, p. 124.

[82] *Scottish Baptist Magazine*, April 1905, p. 66.

[83] These Fifty Years: The Book of the Jubilee of Gilcomston Park Baptist Church 1886-1936, pp. 6-8.

years, he baptized over 500 people and welcomed 720 new members into the church.

Stirling

At a meeting of Deacons on 11 January 1905, Mr Yuille, the minister, expressed the hope that 'the great revival in Wales extend to Scotland and to Stirling and that prayer to this end be offered'.[84] The church was committed to evangelism and appointed a full-time evangelist who engaged in house-to-house visitation. During a mission led by A. Y. McGregor from Edinburgh there were 397 converts. The converts resulting from the mission were described as 'far in excess of any movement in Stirling within our recollection [and] there were no cases dealt with at the police court this week, but this we are told is merely 'a coincidence'.[85] The church increased in membership from 150 in 1903 to 222 in 1906.

Old Cumnock

The church reported a mission in 1905 with 'three Welsh friends' when 'quite a number have professed faith in Christ'.[86]

Dundee

Maxwelltown Baptist Church was formed in 1898, as a church plant from Ward Road Baptist Church. The new congregation of 34 members found itself in the midst of a teeming population of non-Church goers, but 'by house to house visitation, visiting the sick, officiating at the funerals of those who had no Church connection, cottage meetings, and open-air work ... the careless were awakened, drunkards reclaimed, and many brought into the Kingdom of God and added to the Church'.[87] In April 1905 the church reported that 'for the past three months quite a revival movement has been going on here ... with street parades and open air meetings'.[88] In 1908 the pastor, John Dick, left with about 350 members on its roll, a large Sunday school, and numerous active organizations.

---

[84] Records of Stirling Baptist Church, PD 154/2, Deacons' Meeting Book 1890–1911, pp. 210-11.
[85] *Scottish Baptist Magazine*, April 1905, p. 64.
[86] Scottish Baptist Year Book 1906, p. 67.
[87] Yuille, *Baptists in Scotland*, p. 161.
[88] *Scottish Baptist Magazine*, pril 1905, p. 65.

Inverkeithing

In 1904 a Christian Endeavour Society was formed in the town, and the open-air meeting was carried on with great enthusiasm. During the year crowded meetings were held weekly with several conversions. In March 1905 Mr Henry Turner, Alva was invited to lead a mission and began preaching nightly for three weeks. 'The town' the church recorded 'has been moved as it had not been for over 30 years ... some 350 have been converted.'[89] As a result the Mission Committee communicated with the Baptist Extension Committee with a view to the formation of a Church and with 55 founding members[90] a church was formed on 25 March with Mr Turner appointed pastor for six months. Under his ministry the membership steadily increased to 113.[91]

The Role of Women in the Revival

I've already mentioned several churches in Scotland who utilized women in various mission activities such as preaching, evangelism, and singing in meetings. The *Charlotte Chapel Record* mentioned the presence of Miss Davies, Welsh evangelist, being involved in a five-week mission in Coldstream in 1907. In April 1908 the *Record* mentioned Miss Annie McLaren 'recently returned from America is evangelizing with Mr Frank Weaver'.[92] In June 1905 the Alexandria church held a two-week mission with Miss Condie from Wales, and thirty people professed conversion, some of whom joined the church.[93] In May 1905 the Shettleston church in Glasgow held a special mission conducted by Miss Maggie Condie, from Wales, and between 150 and 160 people were converted, with about one hundred of the young converts forming Christian Endeavour societies. The church reported that they had added 15 new members through baptism and 'at present we are having a special season of prayer in view of Miss Condie's return on 15 October. Our sister will be with us for a fortnight, and we are expecting great things from God, and that many souls will be saved.'[94]

In Motherwell, during a conference on revival a Mrs Colville from Cleland spoke on the 'Filling of the Holy Spirit' and J. J. Thomas 'sang some of the favourite Welsh revival hymns'.[95] The Kelso church, in February 1905, invited Joseph W. Kemp to give an account of his impressions of the Welsh revival, and the church began nightly meetings for prayer for revival in the town. These meetings were carried on without a break till 20 August. A three-weeks mission

---

[89] *Scottish Baptist Magazine*, April 1905, p. 64.
[90] *Scottish Baptist Magazine*, April 1905, p. 64.
[91] Yuille, *Baptists in Scotland*, pp. 147-8.
[92] *Charlotte Chapel Record*, April 1908, p. 43.
[93] Scottish Baptist Year Book 1906, p. 70.
[94] Scottish Baptist Year Book 1906, p. 64.
[95] *Scottish Baptist Magazine*, May 1905, p.87.

was held in the church in midsummer at which Miss Davies, from Pontypridd was the missioner, and a few people were converted.[96]

The involvement of women during this period of revival in activities such as preaching appears to challenge the conservative interpretation of scripture that characterized Baptist churches in Scotland. The pragmatic evidence of the work of the Spirit through their lives and ministries appears to have countered other arguments to the contrary.

Modernism

The influence of the Welsh revival, with its 'conservative evangelical ethos',[97] influenced several Scottish Baptist ministers. David Bebbington has argued that one of the results of the Welsh revival was that 'a section of Evangelicalism, albeit a small one, remained firmly committed to the conservative side in the years after the First World War'.[98] During a conference on revival in Charlotte Chapel in April 1904, W. D. Dunn, speaking on the incident of 'Paul and the Vipers', stated that 'there were vipers clinging to the Christian Church today. There was the viper of slander, of pride, of laziness, and last of all, of higher criticism.'[99]

Towards the latter part of the nineteenth century, when developments in natural science, the emergence of higher criticism, led to a severe questioning of biblical faith, many observers believed that the spiritual life of churches was being affected and revival hindered. Baptists were not necessarily opposed to the insights of modern biblical studies. In an address to the Baptist World Congress, A. T. Robertson from Southern Seminary in Kentucky stated that 'Baptists are not opposed to criticism. ... We believe in an open book and an open mind.'[100] A. H. Strong contended that 'I am prepared to believe that this higher criticism may be one of Christ's methods of instructing the world, and just so long as higher criticism is animated by this Spirit of Christ and recognizes Christ's mastery, I have no fear of the conclusions to which higher

---

[96] *Scottish Baptist Year Book* 1906, pp. 68-69.

[97] Ian S. Rennie, 'Fundamentalism and the Varieties of North Atlantic Evangelicalism', *Evangelicalism: Comparative Studies of Popular Protestantism in North America, the British Isles, and Beyond 1700-1990* (Oxford, Oxford University Press, 1994), ed. Mark A. Noll, David W. Bebbington and George A. Rawlyk, p. 342.

[98] D. W. Bebbington, *Evangelicalism in Modern Britain: A History from the 1730s to the 1980s* (London, 1989), p. 196. Richard Riss comments that 'within the context of an awakening, people are almost invariably orthodox theologically with respect to the great basics of the Christian faith. Great emphasis is placed on the Bible and its teachings. Stress is usually laid upon the suffering, cross, blood, death and resurrection of Jesus Christ'. *A Survey of 20th century Revival Movements in North America* (Peabody, 1988), p. 4.

[99] *Scottish Baptist Magazine*, May 1904, p. 97.

[100] Proceedings of the *Congress*, p. 141.

criticism may lead. Therefore I simply open my mind to the truth, from whatever quarter it comes.'[101] However, there were other voices that sounded serious warnings against what they considered to be inroads to truth. During the same Congress in London, Dr A. C. Dixon of Boston pleaded for 'a rallying of the Baptist host around the Baptist standard – God's infallible Book'.[102] Supporters of the revival movement maintained that 'orthodox theology has always proved to be the hidden source of true revival'.[103]

John Shearer felt that the simple gospel that moved men and women during the revival was in danger of being rejected as a result of higher criticism.[104] In his presidential address to the Scottish Baptist Assembly in 1936, Shearer spoke of the 'danger [that] threatens us at the present moment. The new Rationalism that has invaded the Church has taken our feet from the firm ground of our faith and made us to flounder miserably in a quagmire of doubt'. He maintained the need to hold on to the fundamentals of Baptist faith such as belief in the Bible as 'the Word of the Living God' and 'our Lord's Deity' which will oppose the 'insidious Unitarianism that ... is deep seated in the churches of our land'. Thirdly, he spoke of the 'atoning death' of Christ as a 'perfect substitution'. This he contended was 'the central truth of Christianity'. He concluded by mentioning the Lord's Resurrection, the fact of the New Birth which opposed the 'New Rationalism' with its 'system of psychology' and also the Blessed Hope of the Church which he identified as the imminent return of Christ.[105] Although Bebbington argues that Fundamentalism did not make

---

[101] Proceedings of the *Congress*, p. 144.

[102] Proceedings of the *Congress*, p. 237. In a similar vein, Evan Philipps, Moderator of the Welsh Presbyterian Church in 1900, commented that 'a spirit of error fills the air, so that a silent subconscious influence on the minds of men attracts them away from the living God'. Cited by Eifion Evans, *The Welsh Revival of 1904*.

[103] David Matthews, *I Saw the Welsh Revival* (Chicago, 1951), p. 121.

[104] Shearer believed that the preparation he had received for pastoral ministry through Glasgow University was detrimental to the spiritual life of young students. Shearer attended the Moral Philosophy classes of Henry Jones. Jones's teaching led some students to believe that 'the deity of Jesus' was a 'later theological accretion (due in large part to Paul) extraneous, unnecessary, undesirable and illusory'. Later in his life, Shearer commented that 'the Arts course [at the University] displaced the Theological and we were urged [by the College] above all to secure our degree in Arts. It was a false preparation for the ministry and showed the growing baleful influence of Modernism.' Material from John Shearer's personal memorandum notebook in the possession of his daughter, Miss Flora Shearer, St Andrews. When he received the call from Stirling, Shearer commented on the desire which he had 'to preach among you the grand old verities of that old yet ever fresh Theology which are the very life of our life and which were never more needed than they are today'. Minutes of Stirling Baptist Church 1911-1918, for 1 July 1913.

[105] John Shearer, 'Forward: The Call to a Great Advance', in Scottish Baptist Year Book for 1937, pp 153-7.

serious inroads amongst British Baptists,[106] the concern of John Shearer in Scotland was echoed by many people among the churches of the denomination.[107] In Scotland, John Shearer published a series of booklets on Modernism,[108] focusing upon these very doctrines, arguing that at each point Modernism was undermining the evangelical message which for many years had been faithfully preached from Scottish Baptist pulpits. For Shearer, the only hope of the church was to be found in a fresh outpouring of the Holy Spirit and a concentration on issues relating to evangelism.[109]

Kemp and Charlotte Chapel

One of the contacts that Kemp made in America was that of James M. Gray, then dean Moody Bible Institute. In one of his visits to the Chapel on several summers, he delivered Bible Schools and dealt with subjects such as 'Is Jesus God or Man? And 'Is the Bible the Word of God?'[110] These lectures were described by Kemp as 'a tremendous counterblast to the New Theology, and made one feel how flimsy is the foundation on which the pioneers of the new propaganda build'.[111] In one of his studies in 1907, Gray maintained that 'we are living in a day now, when even in the evangelical church, the death and sacrifice of Jesus Christ is being ignored'.[112]

When the Chapel celebrated its centenary in October 1908, Kemp lamented the 'annual statistics sent forth by our different denominations' that indicated 'that the numbers attending our churches are growing less and less'. Kemp was convinced that one remedy was for the 'pew and the pulpit' to

> return to the old truths ... the old words of scripture ... the ancient doctrines ... we must get back to the words of 'the cross', 'the Blood' ... we must emphasise 'sin' its heinousness, deceitfulness, and the awful judgement God has pronounced over it. There must be no two opinions regarding heaven and hell ... there is no need for

---

[106] Bebbington, 'Baptists and Fundamentalism', pp. 320, 326.

[107] For example, J. Sidlow Baxter, minister of Charlotte Baptist Chapel in Edinburgh published one of Shearer's booklets on Modernism in the *Charlotte Chapel Record* for June and July 1944.

[108] See John Shearer, *The Baptist Confession of Faith* (Stirling, n.d.); *Who are the Baptists* (Dundee, n.d.); *Modernism: The Enemy of the Evangelical Faith* (n.p., n.d.); *The Evangelical Faith* (Glasgow, 1946), 2nd edn; *Modernism: The Enemy of the Evangelical Church* (n.p., 1946), 3rd edn.

[109] See John Shearer, *Old Time Revivals: How the Fire of God spread in days now past and gone* (London, n.d.).

[110] Gray wrote the article on 'The Inspiration of the Bible – Definition, Extent and proof' for *The Fundamentals*, published 1910–15.

[111] *Charlotte Chapel Record*, July 1907.

[112] James M. Gray, 'Synthetic Studies in the Epistle to the Romans', *Charlotte Chapel Record*, September 1907, p. 133.

us to depart from our doctrinal basis ... we shall hold forth the Atonement of Christ as the only hope for precious souls'.[113]

Kemp opposed the tenets of Modernism, and frequently made vigorous protests from his pulpit against any who would impugn the deity of Christ, or question the integrity or inspiration of the Scriptures. Kemp argued that Modernism was a menacing factor in the life and work and witness of the church.[114] This antipathy towards any opinion that deviated from the fundamental truths of the gospel was intensified through his two pastorates in America in 1915. When he immigrated to New Zealand in 1917, he took a lead in promoting fundamentalism in the country, actively propagating a biblical literalism, bolstered by the inerrancy theories of Princeton theology, a premillennial dispensationalism and a vigorous defence of the Keswick holiness movement. He preached sermons entitled 'the delirium of the dance', 'the menace of the movies', and 'the Bible in the Billows, an attack on Modernism'.[115] The climax of his influence was foundation of the New Zealand Bible Training Institute founded on the principles of Moody in Chicago. From March 1923, he published a monthly journal called *The Reaper* which contained articles on the inerrancy of scripture, the virgin birth, and the imminent return of Christ.

Conclusion

The impact of the Welsh revival of 1904 on Scottish Baptist churches was limited to particular congregations, scattered through various parts of the country. There is evidence to suggest that pastors who visited the scenes of the revival in Wales, or who employed Welsh evangelists in special missions, were more likely to experience similar movement of the Spirit. Baptist churches in Scotland were already growing at the beginning of the century, although there was a particular surge of growth in 1905 when 1,970 baptisms were reported, a higher than normal statistic.

The lasting impact on Scottish Baptist churches is harder to evaluate. The role of women in public aspects of evangelism did not continue and appears to have been limited to women from Wales who visit Scotland. The influence of the conservative ethos of the revival, in terms of theology however, would have a longer effect on the churches and would appear in the 1930s and 1940s to counteract influences of Modernism that began to appear with the life of the denomination.

---

[113] *Charlotte Chapel Record*, November, 1908.
[114] Kemp, *Joseph Kemp*, p. 116.
[115] Kemp, *Joseph Kemp*, p. 139.

CHAPTER 16

Scottish Brethren and the Welsh Revival of 1904-5[1]

Neil T. R. Dickson

The Scottish Brethren movement was the child of revival. The first known reference to the Brethren in Scotland was in 1838, but over the next two decades such assemblies (as the movement termed its congregations) as came into existence in Scotland tended to have a short lifespan, and by the late 1850s, when the movement had divided into the 'Exclusive' and 'Open' sections, the two divisions of the Brethren possessed perhaps some six assemblies each.[2] The turning point for them was the 1859 revival. The awakenings which emerged in America and Ireland from 1858 onwards quickly spread to Scotland, becoming, in the opinion of Ken Jeffrey, 'the first truly national revival in Scotland'.[3] Revivalism became a marked feature of Scottish church life over the subsequent decade, and it was reinforced by D. L. Moody's mission of 1873-4. One consequence was a flurry of Brethren assemblies being formed. By 1885 there were 115 assemblies belonging to the main branch of the Exclusives and in the following year some 184 Open Brethren ones.[4] Unlike the pre-1859 period, most of these assemblies were to have a long lifespan, and over the next hundred years they were to become a pervasive presence throughout Lowland Scotland and in the northern archipelagos of Orkney and Shetland, often forming in industrial villages the only religious alternative to the Presbyterian Church.

The Open Brethren, with which this chapter is concerned, became the dominant group throughout the United Kingdom.[5] In Scotland especially they saw revival resurgence as both their inheritance and future. This perspective can be seen in the years around the turn of the nineteenth century from the two Brethren journals, *The Witness* and *The Believer's Magazine*, which were

---

[1] The help of Dr Tim Grass with this paper is gratefully acknowledged.
[2] N. T. R. Dickson, *Brethren in Scotland 1838-2000: A social study of an evangelical movement* (Carlisle, 2003).
[3] K. S. Jeffrey, *When the Lord Walked the Land: The 1858-62 Revival in the North-east of Scotland* (Carlisle, 2003), p. 2.
[4] *References [January 1885]* (n.p. 1885); Sprague's list of assemblies quoted in *The Eleventh Hour* (January 1887), p. 4.
[5] For Brethren history, see F. R. Coad, *A History of the Brethren Movement: Its origins, its worldwide development and its significance for the present day*, 2nd edn (Exeter, 1976).

issued from Scotland. 'There are many of the Lord's people praying and longing for a Revival', wrote John Ritchie, the fiercely separatist editor of *The Believer's Magazine*, in 1900. '... And we have not the shadow of a doubt, that when the Lord's people are in real earnest about it, and prepared to receive it in God's appointed way, it will come.'[6] 'Are we about to have another 1859?', William Shaw had asked the previous year in *The Witness*, a more moderate Brethren journal which had become their principal review in Britain. 'There are those among the Lord's watchmen', he answered his own question, 'who believe we are about to be favoured with such a time ... They connect '59 with '99.'[7] Both these writers were themselves the products of awakenings. Ritchie had been converted during a period of revivalism in Aberdeenshire in 1871 out of which the Open Brethren in the region had emerged; and Shaw was a convert of 'the Maybole Revival' in Ayrshire of the early 1870s and was a founder-member of the assembly which had been formed there in 1877.[8] Both men felt that the fervour of the movement had cooled. It was natural, therefore, that they should look for revival to bring increased zeal within assemblies, resulting in further periods of ingathering of converts, and the consequent growth of the movement. The thought of revival was continually held before the Brethren. When, for example, a member of the Brethren in Wales was shown, in 1900, a letter written by Humphrey Jones, the Welsh revivalist of 1859, on 'how to become a truly successful preacher', he translated it into English and published it in *The Witness* as 'a means to stir up other young men to seek to be filled with the same spirit, and go forth in the same way'.[9] The importance of revival was also stressed in preaching. Special conferences at which several speakers would expound biblical topics were a significant feature of Brethren life, and in December 1902 four of the leading preachers of the Scottish movement addressed a 'Revival Conference' held in Glasgow at which they 'gave rousing and edifying addresses'.[10] The movement had institutionalized revivalism as a pattern with a number of itinerant evangelists dedicated to conducting revivalist missions and revivalist activities formed a large part of the weekly life of individual assemblies. But it was revival – a large-scale movement affecting churches and whole communities with substantial numbers of converts – which was perceived by the Brethren as being the primary mechanism of growth.[11]

---

[6] [J. Ritchie], 'Revival', *The Believer's Magazine*, new series [hereafter *BM*, ns] 1 (March 1900), 37.

[7] W. S[haw]., 'The coming revival', *The Witness*, new series [hereafter *W*, ns] 9 (February 1899), 24.

[8] Dickson, *Brethren in Scotland*, pp. 92-9, 142.

[9] H. R. Jones, 'The revival in Wales in 1858-9, and the way it began', *W*, ns 10 (November 1900), 169-70.

[10] 'Intelligence from many lands' [hereafter 'IFML'], *W*, ns 13 (January 1903), end pp.

[11] The distinction between 'revivalism' and 'revival' is senses R2 ('a deliberate meeting or campaign ... to deepen the faith of believers and bring non-believers to faith') and R4

By 1904 the Open Brethren in Scotland recorded the existence of some 285 assemblies.[12] Their expectation of revival resulted in some local outbursts of increased fervour and conversions in the years before the Welsh revival of 1904–5. Locally in the early Edwardian period, many assemblies reported successful missions with converts ranging from some ten to thirty individuals, but particularly profitable evangelistic campaigns appeared to have been held in places with a tradition of revival. In one report *The Witness* alluded to the revivalism in Wigtownshire of the late 1860s which had seen the Brethren movement established in the county: two itinerant evangelists in Stranraer and Lochans were witnessing, it was noted in February 1902, scenes 'similar to the moving times of 33 years ago, which spread to the Mull of Galloway, and went on for years'.[13] A year later in Lerwick in Shetland, where revivalism had again affected the Brethren in the 1870s, 'a work of grace' was reported in February 1903: 'Meetings have been held for a month,' it was reported, 'lasting three or four hours each meeting; the little hall became so crowded that the meetings were removed to a large fishing shed, with boxes, planks &c., for seats'.[14] Other parts of Shetland were affected in the following weeks. Two months later in April, when three Brethren evangelists joined an awakening which had affected the non-Presbyterian dissenting churches in Portessie and Findochty on the Moray Firth, a report in *The Witness* made a comparison to the 1859 revival. 'The Assembly, Wesleyan, and Salvation Army Halls were crowded with anxious enquirers,' it was noted, 'evangelists dealing with souls until midnight, and commencing again early in the morning.' It was reckoned that 'some hundreds of genuine cases of conversion' had occurred.[15] The following year in January 1904 'a remarkable spiritual awakening' was being reported from Westray, one of the Orcadian north isles. Westray had a tradition of revivals, and the assembly had been formed by majority secession from the Baptist church after one in the 1860s. The fresh awakening led to a brief thaw in the frosty relations between the Brethren and the Baptists, allowing them to cooperate in the revival, before they quickly froze over again.[16] By February it was being noted that 'Following on the blessing in Westray and Eday, a

---

('a regional experience of spiritual quickening and widespread conversions') in the typology developed by S. Latham, '"God came from Teman": revival and contemporary revivalism', in A. Walker and K. Aune (eds), *On Revival: A critical examination* (Carlisle, 2003), p. 172.

[12] J. W. Jordan, *List of some Meetings in the British Isles and Regions Beyond* (London, 1904), pp. 128-64.

[13] 'IFML', *W*, ns 12 (March 1902), end pp. The 'IFML' pages, in which the reports appeared, were made up late in the month prior to publication.

[14] 'IFML', *W*, ns 13 (March 1903), end pp.

[15] 'IFML', *W*, ns 13 (May 1903), end pp.

[16] N. T. R. Dickson, 'Revivalism and the limits of cooperation: Brethren origins in Orkney in the 1860s' in N. T. R. Dickson (ed.), *The Worldwide Growth of the Brethren Movement: National and international experiences* (Carlisle, forthcoming).

number have confessed in Sanday, Orkney, and the work seems to be increasing.'[17] These other two islands both had Brethren assemblies; as in Shetland, revivalism had spread from its starting point to other areas. Fishing was an important element in the economy of these coastal places. The pattern of revival in each fits that detected by Ken Jeffrey in the north-east littoral: they took place in winter when the fishing folk stayed at home and were prepared to be active long into the night during days of 'semi-holiday'[18] and in the northern isles, where farming was also important, the winter day was short and the nights were long. It is this freedom from work that probably also explains the intensity of the evangelistic missions in each place as considerable time was devoted to religious activities which invited comparison with earlier, perhaps more impressive revivals. It was in these coastal places that the most fervent Brethren campaigns took place in the years immediately before the Welsh revival.

As might be expected from such a context, news of revival in Wales was swiftly relayed to a specifically Brethren audience. In December 1904 *The Witness* printed a letter from David Jones, a Brethren evangelist in the principality, reporting the events at Loughor and Gorseinon.[19] 'May the work spread far and wide,' John Ritchie was proclaiming the following month, 'and all that would impede or corrupt be kept down.'[20] Ritchie's latter hope was significant, for reservations were expressed about the revival movement. William Shaw found it puzzling that an awakening was sweeping Wales while it did not take place 'among us who have professedly come out to the call of God, and are seeking to carry out His will according to His Word'.[21] That the Brethren should be untouched was also a problem for Ritchie whose theology of revival told him that if God's word was fully obeyed – and that duty most emphatically included adherence to Brethren ecclesiology – then renewal would surely follow.[22] Shaw felt that its absence was a sign that worldliness had taken over. Ritchie maintained that the presence of revival outside the Brethren was God's way in 'times of universal failure and departure from Himself';[23] more subtly he argued that care must be taken to distinguish between what God uses and what he approves of.[24] Assembly members 'have taken the place of separation' and consequently have the greater responsibility to act in accordance with the word of God, therefore they should avoid 'covert

---

[17] 'IFML', *W*, ns 13 (February, March 1903), end pp.
[18] Jeffrey, *When the Lord Walked*, pp.201-6.
[19] D. E. Jones to the editor, *W*, 34 (December 1904), 193.
[20] 'The Lord's work and workers' [hereafter 'LWW'], *BM*, ns 6 (January 1905), ii.
[21] W. Shaw, 'The revival in Wales: has it a voice for us?, *W*, 35 (1905), 28.
[22] The Editor, 'Revival', *BM*, ns 3 (August 1900), 85.
[23] 'Answers to correspondents', *BM*, ns 6 (February 1905), 22.
[24] [J. Ritchie], 'Revival times', *BM*, ns 6 (March 1905), 25.

worldly alliances'[25] – which was code for not engaging in interdenominational cooperation. There were more direct criticisms of the revival phenomena. Alexander Marshall, the doyen of Scottish Brethren evangelists, visited the revival scenes for three weeks early in 1905 and was enthusiastic about what he witnessed. However, he acknowledged that there were 'regrettable incidents' which he appeared to attribute to Evan Roberts's immaturity as a Christian. He deplored a reported comment of Roberts which maintained that the preaching of the conviction of sin or of 'knowledge' was not necessary. The Welsh, like the Scots, Marshall felt, needed to be told they were sinners. He quoted with approval censorious comments about 'carnal excitement and noise' and 'disorderly meetings'.[26] In early 1905 Ritchie had a calendar of criticisms. In January he was counselling a South Wales correspondent against '[f]eelings, testimony, and revival singing' as a diet for new converts;[27] in March he was critical of the Methodist and Baptist 'excrescences contributed by man' to hinder 'the Divine working'.[28] The next month he was warning against imitation of the Welsh revival, especially 'men, women and children being encouraged to take part indiscriminately, without a single reference to God, or the authority of His Word'.[29] Also in April he warned a South Wales correspondent against relying on dreams, a sign which he believed had ceased in the church.[30] In July it was statistics in the press compiled by preachers, men working in 'the world's religious systems', he was criticizing.[31] True revival, he was fulminating in August, was not '"wrought up"', ending in '"smoke"', with '"lady soloists" and other such crutches to help it along', but came from preaching of the 'old Gospel'.[32] In September he was again warning another correspondent against meetings open for all to take part indiscriminately, the object of godly order being to keep watch on the flesh 'like as a policeman does on a "hooligan"'.[33] The Brethren were distinctly uneasy about the more ecstatic and informal features of the Welsh revival. The pronounced cerebralism of their spirituality that acted as a counterforce to its heightened supernaturalism[34] meant that they hankered after an awakening which was more emotionally restrained, less phenomenonally irregular and entirely word-centred.

---

[25] [J. Ritchie], 'Revival and its counterfeits', *BM*, ns 6 (April 1905), 37.

[26] A. Marshall to the editor, *W*, 35 (March 1905), 65-6.

[27] 'Answers to correspondents' [hereafter 'AC'], *BM*, ns 6 (January 1905), 10.

[28] 'Revival times', *BM*, ns 6 (April 1905), 25.

[29] [Ritchie], 'Revival', *BM*, ns 6 (April 1905), 37.

[30] 'AC', *BM*, ns 6 (April 1905), 47.

[31] 'AC', *BM*, ns 6 (July 1905), 83.

[32] 'The Lord's work and workers', *BM*, ns 6 (August 1905), i.

[33] 'AC', *BM*, ns 6 (September 1905), 107.

[34] I. S. Rennie, 'Aspects of Christian Brethren spirituality', in J. I. Packer and L. Wilkinson, *Alive to God: Studies in Spirituality* (Downers Grove, IL, 1992), pp. 190-209; Dickson, *Brethren in Scotland*, pp. 251-85.

But despite this ambivalence, even Ritchie (as was noted above) welcomed the revival. The scale of conversions and the subsequent transformation of lives and rejection of the rougher features of working-class culture was one obvious source of satisfaction for a conversionist movement such as the Brethren with its strong division of humanity into the 'saved' and the 'lost'. The revivalist message that was being preached in Wales, despite its experiential flavour, generally found favour with them and so too did the preaching of the assurance of salvation which, David Jones claimed, 'is so different to almost all Welsh religionists'.[35] Additionally, there were features of the revival which chimed with distinctively Brethren emphases. They rejected any distinction between clergy and laity,[36] and so Evan Roberts's lack of ordination was decidedly in his favour. 'That God should raise up a young collier to do this work, setting aside the ordained "ministry", crowed John Ritchie, '... is a marvellous proof of the Sovereignty of His mighty grace.'[37] The openness of the revival meetings to the leading of the Spirit was another source of satisfaction to the Brethren whose most distinctive service, their communion service or 'breaking of bread', was similarly open to the promptings of the Spirit.[38] Doubtless Alexander Marshall spoke for many Brethren when he cautioned against being aloof and overly-critical. Instead he recommended the expectation of revival, for 'God is as willing to bless and save in Scotland and England as in Wales.'[39] It was the March 1905 edition of *The Witness* in which Marshall published his generally favourable report of his detailed investigations, the same month in which the magazine began a section among its news pages entitled 'Signs of Revival'. A general awakening was hoped for.

The revival undoubtedly affected the Brethren assemblies in Wales. The movement lacked central institutions and usually failed to keep local records which make it difficult to trace Brethren growth. In 1904 the address list of assemblies reported there were thirty-seven in Wales, all of them, with the solitary exception of Wrexham, in South Wales, and Glamorgan alone accounted for twenty-three of them.[40] However, it would appear that outside the urban areas of Cardiff, Swansea, Newport and their environs they were weak, for when one evangelist felt drawn in 1904 to work among 'small and needy'

---

[35] Jones to the editor, *W* (1904), 193.
[36] N. T. R Dickson, '"The Church itself is God's clergy": the principles and practices of the Brethren', in D. W. Lovegrove (ed.), *The Rise of the Laity in Evangelical Protestantism* (London and New York, 2002), pp. 207-35.
[37] [J. Ritchie], Revival times', *BM*, ns 6 (April 1905), 25.
[38] N. Dickson, '"Shut in with Thee": the morning meeting among Scottish Open Brethren 1830s-1960s', in R. N. Swanson (ed.), *Studies in Church History*, 35 (Woodbridge, 1999), 275-88.
[39] Marshall to the editor, *W* (1905), 66.
[40] [J. W. Jordan], *List of some Meetings in the British Isles and Regions Beyond Where Believers professedly gather in the name of the Lord Jesus for Worship and Breaking of Bread in remembrance of HIM, upon the first day of the week* (London [1904]).

assemblies, he thought of South Wales.[41] The strength of nonconformist culture and the lack of Welsh-speaking evangelists probably counted against the movement in the principality. However, there were already some full-time evangelists who worked among the Welsh assemblies, and some of them were Welsh speakers. David Jones was evidently one of them, and he claimed that some of the leading helpers in the initial revival at Loughor and Gorseinon were individuals who had been 'greatly blessed' during a Gospel tent mission he had held during the previous August and September.[42] There were others among Welsh Brethren who embraced the revival. In an unidentified place some fifty miles from Swansea people began crying out for salvation after a service in a Calvinistic Methodist Chapel conducted by a student: it was to the Brethren hall a request was sent for '"men with the words of salvation"'. In another unidentified small town near Cardiff, Alexander Marshall discovered that the assembly had held prayer meetings uninterruptedly for thirteen weeks and had seen some sixty converts.[43] The Cardiff and Swansea assemblies themselves and the ones in areas stirred by the awakening all saw converts. Clearly there were those among Welsh Brethren who were eager to be identified with revival as a transdenominational phenomenon, but, given their generally strongly separatist nature, there were probably more who took the advice of John Ritchie – he evidently had a South Welsh readership – not to compromise Brethren principles but be ready to teach the new converts.[44] Such Brethren, perhaps the majority in the principality, would attract new members through proselytism. Although it is difficult to document, it would seem that apart from the immediate numerical growth of some assemblies, the long-term effect of the revival led to the increase of the movement in Wales. By 1922, when the first address list after the revival appeared, there were fifty-five Welsh assemblies listed, an increase of 48.6 per cent since 1904. This represented twenty-one new assemblies (four earlier ones had been discontinued), and all but one of these were in Glamorgan, a stronghold of the revival, and the solitary exception was at Cross Hands, just over the border in Carmarthen. However, the precise founding dates of less than half of these are known, but from this limited data it would appear that most of them were commenced after World War I. Like the Pentecostal churches and the independent mission halls, which grew in the principality in much the same places at much the same time, the Brethren drew upon residual influences of the 1904–5 awakening through their revivalist missions and individuals seeking for a purified church order.[45] The revival had considerable impact on the movement in Wales.

---

[41] 'IFML', *W*, 34 (February 1904), end pp.

[42] Jones to the editor, *W* (1904), 66.

[43] Marshall to the editor, *W* (1905), 66.

[44] 'AC', *BM*, ns 6 (February 1905), 22; cf. 'LWW', ibid. (March), ii.

[45] D. D. Morgan, *The Span of the Cross: Christian religion and society in Wales 1914-2000* (Cardiff, 1999), p. 13.

Early in 1905 the Brethren in Britain also received reports of contemporary revivals further afield in Norway and Germany which were affecting their congregations, but in England too there were assemblies which profited from the increased fervour of the period. In London the Brethren eagerly listened to reports from Wales (among them Alexander Marshall's) and there were more than ordinarily successful missions in the capital held in Wimbledon and Stoke Newington. In some places in the West Country and Lancashire there were increased conversions, but the most successful Brethren missions in England during the early months of 1905 were, it would appear, in Carlisle and Nottingham which respectively claimed some 250 and 300 converts.[46] Outside Wales, however, it was in Scotland that the effects of the revival on the Brethren were most fully felt. Like their Welsh counterparts, Scottish Brethren profited by transdenominational revivalism, such as happened in Paisley where a mission by an American preacher, Dr Henry, affected the town's Bethany Hall assembly, or in Cockenzie, East Lothian, where the conversions among the Brethren were simultaneous with a stirring in the Seaman's Bethel, a local mission hall.[47] But the Scottish movement in this period was more than capable of generating its own revivalism. Two of the most emotionally intense occasions took place in Broxburn, West Lothian, and in Lockerbie, Dumfriesshire. In the shale-mining town of Broxburn it was reported that there were large open-air processions being held, and that assembly members were on occasion wakened during the night by interested individuals searching for salvation. There were some 200 converts.[48] At the market town of Lockerbie, the evangelist James Anderson was overcome:

> I felt strange – trembling all over. The sorrows of hell seemed to encompass me, and as I spoke the people quailed. The dying love of Christ melted our hearts and the people sobbed. For a few moments we were speechless. The Lord was at hand and I felt He must carry on the meeting, so I quietly left. The people were rivetted to their seats; the Spirit moved.

During his absence there were prayers, hymns and testimonies before he returned after an hour-and-a-half and brought the meeting to a close.[49]

Many other Scottish assemblies reported successful missions over the winter of 1904 and into the spring of 1905, such as the sixty converts reported from Troon, Ayrshire, or the twenty from Kirkintilloch, East Dunbartonshire.[50] Places as far apart as Shetland and Creetown on the Solway Firth were affected, but it was mainly the urban and industrial districts which were moved, particularly Glasgow and a number of Lanarkshire towns. In Glasgow there

---

[46] 'IFML', *W*, 35 (May and June, 1905), end pp.
[47] Ibid. (March and April), end pp.
[48] Ibid.
[49] Ibid. (May), end pp.
[50] Ibid. (March and April), end pp.

were larger than normal numbers of converts in the assemblies in Kelvinside North on the north side of the city; in Bridgeton on the east side; and in Govanhill and Crosshill on the south side. In the skilled working-class district of Kinning Park on the south-west of the city some 200 converts were claimed, and the same number was reported in the industrial town of Cambuslang immediately to the south of Glasgow in Lanarkshire.[51] The Brethren movement in the towns of Lesmahagow and Strathaven, also in Lanarkshire, had been born out of the 1859 revival and both places were moved in 1904–5. At Lesmahagow there had been a successful Brethren tent mission in the neighbouring mining village of Coalburn in the summer of 1904 and many of the converts from there joined in the revivalist activities in the town in the following winter. In the spring of 1905 there was a mission in the town's United Free Church of Scotland in which the Brethren joined, especially in the fervid after-prayer meetings, with converts being made in both the Church and Gospel Hall.[52] The assembly in the nearby textile town of Strathaven also reported a 'work of grace', begun after five weeks of prayer meetings in late 1904. In January 1905 the conversions began in the town followed by others in the neighbouring villages of Chapeltown and Glassford.[53] Further south in the county, in the lead mining village of Leadhills, the Gospel Hall could not contain the people crowded into it, necessitating a move into the Masonic Hall, while in north Lanarkshire in the steel town of Coatbridge the large numbers attending the gospel meetings meant contemplating a move from the Masonic Hall to larger premises.[54] These winter and spring months were ones of increase for many Scottish assemblies.

The converts were achieved mainly though preaching. Perhaps there were other nights in other places like the one James Anderson experienced in Lockerbie when the audience had become sovereign in the manner of the Welsh revival, but if so, any record of them has failed to survive. It had been a Saturday night 'tea meeting' that had proved the catalyst in Strathaven, but the crowded meetings of the preaching campaign held by two evangelists from January to March in the assembly in Motherwell and the preaching and testimonies given at the open-air services outside Dalziel Steel Works during shift breaks, which added sixty to the assembly in 1905, were more typical.[55] The Brethren remained wedded to the preaching of the word. 'The life of God in a soul cannot live on excitement,' Ritchie caustically commented on Wales,

---

[51] 'IFML', ibid. (April), end pp.

[52] James Anderson, 'A Brief Record of the Early Days of the Assembly in Lesmahagow', unpublished MS, 1960, pp. 44-6.

[53] *BM*, ns 6 (January 1905), i.

[54] 'IFML', *W*, 35 (March and June 1905), end pp.

[55] [J. Waddell], *Roman Road Hall Motherwell: Centenary 1875-1975* (Lanark, [1975]), p. 7.

'it needs the milk of the Word of God'.[56] The proof of the power present in the period for the Brethren was the conversion of 'well known sinners', as they were described in a report on Kinning Park, where they included a wrestler and a 'drunkard'. 'Some remarkable cases of conversion' were reported from Strathaven among the 'half-drunks, loiterers &c' invited to the tea meetings, while among the converts in Creetown, where salmon fishing was to be had, were, it was proudly noted, two poachers.[57] Embracing the world-denying Christianity of the movement was another sign of the power of the times. In Glasgow a whole football team was converted, and doubtless its members were expected to foreswear the game, a phenomenon of the Welsh revival which had been noted with approval.[58] Being 'saved' was expected to transform working-class rough culture.

It is difficult to quantify the scale of the revival movement as it affected Scottish assemblies because of the difficulties already noted with Brethren statistics. The membership numbers of two assemblies, Gospel Hall, Lesmahagow, and Elim Hall in the Crosshill district of Glasgow, which were affected by the Welsh revival, are extant for this period, and unusually for the Brethren, their records are relatively full. The achievements of the mission in Coalburn in the summer of 1904 can be seen in the fifty-two new members in the Gospel Hall, Lesmahagow, for that year, but twenty-one of these were added in November, marking the success of the revivalism of the winter (Table 1). A further forty-nine new members were added in 1905, although there was a gross decrease, mainly due to forty-seven individuals leaving to form an assembly in Coalburn. These figures represented a percentage increase of 30.3 for 1904 and a decrease in the gross membership for 1905 of only 8.5 per cent. In Elim Hall, Glasgow, there were five weeks of prayer meetings in the spring of 1905. After a brief visit from two workers in the Welsh revival, the assembly had seen many converts, a number of whom had become members.[59] These conversions largely explain the ninety-five new members the assembly added, making a percentage growth of 14.7 (Table 2). This was a smaller increase than might have been expected, because 1905 and the three subsequent years saw the highest number of people leaving the assembly in the years for which data are available in Table 2.[60]

---

[56] 'LWW', *BM*, ns 6 (January 1905), ii.
[57] 'IFML', *W*, 35 (April and June, 1905) end pp.
[58] Ibid. (March), end pp; Marshall to the editor, *W* (1905), 66.
[59] *Sixteenth Annual Report of the Assembly Meeting in Elim Hall, 5 Prince Edward Street, Crosshill, Glasgow. From 1st January to 31st December, 1905* (n.p., n.d.), [2].
[60] Additions and those leaving are not given for 1900 and the 1901 annual report is not extant.

TABLE 1. MEMBERSHIP OF GOSPEL HALL, LESMAHAGOW, 1900–1910

Year	Additions	Removals/leavers/deaths/plants*	Net gain	Gross membership
1900	15	7/6/2/0	0	94
1901	3	12/3/2/0	-14	80
1902	12	3/1/1/0	7	87
1903	23	6/2/3/0	12	99
1904	52	15/5/2/0	30	129
1905	47	4/6/1/47	-11	118
1906	18	12/12/0/0	-6	112
1907	12	10/5/0/0	-3	109
1908	11	7/3/1/0	0	109
1909	26	17/7/0/0	2	111
1910	12	24/5/1/0	-18	93

Source: Gospel Hall, Lesmahagow, roll books 1876–1907 & 1908–29.

* These categories are: those removing from the district; those leaving the Brethren; those dying; and those leaving to plant a new assembly.

TABLE 2. MEMBERSHIP OF ELIM HALL, CROSSHILL, GLASGOW, 1900–1910

Year	Additions	Losses/deaths/plants*	Net gain	Gross membership
1900	-	-	11	201
1901	-	-	28	229
1902	45	40/1/0	4	233
1903	61	37/3/0	21 (32)†	265
1904	49	34/1/31	-17 (-14)†	251
1905	95	50//6/0	39	290
1906	65	50/0/0	15	305
1907	56	50/1/0	5	310
1908	59	48/2/0	7 (9)†	319
1909	48	36/0/40	-28	291
1910	40	33/2/0	5	296

Sources: Elim Hall Annual Reports, 1900–1910.

* These categories are: those going from the assembly (presumably including both those removing from the district and those leaving the Brethren); those dying; and those leaving to plant a new assembly.

† The numbers in this row do not tally and the figure in brackets is an adjustment.

Unfortunately, unlike the data from Lesmahagow, those from Elim Hall do not distinguish between those removing from the district and those leaving the Brethren. Some of the losses may have been converts leaving the assembly when their ardour had cooled, for some thirty-two or thirty-three (over a third) of those who joined in 1905 left between 1905 and 1907.[61] It is perhaps significant that the assembly in Lesmahagow saw the highest number leaving the Brethren in 1906, although as these individuals are not named they cannot be identified as recent members. However, most of the losses in Elim Hall were evidently of single people, and, although some were possibly defectors from the Brethren among the recent converts, it is probable they mainly reflect the number of young folk in the congregation (particularly the offspring of members) who had to move for employment. The figures for the losses does list separately those who left to plant a new congregation, and the departure of thirty-one members to form Hermon Hall in Govanhill in 1904 explains the percentage decrease of 5.3 in that year. Hermon Hall was another of the Glasgow assemblies noted above which was affected by the Welsh revival. The new assemblies led to a greater overall increase. But in the history of the originating congregations, 1904 was the year in which the Lesmahagow assembly saw the largest number of new members added and the same was true of 1905 for Elim Hall.

TABLE 3. CONVERSIONS AND NEW MEMBERS, 1900–1910

Year	Conversions	Members	Aggregate
1900	47	45	92
1901	44	24	68
1902	36	44	80
1903	39	33	72
1904	43	43	86
1905	42	36	78
1906	36	29	65
1907	33	33	66
1908	23	40	63
1909	26	35	61
1910	23	38	61

Source: 'With Christ', *The Witness*, 33-108 (1903–78).
Note: When an individual's year of joining an assembly is available, the year of conversion (often the same year) has not been tallied to avoid double counting.

---

[61] It is not possible to positively identify one individual. The years of highest losses excludes the forty members who left to form an assembly in Shawlands, another neighbouring district, in 1909.

One way of approaching the question of numerical growth for the whole Scottish movement is through the years of conversion or of joining an assembly in obituary notices printed in *The Witness*. Although there are problems with these data (not least because the years of an individual's significant spiritual dates were sometimes given as an approximation) they do give a suggestive picture.[62] From Table 3 it can be seen that the years 1904 and 1905 stand out in the Edwardian decade as showing a greater increase in growth than the years immediately surrounding it, with 164 Brethren members being reported as being converted or joining an assembly in 1904 and 1905 compared to the 152 of the preceding two years and the 131 of the succeeding two years. One other indicator of growth is the six assemblies whose origins can be directly attributed to the heightened fervour of the revival months. Apart from the new congregation in Coalburn, there were also assemblies formed on the Shetland mainland at Northmavine; in Clackmannanshire in the textile village of Alva and the nearby industrial town of Alloa; and in the coal-mining villages of Saline, Fife, and Overtown, Lanarkshire.

The assembly address list for 1922 gives 335 ones for Scotland, an increase of 17.5 per cent over 1904, although because of the difficulties with statistics, it is not possible to compare this increase with that of the movement in Wales. Some fifty-five new Scottish assemblies had come into existence during 1904 to 1914 alone, although nine of these had been soon discontinued.[63] However, when the causes of their formation are analysed, then it can be seen that most were formed through the routine operations of the movement: the migration of members in search of employment, the transfer from other Christian bodies (especially mission halls), schisms within assemblies, the outreach of existing congregations and the work of itinerant evangelists.[64] According to the data in Table 3, 1900 (a year not singled out for being a revival one) was apparently more productive for conversions or for new members than either 1904 or 1905. The ordinary aggressive evangelistic functions, which the movement had inherited from Victorian revivalism, and the addition of members' children could be, it would seem, more productive of growth than the intense fervour of revival months. There were some later assemblies, possibly, such as the ones which were formed at Halfway, Cambuslang, in 1906 or in the Flemington district of Motherwell in 1908, which indirectly owed their existence to the growth which had visited the parent assemblies in 1905. Revival, as part of the ideology of evangelicalism and as part of the Brethren's own perception that God would favour them uniquely for their more perfect obedience to scripture, continued to be a potent hope for the movement. The Fisherman's Revival of 1921 would later affect Scottish assemblies; but awakenings were a declining factor in their growth, and the expectations of the potentially infectious nature

---

[62] For the problems with these data, see Dickson, *Brethren in Scotland*, p. 16 n.89.
[63] Figures compiled from Dickson, *Brethren in Scotland*, Appendix 3, pp. 411-24.
[64] Ibid., pp. 123-31.

of the Welsh revival were disappointed. It failed to become the longed for national British revival let alone a Scottish one, and even in those places which were affected it can be best described as revivalism at work rather than revival. That is they were not spontaneous folk movements, but were produced by the formalized procedures which the movement had developed for winning converts. At best they were the spiritual enlivening of individual congregations which led to increased conversions in a locality. There was to be no reversal of secularization through contagion by the Welsh revival.[65] There is also more certain evidence than that from Lesmahagow or Crosshill that the adherence of some of the converts or listeners was ephemeral. Perhaps some went to other churches, as had happened to a certain degree in Lesmahagow, but the futures of the assemblies in Lockerbie and Leadhills were not transformed by the winter of 1904–5, as both remained small. The new congregations in Alva and Saline proved to be transitory, and despite meetings being convened in the burgh hall for the converts in Kinning Park, they failed to form themselves into an assembly, a sure sign, given how few people were needed to start one, of a drift away. Although the assembly which met in the Masonic Hall, Coatbridge, had had high hopes of needing a new meeting place, it was not until 1924 that they moved from their rented accommodation. The final instalment of *The Witness* 'Signs of Revival' feature was for reports from May 1905. With the coming of the long Scottish summer days, people's minds in the industrial districts had evidently turned to other things.

---

[65] For the definitions on which these sentences are based, cf. J. Holmes, *Religious Revivals in Britain and Ireland 1859-1905* (Dublin, 2000), pp. xix-xx, 52-3; and senses R2 (see n.10 above) and R6 ('the possible reversal of secularization and 'revival' of Christianity as such') in Latham, '"God came from Ternan"', p. 172.

CHAPTER 17

The Great Awakening of 1905: The Welsh Revival and its Influence on the American Revival

Emmanuel Hooper

The Great Awakening of 1904–5 onwards appears have been more extensive worldwide, than all the preceding Awakenings. The Awakening had its inception in the Welsh revival of 1904 under the ministry of Evan Roberts. Prayer meetings were held around the world for a great awakening at the end of the nineteenth century and towards the dawning of the twentieth century, seemingly, 'a blaze of evening of glory at the end of the Great century'.[1]

The Awakening began in Wales in late 1904, and later through news of the revival and other witnesses and participants, spread to North America and other parts of the world. It is significant therefore to trace the incipient and origins of the 1905 American phase of the awakening to the Welsh revival.

On Friday 4 November, 1904, Evan Roberts wrote to the editor of *Sunday Companion* newspaper, noting that 'We are on the verge of a great grand revival, the greatest the world has ever seen.'[2] The early beginnings of the revival can be traced to the church of Reverend Joseph Jenkins at New Quay, Cardiganshire, as early as February 1904.[3] The youth of the young people's Christian Endeavour Society experienced a revival through the testimony of a young convert, Florrie Evans.[4]

In September 1904, Seth Joshua, who fanned the flames of the revival, arrived at New Quay, and found the place influenced by the spirit of revival, and recorded the following in his diary:

> 19th. Revival is breaking out here in greater power ... the young receiving the greatest measure of blessing. They broke out into prayer, praise, testimony and exhortation.

---

[1] J. E. Orr, *The Flaming Tongue; the impact of twentieth century revivals* (Chicago, 1973), p. 191; cf. Bibliography section B3 – 'The 1905 American Revival: Primary Sources', and Secondary sources in Bibliography Section B1 on Revival.

[2] *Sunday Companion*, in Daniel. M. Phillips, *Evan Roberts: The Great Welsh Revivalist* (London, 1906), pp. 198ff.

[3] *The Christian*, 7 September 1905.

[4] *The Christian*, 7 September 1905; cf. Seth Joshua Diaries, September 1904.

20th. I cannot leave the building until 12 and even 1 o'clock in the morning – I closed the service several times and yet it would break out again quite beyond control of human power.
21st. Yes, several souls ... they are not drunkards or open sinners, but are members of the visible church not grafted into the Vine ... the joy intense.
22nd. We held another remarkable meeting tonight. Group after group came out to the front, seeking the 'full assurance of faith'.
23rd. I am of the opinion that forty conversions took place this week. I also think that those seeking assurance may be fairly counted as converts, for they had never received Jesus as personal Saviour before.[5]

Evan Roberts, then, a student at Newcastle Emlyn Academy, requested special permission with other students to attend the revival meetings of Seth Joshua and, subsequently, came into a revival experience. He declared: 'I felt ablaze with a desire to go through the length and breadth of Wales to tell of the Saviour; and had that been possible, I was willing to pay God for doing so.'[6]

On 31 October, 1904, Roberts obtained permission from Principal Phillips, to return home to testify to his church. Upon arrival in his home church in Loughor, Roberts laid out the four points of his message:

1. You must put away any unconfessed sin.
2. You must put away any doubtful habit.
3. You must obey the Spirit promptly.
4. You must confess Christ publicly.[7]

The response was so overwhelming that the revival continued throughout that week with further meetings the following week. As the revival became more noticeable, the crowds began to pour into the church, and soon the newspapers were filled with the story.

The first newspaper account began with the title 'Great Crowds of People Drawn to Loughor' on 10 November 1904:

A remarkable religious revival is now taking place in Loughor. For some days a young man named Evan Roberts, a native of Loughor, has been causing great surprise at Moriah Chapel. The place has been besieged by dense crowds of people unable to obtain admission. Such excitement has prevailed that the road on which the chapel is situated has been lined with people from end to end. Roberts who speaks in Welsh, opens his discourse by saying that he does not know what he is going to say but that when he is in communion with the Spirit, the Holy Spirit will speak, and he will simply be the medium of His wisdom. The preacher soon after launches into a fervent and at times impassioned oration. His

---

[5] Seth Joshua Diaries, September 1904.
[6] Phillips, *Evan Roberts*, p. 124; cf. *Western Cardiff Mail*, 1904, pp. iii, 31.
[7] Jessie Penn-Lewis, *The Awakening in Wales 1904-1905* (London:, 1905), pp. 18-19; cf. *Western Cardiff Mail*, consolidated reports, 1904, pp. 31ff.

statements have had the most stirring effect upon his listeners. Many who have disbelieved Christianity for years are now are returning to the fold of their younger days. One night, so great was the enthusiasm evoked by the young revivalist that, after his sermon that lasted two hours, the vast congregation remained praying and singing until two-thirty in the morning. Shopkeepers are closing early in order to get a place in the chapel, and tin and steel workers throng the place in working clothes.[8]

On 11 November, a newspaper reporter, from Cardiff described the scene: 'Instead of the set order of proceedings ... everything was left to the spontaneous hour, the people did not make their way home, when I left to walk back to Llanelli, I left dozens about the road still discussing the chief subject of their lives. I felt that this was no ordinary gathering.'[9]

The social impact of the revival was astounding. Miners transformed by the revival changed their profane language that instructed the horses, thus they were misunderstood, causing a slow down in the mines. All segments of the society were transformed. Crime, embezzlements, drunkenness, illegitimate births, and many social malfunctions were drastically reduced to such an extent that policemen, lawyers and judges were out of work. The police were transformed into quartets for churches in some cases.[10]

By 1905 the revival was at its peak, and in two months 85,000 were converted, increasing to over 100,000 in six months.[11] The revival spread through England, Scotland, Ireland, and the European continent.[12] The awakening in Wales was significant in terms of how it affected social structure and church growth. It is the scale of the impact that resulted in the news of the revival reaching America and other parts of the world. Primary sources indicate that contemporaries and eyewitnesses provided insights into actual occurrences. It was these vivid expressions that affected the American continent.

It is essential in unbiased authentic historiography that the primary sources should speak without distortion of evidence. Preceding an analytical and critical assessment of the events, and how the revival originated in America, it is vital to examine the primary sources and establish both authenticity and credibility of the sources in the historiography. The contemporary sources of eyewitnesses

---

[8] *Western Mail*, 10 November 1904.

[9] *Western Mail* consolidated reports 1904, I: 4ff.

[10] *Registrar-General*, Statistics on Births, Deaths and Marriages; cf. Jessie Penn Lewis 1905, pp. 23ff; J. Vyrnwy Morgan, *The Welsh Religious Revival* (London, 1909), p. 247, Oxford University Bodlean Library, UkOxU.UB LCN PY2993; Criminal Statistics, United Kingdom; *The Christian*, February 23 1905; April 13 1905.

[11] J. Vyrnwy Morgan, *The Welsh Religious Revival*, pp. 248ff.

[12] *British Weekly*, 26 January 1905, 9 February 1905, 23 March 1905; *Irish Christian Advocate*, 10, 17 March 1905, *Scottish Baptist Magazine*, 1905, pp. 42-86; *Lutheran Herald*, 8 March, 14 June 1906; 4 April 1907; *Missionary Review of the World*, 1906, p. 310; 1907, pp. 36, 527, *Journal de Evangelisation*, 26 October 1905.

should be analysed prior to a critical assessment, and thus prevent reductionism or distortion of historical primary research.

The following extracts from primary sources are intended to provide an objective, authentic and credible historiographical account of the American revival and its origins in the Welsh revival. Initially, the extent and unusual nature and significance of the Welsh revival should be evaluated to explain how and why it had such an influence in America and other parts of the world. The details below therefore explain why it not only impacted America, but also the secular, religious and social structures of Wales, then Britain, and Europe and other parts of the world.[13]

Dr G. Campbell Morgan, minister of Westminster Chapel in London provided an objective view of the revival:

> I am speaking with diffidence, for I have never seen anything like it in my life; while a man praying is disturbed by the breaking out of a song, there is no sense of disorder, and the prayer merges into song, and back into testimony, and back again into song for hour after hour, without guidance. These are the three occupations – singing, prayer, testimony. Evan Roberts was not present. There was no human leader ... they saw the face of God and the eternities. I left that evening, after having been in the meeting three hours, at 10.30, and it swept on, packed as it was, until an early hour next morning, song and prayer and testimony and conversion and confession of sin by leading church members publicly, and the putting of it away, and all the while no human leader, no one indicating the next thing to do, no one checking the spontaneous movement ... I come across instance of men converted by reading the story of the revival in the 'Western Mail,' and the 'South Wales Daily News.[14]

He summarized the characteristics of the revival as follows:

> What is the origin of the movement? ... You tell me that the revival originated with Roberts. I tell you that Roberts was a product of the revival. You tell me that it began in an Endeavor meeting where a dear girl bore testimony. I tell you that was part of a revival breaking out everywhere. It is a Divine visitation – in which God is saying to us: see what I can do without the things you are depending on; see what I can do in answer to a praying people; see what I can do through the simplest, who are ready to fall inline, and depend wholly and absolutely on Me. ...
>
> What is the character of this revival? It is a church revival ... more than that have been converted, but the churches in Wales have enrolled during the last five weeks 20,000 new members ... Now what effect is this work producing on men? First of all, it is turning Christians everywhere into evangelists. ... Another

---

[13] *The Christian Advocate* (21), 16 February 1905, 261ff; 5, 23 January pp. 17, 123, 127; cf. *Missionary Review of the World*, October 1905; pp. 728ff; *The Watchman*, 7 (87), 16 February, pp. 1, 9-13; March, 1905, 13 April, pp. 11-17.

[14] G. Campbell Morgan, 'The Welsh Revival' (London, 1905; reprinted in *The Watchman*, 16 February 1905, pp. 9-12).

characteristic is that you never know just where this fire is going to break out next ... The whole movement is marvellously characterized by a confession of Jesus Christ, testimony to His power, to His goodness, to His beneficence, and testimony ...

I say to you today, beloved, without any hesitation that this whole thing is of God ... the revival is far more widespread than the fire zone ... even when you come out of it, and go into railway trains, or into a shop, a bank, anywhere, men everywhere are talking of God ... It is a great recognition of the presence and power of the Spirit manifesting itself in the glorification of Christ ... Pentecostal power and fire are being manifested.[15]

Contemporary scholars in both Britain and America witnessed the revival and gave an objective primary account. Dr Arthur Levi, Professor of Law at Aberystwyth University assessed the revival:

The revival has been with us nearly three weeks, and is more than ever; ... this church has held meetings every night. One or two churches hold nightly meetings. All the churches also hold occasional meetings marked with unusual fervour. Some of the meetings have continued until two or three in the morning. I have remained for hours in them without tiring, and felt no wish to leave. There is in truth no excitement; it is like listening to the Divinest music; every meeting is calm, restful, and deliberate; and every event spiritually ordered ... Every kind of meeting, literary, political, theatrical, has had to give way. Our whole town is overjoyed. Our life has shown new possibilities. Our faith has received an enlightenment, which leaves nothing more to be desired. Every man who has attended these meetings is sure in his heart. It is as if Jesus Christ had come to the town of Aberystwyth, and, indeed, He has come.[16]

The assessment of primary evidence of the revival by contemporary scholars elucidates the extent of the revival. Professor W. W. Davies of Ohio Wesleyan University, in his analysis in 1905 of the Welsh revival expressed his expectations of the spread of the revival to America:

The results have been already very great. Over ten thousand conversions were reported up to the second week of December ... It is gradually extending to all over the British Isles and even to our beloved land? ... May the time speedily come when our churches throughout the length and breadth of this great land shall witness scenes such as are now common in Wales![17]

Dr Arthur T. Pierson, the scholarly American editor-in-chief of the *Missionary Review of the World*, gave an eyewitness assessment of the Welsh

---

[15] Campbell Morgan, 'The Welsh Revival', pp. 10-12.

[16] Arthur Levi, in Davies, 'The Great Welsh Revival', *The Christian Advocate* (17), 26 January 1905, p. 137.

[17] W. W. Davies, 'The Great Revival in Wales', *The Christian Advocate* (17), 26 January 1905, pp. 137-8.

revival: 'The Voice of The Holy Spirit in The Welsh Revival: He who hath an ear, let him hear, what the Spirit saith unto the churches' (Revelation 3:22). [18]

> After four to five weeks' tour amid the very centers of the mighty work of God in Wales, addressing crowds of converts, and coming into daily and close contact with the prominent workers in the revival, compels the conclusion that, in a remarkable way and with unusual emphasis, God's Holy Spirit has been saying to the churches words of encouragement and warning that every one who has an ear should reverently and obediently hear.
>
> For many months Wales has been the scene of supernatural working. After making all due allowances for that characteristic 'emotional' Welsh temperament, and, after eliminating all inexact and extravagant statements, there remains a large body of incontrovertible facts which can only be explained by a Divine working on human souls, and, in some cases, on whole communities. ... After making careful inquiry, gleaning trustworthy information from many sources, and diligently observing for one's self, some mature conclusions have been forced upon us which we soberly put before the reader. We believe that it is with a loud, clear voice, rather than a 'murmur of stillness,' such as Elijah heard, that the Holy Spirit is now speaking to all the churches.'

He summarized his primary eyewitness analysis as follows:

> 1. First of all, He is laying a new stress on *confidence in the Inspired Word of God* (Italics his) ...
> 2. The Holy Spirit is voicing to the churches the *Sovereignty of His Divine operations* ...
> 3. Another voice of the Spirit in this revival has been strongly emphasizing the *possibilities of a Spirit filled assembly*. The power of individual prayer, work, and holy living ...
> 4. The Spirit saith unto the churches a solemn word on the power of earnest and united
> 5. *The Spirit is teaching also the power of sacred song* ... It is very noticeable how largely singing has promoted and extended this revival. ... the true character of worship ... an assembly of praise.[19]

The American newspapers reported news of the Welsh revival from the British press. The following editorial illustrates such columns:

> From the eyewitnesses of the Welsh Revival: From the notices of the work of God in Wales with which the English press are filled we cull these picturesque passages: 'A Christly Christmastide': A correspondent of the Christian Commonwealth (London). Writes of what he saw at Christmas tide: ... It can truly be said that the Christmas of 1904 was the first real Christmas many children –

---

[18] A. T. Pierson, Editor-In-Chief, 'The Voice of The Holy Spirit in The Welsh Revival', *Missionary Review of the World*, October 1905, pp. 728-33.
[19] Ibid., pp. 728-33.

> yea, and men and women – of Wales ever had ... The Light of Wales had entered over twenty thousand homes of fair Cambria and had illumined them with His gracious presence ... Enquiries of the police showed that not a single prisoner was detained throughout the holidays ... The Rev. Thomas Davies, of Pontypridd, puts the situation in his church in a few striking words: 'To my church and congregation and the neighborhood the revival has been and still is a great blessing ... The hours slip by without knowing to us. We generally leave chapel about 10.00 pm., but we carry the meeting with us to our respective homes, and on many a hearth there is prayer, Bible reading, and hushed singing going on until the small hours of the morning.
>
> ...
>
> The Methodist Times correspondent of Jan. 5 contributes these additional items: The secular press is still fanning the flame by sympathetic reports of the revival meetings.
>
> Surely the most remarkable fact yet recorded in daily journalism is the 'Revival Edition' of the Evening Express, published in Cardiff on Dec. 27. The managers have found a football edition to pay them well, so they experimented on Tuesday week with a 'Revival Edition,' in which every article, every report, every paragraph, and every portrait, indeed every line, except the advertisements dealt with religious work. It has had such an enormous sale that a similar edition was produced last Tuesday.[20]

Thus, reporting in America, the editors urged their American readers to obtain the reports from the British press for themselves. This resulted in a great impetus for a similar manifestation of revival in North America:

> We advise the readers of the Methodist Times to order for themselves these revival editions of the last two Tuesdays from the Cardiff office, for the sake of the information as well as the of the astounding novelty. It only shows what a magnificent service the church of Christ could command from the news agencies of the world if it were fired everywhere with whole-hearted enthusiasm for the Master's work.[21]

Letters came from America and other parts of the world to Evan Roberts upon hearing of the Welsh revival: 'Evan Roberts himself shed tears of gratitude, and was moved to speak in English, and told how he was receiving letters from England, Scotland, Ireland, Norway, France, Spain, America, and Africa.'[22]

Meanwhile many ministers came from America, Europe, and elsewhere to witness the revival and capture it for their local communities:

---

[20] *The Christian Advocate* (19), 26 January 1905, pp. 138-39; cf. 'Scenes from the Welsh Revival', *The Christian Advocate* (21), 16 February 1905, pp. 261ff.

[21] *The Christian Advocate* (19), 26 January 1905, p. 139.

[22] *The Christian Advocate* (21), 16 February, p. 261.

> Rev. Richard Hartley, pastor of Hope Baptist Church, New York City, recently visited Wales and gave an account of his observations, at the noon meeting at Tremont Temple Boston, Monday March 20. ... I went to Wales at the request of the Bryn Mawr Conference, a company of ministers of New York City for Bible study and evangelism, and I feel that God has something better for us later on ... When the people found we had come from America, they turned the meeting into prayer for America, and I believe we shall see the results of those prayers. ... People were there from all parts of Europe. A company of Scotchmen, who had come to form a judgment of the revival, wept for joy that God had come in blessing to his people. One hundred thousand have been converted.[23]

Reverend Hartley reported his observations of the revival to the American ministers:

> One overwhelming evidence of the fact that God is working mightily is the influence which these meetings have upon ministers and other Christian workers. In the four days I have been in Mr Roberts' meetings I have met and talked personally with scores of Godly men coming from all parts of Europe. Without an exception, all testified to a marvellous quickening of their own spiritual life. Faithful men of God, who have labored faithfully, but with little result, are going back to their homes with a new fire of faith and love burning in their hearts. God is going to spread this Holy flame through these His servants until the world is aglow with a new light shining from the face of our enthroned and glorified Savior ...
> I came from America for the sole purpose of being in these meetings. I would gladly go round the world if need be to receive the blessing which has come into my own life. Words are powerless to describe the things that have been happening, or rather the things that God has been doing.[24]

Even secular observers remarked on the unusual nature and characteristics of the revival:

> Repentance, open confession, intercessory prayer, and above all else, this marvellous musical liturgy – unwritten but heartfelt, a mighty chorus rising ... And all this vast, quivering, throbbing, singing, praying, exultant multitude is intensely conscious of the all – pervading influence of some invisible reality – Now for the first time, moving palpable though not tangible in their midst. They call it the Spirit of God. Those who have not witnessed it may call it what they will; I am inclined to agree with those on the spot.[25]

When the news from the Welsh revival arrived in North America the journals were filled with articles such as this editorial by a widely read

---

[23] Rev. Richard Hartley, 'The Revival in Wales', *The Watchman*, 23 March 1905.

[24] Rev. Richard Hartley, 'The Revival in Wales', *The Watchman*, 16 March 1905, p. 13.

[25] W. T. Stead, 'More about The Revival in Wales', *The Watchman*, 20 April 1905; cf. Stead, 'Evan Roberts', *The Watchman*, 13 April 1905.

interdenominational magazine: 'The Coming Revival: From various parts of the country, the welcome news comes of an earnest deep-seated desire for a revival of religion'.[26] Dr Francis E. Clark, founder of Christian Endeavour, declared to his American interdenominational movement that the Welsh revival had its incipient in their Young People's Society in New Quay, Wales:[27]

> If such a revival can shake Wales, why not America? If the Welsh Awakening began in a Christian Endeavor meeting, why not the America?' In 1904, the reports of the Welsh revival reached the local Ministerial Association in Schenectady, New York and united the denominations in prayer meetings and evangelistic rallies.[28] At the Northfield Conference for Student Volunteers, founded by D. L. Moody, the news of the Welsh revival was personally related by G. Campbell Morgan, which resulted in a revival at the conference.[29] In Virginia early news of the Welsh revival were featured by the religious press. Thus in February, the minister in Norfolk preached on the 'Coming of Great Revival' to America.[30]

In early 1905, the Baptists of South Carolina presented their readers with articles on the Welsh revival and Evan Roberts, and motivated them to pray for revival of prayer, Bible study and conversion of multitudes. This resulted in revival in the Carolinas and Georgia.[31] In Michigan, the Baptists devoted the front pages of their journal to the Welsh revival, with such titles as 'Lessons from the Welsh Revival', by G. Campbell Morgan. Subsequently there were large mobilizations of prayer for revival in Michigan.[32]

When ministers heard of the Welsh Revival in Indiana, they organized prayer groups and conferences in Indianapolis, and other towns in Indiana among various denominations to pray for revival.[33] Similarly in Chicago, when the news of the Welsh revival was reported to praying ministers, a decision was made to operate within the churches as in the Welsh revival.[34]

Soon the news of the Welsh revival spread through the East, the South, Mid-West, the North, and Western states of America, and generated prayer movements for revival along with evangelism.[35]

---

[26] *Christian Herald*, 1 February 1905.
[27] *Christian Endeavor World*, 5 January 1905, cf. 6 April 1905.
[28] *Evening Post*, Schenectady, New York, in *The Christian Advocate*, 26 January 1905.
[29] *The Christian*, 7, 14 September 1905.
[30] *Religious Herald*, Richmond, 2, 23, 30 March 1905.
[31] *Baptist Courier*, Greenville, South Carolina, 9 February 1905.
[32] *Michigan Christian Herald*, 26 January 1905; cf. 9, 16, 23 February, 1 June 1905.
[33] *Baptist Observer*, Indianapolis, February 1905, March 1905ff.
[34] *Pentecostal Herald*, 15 March 1905; *Baptist Argus*, 16 March 1905; *Christian Endeavor World*, 23 March 1905.
[35] *The Standard*, Chicago, 11 February 1905; 6 January 1906; *Baptist Commonwealth,* Philadelphia, March 1-7, 1905; *Baptist Courier*, Greenville, S. C., 9 February, March 2 1905; *Baptist Congress,* Cincinnati, January –April 1905; *Baptist Home Mission*

Analytical Assessment of the Welsh Revival and its Role in the American Revival

In summary, the Welsh revival influenced the American revival as follows:[36]

1. Through direct observation of eyewitnesses from America, and their reporting of the revival in America.
2. The reports of the religious and secular press from Britain.
3. The reports by American correspondents in the religious and secular press in America.
4. The accounts by British eyewitnesses of the Welsh revival in America.

Although one main influence on the American revival was the Welsh revival, there were indications that a degree of religious resurgence had begun in America through some prayer movements, especially in the South along with

---

Monthly, Philadelphia, 1905 pp. 86, 92, 112, 254, 359ff; *Central Baptist,* St. Louis, 13, 27 April 1905; *Christian Advocate,* New York, 4, 17, 25, 26 January; 2, 8, 9, 15, 22 February; 2, 9 March; 6 April; 24 May; 8, 22, 29 June 1905; *Christian Herald,* Philadelphia, 1, 15, 22 February; 22 March; 5, 19 April; 24 May 1905; *The Churchman,* New York, 1905, pp. 11, 218, 256, 409; *Inter-Convention Baptist Congress,* 1905, p.3ff.; *Journal and Messenger,* Cincinnati, Ohio, Vol. 74, Jan 5 1905ff, 2 February 1905; *The Lutheran,* Pennsylvania, 16 February; 30 March; 13, 27 April; 1, 15 June 1905; *Lutheran Herald,* Decorah, Iowa, 1905-1906; *The Lutheran Observer,* Louisville, 3, 10, 15 February; 10 March 1905; *Lutheran Standard,* Columbus, Ohio, 1905; *Lutheran Witness,* 4 May; 15 June 1905; *Methodist Review,* New York, 1905, pp. 998, 999; 1906, pp. 276, 279; *Michigan Baptist Convention,* Lansing, 1905, 1906; *Pacific Baptist,* 11 January; 1, 8 February; 1, 29 March; 19, 26 April; 24 May 1905; *Western Christian Advocate,* Indianapolis, 31 January; 8 March 1905, 17, 31 January, 21 February, 9 May 1906; *Western Recorder,* Louisville, 4 May 1905; *Zion's Herald,* Nashville, Tennessee, 19 January 1916; 28 February 1917.

[36] See full reports of newspapers in Footnotes 6–35, cf. *The Advance,* Chicago, 16, 23 February; 2, 5-9 March; 1905, June 24 1915; 1906, pp. 177, 222; *British Weekly,* London, Jan. 1905; *Christian Herald,* Philadelphia, 1, 15, 22 February; 22 March; 5, 19 April; 24 May 1905; *Christian Herald,* London, 12 January 1905; 22 February; 30 March 1905; 29 June 1905; cf. 1905-1906; *Christian Observer,* Louisville, 8, 15 February; 1, 8, 15, 22 March; 24 May; 7 June 1905; *Christian Endeavor World,* Boston, 23, 30 March; 4, 27 April; June; 13 July 1905; 5 January–6 April 1905; *The Examiner,* New York, 19, 26 January; 2, 16, 23 February; 16 March; 6 April; 11 May 1905; *Michigan Christian Advocate,* Adrian, 21 January; 4, 11, 18, 23 February; 18 March; 1, 8, 15, 23, 29 April, 6 June, December 9, 16 1905; *Methodist Times,* London, 1905; *The Revival* Reports. Later known as *The Christian* (London: Morgan and Chase, 1905ff); *The Student Movement:* Reports of the Student Movement: The Organ of the Student Christian Movement of Great Britain and Ireland. London, 1904-1905: (June-Oct), vol. 7, nos. 1-9; 1905-1906: (June-Oct), vol. 3, nos. 1-9; New York, 1925; *Student Volunteer Movement Students and The Modern Missionary Crusade.* New York: Student Volunteer Movement For Foreign Mission, 1905-1906.

evangelism.[37] On 2 November 1904 businesses, stores, factories and offices, and even saloons and places of amusements were closed to enable employees to attend the mid-day prayer meetings. The Supreme Court of Georgia was also adjourned. In Atlanta the newspapers reported one thousand businessmen united in prayer for revival.[38]

However, it was largely due to the news of the Welsh revival, widely publicized in religious and secular newspapers in America, along with the eyewitness accounts from American visitors to the Welsh revival that generated a greater impetus for prayer movements for revival in America.

The revival resulted in church growth, social change, evangelism, local and international revivals, and missionary outreach, as the news of the revival spread worldwide. The critics however, could not cause a declension in the revival and awakening, instead there was increased momentum between 1904 and 1906. Its effects in North America were greater impetus for a manifestation of genuine revival of churches for conversion, and socio-political reform. The Welsh revival occurred within the churches, and affected the public widely – revivals in coal mines, colleges, universities, and industrial sites, resulting in reduced police services, decreased imprisonments, changes in morality and greater religious fervour and evangelistic outreach.

The American phase of the 1904–6 revival was noticeably parallel to the revival in Wales, but it had its own characteristics, and particularly in the dimension of missions.

The early stages of the American revival were often described as 'revival meetings', however, when the revival actually occurred, the increase in prayer meetings, number of attendees, number of conversions, protracted meetings, overflows in churches, and the closing of businesses to allow employees to attend meetings, and eventual closure of churches for lack of space, all characteristic of the Welsh revival were manifested.[39] The early stages of the awakenings were defined from late 1904 to early 1905, and intensified between January and June 1905, with results more definable in late 1905 and early 1906.[40]

---

[37] *Christian Herald*, 12 January, 1 February, 1905ff; cf. *Western Christian Advocate*, 14 February, 4 July, 19 September, 1900; *Christian Endeavor World*, 5 January 1905.

[38] *Christian Herald*, 12 January 1905.

[39] *Journal and Messenger* (74), 2 February 1905; p. 21; *Christian Observer*, Louisville, Kentucky, 22 February 1905; *Christian Herald*, 12 January, 1905; cf. Lutheran Witness, (24), Jan-Dec., 12 January, 1905.

[40] *The Watchman*, 9, 16 March, 8 June, 1905; Missionary Review of The World, January, July, October, 1905, pp. 729-733; cf. Dr H. J. Carrol, 'Statistics of the Churches in the Unites States,' in *Christian Advocate*, 5 (1905), pp. 17-19; *Western Christian Advocate*, Indianapolis, 31 January; 8 March 1905, 17, 31 January, 21 February, 9 May 1906; *Western Recorder*, Louisville, 4 May 1905; *Zion's Herald*, Nashville, Tennessee, 19 January 1916; 28 February 1917.

CHAPTER 18

The Fruit of Revival in Uganda

Tudor Griffiths

'Revival' is a complex and multi-dimensional term. It is religious and also cultural, indeed it can be cross-cultural, and this is the particular dimension I would like to explore in this chapter, considering some of the links between 'revival' in the UK and in Uganda between roughly 1890 and the middle of the twentieth century. My hope is that the changing shape of revival in Uganda might not only prove interesting for its own sake but may also cast some light on revival studies elsewhere.

When Henry Venn, the Secretary of the Church Missionary Society (CMS) in the mid-nineteenth century, was told that revival had broken out in Ireland in 1859, his response was to send across a deputation in order to *'connect the revival with missionary zeal, for the sake of the revivalists themselves, as well as for our cause'*.[1] But it was in Scotland not Ireland that year that a young man was converted, Alexander Mackay.[2] In due course he became an engineer and offered for missionary service with CMS. He arrived in Uganda in 1878 and never left east Africa before his death in 1890. Mackay was the CMS missionary most closely linked with the Uganda martyrs of the mid-1880s. By 1890 there was something of a new mood in CMS. In Cambridge particularly the impact of Keswick thinking allied with a new confidence about missionary calling led to some very strong criticism of missionary work up to that point. This was most noticeable with regard to west Africa with Brooke and Robinson heading out to correct what they perceived as the mistakes of Bishop Samuel Crowther. But Douglas Hooper, who had been a member of Trinity Hall 1883–85 and subsequently a lay missionary in east Africa, was actively looking to recruit for Uganda on behalf of CMS. He persuaded two Georges, Pilkington and Baskerville, for Uganda. Pilkington was converted in Cambridge under the influence of Moody and Sankey, and he had been interested in going with Hudson Taylor's China Inland Mission, which had the reputation among some Cambridge students of being more *spiritual* than CMS, but Hooper persuaded him otherwise, arguing the need to establish the work in Uganda under more

---

[1] H. Venn, from a private letter, 7 January 1860, quoted in E. Stock, *History of the CMS*, Vol. II (CMSA, 1899), p. 33.
[2] See J. W. Harrison, *The Story of Mackay of Uganda* (London, 1892).

'spiritual lines' than formerly.³ Hooper did not remain long in Uganda, and thankfully the experience of meeting Baganda Christians led both Georges to revise their opinion that the salvation of Africa was solely in the hands of educated Cambridge gentlemen.

By 1893 Pilkington had been in the country for three years. Bishop Tucker had given him the task of translating the Bible into Luganda. He was tired and generally feeling discouraged with the hard graft of missionary work. Both Pilkington and his colleagues felt that many Baganda were becoming Christians for very mixed motives that had little to do with authentic spirituality. Then the church council heard from one Musa Gyabuganda. He communicated that he wanted to leave the fellowship and have his name announced in church that he was no longer a Christian.⁴ On hearing this Pilkington went off to the island of Kome in Lake Victoria to pray. Speaking to Liverpool students in 1896, Pilkington related the story:

> If it had not been that God enabled me after three years in the Mission field, to accept by faith the gift of the Holy Spirit, I should have given up the work. ... A book by David, the Tamil evangelist, showed me that my life was not right, that I had not the power of the Holy Ghost. I had consecrated myself hundreds of times, but I had not accepted God's gift. I saw now that God commanded me to be filled with the Spirit.⁵

At the same time Baskerville recorded in his Journal that they wanted 'a Baptism of the Holy Ghost, first of ourselves and then it will soon spread'.⁶ So when Pilkington returned from Kome to announce that had 'definitely received by faith the baptism of the Holy Ghost', Baskerville and some of the other missionaries were well disposed to hear the news.⁷ Their immediate response was to hold a series of evangelistic meetings. Hundreds responded to the evangelistic call and Baskerville recorded that some of the older catechists came to a deeper understanding of the faith. Incidentally Musa Gyabuganda renounced his decision to leave the church.

Pilkington was fired up by what was at least a personal experience of revival. He was convinced of the principle that 'Africa must be evangelised by Africans'.⁸ The question remained, but how? Pilkington went with the Baganda army to preach to the *bakopi*, the common people. On the way back he called in at the work of Fisher and Sugden at Mityana, about forty miles west of Mengo. He was struck by the systematic plan for evangelization he found there. Fisher

---

[3] F. W. B. Bullock, *The History of Ridley Hall, Cambridge*, Vol. I (Cambridge, 1941), p. 241.
[4] Makerere University Archives, Mengo Church Council Minutes for 6 December 1893.
[5] C. F. Harford-Battersby, *Pilkington of Uganda* (London, 1898) p. 222.
[6] Makerere University Archives, G. K. Baskerville Journal entry for 4 December 1893.
[7] Ibid., 8 December 1893.
[8] G. K. Baskerville and G. L. Pilkington, *The Gospel in Uganda* (London, 1896), p. 24.

had opened about twelve or fifteen reading houses, which he called 'synagogues' at short distances from the main mission station and put a young man in charge of each. Fisher and his colleague, the Reverend Yairo Mutakyala visited these regularly in order to instruct both the people and the teachers. On his return to Mengo, Pilkington decided that Fisher's scheme could be adapted for the whole country. He mapped out the country and suggested a particular European missionary to take charge of each district. He further proposed that twice as many evangelist/teachers be selected as were needed, so they could spend six months in the field and six months in training in Mengo. This was a realistic attempt to relate the work of the evangelists to the task of church planting. It provided the basic model of how evangelization would work through Uganda and beyond even if the term 'synagogue' swiftly passed into obscurity. Whereas at the start of 1894 there were about twenty country 'synagogues', by the end of the year there were over 200 attended by 4,000 people daily and by 20,000 on Sundays.

Parallel with this development in the Anglican Church was a similar movement in the Roman Catholic Church, which was re-grouping in the Province of Buddu in west Uganda, under the leadership of Henri Streicher. Revival language is not commonly found among Catholics but, in 1892, the missionary Moullec wrote to Livinhac, the leader of the mission at the time, 'En verite le vent violent de la Pentecote a soufflé sur ce people.'[9]

That aside, the revival of 1893 was not without its critics. Robert Walker, the Archdeacon, whose evangelical credentials as a former curate of All Soul's Langham Place were quite impeccable, was very cool. Rather than hold missions which might appeal too much to the emotional side, Walker wanted to put his 'faith in the regular daily reading of the Word of God'.[10] When there was a seven-day 'mission' in 1894, Walker saw little difference with what went on every other week. Again writing to his sister he commented on one of his colleagues,

> Mr Roscoe will have a great deal to say about his being filled with the Holy Spirit and about his having been used by God to convey this blessing to others. I do wish he would explain in more definite terms what he means and give more confirming and convincing evidence for his statement. The happiness he feels himself and the happy faces of people seem to me to be indefinite statements, worth much to him and the individuals, but not the objective evidence one reads of in the book of the Acts of the Apostles.[11]

---

[9] R. Oliver, *The Missionary Factor in East Africa* (London, 1952), p. 187
[10] Church Missionary Society Archives (CMSA), R. H. Walker to his sister 5 July 1894.
[11] CMSA, R. H. Walker to his sister 9 June 1896.

Ten years on Baskerville reflected on the growth of the church in Uganda.[12] By 1904 there were well over a thousand places of worship. In most centres the practice had continued from 1893 of monthly missionary meetings at which accounts of work in the villages were given, new teachers/evangelists commissioned and sent out and a collection made for the work of evangelization. However, Baskerville was not alone in sensing a cooling in the mission. The Conference of Missionaries in 1905 decided that the only way to deal with the problems of the church was by means of a solemn spiritual recall. Bishop Tucker, with the wider support of the missionary body, resolved to hold a mission in early 1906. There were a number of reasons for this. There was the feeling that a number of the evangelist/teachers were becoming too concerned about their perceived low level of pay. In parts of Uganda numbers attending church were falling. Additionally missionaries were hearing remarkable stories of revival in Wales and wanted the fire to fall likewise in Uganda. The model of the Torrey and Alexander campaigns in England was seen as the answer. Alexander's 'Glory Song' was translated into Luganda to become the theme song of the mission. More immediately the model was the special mission services held in Koki under the leadership of Mr. Innes. He recorded the aims of the mission as *to pray for and expect the definite conversion of souls and to deepen the spiritual life amongst our Christians, to try and make them more out and out for Christ*. A week was set apart for prayer and then there was a week with a series of meetings and after-meetings. In the week in Koki some 180 people professed to accept Christ as their Saviour. Innes was particularly concerned for follow-up and assiduously saw to it that each new convert was linked up with a more experienced Christian for teaching and discipling. Bishop Tucker resolved to bring this to Mengo and so in March 1906, over eight successive days, special services were held in the Cathedral. Attendance was high with an aggregate estimated at around 50,000 people. With one exception all the preachers were European missionaries. We know the subjects taken day by day through the week:

Monday	Sin
Tuesday	The Penalty of Sin
Wednesday	Salvation
Thursday	Power over Sin
Friday	The Holy Spirit
Saturday	Holiness.[13]

Also in early 1906 there was a series of revival meetings held in Mityana, taking a similar pattern. Some 250 people are recorded as expressing their desire to amend their lives and follow Christ. The follow-up was a series of

---

[12] G. K. Baskerville 'The Spread and Development of the Mission since 1893' in *Church Missionary Intelligencer*, July 1904.

[13] CMS Annual Report 1907, p. 84.

monthly meetings at which each convert was asked to come and bring someone with him or her. At each gathering people were invited to confess Christ openly and pledge to four things: 'to receive Jesus Christ as Saviour, Lord and King; to give himself entirely to God and to serve him henceforth; to ask the Holy Spirit daily to cleanse him and to enable him to abstain from all sinful habits; to persevere in reading God's word daily in church and in prayer for all'.[14]

A number of comments can be made about the revival of 1906. This was very much a constructed revival with the initiative and the programme both in the hands of the European missionaries. It was noticeable that mission services were only held in areas where missionaries were well disposed in principle to revival campaigns. In the east of the country where many missionaries thought the way ahead was through education and schools rather than mission services, there was nothing that could be brought forward as evidence of revival. Secondly, whereas the revival of 1893 led directly to the adoption of a clear pattern of evangelization, there is little discernible fruit from the revival of 1906, except that it did set a pattern for the Anglican Church in Uganda to answer times of spiritual doldrums with an organized mission to stir up the spirits once more.

We come now to what is generally known as the East Africa Revival, which is better understood as a tradition more than an event, looking back to the 1930s in Uganda and Rwanda. The revival is often called the *Balokole* revival, from the Luganda – *Balokole* means 'the saved people'. The roots of this tradition are complex and the course convoluted and still extant.

We can discern four particular roots of the Balokole revival. The first is in the dispute within Anglican mission circles over what was perceived to be 'liberal' theology within CMS. This led to the formation of the Bible Churchmen's Missionary Society (now Crosslinks) in 1922. CMS had steadfastly refused any doctrinal basis beyond the formularies of the Anglican Church, and it has maintained a broadly evangelical identity. Nevertheless CMS included people whose views of Scripture were certainly not fundamentalist and whose churchmanship was more open to what smacked of ritualism to those of more Protestant hue. CMS also contained those who did not include tobacco and moderate alcohol intake as sins to be abhorred by all Christians. The year 1928 saw the formation of what became known as the Ruanda Mission as a self-governing body within CMS.[15] From the start Ruanda missionaries were clearly identified with more Protestant sensibilities and were inclined to be critical of some of their CMS colleagues in Uganda.

Secondly there was mounting criticism of the level of spirituality of the Church of Uganda, although some CMS missionaries were much more sanguine. A. B. Lloyd, a veteran missionary by 1921, wrote of *the clouds in the sky*, identifying drunkenness, immorality, concubinage, continuing belief in

---

[14] CMS Annual Report 1907, p. 91.

[15] G. Hewitt, *The Problems of Success*, Vol. I, p. 262ff.

witchcraft and in the power of the spirits of the dead as present within the church.[16] Some African Christians, including Simeoni Nsibambi and Blasio Kigozi were also critical of the low moral standards in the church. However, alongside this was a marked and deeply rooted cultural reluctance to move to any schism. Critics of the Ugandan church looked to revival and not to schism as the answer to 'worldliness'.

Thirdly, there was a developing feeling on the part of educated Ugandan Christians that something had been lost from the original vision of the church. Alfred Tucker, who had been bishop from 1890 to 1911 had striven to include Africans with real decision-making power in the church. He had tried to be faithful to Henry Venn's vision of moving towards a fully indigenous church, but many of his efforts had been frustrated. The control of the church in the 1920s and 1930s was firmly in the hands of the missionaries. There were no indicators that this was about to change. The argument proposed by the missionaries that the Africans were 'not ready' had become the received wisdom. Educated Ugandan Christians did not feel that they could progress up a hierarchy.

Fourthly, in the 1920s and early 1930s, Nsibambi and others engaged in a personal quest for holiness. A young Ruanda Mission doctor, Joe Church, was close to Nsibambi and the partnership resulted in a number of young educated and committed Baganda Christians going to work at Gahini Hospital in Ruanda. It was here that an 'outpouring of the Spirit' occurred in 1935. In turn this fed back into Uganda.

We can identify several characteristics of the Balokole revival, many of which were in common with other revivals.[17] There was the need for each individual to be born again and have a personal testimony of conversion. Ideally there should be a clear distinction between before and after meeting Christ. A born-again Christian has a narrative of being 'saved'. There was an emphasis on the confession of sin. This took on the dimension of being public as a test of reality and a means of initiation into the Balokole fellowship. What was stressed was the element of brokenness and being humbled rather than any graphic details of sins committed. A particular outworking of this is the readiness to take an initiative to confess a sin to one sinned against. The reason for this is the need for reconciliation. Confession and reconciliation are two strands of what came to be called 'walking in the light'. This element of reconciliation was particularly significant in terms of the relationship between African and European. It was based on the mutual confession of paternalist attitudes and resentment. Revival teams consisted of both European and African Christians, whose evident love and teamwork was a powerful witness. In the early years of the revival, dreams played an important role and were seen as the direct impact of the Holy Spirit. Dreams and phenomena such as

---

[16] Hewitt, *Problems of Success*, p. 239.
[17] Cf. J. V. Taylor, *The Growth of the Church in Buganda* (London, 1958), pp. 100ff.

trembling were later regarded with more suspicion and discouragement. Balokole have a strict moral code with a particular antipathy to tobacco and alcohol. This is combined with a suspicion of church ritual and a conservative approach to the Bible and matters theological. The Balokole have a theme song, *Tukutendereeza*, which functions both as a recognition among themselves and a challenge towards all who are not saved. Finally, there has grown within the Balokole revival a sense of equality between men and women, although this is not universal. Bishop Festo Kivengere was the first to ordain women in Uganda and he traced this back to the equality discovered within the revival teams where Balokole men and women worked in close partnership.

The course of a revival is rarely smooth, and at this point we can focus on the controversy between the Balokole and a Welsh CMS missionary who later went on to be Bishop of Bangor, J. C. Jones. The background question behind this is to ask why J. C. Jones who is revered in Wales is regarded in Uganda a good deal more equivocally. J. C. Jones was born in 1904 and was brought up in a nonconformist home in Carmarthenshire.[18] In 1922 he went to university in Cardiff with the intention of going on to Aberystwyth for ordination training in the Presbyterian Church. However in 1925 he was confirmed by the Bishop of St David's en route to ordination four years later after theological education in Oxford. He served as curate in Llanelli and Aberystwyth before offering to CMS in 1934. With his wife Mary, whom he had married in 1930 and their daughter Ann, Jones left for Uganda in September 1934. He was appointed to teach at Bishop Tucker Theological College in Mukono. When he returned to the college after furlough in 1940 it was to take up the position of Warden. Three things about Jones brought him to the notice of the Balokole: he smoked a pipe, his views on the Bible were those of a liberal evangelical, and he introduced coloured stoles into the worship of the Chapel in Mukono. He was a clear target for the criticism of the Balokole.

Through the 1930s Bishop Stuart in Uganda was concerned not only to keep the Balokole within the Church of Uganda, but also that the wider church should learn from them and that the clergy should be better educated. With this latter aim in mind he persuaded a number of well-educated Balokole to attend Bishop Tucker College with a view to ordination. The most prominent and gifted of these men was William Nagenda. He became the leader of the Balokole group in the college. They gathered for prayer and praise each morning before dawn, a practice that irritated other students. In Easter 1941 a number of Balokole students went on a mission and were convinced that they should be more outspoken in denouncing the various sins in the college and in criticism of the liberal teaching and more catholic churchmanship of Jones. The following term the Balokole decided to initiate a daily time of preaching to their fellow students after their prayer meeting at 6.00 a.m. This was the time when students were supposed to be cleaning their dormitories. Tensions rose

---

[18] Edward Lewis, *John Bangor the People's Bishop* (London, 1962).

between Balokole and non-Balokole students. In October 1941 Jones instituted a new regime with three rules:

1. No student was to leave his dormitory before the rising bell at 6.00 a.m.
2. No student was allowed to preach within the College precincts without permission from the Warden,
3. Students were forbidden to meet together in groups exceeding three in number.

The Balokole met as usual at 4.00 a.m. and, one by one, twenty-seven disobedient students were summoned to the Warden. Two students apologized for their behaviour but twenty-five were expelled from the College plus another who had been ill at the time of the planned prayer meeting. At the time of the expulsion Bishop Stuart was out of the country, but on his return he offered full support to Jones while at the same time writing to the 'rebels' to encourage them to apologize and return. Jones remained as Warden until 1944 when he returned to Wales as Vicar of Llanelli.[19]

This is a basic account of what was an immensely difficult and painful period for all concerned. The way in which the episode has been written up is indicative. Edward Lewis in writing a biography of his friend J. C. Jones, commented on the ordinands at Mukono as men who were *in many ways still children and whose intellectual standards were exceedingly low*.[20] According to Lewis, Jones felt the Balokole were a menace to college discipline and order and he was compelled to expel them before the life and work and daily routine proceeded happily and efficiently. On the other hand Bill Butler's account is much more sympathetic to the Balokole whom he describes as *not angry young men or callow youths accustomed to flouting authority*, but mature men who had already spent several years engaged in full-time Christian service.[21] It was only after spending time in prayer and fasting that they decided in this particular situation they had no alternative but to obey God rather than man.

In spite of the fact that Bishop Stuart and various enquiries after the expulsion exonerated Jones, the most generous assessment of the Balokole in Uganda today is that Jones over-reacted. Bishop J. V. Taylor who succeeded Jones as Warden and did a wonderful job of reconciling Balokole to the college told of how Jones's mother had reacted very badly to the Welsh revival of 1904 and that Jones was very fearful that the emotionalism of the Balokole might have a similar impact on his wife. There is little doubt that Jones himself was deeply wounded by the whole episode and particularly by his reputation as a foe of the revival.[22]

The first missionaries only arrived in Uganda in 1877, and nonetheless we can speak meaningfully of revival in 1893, in 1906 and from 1930s. We may

---

[19] K. Ward, 'Obedient Rebels', unpublished mss, 1988.
[20] Lewis, *John Bangor*, p. 77.
[21] Bill Butler, *Hill Ablaze* (London, 1976), p. 62.
[22] Personal communication 1993.

like to draw a contrast between the revivals of 1893 and 1906 inasmuch as the earlier revival was more spontaneous and the second more constructed. In these terms the Balokole revival was more in the tradition of 1893 than 1906. However, there is something unsatisfactory about the term 'spontaneous', because in both 1893 and the 1930s there was a strong disposition on the part of some Christians towards Revival. This was expressed both in a commitment to prayer and a desire to see a movement that they could recognize to be revival. An important key to understanding revival in Uganda in each case is the concept of 'nominalism'. This term refers to the notion of belonging to the church in name only together with an absence of a testimony of personal conversion and holiness, marked by evangelistic zeal, regular Bible reading and prayer, and the avoidance of drunkenness, sexual unfaithfulness, lying and gambling. Missionaries tended to accept very high standards for themselves and then this extended to high expectations of the African church.

The Balokole tradition has left a major mark on the shape of the Ugandan church. J. V. Taylor referred to the impact it had in terms of the recovery of the indigenous structures of the church. In the earliest days of the church, it was very dependent upon the patronage of chiefs. In the revival movement the local leader, who would most probably be lay, would gather around himself a community of the brethren. In many ways the kinship unit thus gathered became stronger than traditional kinship links in family, clan and tribe.

Secondly, the Balokole revival emphasized the role of the laity. Nagenda after his expulsion from Mukono was never ordained. He interpreted his experience as a call from God to remain a lay evangelist. He remained immensely influential in the revival movement and so within the Church of Uganda. There is a common saying in the revival movement that *at the cross the ground is level.*

Thirdly the revival represented a challenge to the spiritual leadership of Europeans. In doing so it recovered African leadership and responsibility. It was not that European leadership was replaced. Instead there was a strong commitment to a partnership, to which some missionaries felt able to contribute more than others.

Fourthly the revival represented a major step forward in contextualization. This was true to some extent in 1893 and 1906, but it was certainly true in the Balokole revival. The shape of worship, confession, testimony was authentically shaped by African experience and culture in a way which was not the case with the very Anglican liturgy of Sunday services.

Fifthly the revival fed back creatively into western spirituality through the work of such writers as Bill Butler, Patricia St John, Joe Church and Roy Hessian.

However there is one particular point of concern with the revival tradition; that is the way in which its piety has spiritualized all problems, sometimes unhelpfully. In the post-colonial period there was a desperate need for a theology that was politically aware. The Church of Uganda grew up politically in the time of Amin, but by then it was in many ways too late.

Jesus taught that 'you will know them by their fruits' (Matthew 7:20). This statement may be seen as applying to revivals as to individuals. The 1893 revival had a major input in widespread and effective evangelization. The Balokole revival produced Anglican saints in Luwum and Kivengere and others less known. The Church of Uganda today is the second largest in the Anglican Communion. Far from perfect it may be, but nonetheless the fruit of revival in Uganda is wholesome.

CHAPTER 19

The 1904–5 Welsh Revival and Social and Political Action: A Centenary Perspective

Daniel Boucher

It is one of the mysteries of Welsh history that by the 1960s evangelical Christians, who represented the dominant religious tradition in Wales from about 1750 to 1930, were generally considered distinctly odd by most Welsh people. Theological liberalism had done its work very thoroughly, and evangelicals had become a marginalized minority in the Church. The narrow-minded fundamentalism of some of us helped to push us further to the margins'.[1]

The last national revival within the United Kingdom was the Welsh revival of 1904–5. Given this heritage, and the fact Wales had in any event regularly experienced revival during the eighteenth and nineteenth centuries (in a way that had, in the nineteenth century at least, eluded the other British nations), one might suppose that, despite general twentieth-century decline, Wales would be the most evangelical of the British nations. The truth is, however, that with evangelical Christians accounting for perhaps two per cent of the population, Wales is arguably the least evangelical of the UK nations.[2] Why have things swung so violently against Welsh evangelicalism?[3] This chapter suggests that

---

[1] Dewi Hughes, *Castrating Culture: A Christian Perspective on Ethnic Identity from the Margins* (Carlisle, 2001), p. 50. Other references to the dominance of evangelicalism can be found in Dorian Llywelyn, *Sacred Place, Chosen People: Land and National Identity in Welsh Spirituality* (Cardiff, 1999), p. 49; E. T. Davies, *Religion and Society in 19th Century Wales*; Christopher Davies (Llandybie, 1981), p. 65; and Robert Pope, *Seeking God's Kingdom: The Nonconformist Social Gospel in Wales 1906-1939*, p. 3.
[2] This figure is based on work done by the Evangelical Alliance Wales, http://www.eauk.org/wales
[3] The weakness of the revival impact in Wales is noted by Nigel Wright, see 'Does Revival Quicken or Deaden the Church? A comparison of the 1904 Welsh Revival and John Wimber in the 1980s and 1990s', in Andrew Walker and Kristin Aune (eds), *On Revival: A Critical Examination* (Carlisle, 2003), p. 121. The long-term weakness of revival impact in Wales must be qualified by recognition of the fact that it had very significant international implications, see Noel Gibbard, *On the Wings of the Dove* (Brynterion, 2002).

answers to this question lie, in some measure, in the character of the last revival.

The 1904–5 revival, and more importantly its immediate aftermath, fostered a form of evangelical spirituality, whose lack of material concern made for a fairly extreme form of pietism. In the context of real social and economic hardship, and the new opportunities to address this hardship emanating from the growing franchise, this "otherworldliness" resulted in a presentation of the gospel that was, for many, unattractive.[4] It is the specific contention of this chapter that the excesses of this spirituality, in the new socio-political environment, actually undermined the positive impact of the revival and its legacy and damaged the future prospects for Welsh evangelicalism.

Having set out this chapter's central claim, the point must be made that in order to substantiate the idea that something *new* happened in 1904, one must first consider Welsh spirituality's approach to engaging with life beyond the narrowly spiritual domain *before 1904*. This will not actually lay the foundation for the claim that pietism was new to Wales but it will facilitate demonstration of the fact that there was something novel about the intensity of 1904 pietism. Set in the context of great material need and new political opportunities, this research will argue that this intensity had the effect of damaging the long term appeal of Welsh evangelicalism.

Before embarking upon this investigation, however, it is important to pause to define some key terms: evangelical, pietism and otherworldliness.

The term evangelical or evangelicalism refers to a church tradition which, tracing its roots back in relatively recent history to the Puritans, places great emphasis on the Bible which it treats as the inspired 'Word of God'. As a function of this stress upon the scriptures, evangelicals also place great importance on propositional, expository Bible teaching thus differing from those sections of the Church which also allow for truth to emerge from other sources such as 'tradition'. Springing from this emphasis on scripture come attendant emphases on the key biblical challenges: the Cross and the need for personal repentance and therein personal conversion.[5] Having identified these bases for commonality, however, it is important to understand that evangelicalism is far from being an homogenous tradition. It embraces a great diversity of opinion on subjects such as pneumatology, as seen in the great

---

[4] This is unusual in the sense that many revivals have provoked political change. For example see J. Wesley Bready, *England Before and After Wesley: The Evangelical Revival and Social Reform* (Hodder and Stoughton, 1939); and W. T. Stead, *Revivals and the West*, chap. 2.

[5] R. Tudur Jones, *Pwy yw'r bobl efengylaidd* (Casnewydd); and F. L. Cross (ed.), *The Oxford Dictionary of the Christian Church* (Oxford, 1990), p. 486.

debates between Pentecostal and Charismatic theology on the one hand, and secessionist theology on the other.⁶

The term pietism emerged to describe a Protestant movement which arose a century or so on from the advent of the Reformation. Founded by Philip Jacob Spener, pietism challenged the dry formalism that was becoming commonplace in Reformation churches with the need for the Christian to focus on his personal relationship with God and his attendant devotional life in prayer and bible study. Initially, although this challenge to address a lack of spiritual vitality had a rather inward focus, it did not give rise to a rejection of concern for the material world of the here and now. Over time, however, the onus placed on the absolute supremacy of the Christian's inner relationship with God made for a form of introverted, 'hyper-spiritual' spirituality in whose estimation the material world was of marginal significance. In this context engaging in the arts, sports, politics or other 'thisworldly' concerns, was deemed to be a dangerous distraction. As a consequence of the association of pietism with withdrawal and an otherworldly spirituality, 'pietism' has become the shorthand for all forms of evangelical teaching that encourage withdrawal from engaging with the world.⁷

Withdrawal v. Engagement Pre-1904?

The first section will first consider withdrawal v. engagement from the perspective of the 'Wales as Church' paradigm, pointing to a strong, long-term basis for pietism, before it then qualifies this by considering growing evidence of an appetite for engagement in the latter part of the nineteenth century.

Wales as Church

Prior to the 1904–5 revival there was a strong basis for pietism arising from a particular understanding of what scholars have described as the 'Wales as Church'⁸ tradition. Not all of its elements needed to have the effect of

---

⁶ For an example of this division see: Ian Randall & David Hilborn, *One Body in Christ: The History and Significance of the Evangelical Alliance* (Carlisle, 2001), pp. 321-9.

⁷ For a detailed definition of pietism please see: Cheslyn Jones, Geoffrey Wainwright and Edward Yarnold (eds), *The Study of Spirituality* (London, 1994), pp. 93-4, 107-9, 448-52. http://etext.lib.virginia.edu/cgi-local/DHI/dhi.cgi?id=dv3-61 (checked 2.4.04) and F. L. Cross (ed.), *The Oxford Dictionary of the Christian Church*, p. 486. For specifically evangelical critiques see: Francis Schaeffer, *The Complete Works of Francis A. Schaeffer* (5 vol. set) (Good News Pub, 1985). Whilst this research uses the term pietism as another word for withdrawal because this approach has become common practice, it is important to note that this semantic custom actually fails to account for the nuances in sophisticated pietistic theology. Nor does it account for the greater this worldliness in early pietism.

⁸ Llywelyn, *Sacred Place, Chosen People*, p. 78.

spiritualizing Wales, with otherworldly implication, but later (post 1588) historical circumstances have arguably contrived to give it this effect.

Christianity played a crucial role in the formation of Welsh identity on two counts. First, the Welsh language, and thus Welsh identity, emerged between the fourth and fifth centuries at the very time when Christianity was taking hold in the land of Wales.[9] Second, at this same time Welsh identity was strengthened by virtue of its distinction from that of its then neighbours in modern day 'England' who were the initially heathen Anglo-Saxons[10] and then (after experiments with Celtic Christianity) predominantly Roman Catholic (from 664), rather than Celtic Christian as per Wales.[11] In 786 Wales's bishops finally accepted the Roman date for Easter, but made no other significant concessions to Catholicism until the arrival of the Normans.[12] The centrality of religion to Welsh identity can be seen in the fact that at the heart of Owain Glyndwr's rejection of Norman rule was the returning of Welsh ecclesiastical rule from Canterbury to Saint Davids.[13]

The close relationship between Wales and Christianity, however, experienced something of a qualitative transformation in the sixteenth century via the Act of Union. Specifically, the Act 'prohibited all "sinister usages" of the Welsh language in any public sphere'.[14] The language of governance and the law courts thus became English. An exception, however, was made for the churches where it was hoped that the translation of the Bible into Welsh would provide a surer means for the engagement of the Welsh with Protestantism.[15] This was of enormous strategic significance for Welsh identity which was in an important sense spiritualized by the Elizabethan linguistic division of labour. '[T]he association of language and religion gave Welsh something of the odour of sanctity, making it a symbol and a tabernacle of a separate national-religious identity.'[16] The identification of the language, and thus the nation, with the 'spiritual', and its otherworldly implication, is eloquently demonstrated by the following statement from the Rev. William Roberts. 'When the world is spoken

---

[9] Gwynfor Evans, *The Fight for Welsh Freedom* (Talybont, 2000), p. 17.

[10] Gwyn A. Williams, *When Was Wales?: The History, People and Culture of an Ancient Country* (London, 1991), pp. 43-4.

[11] Ibid.

[12] Ibid.

[13] Peter Beresford Ellis, *The Celtic Revolution: A Study in Anti-Imperialism* (Talybont), pp. 77-8.

[14] Llywelyn, *Sacred Place, Chosen People*, p. 47.

[15] Indeed, quite apart from the language of the Bible, Anglican Churches were required by statute to conduct their services in Welsh in those places where Welsh was the dominant language, see Geraint Tudur, 'Howell Harris and the Issue of Welsh Identity', in Robert Pope (ed.), *Religion and National Identity: Wales and Scotland c1700-2000* (Cardiff, 2001), p. 55.

[16] Llywelyn, *Sacred Place, Chosen People*, p. 48; and Beresford Ellis, *The Celtic Revolution*, pp. 78-9.

of on the Sabbath, then let care be taken that one speaks of it in English, lest our ancient Welsh tongue be sullied by such a usage.'[17] If a nation bases its identity on its language and that language is judged to be the 'language of heaven' then it is logical that the nation itself should come to be seen as, in some senses, 'heavenly'/'otherworldly'.

The peculiarities of the above approach to religion and politics fundamentally upset the balance in the Welsh Christian worldview between the spiritual and the material. Instead of Welsh identity existing in a context where the people of Wales were able to confront the 'spiritual' and 'material' in a biblically integrous manner, their identity – that which should have informed their approach to life as a whole – was hived off into a spiritual realm. In this context there is a very real sense in which two Waleses emerged. On the one hand, there was the spiritual Wales, 'Wales as church',[18] that related to the loyalties and identity of the people wherein they chose to live their lives and have their being. On the other, there was a material world related to the world of work, of business, commerce and government, all of which were largely controlled by England, the English or the anglicized. In such a structure it is easy to imagine how one could have lived, with some resignation, a compartmentalized life in which one's heart would have been located in the realm of the spiritual nation, whilst one's physical labour would have been located in subjection to England.[19]

---

[17] Quoted by R Tudur Jones 'Yr Eglwysi a'r Iaith yn Oes Victoria', *Llen Cyymru*, 19 (1996) 165. Trans. Llywelyn, *Sacred Place, Chosen People*, p. 51. On the role of the 'language of heaven' see also W. P. Griffith, 'Preaching Second to No Other under the Sun': Edward Matthews, the Nonconformist Pulpit and Welsh Identity during the Mid-Nineteenth Century', *Religion and National Identity*, pp. 61-83. The significance of this approach is thrown into sharp relief by contrasting it with the theologically disclosed backlash against this otherworldliness seen in R Tudur Jones' (to whom we shall return) twentieth century comments which he made directly in response to the notion that Welsh is 'the language of heaven': '[I]t [Welsh] has been the language of lawyers and canonists, or princes and their councillors, of rogues and ruffians, of farmers, physicians, theologians and craftsmen. In a word, the language of a nation is the rich diversity of its entire social life. And this superb instrument of human communication bound people together in a unique community, distinguished by this very fact from all others'. R Tudur Jones, *The Desire of Nations* (Llandybie, 1975), p. 88.

[18] The 'Wales as Church' paradigm is defined by Dorian Llywelyn, *Sacred Place, Chosen People*, pp. 9-11.

[19] In such a context the quasi-Gnostic statement of Rev. William Roberts (see above) certainly made sense. Quoted by R Tudur Jones 'Yr Eglwysi a'r Iaith yn Oes Victoria', *Llen Cymru* 19 (1996) 165. Trans. Llywelyn, *Sacred Place, Chosen People*, p. 51.

Otherworldliness Qualified?

On the basis of the above one might be forgiven for asking how could Welsh spirituality be made more otherworldly as a consequence of the 1904 revival and, given the success of previous revivals within this epoch and their regular return, how could one ever demonstrate that pietism was/is negatively related to sustainable evangelicalism. The truth is, however, that seminal political changes took place in Wales, especially between 1884 and 1904, which paved the way for a new form of evangelical political engagement, and rendered the implications of non-engagement quite different from those of the preceding era.

After the Act of Union the only Welsh people to be part of the franchise were the gentry who were rapidly anglicized. Given their anglicization, there is a very real sense in which Wales was cut off from political expression. First, it did not have self-government. Second, it did not have any autonomous, 'non-anglicized', 'Welsh' politicians at Westminster. In England, on the other hand, although the working class and many of the middle class could not express themselves politically at the ballot box, Englishness none the less found expression, first, on the basis that government was dominated by England and, second, on the basis that parliamentary representatives were either English or anglicized. In this sense any lack of political engagement in Wales, and specifically any lack of theologically inspired engagement, was primarily a function of Wales being denied political expression. The nineteenth century, however, brought changes that transformed this constitutional settlement, empowering the non-anglicized, Welsh middle classes with the vote. This prompts the crucial question, 'Did the structural change towards 'thisworldliness' challenge traditional pietistic otherworldliness?' The answer – as this chapter will demonstrate – is that in some senses it did, whilst in other senses it did not.

Given the identity of Christianity and Wales, when the franchise began to increase significantly it is not surprising that this should have resulted in Wales's chapels – defined primarily by evangelical religion – gaining new influence. Indeed the increase of the franchise, in the context of the dominance of nonconformist chapel culture, caused Gwyn A. Williams to write of their fusion. 'The historically visible working class embraced that fusion of Dissent and democracy',[20] which resulted in the demise of the Welsh Tories and triumph of the Liberal party. In this context the chapel began to assert some real political influence manifest in, the 1881 Sunday Closing Act, which was a great coup for the Christian temperance lobby, the impact of the 1888 Local Government Act, which provided a new 'local' context for evangelical action, resistance to the 1902 Education Act and in the development of the modern Welsh nationalist movement.

---

[20] Gwyn A. Williams, *When Was Wales?*, p. 216.

A Form of Pietism?

Although, given the above, it would be wrong to suggest that, enfranchised and politically empowered, Welsh non-conformity chose to withdraw from politics, its engagement none the less did have some unusual characteristics which gave it a quality that testifies to an enduring, although weakened, pietism. In order not to overstate the political engagement of the 1884–1904 era, it is now important to unpack this pietism by examining its local focus, avoidance of mainstream political challenges and obsession with disestablishment.

THE HEGEMONY OF 'THE LOCAL'

Specifically, late nineteenth-century Welsh politics – in which the chapels (defined primarily, as we have seen, by evangelical religion) played such a key role – seems to have had a very 'local' focus which resonated with both the romantic Welsh 'communities of communities'[21] ethic and the Celtic tradition.[22] 'The Liberal world', and thus we might add, the non-conformist Welsh world was, according to Morgan, 'a local one. It was, therefore, natural that local government, with all the spectrum of authority and patronage involved, should become a particularly crucial citadel of Liberalism.'[23] The special influence of modern local government for Wales was underlined by the fact that it provided a basis for the assertion of a Welsh distinctive.

> The new county councils created by the Local Government Act of 1888 showed more strikingly in Wales than in any other part of Britain the new transition in democracy. The landed gentry who had dominated the countryside for centuries as justices of the peace were routed in an immense social revolution.[24]

This celebration of the local, which provided a basis for Wales to coherently assert its identity as a liberal bloc, seems to have given Welsh non-conformist politics an almost romantic attachment to 'the local' that made it difficult for it to see some issues, whilst giving it a heightened awareness of others.

AVOIDANCE OF HARD POLITICS

Central to the above romanticism was the principle of 'harmony'. Specifically, Welsh liberals believed that the different classes could live together in 'harmony' and did not appear willing to engage with some of the tough challenges of the class struggle and poverty that exercised the new socialist movement. As Morgan again observes, 'Not until after 1908 did Liberal Associations or denominational assemblies devote time or effort to a serious

---

[21] John Osmond, *Creative Conflict*, (Llandysul and London, 1977), pp. 232 and 239.
[22] Ray Simpson, *Exploring Celtic Spirituality: Historic Roots for Our Future*, (London, 1995), pp. 84-5.
[23] Kenneth Morgan, *Rebirth of a Nation*, p. 52.
[24] Ibid.

examination of issues of class tension or social reform in terms relevant to an industrial community'.[25] A particularly interesting perspective on this point can be seen in the following assessment of the young Lloyd George: 'Until he went to the Treasury in 1908, he had no clear programme of social reform: disestablishment, church schools and temperance captured his attention in a way that the Eight Hours Bill or "the right to work" did not.'[26] In other words had Welsh Liberalism been more willing to recognize and engage with social hardship, it might have been better able to address the rise of socialism. This provides an interesting comparison with nineteenth-century English evangelical political engagement which did not reside on romantic, liberal assumptions in the sense that it moved beyond the challenge of focusing primarily on the individual's moral decision-making capacity (for example, temperance – that is 'to drink or not to drink', a personal moral choice) to structural socio-economic challenges such as working conditions, slavery and prison reform.

DISESTABLISHMENT

Perhaps the most interesting manifestation of this rather otherworldly politics, however, relates to disestablishment. Between 1880 and 1920 a huge amount of energy was devoted to disestablishment. Rather than seeking to assert Welsh identity directly in ordinary political terms, after the failure of Cymru Fydd, many nationalists sought to do so indirectly through addressing the state via the Anglican Church. Now there can be no doubt that there was in the initial grievance a desire to obtain a very material reform, relief from the obligation of paying tithes to an alien church.[27] It does seem strange, though, to anyone not schooled in the 'Wales as Church' paradigm that quite so much *political* energy should have been invested into this apparently primarily spiritual project.

Conclusion

Thus having been impacted very profoundly by otherworldly spirituality especially in the aftermath of the Elizabethan linguistic division of labour, the nineteenth century actually witnessed something of a U-turn. Specifically, the opening of doors to political engagement particularly after 1884, resulted in happy Christian engagement with the new political roles but the quality of this engagement was nonetheless impacted by an enduring pietism which resulted in its adopting a rather unusual sense of priority and perspective. Having considered the pietistic quality of Welsh spirituality pre 1904, the chapter now turns to examine to what extent the 1904 revival challenged this spirituality and to what extent this might have resulted in the erosion of the long term fortunes of evangelicalism in Wales.

---

[25] K. Morgan, *Rebirth of a Nation*, p. 54.
[26] Morgan, *Rebirth of a Nation*, pp. 45-6.
[27] Gwyn A. Williams, *When Was Wales?*, pp. 228-9.

Withdrawal v. Engagement 1904–

It is the contention of this chapter that the part of evangelicalism that was able to hold on to, and define, the 1904 revival and legacy in a distinctively evangelical manner actually embraced a greater measure of pietism than that manifest pre 1904. This development brought with it new implications for evangelicalism, not least because of the fact that Wales was confronting real poverty in the context of a growing franchise and thus greater opportunities for ordinary people to direct government to seek to address that poverty. The chapter will examine the pietism of the revival first by considering it positively, via examination of Welsh evangelicalism during and after the revival (Section 1) and then indirectly by examining non-evangelical responses to the revival (Section 2).

Pietism in The Revival and The Revival Legacy

There was something of an ambiguity in non-conformist, revival theology. On the one hand there was great willingness to point to the positive implications of revival for society at large. On the other hand, however, whilst conscious that revival would have a positive impact on society, there was a reluctance to celebrate direct Christian engagement with politics. Reflecting on this approach, Pope makes the following observation:

> When religion was effective in individual lives it would automatically make a difference to the prevailing principles which governed social and economic attitudes and practices. Thus the chapels and churches of the land were being challenged to lead men and women from an initial evangelical conversion into a life of obedient discipleship that would transform society by individual dedication to the higher, spiritual life and establishment in the world of its values and principles. The result was not a social gospel per se but a recognition that individual conversion practised on a large scale, could not leave the world untouched.[28]

A great example of the above ambiguity can be seen by considering the revival preacher R. B. Jones of Porth and his account of events, *Rent Heavens: The Revival of 1904*. On the one hand, R.B. devotes an entire chapter to list a great many of the positive practical social consequences of revival.[29] On the other hand, however, emphasizing 'the gospel's call to personal repentance and holiness rather than the relevance of its reforming dynamic to economic and

---

[28] Robert Pope, *Seeking God's Kingdom: The Nonconformist Social Gospel in Wales 1906-1939* (Cardiff, 1999), p. 3.
[29] R. B. Jones, *Rent Heavens: The Revival of 1904, Some of its Hidden Springs and Prominent Results* (London, 1930), chap. 4.

social structure',[30] R. B. Jones also celebrated, in this same chapter, loss of concern for "thisworldly" affairs including sport and politics:

'In several places', R.B. wrote approvingly, 'footballs were burned and teams disbanded.'[31] Now, whilst there can be no doubt that in the context of revival it is only natural that attending revival meetings should 'take over' as other issues become shadows in the light of the revival, it is not clear that revival should result in the celebration of a general withdrawal into the spiritual realm, sealed by the deliberate 'burning of footballs', unless one's view of the world has been impacted by an extreme form of pietism.[32]

'Politics also received', R.B. again noted with satisfaction, 'a very definite quietus. Political meetings, so deemed the spiritualised sensibilities of the people were out of the question.'[33] Again the qualification must be made that, whilst it might be natural that people should find political meetings thrust in the shadow of the revival, it does not follow that they should withdraw from political engagement in principle, unless they have embraced an extreme pietism.

The pietistic intensity of the revival legacy can be seen distinctively in both the new publications and the new churches to which the revival gave birth:

PUBLICATIONS

Soon after the revival, Eifion Evans observes, 'a Welsh book ... [J. Henry Williams, *Ar Ei Ben bo'r Goron*] ... specially written for the converts of the revival served to channel their thinking on the purely Keswick principles and limited their view of the Christian life to the horizons of cleansing, consecration, abiding in Christ, and the fullness of the Spirit. This was fundamentally misleading, and it deprived the converts of that humbling, awe-inspiring vision of the whole counsel of God which was at once their spiritual heritage and their greatest need.'[34]

The endurance of this legacy can also be seen through the journal started by two great 1904 revival enthusiasts, R. B. Jones and Nantlais Williams.

> The pages of Yr Efengylydd were redolent with a sincere though narrow pietism which saw sin exclusively in terms of personal shortcomings, usually of the flesh, and was highly dubious of anything resembling a social gospel. Testimonies to conversion gave the impression that the new life in Christ was a matter of

---

[30] Pope, *Seeking God's Kingdom*, p. 15.

[31] R. B. Jones, *Rent Heavens*, p. 69.

[32] R. B. Jones, *Rent Heavens*, pp. 69-70.

[33] Ibid. D. Densil Morgan comments on this evangelical quest to be separate from politics and the arts as seen in the thinking of R. B. Jones and others after the revival see, *The Span of the Cross: Christian Religion and Society in Wales 1914-2000* (Cardiff, 1999), p. 141.

[34] Eifion Evans, *The Welsh Revival of 1904* (Bridgend, 2000), p. 185.

rejecting football, the theatre and politics as though they all belonged to the kingdom of Satan.[35] (Italics added).

NEW CHURCHES

Although revival converts initially joined or reaffirmed their membership of Wales's older denominations, it was not long before significant numbers left to establish gospel halls, independent evangelical churches and Pentecostal churches (the forerunners of a whole series of 'new church' groupings/denominations that would emerge during the twentieth century).[36] Given that it is these church networks/denominations that remained distinctively evangelical as wholes, unlike the other older denominations which became largely liberal, although including many individual evangelicals and indeed evangelical congregations (for instance R. B. Jones technically remained a Baptist and Nantlais Williams a Presbyterian), it is particularly important to understand the revival's legacy through these churches.

Unlike the new churches of the eighteenth-century revivals, which went on to become 'national denominations', locating themselves in the mainstream of civil society the new churches of 1904 deliberately refused the 'mainstream' and in some cases sought to buttress this posture by eschewing the language of 'national denomination', preferring to see themselves as an epistemologically immaculate expression of the Church, the one true transnational Church. They thus never entered into the pantheon of Welsh denominational life and were on occasion pejoratively classed as 'sects' whose non-identity caused them to disappear into the ether as far as their socio-political salt and light witness was concerned. As one commentator recently observed; 'The inheritors of the spirit of the revival were the myriad small sects of the Evangelicals and Pentecostals, English in culture and outlook and *increasingly divorced from the everyday lives of Welsh people*'[37] (italics added). Indeed, it was not so much a case of being more English as much as having one's citizenship in heaven. '[F]or the new evangelical sects and denominations that were springing up, identity was primarily a question of identification with the community of the "saved" rather than the "nation".'[38] None of this sense of 'divorce from everyday life' is to suggest that evangelical churches carrying the revival's legacy refused to deal with 'material need challenges' when presented with them but rather that they did not see this – especially in the context of the development of the welfare

---

[35] D. Densil Morgan, *The Span of the Cross*, pp. 140-1.
[36] E. Evans, *The Welsh Revival of 1904*, pp. 192-9; A. Walker, *Restoring the Kingdom*, p. 250; D. D. Morgan, *The Span of the Cross*, pp. 13-14; R. Pope, *Seeking God's Kingdom*, p. 2; and R. T. Jones, *Faith and the Crisis of a Nation*, p. 368.
[37] Paul Chambers, 'Religious Diversity in Wales', in Williams, Evans and O'Leary (eds), *A Tolerant Nation: Exploring Ethnic Diversity in Wales* (Cardiff, 2003), p. 129.
[38] Chambers, 'Religious Diversity in Wales', p. 130.

state – as priority. If they did engage, moreover, crucially they would tend to do so aloof from mainstream Welsh civil society.[39]

CONCLUSION

Thus, whilst it is not the purpose of this chapter to suggest that the revival had the effect of stopping ongoing Christian political activity (after all, the old priorities of education, temperance and disestablishment seen before 1904 continued afterwards) it is its purpose to contend that "thisworldly" political engagement was not generally encouraged from within the centre of the evangelical tradition which was informed by the strongly pietistic legacy of the revival. The people that had been really touched by 1904–5, and remained fervently evangelical, at best did not tend to see mainstream socio-political engagement as a priority and at worst considered it to be an inappropriate field of activity for the Christian. In the context of Wales's significant socio-economic difficulties, and the increasing franchise, this sharper pietism made evangelicalism an unattractive, un-holistic gospel for anyone with a significantly earthly orientation. Whilst recognizing that there were other bases for the development of Welsh pietism post 1904, therefore, it is the purpose of this chapter to suggest that 1904 pietism was, in an important sense, the twentieth-century foundation upon which subsequent developments built.

Revival Pietism seen via the Reaction Against It

Having assessed the nature of the revival's strongly pietistic spirituality, and its legacy for Welsh evangelicalism, by examining it positively (in Welsh evangelicalism), this chapter must now consider it negatively. Specifically, this means examining a phenomenon that developed as a reaction against the revival mindful that, thus constituted, it provides an interesting negative perspective on the character of the revival.

As Robert Pope notes, one of the most important developments in the immediate aftermath of the revival was the rapid advance of the social gospel movement. 'The fact was, then, that the promulgation of a socially oriented gospel grew either naturally from, or as a reaction to the experience of

---

[39] This should be considered in the context of an appreciation of the fact that, whilst not engaging with the political process to any significant extent prior to 1884, chapels were none the less very 'thisworldly' in the sense that they were very much involved in the provision of community welfare services in the fields of temperance, cultural activities and education. Circulating Schools, see: G. A Williams, *When Was Wales?*, pp. 154-5; Sunday schools (which taught people to read) D. Gareth Evans, *A History of Wales 1815-1906* (Cardiff, 1989), pp. 118-23; schools, ibid., pp. 97-110 and G. A. Williams, *When Was Wales?*, pp. 204-5; providing alternative activities to drinking see, D. G. Evans, *A History of Wales*, p. 88 and regarding cultural/educational activities during the week see E. T. Davies, *Religion and Society in Nineteenth Century Wales*, p. 64, pp. 85-9 and D. G. Evans, *A History of Wales*, p. 220.

widespread individual salvation during the revival.'[40] To be precise, the revival ended in 1905 and the new liberal (and thus not evangelical) epoch which nurtured the social gospel movement, began to have significant effect, according to Pope, in 1906. 'During the religious revival of 1904–5 men and women had sought, and discovered, a religion dedicated to external life in the hereafter. In the following ten years, a variety of factors transformed this into an expectancy that religion, to be of any value at all, had to create a better environment and establish justice and righteousness in this life and in this world.'[41]

It is the contention of this chapter that the social gospel was actually largely a reaction against, rather than an affirmation of, the 1904–5 revival, and specifically the 'thisworldly' versus 'otherworldly' balance to which it subscribed. Having fostered a new idealism at a time of great social need, which could not find any practical form of outward, thisworldly expression, revival spirituality generated a pressure that helped move the prevailing theology of the day from one (hyper-spiritual, evangelical-pietist) extreme to the other (hyper-material, social gospel). Specifically, faced with no obvious means by which they could seriously apply their evangelical faith to welfare concerns, theological liberalism's social gospel became increasingly attractive to converts and revival Christians with a strong social conscience. Far from simply affirming the engagement of the 1884–1904 epoch that revival pietism was now questioning, the social gospel went much further, championing a very much more radical faith-disclosed approach that addressed structural socio-political challenges.

The following observation from E. T. Davies is very helpful both for blowing a hole in the thought that renewed political activity was somehow positively related to the revival and then for clearly demonstrating the sense in which the new politicization was a reaction against it.

> [A] number of nonconformist ministers became politically active during the first decade of the present century and combined theological liberalism with socialism. The activities of these ministers are sometimes attributed to the 1904-5 religious revival: not only is there no evidence to show that they took an active part in this revival, but it is highly probable that they were responding to ideas and pressures in industrial areas which were felt before 1904. Like many of their co-religionists, they reacted against the spiritual individualism which had been so long prevalent, and which the last Welsh revival had temporarily strengthened.[42]

The imbalance of the revival and its unlikely politicizing implications are hinted at by R. Tudur Jones who asserted that '[t]here is something lamentable rather than creative about this revival ... no sooner was the revival over than

---

[40] Pope, *Seeking God's Kingdom*, p. 4.
[41] Pope, *Seeking God's Kingdom*, p. 26.
[42] E. T. Davies, *Religion and Society in Nineteenth Century Wales*, pp. 94-5.

people's interests turned to politics, to the new theology and social struggles'.[43] Crucially, as suggested above, this was not because of the fact that revivalists had a weakness for political distraction such that political and social issues became all important to non-conformity post 1905. No, the whole point was precisely the complete failure of revival theology to sustain adequate 'thisworldiness' to uphold the breadth of authentic Christian witness. Thus, whilst a positive movement in so many ways, the revival was made 'lamentable' in some senses by the unbalanced and unbiblical responses of the revivalists, and more importantly the revival churches (especially in the immediate aftermath of revival), to the material world of the here and now. It stirred up idealism but only provided otherworldly means through which this could find expression and this, in turn, provoked a corresponding, thisworldly reaction. In this regard Gwyn A. Williams includes an interesting personal anecdote in *When Was Wales?*:

> If I may be permitted a personal note, two collier uncles of mine who had been rather routine members of an Independent chapel and Liberal voters, were swept up in it [the 1904 revival]. Their passion did not last ... they moved straight from the Revival into the Independent Labour Party.[44]

Of course, becoming a member of a political party is precisely the kind of initiative one would expect from a balanced 'thisworldly-otherworldly', non-pietist evangelical. The point is, however, that converts were not encouraged to see social and political activity, in the interests of social justice, as part of evangelical Christian ministry. In taking this step, therefore, Williams's uncles were taking a step away from evangelical, and towards liberal, Christianity.

Kenneth Morgan makes a similar observation about the revival:

> What the revival had done was to provide countless men and women with new hope and comfort in the face *of brutalizing material conditions* [emphasis added] ... Certainly the Independent Labour Party was one beneficiary of the revolutionary impact of the revival; the political impulses of young men like Frank Hodges and James Griffiths were quickened accordingly.[45]

This generally meant, as Pope observes, that the likes of James Griffiths were soon converts to the liberal 'social gospel'.[46]

Thus, by considering the otherworldliness of the revival from the negative perspective of the way in which some people reacted against it and turned to the social gospel, this section further underlines the intense pietism of the

---

[43] E. Evans, *The Welsh Revival of 1904*, p. 185.
[44] G. A. Williams, *When Was Wales?*, p. 240.
[45] K. Morgan, *Rebirth of a Nation*, p. 135.
[46] Pope, *Seeking God's Kingdom*, p. 15.

1904–5 revival. Having concluded Part 2, it is now possible to turn to the overall summary and conclusion of this chapter.

Conclusion

It is the contention of this chapter that, whilst there has been a close association between Wales and Christianity since the fifth century, giving rise to the 'Wales as Church paradigm', from 1588 into the nineteenth century this association helped sustain a strongly otherworldly, pietistic theology as far as politics was concerned. This was qualified by the advent of greater opportunity for political expression within Wales, especially after 1884, albeit of an individualist, quasi-pietist nature. The spirituality of 1904–5 revival, however, re-energized a strongly pietistic theology with the effect that evangelical political engagement was frowned upon in many quarters. Such was the introverted pietistic individualism of revival theology that it generated a hunger for thisworldliness which, given the climate of evangelical thought, could only really be addressed through the social gospel and thus liberal theology. It is thus the contention of this chapter that ironically the otherworldliness of revival spirituality at a time of real practical need and an increasing franchise was such that it greatly assisted undermining the long-term influence of evangelicalism, contributing to the triumph of liberal theology in Wales. One wonders what would have happened had the revivalists themselves, and the revival churches, demonstrated a way in which those impacted by the revival, and yet troubled by material conditions, could express their concern as part of their evangelical Christian witness?

In closing it is interesting to contrast 1904 pietism with an observation from Alistair Petrie of the Sentinel Group, which studies revivals across the world. Petrie's research demonstrates that where revivals are not otherworldly in the sense that they deliberately seek to engage with the 'thisworldly', for example, politics, the arts etc., as well as the saving of souls narrowly conceived, this has resulted in community transformation *that lasts*. Where revivals have a very narrowly spiritual posture on the other hand, their impact *is relatively short lived*.[47]

Future Research

There is a need to assess the relationship between 1904 pietism and the wider and later pietistic movement emanating from the publication of 'The Fundamentals' in the United States in the second decade of the twentieth century.[48] To what extent could the Welsh experience in the previous decade

---

[47] Alistair P. Petrie, *Transformed: People, Cities, Nations* (Grand Rapids, 2003), pp. 29-30 and p. 200.
[48] D. D. Morgan, *The Span of the Cross*, p. 138.

have encouraged or laid the foundation for this pietism? Work also needs to be done to assess how the 'new churches' that emerged on the back of the Welsh revival (and that have since developed)[49] have adjusted their pietism, and in many cases – influenced by the rejection by much of international evangelicalism following developments such as the Wheaton Declaration (1964), the Lausanne Covenant 1974 and the Consultation on the Relationship between Evangelism and Social Responsibility (CRESR, 1982) – jettisoned it entirely.[50] Could this new approach that exhibits a greater balance between the 'thisworldly' and the 'otherworldly', contribute to a revival of Welsh evangelicalism in the twenty-first century?

---

[49] The Evangelical Alliance Wales, *The Churches Diversity Index*, 2003.
[50] Daniel Boucher, *Taking Our Place: Church in the Community* (Cardiff, 2004), chap. 2.

CHAPTER 20

Revival Movements in the Twentieth Century as an Urgent Task of the International Research Network

Wolfgang Reinhardt

The Deficit

It is hoped that in the future the last Welsh revival will get more attention in countries like Germany, where it is nearly unknown, but this is only part of a greater challenge and task.

If you compare studies on revival movements in continental Europe, Britain and North America you find that there is often a very *limited view and arbitrarily selection of revivals* mentioned and described. You would be surprised by searching the internet to find out what English-speaking overviews and histories say about revivals in Germany.[1] One example is the mention made of the meeting of 13 August 1727 in the Moravian church in Herrnhut (which was important for the unity and development of the Moravian church but usually is not mentioned in our histories of the European revival movements). Another example is the revival in connection with Christoph Blumhardt (which was only local though spectacular, as it was a result of the famous long-lasting exorcism in Blumhardt's little town Möttlingen which ended with his triumphant cry 'Jesus is Victor'). However, you wonder why the more widespread regional revivals in nearly all provinces of Germany in the nineteenth century are not mentioned at all. The German revival movement in the nineteenth century was largely connected with the revival preaching of mostly Lutheran pastors like Hofacker in Württemberg, Henhöfer in Baden, Volkening in East Westphalia, Ludwig and Claus Harms in Northern Germany and many other, more reformed, preachers in Western Germany but also the

---

[1] Compare (though these examples are not scientific histories): H. H. Osborn, *Revival, God's Spotlight. The significance of revivals and why they cease* (Godalming, 1996), pp. 43f; 91f; Geoff Waugh, 'Revival Fire', *Renewal Journal* 1 (93:1), pp. 33-65. Other overviews don't even mention the continental revivals at all, see most works in the chapter 'Revival histories' on the Revival Library CD by Toni Cauchi (ed.), new and rev. edn (Bishop's Waltham, 2004).

revival in Bavaria beginning among Roman Catholic priests.[2] It had great social and missionary effects: most of the big diaconical institutions of our present time and missionary societies were founded as effects of the revival of the nineteenth century, although the first Protestant missionaries worldwide were sent out from Halle and Herrnhut a hundred years before (also long before William Carey). There were intense international connections by correspondence, visits, and mutual inspirations between Germany, England, Switzerland and other parts of Europe – the 'Christentumsgesellschaft' in Basel (partly also the 'diaspora workers' of the Moravian church)[3] playing the most important role in this vital fascinating exchange among the revival Christians.

On the other side, on continental Europe, *our* narrow view and failures can be seen. Dealing with the revival movements of the twentieth century you realize that there is a big gap in our Mid European research. For example, there is not even one monograph or a newer article on the last great revival in Wales written in German! However, more generally, if you review our big lexica, general church histories and special monographs and articles on 'revival movements', you will find little or nothing concerning the twentieth century. Nearly all German theological *lexica*[4] stop by the end of the nineteenth century when dealing with the topic 'Revival Movement'.

An exception is the newest, the fourth edition of the *Religion in Geschichte und Gegenwart* (*RGG*). But on one side the article on revival movements in North America is too undifferentiated, including all famous evangelists and the juvenile enthusiasm for Christian rock festivals.[5] On the other side there is a paragraph under the problematic (because partly anachronistic) title 'Awakening in Missions.' It should be 'Awakening in the new churches of all continents.' Here the author criticizes a shortcut identification of mass conversions like in Indonesia and Korea as revivals or effects of the Holy Spirit,[6] mentions correctly the manifold non-religious factors but falls into the other extreme: to explain these growth processes *only* in political and sociological, but not at all in theological terms.

---

[2] Compare for all phases: *Geschichte des Pietismus* [*GdP*], III (Göttingen, 2000), pp. 87ff; Erich Beyreuther, *Die Erweckungsbewegung* (KIG 4/R/1) (Göttingen, 1963), pp. 22ff, and the lexica in n.3.

[3] Horst Weigelt in *GdP*, III, pp. 113ff.

[4] Kurt Algermissen, 'Erweckungsbewegung', *LThK* 3 (1959), pp. 1063ff; Gustav Adolf. Benrath, 'Erweckung/ Erweckungsbewegungen, I. Historisch', *TRE*, 10 (1982), pp. 205-20; Erich Beyreuther, 'Erweckung/ Erweckungsbewegungen im 19. Jahrhundert', *RGG*, 2 (1958), pp. 621-9; Ulrich Gäbler, 'Erweckungsbewegung', *EKL*, 1, pp. 1081-8; Wolfgang Philipp, 'Erweckungsbewegungen', *WKL* (1960), pp. 353-6; Gerhard Ruhbach, 'Erweckungsbewegung', *ELThG*, 1 (1992), pp. 521-6.

[5] Charles E. Hambrick-Stowe, *RGG*, pp. 1495-8. An exception is also L. Rott,. 'Erweckungsbewegung', *Ökumene-Lexikon*, 2 (1987), p. 335.

[6] Christoffer H. Grundmann, *RGG*, 2 (1999), p. 1499.

Most scholarly histories of 'Pietism' and on 'The Revival Movement' usually exclude the twentieth-century revivals. One reason for this fact is that some scholars want to confine the term 'The Revival Movement' to the one renewal movement in the context of the Enlightenment in Europe and North America.[7]

There is an analogy in the heated debate among scholars as to whether the technical term 'Pietism' ('Pietismus') should be restricted to the historical period of the original 'Pietismus' in the last part of the seventeenth and the first half of the eighteenth centuries (which view Johannes Wallmann pugnaciously takes).[8] The majority of scholars like Hartmut Lehmann,[9] and Martin Brecht (the editor of *Geschichte des Pietismus*)[10] contend that Pietism ('Pietismus') in a broader sense should include the later 'Pietism' in the nineteenth and twentieth centuries, so comprising the European and North American revival movements of the nineteenth century too. There would be no problem if Wallmann would agree on the evident proposal to differentiate in the use of the term 'Pietismus': first a narrower sense as a term for an epoch and secondly as a wider phenotypical term;[11] 'Pietismus' for the whole continuity of those movements from the seventeenth to the twentieth century (a larger number of them consider themselves as 'Pietists' today) and whose similarities and continuities are more evident and numerous than the differences and discontinuities.[12]

Even more unacceptable is to use the term 'Erweckungsbewegung' ('*The Revival Movement*') only in the narrow sense because of two reasons: first, it looks arbitrary to claim the historical terms *Erweckung, Revival, Reveil* only for a historic manifestation at the end of the eighteenth and the beginning of the nineteenth centuries. The earlier *First Great Awakening* in America would not be included and, what is more relevant, the many later and widespread revivals like the Welsh revival of 1904–5 would be excluded from the historical field of 'Revival' research. Second, the historians who research revival movements in other continents would be excluded too. This Euro-centrism is not sustainable.

---

[7] Ulrich Gäbler, *Auferstehungszeit. Erweckungsprediger des 19. Jahrhunderts* (München 1991), p. 179, n.7; idem. 'Erweckungsbewegung' in *EKL*, 1, pp. 1081-8.
[8] J. Wallmann, 'Pietismus – mit Gänsefüßchen', *ThR* (2001), pp. 462-81; ibid., 'Fehlstart. Zur Konzeption von Band 1 der neuen "Geschichte des Pietismus"', *PuN*, 20 (1995), pp. 218-35.
[9] 'Zur Definition des ‚Pietismus', in Martin Greschat (ed.), *Zur neueren Pietismusforschung* (*WdF* 440) (Darmstadt 1977), pp. 82-90.
[10] M. Brecht, 'Einleitung', in *Geschichte des Pietismus* (*GdP*), I (Göttingen, 1993), pp. 4ff.
[11] So Hartmut Lehmann, passim in oral statements. Wallmann mentions the differentiation without accepting the complementarity: 'Pietismus ein Epochenbegriff oder ein typologischer Begriff, – darum geht der Streit.' Gänsefüßchen, p. 464.
[12] See M. Brecht, 'Einleitung' in *GdP*, I, pp. 4ff.

Even the third volume of the big and most detailed *Geschichte des Pietismus* (History of Pietism), which has some chapters on the twentieth century, is insufficient under temporal and regional aspects: revival movements of the last century are mentioned only very scarcely.[13]

Wales with its great revivals, especially the last one in 1904–5 with its effects on all continents, deserved its own chapter. But it is at least mentioned in two contributions dealing with other countries. Let us have a short look at this treatment of the Welsh revival as an example where further research is needed. Mark Noll in his chapter on 'Evangelicals and Fundamentalism in North America' refers to it briefly in connection with the events of 1906 in Azusa Street, Los Angeles, and the Latter Rain Movement.[14] It has been noted that there are real connections and influences between Wales and the beginning of the Pentecostal movement, but this needs more scholarly attention.

More detailed is the chapter on the 'Fellowship Movement' ("Gemeinschaftsbewegung") in Germany of the nineteenth and twentieth centuries[15] by Jörg Ohlemacher (older books had briefly described the Welsh revival before).[16] He describes the long expectations of a worldwide revival that seemed to be ahead of the great revival in Wales, other European countries and India. All these events owed themselves to impulses of the Anglo-Saxon Holiness Movement and its conception of the work of the Holy Spirit. He names the elements of the revival meetings of Evan Roberts, especially a certain atmosphere of the spirit and corresponding of a ban that lay on the gathering if sin was not confessed which would hinder the work of the Spirit.

He states that new elements were introduced in the revival too by the events of Wales and Keswick, which were already present before as single elements but never in this combination. He lists the following elements and their connection to similar ideas in America and Germany:

---

[13] Penti Laasonen in his contribution on 'Erweckungsbewegungen im Norden im 19. und 20. 'Jahrhundert' mentions only very little of the twentieth century and only about Finland but insufficiently as 'Evangelisationsbewegung' and as a revival Christianity of Anglo-American type of the Pentecostal movement which works from outside the Lutheran church. *GdP*, III, p. 346.

[14] *GdP*, III, p. 513; idem, *Das Christentum in Nordamerika* (*KGiE* IV/5) (Leipzig, 2000), p. 155.

[15] Jörg Ohlemacher, 'Gemeinschaftschristentum in Deutschland im 19. und 20. Jahrhundert', *GdP*, III, pp. 430ff.

[16] Paul Fleisch, *Die moderne Gemeinschaftsbewegung in Deutschland, Ein Versuch, dieselbe nach ihren Ursprüngen darzustellen und zu würdigen*, 3 (Leipzig, 1912), pp. 442-8; Ernst Giese, *Und flicken die Netze. Dokumente zur Erweckungsgeschichte des 20. Jahrhunderts* (Marburg, 1976), pp. 35-42; Dieter Lange, *Eine Bewegung bricht sich Bahn. Die deutschen Gemeinschaften im ausgehenden 19. und 20. Jahrhundert und ihre Stellung zu Kirche, Theologie und Pfingstbewegung* (Berlin, 1979).

1. the public exposition of sinners and sin in the meetings
   - intensifying the concepts of purity of the premillenarian church as a bride
2. the role of women and girls as evangelists
   - having its patterns already in Phoebe Palmer among others
3. the stress on demonological notions
   - prepared in the dualistic worldview of the holiness movement, in Germany connected with the experiences of Christoph Blumhardt
4. spectacular healings
   - fortifying motives of the holiness movement too
5. and the guidance of the meetings by the Holy Spirit

The Effects of the Welsh Revival on Germany

A brief mention of the effects of the Welsh revival in Germany will follow:

There were Personal Blessings

In an atmosphere of expectation of a revival, adherents of the German holiness movement travelled to the British Isles and in 1905–6 to Wales. Meanwhile, the fundamentally over-denominational attitude of the Anglo-Saxon holiness movement had spread also in Germany: Didn't God gather his people from all nations, churches, and Christian associations? Noel Gibbard has written more details in his chapter on the effects in Germany in his pioneer book on the worldwide effects of the Welsh revival.[17] But, understandably, as he did not have direct access to the German sources detailed research must go on. It is well known that among the German visitors there were several noble women, some had leading positions in parts of the 'Fellowhip Movement' and societies being formed in Germany.

An example of this is found in 1900 when the 'Deutsche Frauenmissions-Gebetsbund' (DFMGB = German Women's Alliance of Prayer for Missions) was founded by four aristocratic women and it had grown to 14,000 members in 30 years.[18] They did not only pray and support mission at home and abroad but also organized big conferences and sent women into the mission field for example to China. Most women of the early leading board made their way to Wales: Countess Elisabeth Waldersee and Jenny von Plotho, Ms von Hochstetter, and Jeanne Wasserzug. They came back enthusiastically and gave testimony of the miracles of this revival, and invited others to come with them next time. On one side, there were positive reactions as in the well-known

---

[17] Noel Gibbard, *On the Wings of the Dove, The International Effects of the 1904-05 Revival* (Bridgend, 2002), pp. 36-47.

[18] Maria von Oertzen, *Mein Leben. Eine Selbstbiographie* (Lahr-Dinglingen, no date), pp. 111-16.

autobiography of Eva von Tiele-Winckler, the founder of a growing sisterhood of deaconesses and the 'Friedenshort' for homeless children and others in Miechowitz (Upper Silesia).[19] On the other hand, Hedwig von Redern was a bit disappointed by her visits to Keswick and Wales after her high expectations – perhaps due to her character and the weakening of the revival already in 1906.[20]

There were Regional Awakenings

In consequence of visits of members of the German 'Gemeinschaftsbewegung', there were regional awakenings in some parts of Germany. In March 1905, the first revival following the example of Wales happened in Mülheim an der Ruhr. They practised in their meetings the direct leadership of the spirit and public confessions of sin. In the autumn of 1905 other revivals followed in other parts of Western Germany, also in the north, middle and east.[21]

There were Open Debates pro and contra

In Hamburg, one Lutheran pastor published a booklet: 'Wittenberg or Wales? A serious question.' Another Lutheran pastor answered by his writing, 'Wittenberg and Wales!'[22]

More Important were the Discussions on the Big Conferences of Evangelicals in Germany

The conference of the Evangelical Alliance in Blankenburg 1905 was enthusiastic. The report described the events in the conference after the teachings of Dr Torrey on the Baptism of the Holy Spirit as an answer to many prayers and a revival 'as it could not have been expected more powerful in the spirit and more deeply by the 1300 guests of the conference'. It mentions that

---

[19] On her visits to Wales and Keswick see: *Denksteine des lebendigen Gottes. Aufzeichnungen selbsterlebter Führungen* (Gießen/Basel, 1963), pp. 36-49; Walter Thieme, *Mutter Eva. Die Lobsängerin der Gnaden Gottes. Leben und Werk der Schwester Eva von Tiele-Winckler* (Berlin, 1966), pp. 150-6.

[20] Hedwig von Redern gives also an example of the vivid connections over the channel in these years, she accompanied Elisabeth Waldersee and Jenny von Plotho in 1906 and described her journey in *Knotenpunkte, Selbstbiographie* (Lahr-Dinglingen, 1938), pp. 86-91.

[21] Summary in: J. Ohlemacher, 'Gemeinschaftschristentum in Deutschland im 19. und 20. Jahrhundert', *GdP*, III, p. 432. Gerhard Ruhbach underestimated the effects in Germany in his short article 'Die Erweckung von 1905 und die Anfänge der Pfingstbewegung', *PuN* 15 (1989), pp. 84-94.

[22] Max Glage, *Wittenberg oder Wales? Eine ernste Frage* (Hamburg, 1905). R. Mumssen, *Wittenberg und Wales! Erwiderung auf P. Glage's Schrift: Wittenberg oder Wales?* (Neumünster, no date).

this was not a simple imitation of Wales as some had feared.[23] During the Gnadauer Konferenz 1906 (conference of Pietism within the established Evangelical Church) there were several references to the Welsh revival too and what could be learned from it, but in general it was less enthusiastic.[24]

The influence of Speaking in Tongues, the 'Tongue Movement' and Pentecostalism

A later event in indirect connection with Wales would become most influential and tragic for the development of the German Fellowship Movement. In 1907 Pastor Heinrich Dallmeyer had invited two female Norwegian evangelists to Kassel whom he had met at the Hamburg Strandmission. Its leader, Emil Meyer, had been so impressed hearing them speaking in tongues in the capital of Norway, Christiana, that he had invited them to Hamburg; here they initiated speaking in tongues too. The young ladies were part of the 'tongue movement' in Norway influenced by the Methodist Thomas Ball Barratt who claimed to have received this gift in the USA. Therefore, there is a chain between Los Angeles, Christiana, Hamburg, and Kassel. Initially some leaders were impressed by the singing and testimony of the Norwegian women. But the gatherings which were blessed at first got so much out of order with men and women with paroxysmal manifestations, the public of the town of Kassel read about it in the newspaper and scoffed at it. The events got such a devastating reputation that even the police had to intervene and the leadership of the Evangelical Church decided to forbid everybody from participating in these meetings.[25] An initially positive evaluation by some leading pastors changed to the opposite. The events and the theology were condemned by the *Berliner Erklärung* 1909.[26] These events were said to be 'from below', by Satan or by human emotions but not by God's Spirit. However, the Gnadau brethren opposed also the words and writings of Pastor Jonathan Paul on the pure heart and the possibility to get rid of sin and the teachings of a Baptism in the Spirit as a separate act after conversion as not consistent with the doctrines of the reformation. They rejected the expectation of a 'new Pentecost' as it was obvious already in Irvingianism with all its failures. On the Gnadau Conference of 1910 there was not only a reaction against the rising Pentecostalism but more

---

[23] *Reden und Ansprachen der zwanzigsten Allianz-Konferenz zur Vertiefung des Glaubenslebens, 28.August bis 2. September 1905* (Blankenburg, 1905).
[24] *Verhandlungen der achten Gnadauer Pfingstkonferenz gehalten zu Schönebeck a. d. Elbe vom 5. – 8. Juni 1906* (Stuttgart, 1906); references to Wales mainly in the report of the eyewitness P. Simsa in his paper 'Vorbedingungen einer Erweckung', pp. 27-34; passim pp. 42, 112f, 128.
[25] For the events in Kassel and Hessen see Paul Fleisch, *Geschichte der Pfingstbewegung in Deutschland von 1900 bis 1950* (Marburg, 1983), pp. 36-51.
[26] Lange, 'Bewegung', *GdP*, III, pp. 287-90.

generally against the (American–British) influences which were considered to be foreign to the rich theological tradition of the reformation in Germany.[27]

So unbalanced adoptions of Anglo-Saxon influences on Holiness and the Baptism by the Spirit, some excesses in Kassel and the radical opposition of the largest part of the inner-church 'evangelicals' led to a deep split within the German Fellowship Movement and the formation of a Pentecostal movement outside the (established) Evangelical Church of Germany. This was to poison the relationship to the later Pentecost and charismatic movement in Germany for about a hundred years up to today. These events certainly affected later evaluation and the silence on the Welsh revival too, although the positive effects on the revival in Germany 1905–6 were obvious. The influence of Jesse Penn-Lewis in Germany, who had been there and also kept correspondence, is still to be investigated.

The Task of Future Research

As the majority of World Christianity is no longer living in the Western and Northern world (as the new *World Christian Encyclopedia*[28] shows more than ever before) the revivals in the new churches must be part of future church histories and historical research.

This is true for the majority of 'Pietists' which we find worldwide under the name of 'evangelicals' too. Though it is accepted that the semantic denotation and connotations are not completely the same it seems obvious that the huge majority of characteristics of 'Pietists' and 'Evangelicals' are identical. In addition, the English (technical) term 'evangelical' is much older than the German term 'Evangelikale' including classic Pietism as, for example, the work of the British historian W. R. Ward, *The Protestant Evangelical Awakening*,[29] shows.

The synchronic (regional) and diachronic links and network between European and non-European revival movements must be taken serious, so the narrow German term 'Die Erweckungsbewegung' or French 'Le Réveil' or English 'The Revival' can only be adopted to the European-North American revival movement of the eighteenth and (beginning of the) nineteenth centuries. 'Revival Movement' but must not exclude scholars from Asia, Africa, and

---

[27] E. Schrenk, 'Man muß aufhören, immer neue Lehren erfinden zu wollen, immer wieder auf Ausländisches hineinzufallen und das gering zu achten, was Gott uns Deutschen durch eine Wolke deutscher Zeugen geschenkt hat....' *Verhandlungen der achten Gnadauer Pfingstkonferenz gehalten zu Wernigerode. 17.-19, Mai* (Stuttgart, 1910).

[28] D. B. Barrett, G. T. Kurian, T. M. Johnson (eds), *The World Christian Encyclopedia: A Comparative Survey of Churches and Religions in the Modern World* (Oxford, 2001); Klaus Wetzel, *Wo die Kirchen wachsen. Der geistliche Aufbruch in der Zwei-Drittel-Welt und die Folgen für das Christentum* (Wuppertal, 1998), 12ff.

[29] W. R. Ward, *The Protestant Evangelical Awakening* (Cambridge, 1992).

Latin America from calling the subject of their historical studies 'Revival' too. In this respect, this author disagrees with Ulrich Gäbler. However, his demand to investigate the mutual incitation, impact, and imitation across borders of countries and languages[30] is appreciated, but it must be referred to as *revival* in the twentieth century too.

Important preparatory investigational work has been done by J. Edwin Orr who probably had the largest knowledge and overview in historical and regional respect due to his many visits to all continents and his life-long investigations of revival movements. The reader is reminded of his temporally built trilogy on the three periods of 'Evangelical Awakenings 1790–1830', 'the worldwide impact of the great Awakening of 1858' and 'the impact of the twentieth century revivals'.[31] However, maybe even wealthier is the material he had collected in his five-volume regionally structured work on *Evangelical Awakenings* in Africa, Latin America, East Asia, South Asia, and the South Seas.[32] He has not been surpassed in the wealth of his knowledge about revival movements in all continents. His attempt at classification of the periods of revivals was also most influential. He changed it several times but in his last classification he saw five major awakenings – beginning from 1725, 1792, 1857, 1904 and 1948, and two significant resurgences in the years from 1830 and 1880 and many smaller and regional awakenings.[33] Certainly, his works are methodically weak and scientifically unsatisfying. This author would agree with the appreciation and critique of R E. Davies: 'Orr is often doing no more than chronicling a long series of facts without much attempt at assessing their significance ... sometimes he sees revivals where there are none!' But

> He is the only researcher who has done any work at all on revivals in certain periods and places. Orr's pioneering work needs to be supplemented, and at times, possibly be corrected by further study, but for the present, his is the only work

---

[30] 'Die Erforschung der "wechselseitigen Anregung, Beeinflussung und Nachahmung" über Landes- und Sprachgrenzen hinaus', *GdP*, III, p. 27; idem, *Auferstehungszeit. Erweckungsprediger des 19. Jahrhunderts. Sechs Porträts* (München, 1991), p. 168.

[31] J. Edwin Orr, *The Eager Feet, Evangelical Awakenings 1790-1830* (Chicago, 1975); *The Fervent Prayer. The Worldwide Impact of the Great Awakening of 1858* (Chicago, 1974); *The Flaming Tongue. The Impact of the Twentieth Century Revivals* (Chicago, 1973).

[32] J. Edwin Orr, *Evangelical Awakenings in Africa* (Pasadena, 1974); *Evangelical Awakenings in Eastern Asia* (Minneapolis, 1975); *Evangelical Awakenings in Latin America* (Minneapolis, 1978); *Evangelical Awakenings in Southern Asia* (Minneapolis, 1976); *Evangelical Awakenings in the South Seas* (Minneapolis, 1976).

[33] J. Edwin Orr, *The Re-Study of Revival and Revivalism* (Pasadena), pp. 1-64.

which has been done in bringing together the host of evidence present in newspaper and magazine reports, and other contemporary writings.[34]

Again, it is argued that it would be correct to contradict Gäbler, who criticises Orr, because his area of application of the term revival would be too broad and inept as a historical term by talking about five revival movements. It will be remembered that Gäbler wanted to restrict 'Revival Movement' as a technical term for a certain epoch. It would be preferable then to speak of the 'European-North-American revival movement in the eighteenth and the first part of the nineteenth century'. The big revival movements which Orr describes must be included in further research not only because of factual research in these continents but also because of the historical connections between the nineteenth-century revivals in Europe and North America and those of the twentieth century in Asia, Africa, and Latin America.

The huge task of a comparative investigation of the phenomenology of revival movements is still ahead. Gäbler is surely correct – not restricting it on his just-mentioned restricted understanding of 'Revival Movement' – when he states that the revival movement does not enjoy a lot of popularity among historians and church historians outside the Anglophone world. The research in the United States and Great Britain seems to be most advanced.[35]

A presupposition is the discussion and possibly a consensus on the definition of 'Revival Movement' in comparison with related but not identical terms like 'mass conversion', 'church growth', 'renewal' etc. This task is very difficult, but it would be wrong to overestimate the danger of all definitions.

Among many proposals, two interesting attempts[36] can be quoted which could serve as a basis for future discussions. They offer theological and phenomenological inductive definitions which include constant and variable, unusual internal and external effects. In the words of R. E. Davies:

> A revival is a sovereign outpouring of the Holy Spirit upon a group of Christians resulting in their spiritual reviving and quickening, and issuing in the awakening of spiritual concern in outsiders or formal church members; an immediate, or, at other times, a more longterm, effect will be efforts to extend the influence of the Kingdom of God both intensively in the society in which the Church is placed, and extensively in the spread of the gospel to more remote parts of the world' '... an event or series of events in which a number of people, in the same locality and

---

[34] R. E. Davies, *I Will Pour out My Spirit. A History and Theology of Revivals and Evangelical Awakenings* (Tunbridge Wells, 1992), p. 13.

[35] 'Im allgemeinen erfreut sich die Erweckungsbewegung bei Historikern und Kirchenhistorikern außerhalb des englischsprachigen Gebiets keiner großen Beliebtheit. Die Forschung in den Vereinigten Staaten und in Großbritannien scheint am weitesten fortgeschritten zu sein.' U. Gäbler, *Auferstehungszeit. Erweckungsprediger des 19 Jarhunderts. Sechs Porträts* (München, 1991), p. 169.

[36] Davies, *Spirit*, p. 15. Osborn, *Revival, God's Spotlight*, p. 15.

at the same time, experience an extraordinary powerful and unmistakable sense of the reality and presence of God, accompanied by an overwhelming conviction of truth, especially as it relates to the relationship between them and God. ... These powerful inner convictions and outward manifestations are then followed by clear and lasting evidence of lives changed from wickedness and immorality to purity of character and uprightness of behaviour, from timidity and ineffectiveness in witness to the world, to a bold, powerful affirmation of biblical truth, especially that which relates to God´s reconciling work through the Cross of Jesus Christ.[37]

H. H. Osborn, who has mainly worked on the East African Revival and especially on Rwanda, names variable and also dispensable elements: 'This powerful working of God in the spirit may or may not be evidenced by dramatic, outward, physical manifestations but is always characterised by very strong inner convictions and emotions.'[38]

An interesting and difficult question is in how far the Pentecostal and Charismatic movements of the twentieth century are to be understood as 'revival movements' and by which criteria. Here you will not be able to answer simplistically by YES or NO'.[39] As it is true that Pentecostal and Charismatic movements cannot be excluded from a history of Pietism and Revival movements, so ignorant it would be mentioning only these movements when revivals of the twentieth century are concerned – as you can find it unfortunately in some ecumenical and missiological studies.[40]

Two special tasks for future international linked investigations are mentioned:

The Revival Movement in the First Decade of the Twentieth Century

Some considered this the most far-reaching revival of all times, especially in Wales 1904–5 but including many other countries in all continents.[41]. Not all will know that the Welsh revival was not the actuator of the *whole* movement

---

[37] Davies, *Spirit*, p. 15.

[38] Osborn, *Revival, God´s Spotlight*, p. 15.

[39] For an example of the difficulty in this area, see Holger Böckel, *Gemeindeaufbau im Kontext charismatischer Erneuerung. Theoretische und empirische Rekonstruktion eines kybernetischen Ansatzes unter Berücksichtigung wesentlicher Aspekte selbstorganisierender sozialer Systeme* (Leipzig, 1999).

[40] For example in the series *Studien zur interkulturellen Geschichte des Christentums*. among 116 volumes you find 8 monographs to Pentecostalism, but not a single title to revival movements – perhaps due to the influence of one of the founders of this series, Walter Hollenweger, who understands himself as somebody like a 'Pentecostal of higher order.' Among these studies of Pentecostalism there is also the paper of Michael Bergunder, 'Die südindische Pfingstbewegung im 20. Jahrhundert. Eine historische und systematische Untersuchung' (vol. 113) (Frankfurt, 1999), which at least briefly mentions some revivals in India which are not in direct connection to the Pentecostal movement but were influenced by the Welsh revival like the *Mukti Mission* .

[41] For example, Orr, *The Flaming Tongue*.

in the beginning of the twentieth century but probable the most impressive and effective partial movement because of its great individual and social consequences in Wales itself and literally on all continents.[42]

Future research has to include the perspective of other continents too like the view of the church of Korea who has experienced several waves of revivals[43] and in the context of a history of persecutions. It is not by chance that the church of Korea belongs to the churches that have grown most and have sent an enormous number of missionaries to the world. But there were big revivals in India, East Asia, on the continent of Australia and the Pacific islands as well as in Latin America, and last not least in Africa.

The East African Revival Movement

The East African Revival Movement was said to be the most long-lasting revival of history[44] that happened mainly in the established Anglican and Lutheran churches. It was of great importance for the church history and the societies of East Africa and was called one of the most vital movements of Africa.[45] Also its sociological influence is remarkable.[46] In many countries the consequences of the East African Revival are visible today. Many church leaders are influenced by it as visitors of the churches in East Africa can notice.

The relations to the European revival of the nineteenth century and the Keswick Holiness Movement and its effects on world missions also on this genuine African movement are interesting[47] and deserve further research. A

---

[42] Gibbard, *On the Wings of the Dove*, p. 17.

[43] W. Blair and B. Hunt, *The Korean Pentecost and the Sufferings Which Followed* (Edinburgh, 1977); Allan D. Clark, *A History of the Church in Korea* (Seoul, 1971); Bram Krol, *De Kerk van Korea. Haar geschiedenis en de huidige situatie* (Doorn, 1984); Mo-Un Lee, *Die erste Kirchengeschichte* (The Christian Literature Society of Korea, 1970); Ro Bong-Rin and Martin L. Nelson (eds), *Korean Church Growth Explosion. Centennial of the Protestant Church (1884-1984)* (Seoul, 1983).

[44] Andrew F. Walls, 'The Evangelical Revival, the Missionary Movement, and Africa', in *The Missionary Movement in Christian History. Studies in the Transmission of Faith* (Edinburgh, 1996), pp. 79-101; Richard Gehman, 'The East African Revival', *EAJET*, 5 (1986), pp. 36-56.

[45] F. B Welbourn, *East African Christian* (London, 1965), p. 142.

[46] Catherine E. Robins, 'Tukutendereza. A Study of Social Change: Sectarian Withdrawal in the Balokole Revival in Uganda' (D. Diss., Columbia University 1975), *Occasional Research Papers* (Makarere University, 1987).

[47] Walls, 'The Evangelical Revival, p. 100: 'In its origin this revival affected both European missionaries and Africans, and its antecedents can be found in both traditions. It has developed as an essentially African movement, though it has had a certain impact on evangelical life in the West, especially in Britain'; Robin Anker-Peterson, 'A Study of the Spiritual Roots of the East African Revival Movement with special Reference to it's Use of Confession of Sins in Public' (unpublished M.Th. thesis, University of Aberdeen, 1988).

fertile field of comparative historical research are the analogies and peculiarities in comparison to earlier revivals,[48] for example:

- the open confession of faith;[49]

- small revival groups (in a certain analogy to the 'conventicles' of classical Pietism);[50]

- ecstatic phenomena like in early Pietism in Germany or during the *First Great Awakening* described and interpreted so meticulously by Jonathan Edwards. It was probably one of the strengths of the East African Revival that these unusual phenomena were never in the centre. 'Jesus satisfies' and 'Jesus alone' were the watchwords of the great East African revival conferences in Rwanda and Uganda.[51]

- As in all revival movements there were tensions between the 'revived' and the leaders and theological schools of the established church, but it was special to the revival in East Africa that the revivalists nearly always stayed within the established churches and could contribute to renewal from within. And as on the other side many church leaders opened themselves for the revival so it is not so surprising that even today you find many bishops and other church leaders close to or at the top of the revival groups.

- There were many social impacts on society, for example the self-esteem and social status of women were not unessentially altered by the revival.[52] In Rwanda it effected also opposition against the hate propaganda among the

---

[48] R. G. Calderwood, 'Revival in East Africa', in *World Dominion* (London, 1951), p. 265: 'There can be no clearer proof of the genuineness of the movement than the fact that hundreds of Africans who knew no church history give their testimony in terms almost identical with those of the comments of the great evangelical revival of the 18th century, or the Sankey and Moody revival in the 19th century'.

[49] Robin Anker-Peterson, *Joe Church: Awake. An African Calling. The Story of Blasio Kigozi and His Vision of Revival* (London, 1937); idem, *Quest for the Highest. An Autobiographical Account of the East African Revival* (Exeter, 1981).

[50] In which concrete sins are confessed before others to prevent a backsliding and self-deception, proved in her great study on the early evangelization of Uganda by indigenous Christians the purifying and refreshing effects of this way of liberation, which usually were missing in average Protestantism. See M. Louise Pirouet, *Black Evangelists. The Spread of Christianity in Uganda 1891-1914* (London, 1978).

[51] Anker-Peterson, *Joe Church: Awake*; idem, *Quest for the Highest*; Festo Kivengere, 'The Revival that was and is', *Christianity Today*, 20 (1976); H. H. Osborn, *Fire in the Hills. The Revival which spread from Rwanda* (Crowborough, 1991).

[52] Brigitta Larsson has investigated the influence in Tanzania: *Conversion to Greater Freedom? Women, Church and Social Change in North-Western Tanzania under Colonial Rule* (Uppsala, 1991).

groups of Hutu and Tutsi,[53] up to shaking examples of courage, solidarity and common martyrdom with the endangered Tutsi[54] during the most terrible genocide of 1994. After Rwanda had been forsaken by the whole world – the biggest shame of the UN and the international community – it is worth reminding people not only of the horrors and the failure of the parts of the churches in 1994, but also these 'testimonies of Christian bravery' and the many miraculous changes of healing, holistic development, forgiveness and reconciliation today.[55]

- Lastly here – as in all revivals – both dimensions have to be taken seriously: the non-theological contextual conditions as well as the spiritual, ecclesiastical, theological origins of the revival. A merely sociological explanation will be as little sufficient as a merely theological approach. One might compare the investigations of the revival and the phenomenal growth of the Korean church.[56] However, already the growth of the first church – if you want to call it a 'revival' of the people of God – can be understood historically and according to the testimony of the Acts of the Apostles only by these complementary aspects.[57]

Practical Consequences

First of all this gap and desideratum, at least in European scholarship, to include the big twentieth-century revivals on all continents in the historical and

---

[53] Osborn, *Fire in the Hills*; Meg Guillebaud, *Rwanda: The Land God Forgot? Revival, Genocide and Hope* (London, 2002), p. 324.

[54] Antoine Rutayisire, *Faith under Fire. Testimonies of Christian Bravery* (1995). I have edited an updated and enlarged German translation: idem, *Und trotzdem reiche ich dir die Hand. Ruanda zwischen Völkermord und Versöhnung* (Moers, 2001).

[55] I would like to highlight from my own experience over many years the indigenous organization *Solace Ministries* founded by Jean Gakwandi, a survivor of the genocide himself, which has helped thousands of widows and orphans during the last years in many projects of inner healing and holistic help. But we must mention also the traditional organization Africa (Evangelistic) Enterprise (AEE), which played an important role in the East African Revival Movement (e.g. by the also in Europe well known bishop Festo Kivengere) who tried under risk of his own life to work for reconciliation under the terror of Idi Amin. Today AEE is probably the most important work for reconciliation in Rwanda working by seminars and activities, e.g. in the prisons of Rwanda – beside the National Commission for Unity and Peace, whose vice president, Antoine Rutaysire, is also the leader of AEE.

[56] Ro and Nelson (eds), *Korean Church*, p. 46.

[57] Wolfgang Reinhardt, *Das Wachstum des Gottesvolkes. Biblische Theologie des Gemeindewachstums* (Göttingen, 1995); idem, *The Population Size of Jerusalem and the Numerical Growth of the Jerusalem Church, The Book of Acts in its Palestinian Setting (Acts in the First Century Setting vol. 4)* (Carlisle, 1995), pp. 237-65.

church historical research, has to be realized and discussed. Some specific proposals follow:

1. This big task cannot be undertaken by isolated scholars but only with cooperation of the best experts and institution of all continents. There may be already some systematic research in the USA (maybe in Wheaton, Asbury and Fuller) but it should be related to European universities and centres like the Interdisciplinary Centre of the Study of Pietism in Halle – they should be convinced to include the Pietism and revivals of the twentieth century too. There is a need for international cooperation for the research on revival movements in the twentieth century also in Europe! Certainly, scholars in the other continents should be detected and invited. An attempt should be made to try to find cooperation with evangelical and ecumenical missiological societies, though it should be noted that the topic is not simply delegated to the discipline of missiology – it is mainly a part of general history and church history.

2. There should be a centre for the research on revival movements in the twentieth century that should try to get an overview, collect all available literature, and publish the bibliography on the internet. Sponsors should be found to encourage research in new fields. Maybe there can be also in Europe a chair for the research and teaching on this topic (maybe with visiting professors from all over the world).

3. An international congress in the next two or three years should be well planned including the mentioned experts from all continents.

4. The result maybe the first comprehensive volumes about larger revivals of the last century on a scientific level, perhaps a series on new revival movements. A start could be a fifth volume of the most comprehensive *Geschichte des Pietismus* (History of Pietism).

In concluding this chapter, mention must be made of the relevance of the subject for the churches in reference to the Lutheran bishop of the hosting church at the first *International Congress on the Research of Pietism* who had admonished the scholars in Halle 2001, 'Let us not forget the relevance of our research for the people in our churches and the secularised people outside.' Could there be something better for our (at least in Europe) rather weak and normally shrinking churches than to be challenged by the dynamics of revivals: the Welsh revival which we commemorate in this volume and the power of the non-European growing churches, part of which enjoy the consequences of past or the reality of present revival movements?

CHAPTER 21

Dream/Vision: A Language of the Soul

Susan Gabriel Talbot

Charlotte Bronte wrote in *Wuthering Heights*,

> I have dreamed dreams in my life, dreams that have stayed with me ever after ...
> They've gone through and through me like wine through water, and altered the *colour of my mind*.[1]

Freud was not the first man to study the significance of the dreaming mind but was the pioneer in Western culture of an understanding of this everyday occurrence as being of scientific interest. It is certainly the case that they are present universally in human experience and their place within human consciousness is cross-cultural. After years of questioning both personally and as a scholar of dreams that have occurred within a cross-over area between dreaming and vision as understood within religious experience, it seems that what a poet has said in both warning and as tantalising exhortation regarding the sense of meaning that lies at the heart of claimed religious experience may well be something of which we need to take note.

> Was it a vision?
> Or did we see that day the unseeable
> One glory of the everlasting world
> Perpetually at work, though never seen
> Since Eden locked the gate that's everywhere
> And nowhere?[2]

For some it would appear, even now, even today, the road into a sense of the holy and even of glory maybe a dream-vision that is so powerful it is effortlessly remembered down the years, carrying within it both a sense of message, challenge and question that raise important issues related to our sense of what is real and what matters.

I have come to a not dissimilar conclusion to Erich Fromm but I would now suggest an added dimension indicated by patterns observed from empirical research for the BBC and at Manchester University. Dream and Vision are not

---

[1] Charlotte Bronte, *Wuthering Heights* (1858 edn), p. 81.
[2] Edwin Muir, 'The Transfiguration'. Quoted by Richard Hollway, in *Crossfire* (London, 1988), p. 160.

only a language of the 'soul' but they also may become major pathways of grace as well as of truth. Certain visionary-dream experiences can become a universal Jacob's ladder, by which the things of the earth and the realities of the transcendent realm may connect.

For Evan Roberts and the experience of the Welsh Revival of 1904, although his religious experience was essentially strongly 'word based' vision came to have its place. This place was disputed and some possibly wisely in his case, were of the view that these visions were essentially for his own encouragement and should not have been as widely shared, particularly with the media as they were.

One of the most striking of Evan Roberts's visions, many of which were of fairly standard symbolic pattern of known religious imagery, was the vision in the garden of Ty Llwyd. It was unusual in that two people saw this at the same time. Evan Roberts and his friend Sydney Evans both reported seeing,

> a kind of arm stretching out from the moon in direction of earth ... I saw something of the sort. I do not usually get visions, but I saw it also ... We both had a vision that night.[3]

The image that Evan Roberts and his friend both saw seemed to them a confirmation of their longing for a revival of faith in Wales. The image seen was understood as affirming that this was within the will and action of God's Spirit who was reaching down to touch the lost earth.

What is vital before understanding can take place is the 'key to the code' of the imagery deployed within altered states of consciousness and occurring within visionary or dream experience. Those reflecting on the meaning of dream-visionary experience need knowledge of the common themes and archetypal symbols that are important within the primary culture that is inhabited by the dreamer or visionary.

For many research projects the scientific method of clinical testing and double-blind trials is understood as the preferred and most trustworthy way by which we endeavour to understand our world and ourselves. However, within the human realm such methods of scrutiny may be neither possible nor desirable, either ethically or in relation to the nature of what is under examination. Not all phenomena within the human realm of behaviour and consciousness can be so examined. When transcendence is the area which is examined the intrinsic nature of what is being observed may be affected by both the Heisenberg principle related to quantum phenomena, that is, that observation itself affects the phenomenon under scrutiny, as well as the possibility that the nature of a spiritual realm has to be dealt with differently to that of the workings of bone, the digestive system and the affects of

---

[3] R. Smith, *When the Fire Fell: The Great Welsh Revival of 1904 and its meaning for survival today* (Remo, 1996), p. 17.

pharmacology on the human body. One of the ways forward in such a context is the use of qualitative methodologies which look closely in a disciplined and structured way at individual human experience, watching for parallel and clustering repeating patterns of phenomena which can be important indicators of significance and meaning.

Parallel and clustering repeating patterns of phenomena and experience can be important indicators of significance and meaning. Within the sociological and psychological areas of study, repeating patterns and clustering of phenomenon are regarded as reasonable indicators of possible significance.

In the 1980s a most unusual dream/vision was recounted to me by a woman who had worked for some time in Nigeria with CMS. It had had a particular impact on her for two reasons; one reason was its inherent quality and atmosphere and the other because she had been asked to be the interpreter for this Hausa native man from the north of the country.

The dream/vision described correlated to a surprising if not astonishing degree with a story described in Bede's *History of the English Church and People*. It is now a famous description of a visionary experience of a cowhand who was a lay brother at Whitby Abbey.

Bede described an ordinary man's encounter with an angelic vision. Caedmon helped with the cattle at the monastery of Whitby. In the summary described by Bede, Caedmon, *who was not musical*, had retreated to his cell when the time for passing the harp round had come after the meal in the refectory. There he,

> lay down at the appointed time and fell asleep, and in a dream he saw a man standing beside him who called him by name. 'Caedmon,' he said, 'sing me a song.' 'I don't know how to sing,' he replied. 'It is because I cannot sing that I left the feast and came here.'... 'The man who addressed him then said: 'But you will sing to me'...[4]

This account, which was written somewhere around the mid-eighth century, has a surprising correlation with a twentieth-century account told to me in a preliminary research period for a programme with the BBC and was one of the incidents that became a stimulus and challenge to further research.

The account given below was told to me by Sue Davies who worked for CMS in northern Nigeria and who could speak fluent Hausa. She acted as interpreter when the man in question told the story of what had sent him on a long trek to find the 'people of the book', which from his dream he had known to be Christians. The nearest Christian community was about 25 miles distant from his village. The Hausa tribesman was in mid-life and was asking the questions of his gods as to how one could live a life of integrity, grow in wisdom, and live a 'good' life.

---

[4] Bede, *A History of the English Church and People* (Penguin, 1965 edn), p. 243.

During this period of questioning and concern a night came in which still pondering on such matters, the man lay down in his room, as Sue Davies reported,

> It seemed that the whole room was filled with light and he opened his eyes and looked and saw an angel. The angel was bringing a book and the angel said to him, 'Read the book!' But he said, 'I can't read, 'you read it to me.'
> So the angel read to him from the book and it was all about the kind of man God wants to work for him. Then the angel closed the book and went away and the light died down ... so (said the man) I closed my eyes and tried to sleep.
> Then again the room was filled with light and exactly the same thing happened again and the angel read the same words again. This happened three times. At the end of the third time, the man asked, 'What shall I do? What does this mean? I don't understand it. And the angel said that he should go and find someone to read him from the book.'
> The next morning, unable to forget the dream/vision, the man decided he had to go in search of people who could indeed read to him from the book like he had seen in his vision. After a long journey he stayed with a Christian community while they read to him from the New Testament. 'He identified the exact passage the angel had read. It was from Paul's letter to Timothy and described the characteristics of a good leader. When this Hausa man heard this passage, he said,
> 'That is what God has called me to do.'

This description given by the woman-worker who interpreted this account for the Christian community has interesting parallels with Bede's ninth century account of the vision of Caedmon (1965). In both experiences a man encounters an angelic figure. In the Anglo-Saxon description, as in the ancient Hebrew text, the word used for the 'messenger' is ambivalent. It can be translated as either angel – with all the transcendent implications of the more visionary accounts of such beings – or equally accurately as a human messenger. Both men's lives ultimately were changed in pattern and purpose. The Hausa man became a Christian pastor in Nigeria after completing theological training. The Anglo-Saxon cowhand became the chief singer and composer of music for a monastic order in Whitby. In both accounts the effect was of a change of direction of life. The meaning of the experience was in the message but the medium by which the message came was what carried its impelling and compelling force.

Although the visual imagery at work here gives a glimpse or sense of other realms of being, the content of the dream appears to be related to the ultimate vocation and calling in life of the dreamer.

It may well be that at the heart of such experiences is a common core of revelationary phenomena described elsewhere in the seminal works of Religious Experience written by Huxley (1946), James (1928), Ward (1994) and occurring within the twentieth-century charismatic revivals as well as the Welsh revival of 1904.

Within the beloved 'Word *of God*' of the Protestant tradition is, I would suggest, a similar experience of the numinous ... that in other traditions would find a different outlet within consciousness. In the Roman Catholic Tradition, visionary imagery is the more common phenomenon. But in the 1904 revival although visionary experience was experienced quite markedly by Evan Roberts the more common motif was the impact of a particular 'word' or phrase of scripture that was experienced as 'spoken' to the man or woman in prayer. This emphasis on the numinous impact of certain words of scripture lasted and survived within the charismatic and the evangelical tradition. The known phenomenon of the experience of *some particular 'words' of Scripture – as being charged with spiritual presence and having an impact beyond the simplicity and often brevity of the words themselves*, described by such different personalities as Francis of Assisi, Augustine, Teresa of Avila, Ignatius, George Fox, Joan of Arc and Julian of Norwich, the research evidence collected by David Hay,[5] and my own research data would suggest that such phenomena are still occurring.

It is the atmosphere and emotional 'charge' that is such a key part of this experience that is similar to certain dream/visionary phenomena experienced today, which are not unlike those recorded within the biblical tradition.

The biblical records include over a hundred and thirty references to dreams and almost a hundred to visions in both Old and New Testaments. In addition to these well-known historical records, first-hand interviews collected during the course of radio and university research replicated the findings of David Hay and Huxley in their description of contemporary religious experience.

The data suggest that such experiences of visionary seeing are not unknown in our own contemporary experience. But these things are not well known or acknowledged, due to a continuing taboo and lack of acceptable contemporary models who admit to such phenomena. There is also a very real medical danger of being regarded as having been subjected to a psychotic episode and labelled as 'schizophrenic' if such experiences are shared with any beyond the most trusted circle. This was the case as reported by one of the BBC research contributors. For some within the traditional, essentially secular, schools of psychological thought their may be a direct correspondence of assumption that what a religious person regards as a 'vision' would be regarded as essentially an affect of psychosis.[6]

The reasons for this are complex. Our world-view is predicated on the essential primacy of a scientific, technologically based society, in which in a

---

[5] D. Hay, *Exploring Inner Space* (London, 1982); *Religious Experience Today* (London, 1990).

[6] S. G. Talbot, 'Altered States of Consciousness: Spiritual Experience in Dream and Vision', unpublished PhD thesis, Manchester Victoria University (2000); also W. West, *Psychotherapy and Spirituality: Crossing the line* (London, 2000); *Spiritual Issues in Therapy, Relating Experience to Practice* (Macmillan, 2004).

number of senses 'seeing is believing'. But it is only a certain kind of seeing which we regard as a route to knowledge.[7]

Scientific testing and double-blind trials are now the essential tools of any research method that is to be taken seriously within the scholarly community and I have no quarrel with this but to embrace and learn from all aspects of our human experience we need 'Both/And' not 'Either/Or'.

This is also true of access to the knowledge that our minds can gain through the different functions of the brain. The human brain has about as many nerve cells as the Amazon rainforest and about as many synapses as the Amazonian rainforest has individual leaves upon those trees. Its working is complex, multifaceted with much as yet unknown. What is clear is that the two hemispheres of the brain, although having some crossover capabilities, work with fairly clear foci on different functions within human consciousness. In the left part of the brain are the centres for logical thought, language and sequenced problem-solving. The right hemisphere specializes in motor skills, artistic creativity, intuition, visual imagery and memory of the present moment. We need both skills, both ways of perceiving.

According to one scientific researcher into some of the detailed functioning of the two hemispheres of the brain, the left part of the brain, the area that deals with language, logical cognitive ability and problem-solving, is not always as reliable as we may think. The left part of the brain endeavours to interpret the world it receives, fitting input into a meaningful context and framework. It creates an overall view that will make sense but this sense may in fact not be the truth. Logical and coherent it may be but true it may be not. The right brain, the guardian and seat of image, symbol, emotion and the present experience, does not lie or so one researcher into mind–brain function would suggest.[8]

To be using in adult life, essentially, often only one half of the brain, the left side with its logical, linear skills, uninformed by the language of the soul and heart of the right side of the brain, is clearly to limit our understanding of ourselves and our capacity to respond aright to internal and external events. There is a power within the language of Dream, Image, Symbol and Vision that has the capacity to carry within itself, something of the true and the holy, which at rare and special moments may speak to us of a transcendent realm, where nothing is wasted, nothing forgotten and all things have their place and meaning.

Naomi Rachel Remen was Head of Paediatric medicine at Mount Zion Hospital in an inner city area in San Franscisco. The following is an abbreviated summary of key aspects of an account told in full in a book somewhat mis-entitled, *Kitchen Table Wisdom*. The book is rather the spiritual journey and reflections of a doctor interested in healing of the whole person, which includes issues of spirituality.

---

[7] D. Jenkins, *Guide to the Debate about God* (London, 1985).

[8] M. Gazzaniga, 'The Split Brain Revisited', in *Scientific American* (August 2002).

She arrives at work to hear angry voices coming through her closed office door ... at the centre of the row: Was a 5 year old boy, one of her patients? That morning, he had told the nurse who had woken him that he was going home that day....

'Help me pack my things' he had demanded, pointing with excitement to his tiny suitcase in the cupboard.

Who could have said such a thing? And to such a very sick child?

He was, the doctor informs us, a child who had hardly any white blood cells and could bleed to death from the slightest injury ... The nurse had asked all the other nurses on the shift. No one had said a word. The outraged nurses had accused the young doctors ... The doctors were incensed at the suggestion that it was one of them ... The row was going on in Dr Remem's Officer ...

Could they send him home in an ambulance for maybe just one hour so as not to disappoint him?

Dr Remen had decided she had to go and see this little boy in her care and decide how to deal with the row after she had seen him. Doctor Remen went to the boy's room and saw how very sick and fragile he was ... Then somehow ... there was a sense of change of light ...

... a meeting of look ... a sense of an immense presence ... of being out of time ... a sense of mutual respect ... Then this very young, very sick little boy, spoke to his doctor ... In a voice filled with joy, he said ...

'Dr Remens, I'm going home'

Dr Remen, speechless, mumbled something like, 'I'm so glad' ... and backed out of the room ... She went back to her office and suggested the medical staff just calm down and wait for a while ... A few hours later, the child said he was tired.

He lay down, pulled the sheet over his head, and died.[9]

I have no quarrel with the hard sciences apart from its sometime arrogance. But it is important to bear in mind, that to have knowledge as to process, is not to have access into meaning, compassion or wisdom. My own view is that we need both 'eyes', both ways of truth gathering: twin avenues to truth and that within each sphere, within each genre and skill of observation and knowledge-acquisition can be pathways of grace, depending on our attitude and our desire.

We are fearfully and wonderfully made, a little lower than the angels and yet of the stuff of dust. We need both hemispheres of the brain to function at our optimum best. We need to interpret our world, to be able to see the wider picture so that we can correctly interpret social, psychological and self-preservative responses.

We also need the intuitive, the creative and the emotional sense of the 'field' or gestalt of an event as well as logical analysis. The two together keep us on track and enable us to know who we are and who and what the truth of our deepest self is. There is a part of ourselves it seems, that if we desire to know truth, no matter what, will tell us how it is. And that hidden self speaks to us often, particularly if we are playing deaf, in image/vision and dream.

---

[9] R. N. Remen, *Kitchen Table Wisdom* (New York, 1997), pp. 95-7.

The Talmud says, 'Dreams which are not interpreted are like letters which have not been opened.' Letters are of little use unless opened and read. Other peoples and other times have given the dreaming mind much serious study and have described its potential as a mode of knowledge which may give human beings access to information not available to them from other sources.

The question of how experience may inform, challenge or even ultimately destroy long-held opinions as well as the philosophy on which are built value systems and their practical outworking, is an issue within the scientific and human realm.

How to interpret those influences that impinge on our consciousness from the inner and outer world may become in certain instances a vital, pragmatic and pressing question. The film 'Kundun' (Scorsese, 1998), based on the early life of the Dalai Lama, shows true and helpful information being given through the altered state of consciousness of the prophet/shaman figure. Through prophecy, the oracle advises the Dalai Lama of how to escape from the encircling Chinese troops.

For many individuals whom I have interviewed, there has been great difficulty as to how to integrate these experiences. Some still struggled years after the event to make sense of it. Others just kept it on a back shelf in the mind. But even if purposively forgotten or neglected, experience itself cannot be wholly denied.

Being generally predates thinking. It is the ground-base of life. But how we understand our experience or integrate it into our world-view is another matter.

The mystery and question of the human condition challenges thoughtful men and women in every age and in a variety of disciplines. It is not only within the scientific discipline that such difficulties are known. Marlowe, a sixteenth-century playwright, succinctly summarized the challenge of experiences, which may come to us bidden or unbidden, that do not fit the current intellectual climate or a philosophy that we might prefer.

Faustus   First will I question with thee about hell,
            Tell me, where is the place that men call hell?

Mephistopheles   Hell hath no limits, nor is circumscribed
                   in one self place; but where we are is hell,
                   And where hell is, there must we ever be
                   And to be short, when all the world dissolves,
                   And every creature shall be purified,
                   All places shall be hell that is not heaven.

Faustus   I think hell's a fable.

Mephistopheles   Ay, think so still, till experience change thy mind.

(*Doctor Faustus*, Act 11 sc. 1 lines 115 ff.)

'The English mystics of the fourteenth century, and the Spanish mystics of the sixteenth century, may well have known things, which we shall only learn by apprenticing ourselves to their insights.'[10]

---

[10] J. Polkinghorne, *Science and Christian Belief* (London, 1994), p.33.

Index

Aberdare. 134, 140, 170.
Aberdeen. 202.
Aberporth. 111, 155.
Aberthyn. 30-31, 33-35.
Aberystwyth. 36, 42-43, 112, 239.
Aldersgate. 14.
Anglesey. 114.
Arbroath. 71.
Aubrey, T. 40, 44.
Baskerville, G. 233-234, 236.
Bellshill. 200.
Bethesda. 139-144, 146-149.
Blaenannerch. 110, 155.
Boddington, T. 16, 26.
Bodie, W. 165.
Bois, H. 108, 114, 175.
Booth, W. 192.
Bootle. 159, 162.
Bonar, A. 70, 81.
Boston. 47.
Brady, N. 47.
Brewster, J. 68-70, 84, 87.
Bristol. 14.
Buchanan, D. 54-55.
Burns, W.C. 186.
Cardiganshire. 2, 5-6.
Cennick, J. 24-25, 51, 60-61.
Chauncey, C. 129.
Chicago. 230.
Church, J. 238-239.
Clark, F.E. 230.
Coke, T. 38.
Cotton, J. 47.
Cowbridge. 27, 35.
Crosby. 159.
Davies, A. 110.
Davies, H. 2-3, 8.
Davies, O. 38.
Davies, S. 46, 55, 62.
de Fursac, M. 108.
Dennistoun. 199.
Dodderidge, P. 64.
Donne, J. 29.
Dowlais. 107.
Dundee. 203.

Dyffryn. 134.
Edinburgh. 186, 194-196, 201-202.
Edwards, J. 13, 22, 39, 49-51, 86-87, 108-109, 113, 187.
Edwards, T.C. 36.
Elias, J. 38.
England. 14, 18-21, 23, 129, 224.
Evans, C. 38.
Ewer, J. 27, 30, 34.
Ferryden. 65-94.
Fetter Lane. 14, 16-17, 19, 25.
Finney, C.G. 13, 36-41, 44, 96-98, 103, 108, 113-114, 187, 194.
Forbes, J.T. 188.
Forlong, G. 73, 80, 82, 90.
Fuller, A. 38, 102.
Galashiels. 201.
George, D. 56.
Glamorgan. 27, 213.
Glasgow. 186-188, 192, 195, 197-198, 203, 209, 215-219.
Grant, H.M. 66-67, 71, 73, 80, 82, 90, 92.
Griffiths, A. 62-63, 108, 112-114.
Guyse, J. 50.
Harper, G. 200.
Harper, J. 197-198, 200.
Harris, H. 2, 8-11, 18-21, 24-26, 53-54.
Hartley, R. 229.
Hartsough, L. 46.
Holyhead. 152.
Hooper, D. 233-35.
Howell, D. 151.
Hughes, H. 143-144.
Hughes, J. 38.
Hutton, J. 16.
Indiana. 230.
Innes. 236.
Inverkeithing. 203.
Jenkins, G.H. 1.
Jenkins, J. 38, 143-144, 147, 158, 160, 170, 222.
Job, J.T. 139-149, 158.
Johnston, F. 98-106.
Jones, D. 211, 213-214.
Jones, G. 2, 3, 9, 20.

Jones, H. 36, 40-44, 113, 209.
Jones, J.C. 239-240.
Jones, M. 134-135.
Jones, T. 39.
Jones, W.O. 159-161, 163, 165-166, 168.
Kemp, J. 194-196, 201, 206-208.
Keswick. 116, 119, 127, 151, 190, 196, 207, 233, 252.
Kirk, J. 96, 98-101, 105.
Kivengere, F. 239, 242.
Lambert, F. 14, 20.
Leicester. 107-108, 114, 180-183.
Levi, A. 226.
Lewis, J. 13, 16, 18-26.
Lillingston, C. 153.
Lister, J. 83, 91.
Liverpool. 114, 149, 159-168.
Llandybie. 142.
Llanfairfechan. 40.
Llangeitho. 2.
Llanblethian. 27.
Llantrisant. 6.
Llanwenog. 3.
Lledrod. 6.
Lord Penrhyn. 140-141.
Loughor. 107, 149, 154-155, 161, 170, 211, 223.
Mackay, A. 233.
Marshall, A. 212-215.
Marshall, H. 83, 91.
McLean, J. 189, 193, 198.
Merthyr Tydfil. 40.
Meyer, F.B. 192.
Michigan. 230.
Miles, W. 27-28, 30-35.
Mitchell, H. 67, 69, 83-84, 87-88, 92.
Montag, W. 29-30.
Montrose. 65-67, 69-71, 73, 76-78, 80, 83-84, 86, 88, 90, 92.
Moorfields. 15.
Morgan, C. 190-192, 225, 230.
Morgan, D. 40, 42-44.
Morgan, J.V. 107, 151.
Morison, J. 97-99, 101-104, 187.
Motherwell. 200, 203, 216.
Mudie. 71, 80.
Murray, A. 119.
Nancwnlle. 2.
New Quay. 143-144, 149, 155, 222.
Nietzsche, F. 30, 33.

Nixon, W. 66, 68-69, 71-74, 76-77, 79-83, 85-93.
Northampton. 51, 64.
Orkney. 208, 211.
Oxford. 27.
Partick. 199.
Penn-Lewis, J. 107-108, 113-115, 116-123, 125-128, 171-172, 180-184.
Philadelphia. 53.
Phillips, D.M. 107, 161, 164-165, 191.
Pierson, A.T. 226.
Pilkington, G. 233-235.
Pontrhydygroes. 42.
Price, P. 107, 170, 176-177, 179.
Rees, W. 45.
Rhys, M. 46.
Rice, T. 153-154.
Richard, J. 5, 7, 9.
Richard, T. 36.
Ritchie, J. 209, 211-214, 216.
Robe, J. 129.
Roberts, Evan. 1, 46, 107-116, 120-128, 130-139, 145-146, 148-149, 154-156, 158, 169-172, 176-184, 189-192, 200, 212-213, 222-223, 225, 228-230, 275, 278.
Roberts, J. 39.
Robinson, R. 57.
Rowland, D. 2, 3, 5, 10-11, 20, 54.
Scotland. 14, 21, 49, 55-56, 66-69, 80, 83-84, 86, 96-98, 101-102, 104-106, 185-189, 192-194, 196-204, 206-210, 213, 215-216, 220, 224.
Rwanda. 237.
Shaw, W. 209, 211.
Shearer, J. 200-201, 205-206.
Shetland. 208, 210-211, 215, 220.
Smith, Gypsey. 192.
Spener, P.J. 245.
Spurgeon, C.H. 186, 197.
Stead, W.T. 45-46.
Steele, A. 62.
Stirling. 202.
Stoddard, S. 95.
Stuart, M. 80-81, 91.
Swift, J. 29-32.
Talbot, Lord. 27.
Talgarth. 3.
Tate, N. 47.
Tibbot, R. 7.
Toxteth. 159-160.
Trefeca. 8.

Tregaron. 6.
Tre'r Ddôl. 36, 40-41.
Wales. 1, 2, 8, 12, 14, 18-21, 23, 36-42, 44-46, 49, 53-56, 58, 64, 129-131, 134-135, 138-140, 146-148, 159-161, 167, 169-171, 173-177, 182, 222-228, 230, 243-254, 256-257.
Tucker, A. 234, 236, 238-239.
Uganda. 233-242.
Watford. 19.
Watts, I. 46, 48-51, 55, 57, 64.
Wesley, C. 51, 57, 58, 60, 63.
Wesley, J. 14, 18, 48, 51-52, 58, 61, 129.
Wesley, S. 47.
Whitefield, G. 9-10, 14-20, 23-26, 53-54, 60, 194.
William, D. 58.
William, J. 11-12.
Williams, C. 153-154, 158.
Williams, J. 159, 163-165, 167-168.
Williams, William. 1-5, 8, 10, 45, 54, 58, 108, 112-113, 140.
Woodward, J. 47.

www.ingramcontent.com/pod-product-compliance
Lightning Source LLC
Chambersburg PA
CBHW050625300426
44112CB00012B/1664